Thinking, Reading, and Writing Critically

www.prenhall.com/troyka

Thinking, Reading, and Writing Critically

Grammar Basics

Tips for Multilingual Writers

Punctuation and Mechanics

Special Kinds of Writing

DIVIDER DIRECTORY

Welcome to the fourth edition of Lynn Troyka's *Quick Access Reference for Writers*. This edition is designed to help you quickly find answers to all the questions you may have about writing.

Use the following QUICK ACCESS guides to find information quickly:

- The Divider Directory to the left lists all the parts and chapters. Turn this page to find a list of Response Symbols and Proofreading Marks.

- The Quick View Contents inside the back cover provides a detailed table of contents.

- The back of each divider lists the complete contents for its part.

- Plus, the QUICK ACCESS e-book is available online in a searchable format at **www.prenhall.com/troyka**

RESPONSE SYMBOLS AND PROOFREADING MARKS

Your instructor might use correction symbols to show where writing should be edited or revised. You can use proofreading symbols to mark hard copy for editing or revision.

CORRECTION SYMBOLS

ab	abbreviation error	425	pro agr	pronoun agreement error	343	
ad	adjective or adverb error	354	pro ref	pronoun reference error	345	
ca	pronoun case error	348	p	punctuation error	382–408	
cap	needs a capital letter	418	,/	comma error	382	
cl	revise a cliché	115	;/	semicolon error	395	
coh	needs coherence	37	:/	colon error	396	
coord	faulty coordination	83	ˇ	apostrophe error	398	
cs	comma splice	68	"/"	quotation marks error	401	
dev	needs development	34	rep	too much repetition	81	
dm	dangling modifier	79	ro	run-on sentence	68–71	
e	needs exact language	110	shift	sentence shift	72	
emph	needs emphasis	90	sl	revise slang	113	
frag	sentence fragment	65	sp	spelling error	118	
hyph	hyphen needed	415	subord	subordination error	85	
inc	incomplete sentence	65	sxt	sexist language	116	
ital	italics error	423	t, tense	verb tense error	331	
k	awkward	72, 77, 79, 110	trans	needs transition	38	
lc	needs lowercase letter	418	u	needs unity	35	
mixed	mixed construction	72	us	usage error	93	
mm	misplaced modifier	77	v	verb form error	327	
¶	new paragraph	34	v agr	verb agreement error	336	
no ¶	no new paragraph	34	var	needs sentence variety	89	
//	faulty paralellism	88	w	wordy	79	
pass	passive voice	335	wc	word choice error	110	
pl	faulty plural	118	ww	wrong word	110	

PROOFREADING MARKS

⌦	delete	take ~~this~~ this out
¶	new paragraph	This is the end. ¶ This is a new beginning.
∩	transpose letters	transpoe͡s letters
⌐	transpose words	words transpose
∧	insert	caret A ∧ signals an addition
#	add space	add # space
⌣	close up space	clo ⌣ se up space
SP	spell out	They live in WI. SP
rom	use roman type	That sounds *silly.* rom
ital	use italic type	Washington Post ital
cap	use capital letters	anne tyler cap
lc	use lowercase letters	Drive North and then East. lc

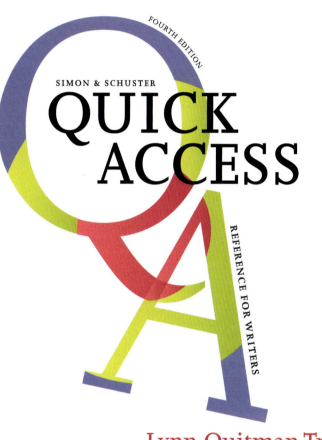

FOURTH EDITION

SIMON & SCHUSTER

QUICK ACCESS

REFERENCE FOR WRITERS

Lynn Quitman Troyka

PEARSON
Prentice
Hall

Upper Saddle River, New Jersey 07458

Library of Congress Cataloging-in-Publication Data

Troyka, Lynn Quitman
  Simon & Schuster quick access reference for writers/Lynn Quitman Troyka.—4th ed.
    p. cm.
  Includes index.
  ISBN 0-13-140081-9
    1. English language—Rhetoric—Handbooks, manuals, etc. 2. English
language—Grammar—Handbooks, manuals, etc. 3. Report writing—Handbooks, manuals,
etc. I. Title: Simon and Schuster quick access reference for writers. II. Title: Quick access
reference for writers. III. Title.

PE1408.T6964 2003
808'.042—dc21   2003051796

 For David, my husband and sweetheart

Editor in Chief: Leah Jewell	*Director of Marketing:* Beth Mejia
Acquisitions Editor: Stacy Best	*Executive Marketing Manager:*
Assistant Editor: Karen Schultz	Brandy Dawson
Editorial Assistant: Steve Kyritz	*Marketing Assistant:* Christine Moodie
VP/Director of Production and	*Creative Design Director:* Leslie Osher
Manufacturing: Barbara Kittle	*Art Director:* Anne Bonanno Nieglos
Senior Production Editor:	*Interior and Cover Designer*:
Shelly Kupperman	Anne DeMarinis
Production Assistant: Marlene Gassler	*Art Coordinator:* Guy Ruggiero
Copyeditor: Kathy Graehl	*Electronic Artist:* Mirella Signoretto
Manufacturing Manager: Nick Sklitsis	*Development Editor in Chief:*
Assistant Manufacturing Manager:	Rochelle Diogenes
Mary Ann Gloriande	*Development Editor:* Elizabeth Morgan

Grateful acknowledgment is made to all copyright holders for permission to use copyrighted material.
Page 7, Excerpt from "Sports Only Exercise Our Eyes" from *The Best of Sydney J. Harris.* Copyright ©
1975 by Sydney J. Harris. Reprinted by permission of Houghton Mifflin Company. All rights reserved.
Page 41, Excerpt from "Safe Lifting Techniques" by John Warde. Copyright © the *New York Times.*
Reprinted with permission. Page 59, Student paper reprinted with permission of Lacie Juris. Page 437,
"Blackberries" from Pleasure Dome by Yusef Komunyakaa. Copyright © 2001. Reprinted by permission
of the publisher, Wesleyan University Press.

This book was set in 9/11 New Century Schoolbook by Pine Tree Composition, Inc.
and was printed and bound by R. R. Donnelley & Sons, Inc.
The cover was printed by Phoenix Color Corp.

PEARSON
Prentice Hall © 2004, 2001, 1998, 1995 by Lynn Quitman Troyka
Published by Pearson Education, Inc.
Upper Saddle River, New Jersey 07458

Printed in the United States of America
10 9 8 7 6 5 4 3 2

ISBN 0-13-140081-9

Pearson Education LTD., London
Pearson Education Australia PTY, Limited, Sydney
Pearson Education Singapore, Pte. Ltd
Pearson Education North Asia Ltd, Hong Kong
Pearson Education Canada, Ltd., Toronto
Pearson Educación de Mexico, S.A. de C.V.
Pearson Education—Japan, Tokyo
Pearson Education Malaysia, Pte. Ltd
Pearson Education, Upper Saddle River, New Jersey

PREFACE

TO STUDENTS

A personal message from Lynn Troyka to students

Many of you as writers have much in common with me. Sure, I've been writing longer, so I've had more practice, and lots of rules are cemented in my head by this time (though some stubbornly refuse to stick, and I still need to look them up). Rather, our shared experiences during the act of writing define our commonalities. After all, we're each trying to put into words ideas worthy of someone else's taking the time to read them.

When I write, I'm often unsure of how to begin (starting in the middle and then working backward and forward usually helps). Not infrequently, I'm stuck for examples sufficiently effective to get my point across (running my thoughts past my friends can often get me going). Somewhat regularly, the precise expression that I'm looking for eludes me as I rummage through the clutter of words in my mind (using a thesaurus commonly helps me sort things out, as long as I attend to the subtle differences in meanings of synonyms).

I offer this book to you as my partners in the process of writing, hoping that its pages suggest strategies that enhance your abilities to give voice to your thoughts. You're always welcome to write me at <LQTBook@aol.com> to express your reactions to my book and to share your own experiences as a writer.

I'd like to end this message with a personal story. When I was an undergraduate years ago, handbooks weren't as common as they are now. Questions about writing nagged at me, and no one seemed to have the answers I sought. One day, browsing through the library, I found a dust-covered book sitting on the wrong shelf. Its title included the words "handbook" and "writers." I read that book hungrily and often. Back then, I could never have imagined that someday I might write such a book myself. Now that I've completed the *Simon & Schuster Quick Access Reference for Writers,* Fourth Edition, I'm amazed that I ever had the nerve to begin. What this proves to me—and I hope to you—is that anyone can write. Students don't always believe that. I hope you will.

With cordial regards,
Lynn Troyka

HOW TO USE QUICK ACCESS

Your *Simon & Schuster Quick Access Reference for Writers* is a reference book, like a dictionary or an encyclopedia.

STEP 1 Scan the following lists to decide where to start looking.

- Scan the Divider Directory inside the front cover.
- Scan the Quick View Contents inside the fold-out back cover.
- Scan the detailed contents on the back of each divider.
- Scan the list of boxes at the back of the book.
- Scan the index at the back of the book.

STEP 2 Find a number tied to the information you want.

- Find the number of the chapter.
- Find the number-letter combination of your question.
- Find the page number of the box you want.

STEP 3 Check page elements illustrated on the opposite page.

- Check the chapter number in the tinted rectangle.
- Check the page number at the top of page.
- Check for your question and its number-letter combination.
- Check for a box number and/or title.

STEP 4 Read and use the special features illustrated on the opposite page.

- Read terms in small capital letters as being defined in the "Terms Glossary" on pages 467–485.
- Read Alerts 👁 , Computer Tips 💻 , and cross-references.

Icon shows this is a checklist box

■ **BOX 7** ■   Box number

✔ **Basic requirements for a thesis statement**   Box title

✔ It states the essay's subject, but it does not repeat the title of the essay.

✔ It indicates the essay's PURPOSE but it does not announce it with "The purpose of this essay is . . . "

✔ It conveys the writer's point of view toward the subject.

✔ It makes a general statement that leads to a set of main ideas and supporting details; that is, it's much more than a statement of fact that leads nowhere.

✔ It uses specific language and avoids vague words.

✔ It may give the major subdivisions of the topic.

Small capitals show words defined in Terms Glossary

Number-letter of this section

7b **Can a thesis statement and an essay title help me revise?**

Question to be answered

Use the THESIS STATEMENT to guide your revision. At the end of every paragraph, ask yourself, *"How does this paragraph relate to my thesis statement?"* If your thesis statement does not match what your essay says, revise either the thesis statement or the essay or both.

Answer

Your essay title can also play an important part in revising, so do not wait until the last minute and merely tack on a title. A direct title tells exactly what the essay will be about: for example, *"Women Can Pump Iron, Too."* An indirect title hints at an essay's topic: *"Why Not Try Pumping Iron?"* Indirect titles can be very effective as long as the connection is not too obscure.

👁 **ALERT:** A title stands alone. Do not open an essay by referring to the title as though its words are in the essay's first sentence. Carol Moreno titled her paper *"Women Can Pump Iron, Too."* The NO example shows an unacceptable first sentence for that essay because it refers to the title. The YES example shows the way Carol Moreno's paper actually begins.

Alert starts

NO They certainly can, and I'm living proof!

YES When my grandmother fell and broke her hip last summer, I wanted to help take care of her. 👁

Alert ends

Computer Tip starts

💻 **COMPUTER TIP:** The mechanics of revising are easy on a computer. You can add, delete, and rearrange anything from a word or a sentence to a paragraph without the agony of retyping your entire essay. (1) If you are undecided about a revision, create several versions on your paper. (2) Experiment by reordering your body paragraphs. 💻

Computer Tip ends

Quick Access Reference for Writers gives you "quick access" to all the information you need about the writing process from mastering grammar to using correct punctuation, from writing research papers to documenting sources, and from writing for the Web to creating oral presentations. In addition, *Quick Access* is carefully designed for easy use and speedy entrée into all topics. The spiral binding allows *Quick Access* to stay open and lay flat, which is especially convenient for use at a computer. Here's a preview of *Quick Access*:

Quick Access E-Book Online

Every page of *Quick Access,* Fourth Edition, is available online for you to search effortlessly by index, rule number, and chapter number.

Quick Access to Contents

The Divider Directory inside the front cover gives you a brief list of the contents in *Quick Access*. Simply open the book to see instantly which divider—one of the twelve tabbed pages—you need. Or, for a more detailed overview of the contents, go to the Quick View Contents inside the fold-out back cover. Or, to find a specific topic, use the Index that follows the last divider.

Quick Access to All Topics

Twelve dividers separate major topics into sections. Glance over the divider tabs; so that with a flip of your finger, you're where you want to be. On the back of each divider, you'll find a detailed list of contents of that section. Numbered chapters contain uncomplicated discussions in small "chunks" of information. Every chunk has a chapter number plus a letter in alphabetical order within the chapter. To return quickly to a page that you consult frequently, personalize your book by attaching a sticky note that overhangs the specific page and writing your individualized label on both sides of the overhang.

Quick Access to Page Information

The spiral binding lets you open the book flat and fold it over flat. You'll never lose your place. Major headings are worded to resemble FAQs (Frequently Asked Questions) to match the questions you'll likely be asking when you consult *Quick Access*. Look for the FAQ repeated in a "running head" at the top of each right-hand page to help you navigate smoothly through the book. Also, use the color rectangle at the top-outside corner of each page to check what chapter you're using.

Quick Access to Special Elements Throughout

Each of the eighty-nine *Quick Access* boxes is a special element providing a thumbnail sketch of key information. The symbol at the top of each box carries a message: ⦿ means the box serves as a summary; ◆ signifies that the box shows a pattern; and ✔ indicates that the box provides a checklist. Also, 👁 signals an Alert to remind you about a related rule or other relevant information—for example, in a sentence discussion, an Alert might remind you of a comma rule that applies.

Quick Access to Documentation Styles

When looking for MLA documentation, locate the MLA divider. On the divider's back is a handy directory of where you can find how to document books, articles, nonprint media, and electronic sources. When looking for APA documentation, locate the APA divider, which has its directory on the back. When looking for the documentation guidelines of the *Chicago Manual* (CM), the Council of Science Editors (CSE), or the Columbia Online Style (COS), locate them all in the same divider section immediately after the APA listings.

Quick Access to Sample Research Papers

Quick Access contains five complete examples of student writing. Of these, three are student research papers: at the ends of Chapter 10 ("Writing to Argue"), Chapter 30 ("A Student's MLA Research Paper"), and Chapter 33 ("A Student's APA Research Paper"). Two are non-source-based student essays that appear at the ends of Chapter 9 ("Writing to Inform") and Chapter 62 ("Writing About Literature").

Quick Access to Help for Native Speakers and Multilingual Students

Whether English is your native language or you're multilingual, you'll find quick answers in *Quick Access* to your questions about standard American English grammar, punctuation, and sentence correctness and style. In addition, there's an entire section devoted to questions of special concern to multilingual students.

PREFACE
TO INSTRUCTORS

What's NEW in the Fourth Edition

NEW **Companion Website™ powered by *My Handbook* located at www.prenhall.com/troyka offers:**

- *Quick Access* **E-Book available online** 24/7 in a searchable format that enables users to find information quickly and easily.
- **A self-graded diagnostic test** that helps students identify specific problem areas by creating for each student a personalized online handbook called *My Handbook* and by offering tutorial-style exercises. A progress checker, available to instructors, assists in monitoring students' progress.
- **Hundreds of interactive, text-tied, and self-graded exercises,** which include editing activities.
- **Access to *Research Navigator*™** designed especially to help students use their research time efficiently and effectively. It facilitates and offers three exclusive databases filled with relevant and reliable source material, including EBSCO's *ContentSelect*™ Academic Journal Database, the *New York Times* Search-by-Subject Archive, and the *Best of the Web* Link Library.

NEW **Discussion of the research process increased from five to six chapters**. Provides the latest information about developing a research project, building a search strategy, finding and evaluating library resources, finding and evaluating online resources, avoiding plagiarism, and writing the research paper.

NEW **More highly developed discussion of practical ways to avoid plagiarism** (Chapter 26), emphasizing the students' role as student-scholars. Suggests how students can check whether their paraphrases and summaries are sufficiently revised from their original sources.

NEW **Up-to-date documentation guidelines, including MLA 2003 and APA 2001.** Entire sample student research papers complete the MLA and APA documentation sections.

NEW **MLA research paper on a new topic with greatly expanded writing guidance.** Opposite each page of the research paper is a page of "Commentary" that describes the researching, thinking, and writing processes. Annotations run along the sides of the paper to describe technical aspects of the writing.

NEW **Guidelines for the Columbia Online Style (COS) of documentation.**

NEW **Chapter 3 on the connections between thinking, reading, and writing.**

NEW **Chapter 10 on writing arguments,** which ends with a complete source-based student essay.

NEW **Chapter 62 on writing about literature,** which ends with a complete student essay that analyzes a poem.

NEW **Chapter 64 on oral presentations,** which explains how to plan, create, and deliver speeches and talks.

NEW **Exceptionally outstanding four-color design** that expertly highlights each key concept to help you navigate *Quick Access* more easily than ever.

Supplements

Resources for Instructors

- *Strategies and Resources for Teaching Writing with* **Quick Access,** Fourth Edition, offers guidance to new and experienced instructors for teaching in the composition classroom. ISBN 0-13-182909-2

- *Educator's Access for* **Quick Access,** Fourth Edition, **Companion Website™ powered by** *My Handbook* provides faculty-only access to instructor's tools, such as *Progress Tracker*, which reports students' progress when they submit the online exercises and activities; *Syllabus Tools*, which helps build your syllabus and post multiple syllabi; *Class Calendar*, which helps organize your courses; and *Communication Tools*, which allows you to post class messages on each student's *Quick Access* home page, send class bulletins via e-mail, and insert comments and highlights in the *Quick Access* E-Book.

- Course management solutions for *BlackBoard™, Course Compass™,* and *WebCT™,* adapted for *Quick Access*, Fourth Edition, provide extensive book-specific content, including **the entire Quick Access Handbook online as a searchable E-Book** as well as **online exercises for each chapter.** Access Code Cards for these course management solutions are available free in Value Packs with new copies of *Quick Access*, Fourth Edition. Contact your Prentice Hall representative for complete information.

- **Prentice Hall Resources for Teaching Writing,** individual booklets covering some of the most effective approaches and

important concerns of composition instructors today, are available to use with your students and teaching assistants. Contact your Prentice Hall representative for copies of:

- *Distance Learning* by W. Dees Stallings. ISBN 0-13-088656-4
- *Classroom Strategies* by Wendy Bishop. ISBN 0-13-572355-8
- *Portfolios* by Pat Belanoff. ISBN 0-13-572322-1
- *Journals* by Christopher C. Burnham. ISBN 0-13-572348-5
- *Collaborative Learning* by Harvey Kail and John Trimbur. ISBN 0-13-028487-4
- *English as a Second Language* by Ruth Spack. ISBN 0-13-028559-5
- *Teaching Writing Across the Curriculum* by Art Young. ISBN 0-13-081650-7

Resources for Students

- **Companion Website™ powered by *My Handbook*** at **www.prenhall.com/troyka**, offers *Quick Access,* Fourth Edition, as an **online E-Book** available 24/7 in a searchable format. It also includes a **self-graded diagnostic test** to assist in identifying specific problem areas and creating a personalized handbook called *My Handbook;* **hundreds of interactive exercises,** text-tied and self-graded; and access to *Research Navigator*™.
- *Research Navigator*™ is designed to help students use their research time efficiently and effectively. It facilitates the research process and offers three exclusive databases full of relevant and reliable source material, including EBSCO's *ContentSelect* Academic Journal Database, the *New York Times* Search-by-Subject Archive, and the *Best of the Web* Link Library.
- **Exercise Booklet,** which contains exercises and activities to help students improve their writing skills, can be packaged with *Quick Access*, Fourth Edition. ISBN 0-13-182906-8
- **Answer Key** provides answers to the exercises in the Exercise Booklet. ISBN 0-13-182907-6
- *The New American Webster Handy College Dictionary* or *The New American Roget's College Thesaurus in Dictionary Format* is available to package free with *Quick Access*, Fourth Edition. Contact your Prentice Hall representative for ordering information.
- *A Writer's Guide to Research and Documentation* by Kirk G. Rasmussen, available free in Value Packs with new copies of *Quick Access*, Fourth Edition, features the most recent information on MLA, APA, CSE, and CM formats and covers the research process. ISBN 0-13-177997-4

- *A Writer's Guide to Writing in the Disciplines and Oral Presentations* by Christine Manion, available free in Value Packs with new copies of *Quick Access*, Fourth Edition, helps students write successfully in different academic disciplines, and offers advice and information on preparing oral presentations. ISBN 0-13-018931-6
- *A Writer's Guide to Writing About Literature* by Edgar V. Roberts, available free in Value Packs with new copies of *Quick Access*, Fourth Edition, prepares students for writing about literature by providing information on research and literature, as well as additional sample student papers. ISBN 0-13-018932-4

ACKNOWLEDGMENTS

With this fourth edition of the *Simon & Schuster Quick Access Reference for Writers,* nicknamed *QA,* I heartily thank the students who, to my great luck, have landed in my writing classes. They and their counterparts across the United States and Canada inspire me with their gritty determination to write skillfully, think critically, and communicate successfully in college courses and beyond.

My warm special thanks go to the individual students who have given me permission to make them "published authors" by including their exemplary writing in this handbook. Their names accompany their work. Additionally, I thank the hundreds of students who have written me e-mails or letters with their reactions to, and questions about, *Quick Access* or related matters. I take your comments very seriously and strive to improve my books accordingly. Any student now holding *QA* is welcome to get in touch with me at <LQTBook@aol.com> or c/o Senior English Editor, Pearson Education, One Lake Street, Upper Saddle River, NJ 07458. I promise to answer.

Three colleagues contributed significantly to this edition of *Quick Access*. Carolyn Calhoun-Dillahunt, Director of the Writing Center and Professor of English at Yakima Valley Community College, shared her delightful, natural talent as writer and teacher by drafting the new chapter about writing essays of argument and by finding its accompanying student paper. Doug Hesse, Director of the Center for the Advancement of Teaching and Professor of English at Illinois State University, lent his outstanding skill, insight, and refinement by drafting the new chapter on writing about literature and by finding its accompanying student paper. Additionally, Doug brought his impressive knowledge to expanding my discussion of plagiarism and research writing. Kip Strasma, Professor of English at Illinois Central College, drew on his impressive experience with computers in the classroom to develop the new chapter on Web-based writing.

For their helpful analytic reviews of the third edition of *Quick Access* toward my preparing this fourth edition, I sincerely thank Marilyn Barry, Alaska Pacific University; Janet Cutshall, Sussex Community College; Dawn Elmore-McCrary, San Antonio College; Sheryl Forste-Grupp, Villanova University; Joe Glaser, Western Kentucky University; Jimmy Guignard, University of Nevada at Reno; Kimberly Harrison, Florida International University; Rodney Keller, Brigham Young University, Idaho; Martha Marinara, University of Central Florida; Michael Matto, Yeshiva University; Pamela Mitzelfeld, Oakland University; Rhonda Morris, Lake City Community College; Roark Mulligan, Christopher Newport University; Alyssa J. O'Brien, Stanford University; Beverly J. Slaughter, Broward Community College; Martha A. Smith, Brookhaven College; Scott R. Stankey, Anoka Ramsey Community College; Michael Strysick, Wake Forest University; and Susan Swartwout, Southeast Missouri State College.

I renew my gratitude to the members of each Regional Advisory Board for Prentice Hall, who set aside precious days in their busy lives to discuss with me effective strategies for teaching writing. In the Southeast, they are Peggy Jolly, University of Alabama at Birmingham; Stephen Prewitt, David Lipscomb University; Mary Anne Reiss, Elizabethtown Community College; Michael Thro, Tidewater Community College at Virginia Beach; and the late Sally Young, University of Tennessee at Chattanooga. In the Southwest, they are Jon Bentley, Albuquerque Technical-Vocational Institute; Kathryn Fitzgerald, University of Utah; Maggy Smith, University of Texas at El Paso; Martha A. Smith, Brookhaven College; and Donnie Yeilding, Central Texas College. In Florida, they are Kathleen Bell, University of Central Florida; David Fear, Valencia Community College; D. J. Henry, Daytona Beach Community College; Marilyn Middendorf, Embry Riddle University; Phillip Sipiora, University of South Florida; and Valerie Zimbaro, Valencia Community College.

I'm also grateful to past reviewers of my various handbooks: Nancy Westrich Baker, Southeast Missouri State University; Norman Bosley, Ocean Community College; Phyllis Brown, Santa Clara University; Judith A. Burnham, Tulsa Community College; Robert S. Caim, West Virginia University at Parkersburg; Ann L. Camy, Red Rocks Community College; Joe R. Christopher, Tarleton State University; Marilyn M. Cleland, Purdue University, Calumet; Thomas Copeland, Youngstown State University; Esther DiMarzio, Kishwaukee College; Rita Eastburg, College of Lake County; Joanne Ferreira, State University of New York at New Paltz and Fordham University; Carol L. Gabel, William Paterson College; Barbara Gaffney, University of New Orleans; Anne Gervasi, DeVry Institute of Technology; Joe Glaser, Western Kentucky University; Michael Goodman, Fairleigh Dickinson University; Mary

Multer Greene, Tidewater Community College at Virginia Beach; Julie Hagemann, Purdue University, Calumet; John L. Hare, Montgomery College; Lory Hawkes, DeVry Institute of Technology, Irving; Lorraine Higgins, University of Pittsburgh; Janet H. Hobbs, Wake Technical Community College; Frank Hubbard, Marquette University; Rebecca Innocent, Southern Methodist University; Ursula Irwin, Mount Hood Community College; Denise Jackson, Southeast Missouri State University; Margo K. Jang, Northern Kentucky University; Margaret Faye Jones, Nashville State Technical Institute; Myra Jones, Manatee Community College; Judith C. Kohl, Dutchess Community College; Scott Leonard, Youngstown State University; James C. McDonald, University of Southwestern Louisiana; Darlene Malaska, Youngstown Christian University; Christine M. Manion, Marquette University; Martha Marinara, University of Central Florida; Michael J. Martin, Illinois State University; Barbara Matthies, Iowa State University; Susan J. Miller, Santa Fe Community College; Rosemary G. Moffett, Elizabethtown Community College; Bethany Paige Nowviskie, University of Virginia; Jon F. Patton, University of Toledo; Pamela T. Pittman, University of Central Oklahoma; Nancy B. Porter, West Virginia Wesleyan College; Kirk Rasmussen, Utah Valley State College; Edward J. Reilly, St. Joseph's College; Peter Burton Ross, University of the District of Columbia; Mary Ruetten, University of New Orleans; Matilda Delgado Saenz; Eileen Schwartz, Purdue University, Calumet; Lisa Sebti, Central Texas College; Eileen B. Seifert, DePaul University; John S. Shea, Loyola University at Chicago; Tony Silva, Purdue University; Paulette Smith, Reference Librarian, Valencia Community College; Bill M. Stiffler, Hartford Community College; Jack Summers, Central Piedmont Community College; Vivian A. Thomlinson, Cameron University; Matt Turner, Iowa State University; William P. Weiershauser, Iowa Wesleyan College; Joe Wenig, Purdue University; Carolyn West, Daytona Beach Community College; and Roseanna B. Whitlow, Southeast Missouri State University.

At Prentice Hall, exceptional people facilitated my work on *Quick Access,* Fourth Edition. Elizabeth Morgan, Development Editor, offered her uncanny ability as perceptive reader and patient organizer of a multivariate project. Additionally, the energetic vision of these talented people supported my goals indispensably: Leah Jewell, Editor in Chief for English and Psychology; Corey Good and Stacy Best, Senior Acquisitions Editors for English Composition; Brandy Dawson, Executive Marketing Manager for English Composition; and Karen Schultz, Assistant Editor for English. Serving officially as Senior Production Editor and unofficially as protector of my pedagogic goals, Shelly Kupperman once again demonstrated how vital to my writing are her keen reader's eyes. Others include Christy Schaack, Media Editor for

English; Christina Scalia, Editorial Assistant to Leah Jewell; Steven Kyritz, Editorial Assistant to Corey Good and Stacy Best; and Christine R. Moodie, Marketing Assistant to Brandy Dawson.

My family and friends bless me generously with safe harbor no matter how challenging the seas. Ida Morea, my Administrative Assistant and dear friend, daily enhances my work with her graceful ability to skillfully handle myriad tasks with good humor and warmth. Kristen Black, child of my heart if not my womb, along with her beloved family Dan, Lindsey, and Ryan, sustains me with her indomitable spirit, vision, and brilliance. My other wonderful pals and relatives include Susan Bartlestone; Florence Bolden; Carol Carter; Rita and Hy Cohen; Elaine Gilden Dushoff; Alan, Lynne, Adam, and Joshua Furman; Elliott Goldhush; Warren Herendeen.; Cynthia Lester, my extra-special new friend; Edie and Alan Lipp; Brenda and John Lovas; Edith Klausner, my treasured sister; Jo Ann Lavery, my "sister" and much-loved buddy through thick and thin, and her husband, Tom Lavery; Lois Powers; Betty Renshaw; Magdalena Rogalskaja; Avery Ryan, my cherished "niece" and her delightful Jimmy, Gavin, and Ian Ryan; Shirley and Don Stearns; Marilyn and Ernest Sternglass; Joseph Wayne Thweatt; Lisa Wallace, my dearly loved, clever "niece" and her delightful husband, Nathaniel Wallace; Muriel Wolfe; Douglas and Anna Young; and Tzila Zwas. Above all, David Troyka, my husband, is my rock, my perceptive partner, and the love of my life.

Lynn Quitman Troyka

Photo by Ida Morea

ABOUT THE AUTHOR

Lynn Quitman Troyka earned her Ph.D. at New York University and taught for many years at the City University of New York (CUNY), including Queensborough Community College; the Center for Advanced Studies in Education at the Graduate School; the graduate program in Language and Literacy at City College; and, as Senior Research Associate, in the Instructional Resource Center, CUNY.

Former editor of the *Journal of Basic Writing* (1985–1988), Dr. Troyka has published in journals such as *College Composition and Communication, College English,* and *Writing Program Administration* and in books from Southern Illinois Press, Random House, the National Council of Teachers of English (NCTE), and Heineman. She wrote the composition/rhetoric essay for the *Encyclopedia of English Studies and Language Arts* (Scholastic, 1993), as well as the basic writing essay for the *Encyclopedia of Rhetoric* (1994). She has conducted workshops at numerous colleges and universities and at national and international meetings.

Dr. Troyka is the author of many textbooks, including the *Simon & Schuster Handbook for Writers,* Sixth Edition (Prentice Hall, 2002); the *Simon & Schuster Handbook for Writers,* Third Canadian Edition (Pearson Education, 2002); the *Simon & Schuster Quick Access Reference for Writers,* Second Canadian Edition (Pearson Education, 2004); *Structured Reading,* Sixth Edition, with Joseph W. Thweatt (Prentice Hall, 2003); and *Steps in Composition,* Seventh Edition, with Jerrold Nudelman (Prentice Hall, 1999).

Dr. Troyka is a past chair of the Two-Year College Association (TYCA) of NCTE, the Conference on College Composition (CCCC), the College Section of NCTE, and the Writing Division of MLA. She was named Rhetorician of the Year in 1993; earned the Nell Ann Pickett Award for Service in 1995; and received the 2001 CCCC Exemplar Award, the highest CCCC award given for scholarship, teaching, and service. She serves on the NCTE Leadership Committee for Preparing Future Faculty (PFF), a project of the Council of Graduate Schools and the American Association of Colleges and Universities.

"All this information," says Dr. Troyka, "tells what I've done, not who I am. I am a teacher. Teaching is my life's work, and I love it."

xvii

Why begin a book about college writing with chapters on critical thinking and reading? The amswer is simply this: Being successful in your college career and beyond involves your developing a careful mind and a clear eye. You pause to examine ideas. You challenge ideas instead of passively accepting them. You question conclusions instead of agreeing with them without reflecting on them.

Critical in this context does not mean finding fault, as when one person criticizes another for doing something wrong. Thinking and reading critically means your mind never slips into "automatic pilot." By being critical, you move beyond the obvious to an understanding that goes below the surface to deeper meanings.

1 THINKING CRITICALLY

1a What is critical thinking?

Thinking is not something you choose to do, any more than a fish chooses to live in water. To be human is to think. Yet, while the process of thinking may come naturally, awareness of how you think does not. Thinking about thinking is how you think critically.

1b What steps do I use to think critically?

Critical thinking is a process of contemplation and deliberation. It begins with understanding and progresses to reaction. Actually, critical thinking is something you do every day. It applies to what you read, hear, and see. For example, when you picked a college, you reflected on the information you gathered about the school. When you start a new job, you engage in critical thinking to learn and master how to do the work, to decide whether the job is in line with your abilities, and to form your opinion of the job.

The steps of the critical thinking process rarely proceed in a rigid order. I discuss each step separately in this handbook, but in reality, the steps interweave and loop back and forth. As you work through the process, you can expect to combine steps, reverse their order, or return to earlier parts of the process when you get to the end.

■■■ BOX 1 ■■■

 Steps in the critical thinking process: SASE

1. **S = Summarize:** Extract and restate the material's main message or central point (4a). Use only what you see on the pages. Add nothing.

2. **A = Analyze:** Examine the material by breaking it into its component parts. By seeing each part of the whole as a distinct unit, you discover how the parts interrelate. Consider the line of reasoning as shown by the evidence offered (27b) and the logic used (10f). Read "between the lines" to draw inferences about information that is implied but not stated (2b). When reading or watching a performance, notice how the writing style and choice of words work together to create a tone (2b).

3. **S = Synthesize:** Pull together what you have summarized and analyzed by connecting it to your own experiences, such as reading, talking with others, watching TV and films, and so on (4b). In so doing, you create a new whole that reflects your newly acquired knowledge and insights combined with your prior knowledge.

4. **E = Evaluate:** Judge the quality of the material now that you have become informed by the activities of analysis and synthesis (2b). Resist the very common urge to evaluate before you summarize, analyze, and synthesize.

2 READING CRITICALLY

2a What is critical reading?

To read critically is to think about what you are reading—during the time that you're reading and afterward. Critical reading is similar to critical thinking (1b). As you read, you actively think about the material you are looking at. Reading is an active process, a dynamic interaction between the page and your brain. Understanding how this interaction works can help you become a better reader.

● Steps in the critical reading process

1. Read for *literal meaning:* Read "on" the lines to see what is stated. Be sure not to stop here. Steps 2 and 3 give you a complete understanding of the material.

2. Read to draw *inferences:* Read "between" the lines to analyze the material. Figure out what is implied but not stated. See how the writer uses language and style to create a tone. Assess the reasoning to check whether it is faulty (10f).

3. Read to *evaluate:* Read "beyond" the lines to mold your informed opinion about the material.

2b What steps do I use to read critically?

Without being conscious of it, as you read, you make split-second predictions. Your mind is constantly guessing what ideas and words are coming next. When your mind does see what has come next, it instantly confirms or revises its prediction and moves on. For example, when you glance through a magazine and come upon the title "The Heartbeat," your mind starts guessing: Is this a love story? Or is this about how the heart pumps blood? Or maybe it tells the story of someone who had a heart attack. As you read the first few sentences, your mind confirms which guess was correct. If you see words like *romance* and *kisses,* you know that the material involves a human relationship. On the other hand, if you see words like *electrical impulse, muscle fibers,* and *contraction*, you know instantly that you're in the realm of physiology. As you read further, you narrow your predictions to the heart as pump, or a heart suffering an attack, or a related topic.

To help your mind make predictions efficiently, determine in advance your **purpose** for reading. People generally read for two reasons—to relax or to learn—though the two often go together. Both types of reading are enjoyable, but they involve different approaches. Reading a popular novel or current biography usually helps you relax—and possibly learn. Reading for college courses calls for you to understand and remember the material—and possibly enjoy it. When you read to comprehend and retain information, you can rarely read something just once. A single encounter with new material usually is not enough to help you learn it. Most students repeatedly reread sections of textbooks, lab manuals, research sources, and lecture notes.

What role does reading speed play in critical reading? That depends on what you want to accomplish. If you are hunting for a particular fact, you need to skim until you find it. If you are reading about a subject you know well, you might read reasonably rapidly, although you certainly would slow down when you encounter material that's new to you. If you don't know a subject well, you would proceed more slowly, to give your mind time to understand and absorb the new material. No matter what your reading speed in each situation you need to be critical as you read. Therefore, you want to attend to the literal meaning of the material, to make some inferences about the material, and to evaluate it.

Determining literal meaning

Reading for **literal meaning** involves reading to comprehend. This isn't the time to go beyond what's "on the line." Your goal is to discover the main ideas and supporting details or, in a work of fiction, the central details of plot and character. If you find reading on the literal level difficult, the cause might be a writer's complex style. Try breaking the sentences into shorter units or rewording them in a simpler style. Think about the vocabulary used and what the words mean. Resist the temptation to add your own interpretation to the literal meaning of the material. Take your time. Rushing through material to cover it, rather than to understand it, wastes your valuable time.

SUGGESTIONS FOR IMPROVING YOUR READING COMPREHENSION

- Associate new material with what you already know, especially when you're reading about an unfamiliar subject. Many readers locate an easier book on the subject and read it before they tackle the more complex material.

- Remain fiercely determined to concentrate, especially if your mind tends to wander. Imagine putting on blinders, like those that keep horses from looking around. Arrange for silence or music, for being alone or with others in the library. Try to complete your reading at your best time of day. Do whatever it takes.

- Allow sufficient time to read, reflect, reread, and study. Discipline yourself to balance your time for reading and studying with time for classes, working, socializing, and family activities. Reading and studying take time. Nothing prevents success in college as much as poor time management.

- Keep an up-to-date college edition dictionary at hand or on your hard disk. As you encounter new words, try to figure them out from the context in which they appear. You'll find that the rest of the sentence, or a nearby sentence, often cues you to what the word means.

If the context doesn't hint at a word's meaning, look in your textbook's glossary, which appears either at the end of each chapter or in the back of the book.

- Work efficiently. Don't waste time looking up a word more than once. Tape a list of new words into each textbook or inside your dictionary, or paste the list into a document you create on your computer for that purpose. Take time as often as possible to look over the list to remind yourself of the meanings. This is a quick, easy way to build your vocabulary.

Making inferences

Making **inferences** is something you do all the time. For example, if you see a large crowd at a bus stop and many of the people look annoyed, you can infer that the bus is late. To make inferences, you need to read "between the lines," a central concept in reading critically. This process involves detecting a writer's assumptions, telling the difference between fact and opinion, discovering a writer's bias, and recognizing a writer's tone.

A WRITER'S ASSUMPTIONS

All writers make **assumptions** about the readers who will be reading their material. Writers suppose that readers come to the material with a certain level of knowledge about the subject, ranging from zero to advanced. In addition, some writers take for granted that readers already know certain facts about them: their background, reputation, personal history, religious or ethical beliefs, or point of view. To read critically, you need to sort out a writer's assumptions. Once you do, you can read with greater understanding of the writer's stance toward the subject—and greater insight into how the writer expects you to react. Most importantly, you can resist being manipulated by such assumptions, if that is the writer's intention.

FACT VERSUS OPINION

Some writers intentionally blur the difference between fact and opinion. **Facts** are statements that people can verify objectively by observation, experiment, or research. That Abraham Lincoln was sixteenth president of the United States is a fact. That Abraham Lincoln was the greatest U.S. president is an **opinion**—a statement with which you may or may not agree. Critical readers know the difference.

In making judgments, remember that "facts" sometimes change as time passes. For example, a person once thought to be a hero might later turn out to be a criminal. As facts change, knowledge grows. Always use current knowledge to assess the accuracy of facts.

To differentiate between fact and opinion, you want to think beyond the obvious. For example, is the following statement a fact or an opinion: "Strenuous exercise is good for everyone's health"? Though this statement carries the ring of truth, it doesn't apply to people with advanced heart disease or other medical limitations. It is, therefore, an opinion.

A WRITER'S BIAS

When you make inferences, you may encounter viewpoints based on **bias** rather than facts or evidence. If a writer makes rude or cruel remarks, you can infer that the author dislikes certain ideas or people. Be critical of such bias and **prejudice**, because it slants the material toward the writer's beliefs and attitudes and away from facts or evidence. You might find that the author uses positive language to cover up prejudice. For example, in the statement "Most women are too nice to succeed in business," *nice* sounds complimentary, but the underlying assumption is negative and prejudicial.

A WRITER'S TONE

By recognizing the **tone** that emerges from a writer's use of words and ways of presenting ideas, you're making inferences. Reading with an ear for tone is a major critical reading skill. Tone can be serious, respectful, friendly, humorous, slanted, sarcastic, or angry. Most writers of textbooks and academic journals choose language that is neutral, direct, and neither overly relaxed nor stiff. When the tone doesn't fit the occasion, the writer may be seeking to manipulate readers rather than to influence their reasoning. Critical readers view such writing with suspicion.

Making evaluations

Critical readers **evaluate** what they've read only after dealing with the literal and inferential meanings in the material. Making evaluations calls for reading "beyond the lines," to come to conclusions about whether a writer's reasoning is sound, and the presentation and word choice are balanced.

2c   How do close reading and active reading work?

The secret to reading closely and actively is annotating. When you **annotate,** you write notes to yourself in a book's margins, occasionally underlining or highlighting major passages or using asterisks and other special marks to focus your attention.

Close reading means annotating for content and meaning. You might, for example, number and briefly list the steps of a process or summarize major points in the margin. Where you underline or highlight, also jot key words or phrases in the margin. When you review, these marginal notes will jog your memory. Your goal is to extract meaning on the literal, inferential, and evaluative levels (2b).

Active reading means annotating to make connections between what you already know or have experienced and the material you're reading. This is your chance to converse on paper with the writer. Give your mind free range to see what associations arise between what you know and what you are learning. Consider yourself a partner in the making of meaning, a full participant in the exchange of ideas that characterizes a college education.

The example below shows annotations for both close reading and active reading.

The act of annotating pages has a proud history that dates back to the Middle Ages. However, if you can't bring yourself to write in a book, design for yourself a double-entry notebook. On one side of each sheet

Although I like to play, and sometimes like to watch, I cannot see what possible difference it makes which team beats which. The tactics are sometimes interesting, and certainly the prowess of the players deserves applause but most men seem to use commercial sports as a kind of narcotic shutting out reality, rather than heightening it.

There is nothing more boring, in my view, than a prolonged discussion by laymen of yesterday's game. These dreary conversations are a form of social alcoholism, enabling them to achieve a dubious rapport without ever once having to come to grips with a subject worthy of a grown man's concern.

It is easy to see the opiate quality of sports in our society when tens of millions of men will spend a splendid Saturday or Sunday fall afternoon sitting stupefied in front of the TV, watching a "big game," when they might be out exercising their own flaccid muscles and stimulating their lethargic corpuscles.

Annotations (handwritten):
- Doesn't matter who wins, but tactics and prowess can be admired.
- Sports talk is boring.
- When my son and husband watch together, the rapport is very real.
- Other examples include soap operas and sitcoms.
- Instead of watching men should exercise.

Annotations for close reading (content) and active reading (synthesis). Active reading notes are circled.

of paper, write close reading notes on the content; on the other side, enter active reading notes on your thoughts as you synthesize the material.

2d How does systematic reading work?

When you **read systematically,** you follow the structured plan of **PRR.**

- **P = Preview:** Before you start reading, look over the assignment or the chapter's list of contents to get an idea of what is ahead. This activity helps you make efficient predictions and ask yourself questions that engage you to think about the material (2b). You won't have answers at this point, but research has revealed that questions prepare the mind to learn actively. To preview a textbook chapter, begin by reading the summary at the end of the chapter, if there is one. Then skim through the chapter, reading all the headings, large and small. Read any words in boldface, because they're the key terms in the chapter. Next, look at all figures, tables, charts, drawings, and photographs—always reading the captions. Think about what the summary covers. Finally, read the first and last paragraphs of the major sections of the chapter.

- **R = Read:** Read the chapter closely and actively. Seek meaning at all three levels: literal, inferential, and evaluative (2b). Always expect to read more than once. College-level material is rarely understood fully and absorbed in one reading. Budget your time accordingly.

- **R = Review:** To review, repeat the preview process by looking at the chapter summary, the headings, the boldface terms, the first and last paragraphs of major sections, and once again, the chapter summary. Ask yourself the same questions that you asked during your preview, but this time answer your questions. If you have trouble with an answer, reread that section of the chapter and try again.

For best success, review in **chunks**—small sections that you can capture comfortably. Don't try to cover too much at once. Give your mind a chance to absorb the new material. Repeat your review the next day, again about a week later, and at frequent intervals during a course. This process reinforces your learning and makes it yours forever. The more you reinforce your new learning, the better. Another system for reinforcing your learning is to work collaboratively with a friend or classmate. When you've reached the same knowledge level, test each other orally. An equally effective strategy is to teach the material to someone who needs help understanding it.

3 CONNECTING THINKING AND READING TO WRITING

3a How will other people read my writing?

The following statement might seem obvious, but it carries a message that goes beyond its simple words: *When you write for college, one or more readers will read and think critically about your material.* This statement explains why the first two chapters of this writer's reference cover the topics of critical thinking and critical reading.

When you write, you're writing for people—no matter what their backgrounds or your topic—who will read your material

- at the literal, inferential, and evaluative levels (2b)
- closely and actively (2c)
- systematically (2d)
- while thinking critically about it, by going through the steps of summary, analysis, synthesis, and evaluation (1b).

Because the people who read your writing—whether your peers, your instructor, specialized experts on your topic, or all of these—use these processes of critical reading and thinking, you want to keep the steps of each process in mind as you write. Use Chapters 1 and 2 to help you read your writing as others will.

3b Who are the people who will read my writing?

The people who read your writing are your **audience,** a term that refers to the specific people who read a specific piece of writing. These people read your writing in light of their own backgrounds and prior knowledge of your topic. The more general term *readers* includes your audience, but goes beyond it to all human beings who read any sort of writing.

When you write for yourself, you're free to focus only on what matters to you. Often, in such situations, this includes what you're writing about (your topic) as well as your choice of words and stylistic techniques (your writing style). If, however, you're writing for a specific audience, you need to maintain a keen awareness of their presence as you focus on your topic and writing style. See 5c for suggestions on how you can determine the characteristics of your audience in each of your specific writing situations.

4 DISTINGUISHING BETWEEN SUMMARY AND SYNTHESIS

As a person with a reflective mind, you need to recognize the difference between summary and synthesis. Box 1 (p. 2) gives the steps in the critical thinking process, known for short as SASE. Notice that in the steps, summary always comes before synthesis. They are two different steps, but it is easy to confuse them. Be careful not to.

4a What is summarizing?

Summarizing extracts the main message or central point of a passage. A **summary** tells what is written or said, without any additions from your personal thinking and reacting.

4b What is synthesizing?

Synthesizing weaves ideas together. A **synthesis** connects material that you have summarized, analyzed, and interpreted to what you already know. When you synthesize, you draw on ideas from what you have read, listened to, and experienced. In so doing, you create a new whole that is your own. Don't be afraid to synthesize. I'm always surprised when I find that some students assume that what they think has no value. Nothing could be farther from the truth—simply use your life experiences, television watching, reading, and everything else you can think of. With practice, you will become increasingly at ease with and more skilled at synthesizing.

Synthesizing from multiple sources

Wrap your mind around the multiple sources that you have encountered (Ch. 23). Work toward synthesis by making connections among concepts, ideas, and information that you have read, heard, and experienced. Unsynthesized ideas and information are like separate spools of thread, neatly lined up, possibly coordinated, but not woven together or integrated. Synthesized ideas and information are like threads woven into a tapestry that becomes a new whole. By synthesizing, you show evidence of your ability to tie ideas together in the tapestry of what you learn, know, and experience. Here are some specific techniques.

- Make comparisons among concepts, ideas, and information.
- Think of contrasts among concepts, ideas, and information.

- Create definitions that combine and extend definitions you encounter in the separate sources.

- Use examples or descriptions from one source to illustrate ideas in another.

- Use processes described in one source to explain those in others.

👁 **ALERT:** Never do "synthesis by summary." That is, avoid merely listing who said what about a topic. Such a list isn't a synthesis. It does not create new connections among ideas. 👁

Synthesizing with one source

If you're working with only one source, you need to rely even more on what you remember, known as your prior knowledge. Here are some specific techniques.

- Use your powers of play. Mentally toss ideas around, even if you make connections that seem outrageous. Try opposites (for example, read about athletes and think about the most nonathletic person you know). Try turning an idea upside down (for example, if you have read about the value of being a good sport, list the benefits of being a bad sport). Try visualizing what you are reading about, and then tinker with the mental picture (for example, picture two people playing tennis, and then substitute dogs playing Frisbee or seals playing Ping-Pong).

- Use the technique of clustering (5g) to lay out visually the relationships among elements in your source and other ideas that come to mind.

- Make word associations, think up song lyrics, draft a TV commercial. Your goal is to jump-start your thinking so that you see ideas in new ways.

- Discuss the source with another person. Summarize its content and elicit the other person's opinion or ideas. Deliberately debate that opinion or challenge those ideas. Discussions and debates can get your mind moving. (If in your writing you use that other person's ideas, be sure to give that person credit as your source (Ch. 26).)

- Write a critical response to the material. Summarize its content and then write your personal response to it. Explain whether you agree or disagree and also the reasons why you respond as you do. Connect your reasons with your prior knowledge and experiences so that the synthesized material becomes your own.

Writing Process

www.prenhall.com/troyka

Writing Process

5 GETTING STARTED

5a What is the writing process?

Many people assume that a real writer can magically write a finished product, word by perfect word. Experienced writers know better. They know that *writing is a process,* a series of activities that starts the moment they begin thinking about a topic and ends when they complete a final draft. In addition, experienced writers are aware that good writing is actually rewriting—again and yet again. Their drafts contain additions, deletions, rewordings, and rearrangements. For a real-life example, see this paragraph as I drafted and revised it below.

Many people assume that a real writer can ^*magically* write a
finished product, *word by perfect word.* ~~easily.~~ Experienced writers know
~~better than~~ that; writing is a process, ~~that involves~~
the moment they begin
a series of activities that start ~~when the writers start~~
about a topic *when they complete* ^
thinking ^and end ~~with~~ a final draft. ^

Draft and revision of the beginning of the first paragraph in 5a

As you work through the writing process as described in Box 3 on the next page, remember that writing is a so-called *recursive* activity, which means that writers often move back before moving ahead, skip a step and go back to it later, or finish a section but then decide to return to it again. As the circles and arrows in the diagram of the writing process show, planning is not over when drafting begins; drafting is not over when revising begins; editing might take you back to revising; and so on.

For example, consider that a college essay has an introductory paragraph (8b), as many **body paragraphs** (8d) as you need to cover your topic, and a **concluding paragraph** (8g). As you're writing, you might discover you need to think of a new topic for one of your body paragraphs

BOX 3

🎯 An overview of the writing process

- **Planning** means gathering ideas and thinking about a focus for your writing.
- **Shaping** means considering ways to organize your material.
- **Drafting** means writing your ideas in sentences and paragraphs.
- **Revising** means evaluating your draft and then rewriting it by adding, cutting, replacing, moving, and often totally recasting material.
- **Editing** means checking for correct grammar, spelling, punctuation, and mechanics.
- **Proofreading** means checking your final draft for typing errors or handwriting legibility, so that what you hand in is as clean as possible.

so that it's in line with your introduction. Similarly, as you write your concluding paragraph, you might realize that a body paragraph or the introductory paragraph needs revision to flow smoothly with the style and tone of the rest of your essay. Paths differ for each writer and for the same writer in each new WRITING SITUATION.*

Here's my personal advice from one writer to another: Most writers struggle with ideas that are difficult to express, sentences that won't take shape, and words that aren't precise. Be patient with yourself; writing takes time. The more you write, the easier it will become—though writing never goes easily for anyone.

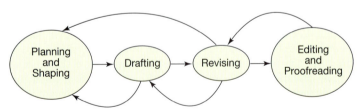

Visualizing the writing process

* Words printed in small capital letters (such as WRITING SITUATION) are defined in the Terms Glossary on pages 467-85.

BOX 4

⊙ Purposes for writing*

- to express yourself
- to inform a reader
- to persuade a reader
- to create a literary work

*Adapted from James L. Kinneavy, in *A Theory of Discourse*. New York: Norton, 1980.

5b What are the purposes for college writing?

A writer's **purpose** for writing is the motivating force behind what that writer wishes or is assigned to write. You need, therefore, to choose among the four major purposes of writing, listed in Box 4.

In this book, I concentrate on the two major purposes for most **academic writing**—the writing people do for college and scholarship: to inform a reader and to persuade a reader. The two remaining purposes listed in Box 4 are important for contributing to human thought and culture, but they do not relate directly to college writing.

Informing a reader

Informative writing, also called *expository writing,* seeks to give and explain information to readers. It expounds on—that is, systematically tells about—observations, ideas, facts, scientific data, and statistics. Typically, you can find informative writing in textbooks, encyclopedias, technical and business reports, nonfiction books, newspapers, and many magazines. Here's an example of an informative paragraph.

In 1914 in what is now Addo Park in South Africa, a hunter by the name of Pretorius was asked to exterminate a herd of 140 elephants. He killed all but 20, and those survivors became so cunning at evading him that he was forced to abandon the hunt. The area became a preserve in 1930, and the elephants have been protected ever since. Nevertheless, elephants now four generations removed from those Pretorius hunted remain shy and strangely nocturnal. Young elephants evidently learn from the adults' trumpeting alarm calls to avoid humans.

—Carol Grant Gould, "Out of the Mouths of Beasts"

Persuading a reader

Persuasive writing, also called *argumentative writing,* seeks to convince readers about a matter of opinion. Examples of persuasive writing include newspaper editorials, letters to the editor, opinion essays in newspapers and magazines, reviews, sermons, books that argue a point of view, and business proposals. Chapter 10, "Writing to Argue," covers the specific requirements of persuasive writing. Here's an example of a persuasive paragraph.

> The most visible evidence that commercialism now dominates religious holidays in the United States comes from the push to spend money rather than honor special observances. Individuals and businesses buy and mail huge quantities of Christmas cards. How many people can resist the social and business pressures of sending cards? Additionally, exchanging often-expensive gifts has become standard practice on Christmas Day and for weeks beforehand. Many people go into credit-card debt that lasts for half a year or longer merely to support the costly cycle of giving and receiving presents. The advertising industry makes huge profits from writing ads that set high expectations among children and adults alike. Can homemade cookies compare to a microwave oven? Can a well-constructed bookrack compare to an electric saw?
>
> —Lind Brighteyes, student

5c What does "audience" mean for writing?

Your **audience** consists of everyone who will read your writing. After college, your audience will be readers of your business, professional, and/or public writing. In college, you address a mix of audience types, each of which expects to read **academic writing**—the writing assigned in your courses. These audiences include

- your peers (fellow students)
- a general audience (educated, experienced readers without specialized knowledge of your topic)
- a specialized audience (experts on your topic)
- your instructor

The more specifics you can assume about your audience for your academic writing, the better your chances of reaching it successfully. For example, if you're writing a sales report for your supervisor, you can use terms such as *product life cycle, breakeven quantity, nonprice com-*

BOX 5

 ## Characteristics of reading audiences

WHAT SETTING ARE THEY READING IN?
- academic setting
- workplace setting
- public setting

WHO ARE THEY?
- age, gender
- ethnic backgrounds, political philosophies, religious beliefs
- roles (student, parent, voter, wage earner, property owner, veteran, etc.)
- interests, hobbies

WHAT DO THEY KNOW?
- level of education
- amount of general or specialized knowledge about the topic
- probable preconceptions and prejudices brought to the topic

petition, and *markup.* In contrast, if general readers were your audience for this information, you would want to avoid specialized, technical vocabulary—or if you had to use some essential specialized terms, you would want to define them in a nontechnical way. Ask yourself the questions in Box 5 to pinpoint the characteristics of your audience.

⊕ **ESL NOTE:** As someone from another culture, you might be surprised—even offended—by the directness with which people speak and write in the United States. If so, I hope you'll read my open letter to multilingual students about honoring one's native culture (see pp. 359–60). The idea is that for U.S. college writing, you need to adapt to U.S. writing style. Your own written-language traditions may expect elaborate and/or ceremonial language, call for you to introduce the central point in the essay's middle, and prefer tactful, indirect discussions (at least in comparison to U.S. style). In contrast, U.S. writing contains language and style that's very direct, straightforward, and without digressive embellishments. College instructors in the United States expect ACADEMIC WRITING to contain a thesis statement (usually at the end of the introductory paragraph), to demonstrate a tightly organized presentation of information from one paragraph to the next, to make generalizations that are always backed up with strong supporting details, and to end with a logical concluding paragraph. In addition, you need to use standard English grammar, as spoken by most announcers on TV network news programs. 🌐

Writing for a peer-response group

Instructors sometimes divide the students in a class into small **peer-response groups.** Participating in a peer-response group makes you part of a respected tradition of colleagues helping colleagues. Professional writers often seek comments from other writers to improve their rough drafts. As a member of a college peer-response group, you're not expected to be a writing expert. Rather, you're expected to offer responses as a practiced reader and a student writer who knows the difficulties of writing well. Hearing or reading comments from your peers can be very informative, surprising, and helpful.

As you work with your peers, you'll not be able to avoid the sometimes sticky issue of how to take criticism of your writing. Here's my personal advice as a writer for being able (or at least appearing able) to take constructive criticism gracefully. First, know that most students don't like to criticize their peers. They worry about being impolite or inaccurate or losing someone's friendship. Try, therefore, to cultivate an attitude that encourages your peers to respond as freely and as helpfully as possible. Show, also, that you can listen with an open mind, without getting angry or defensive.

Second, realize that most people tend to be a little (or quite a bit) defensive about even the best-intentioned and tactful criticism. Of course, if a comment is purposely mean or sarcastic, you and all others in your peer-response group have every right to reject it. Third, if you don't understand a comment fully, ask for clarification. Otherwise, you might misunderstand and go off in the wrong direction. Finally, no matter what anyone says about your writing, never forget that it remains yours alone. You retain "ownership" of your writing, so use only those comments that can move you closer to reaching your intended audience.

Writing for an instructor

As your audience, your instructor plays three roles. An instructor (1) represents either general or specialized readers, (2) acts as your writing coach, and (3) becomes the eventual evaluator of your final drafts.

Instructors know that few students are experienced writers or experts on their topics. Still, instructors expect your writing to show that you took serious time to learn something worthwhile about a subject and then to write about it clearly. Instructors are experienced readers; they recognize a minimal effort almost at once. In addition, instructors are people whose professional lives center on intellectual endeavors. You want, therefore, to write within the constraints of academic writing, and to write on topics that have some built-in intellectual interest.

If you're a relatively inexperienced college writer, you might wrongly assume that your instructor can mentally fill in what you haven't bothered to say fully. You might think incorrectly that you would be wrong, or even insulting, if you tried to extend your discussion beyond simple statements. Instructors—indeed, all readers—are not mind readers, however, and they become annoyed if you don't write fully on a topic. It's never wrong to go beyond stating the obvious or to show that you know how to develop your material beyond bare-bones basics.

5d How does the tone of my writing affect my audience?

Tone is more than what you say; tone is how you say it. Tone in writing operates like tone of voice in speaking, except that in writing, you can't rely on your facial expressions and voice intonations to communicate your meaning. If your tone is inappropriate for your audience or your topic, it can ruin your essay, no matter how well you handle other matters.

Your choice of words, level of formality, and writing style create your tone. You can use slang and other highly informal language in a note to your roommate, but not in ACADEMIC WRITING or BUSINESS WRITING. When you write for audiences such as your teachers or your supervisor, use more formality. "More formality," however, doesn't mean dull and drab. In fact, in a serious discussion, lively language can enhance your message and strike the right tone.

Academic writing almost always calls for a medium-to-formal tone. For details about how to achieve such a tone, see the discussions of word meaning (Ch. 19) and gender-neutral language (Ch. 20) in the Words section of this book.

5e How do I work with a writing topic?

Situations vary. Some assignments are very specific about your topic. For example, "Explain how oxygen is absorbed in the lungs" leaves no room for choice. You would need to write about that topic precisely, without going off the topic. However, only rarely are writing-class assignments as specific as this.

More often, your instructor will ask you to select your own topic, to narrow a broad topic, or to broaden a narrow topic. As you do this, the overriding principle is always this: **What separates most good writing from bad is the writer's ability to move back and forth between general statements and specific details.**

Selecting your own topic

If you need to choose a topic, don't rush. Take time to think through your ideas. Avoid getting so deeply involved in one topic that you can't change to a more suitable topic in the time allotted. Not all topics are suitable for ACADEMIC WRITING. Your topic needs to allow you to demonstrate your intellectual thinking and writing abilities.

Think through potential topics by breaking each into its logical subsections. Then make sure you can supply sufficiently specific details to back up each general statement. Conversely, make sure you don't drown your essay with so many details your readers can't figure out what generalizations they are supporting. Work toward balance by finding a middle ground. Beware of topics so broad that they lead to vague generalizations (for example, "Education is necessary for success"). Also, beware of topics so narrow that they lead nowhere after a few sentences (for example, "Jessica Max attends Tower College").

Narrowing or broadening an assigned topic

Suppose that "marriage" is your assigned topic for a 1,000-word essay. You'd be too broad if you chose "What makes a successful marriage?" Conversely, you'd be too narrow if you came up with "Alexandra and Gavin were married by a Justice of the Peace." You'd likely be on target with a topic such as "In successful marriages, husbands and wives learn to accept each other's faults." You could use 1,000 words to explain and give concrete examples of typical faults and discuss why accepting them is important.

Carol Moreno, the student whose essay appears in 9b, knew that her assigned topic—"Write about a challenge you faced and tried to meet"—was too broad. She had to be specific. She wanted to write about having faced the challenge of how to get physically fit. She realized that "getting physically fit" or even "women's fitness" was still too broad. She thought of some narrower topics, such as "organized sports," "power walking," and "weight training." In the end, she chose "weight training," because she knew about it from personal experience and could think of both generalizations and specific details to use in her essay. In addition, Moreno knew that if her assignment called for research, she could find many sources on weight training in books and magazines and on the Internet.

✔ **Guidelines for analyzing each writing situation: TPAS**

- **T = Topic:** What is the topic you'll be writing about? (5e)
- **P = Purpose:** Is your purpose to be INFORMATIVE or PERSUASIVE? (5b)
- **A = Audience:** Who are your readers? (5c)
- **S = Special requirements:** How much time do you have to complete the assignment? What is the length requirement?

5f What is a "writing situation"?

The **writing situation** of each assignment involves four elements: *topic, purpose, audience,* and *special requirements.* Use the questions in Box 6 to analyze each element. (Memory hint: The first letter of each word forms TPAS, pronounced "T pass.")

5g How can I find ideas for writing?

Do you ever worry that you have nothing to write about? You're not alone. Most people know more than they give themselves credit for. The techniques listed here can help you uncover ideas and details to use in your writing. If one technique doesn't provide enough useful material, try another.

Keeping a journal

Writing in a journal is like having a "conversation on paper" with yourself. You can write about anything you like—your experiences, observations, dreams, creative ideas, reactions to your reading.

Why do it? First, writing every day gives you the habit of productivity. The more you write, the more you get used to the feeling of expressing yourself on paper. Second, writing regularly in a journal helps you think through ideas that need time to develop. Third, your journal becomes a source of ideas when you need to choose your own writing topic (5e).

Freewriting

Freewriting means writing down whatever comes into your mind about whatever topic that surfaces, without stopping to worry about whether your ideas are good or your spelling is correct. Such writing is a way of discovering, of allowing your thoughts to emerge as the physical act of writing is under way. **Focused freewriting** means starting with a favorite word or sentence from your journal, a quotation you like, or perhaps a topic you are studying for a course.

When you freewrite, do not interrupt the flow. Keep writing. Do not censor your thoughts or flashes of insight. Do not review or cross out. Sometimes, when you finish and read over your freewriting, it might seem mindless to you. But other days it might startle you with its interesting ideas.

COMPUTER TIP: When you write at a computer, dim the screen so that you cannot see what you are writing. This way, you record your thoughts, but you resist the temptation to censor yourself. When you brighten the screen, your freewriting will be visible.

Brainstorming

Brainstorming means listing everything you can think of about a topic. Let your mind range freely, generating quantities of ideas before analyzing them. After you have brainstormed, look for patterns and ways to group your ideas. Discard items that do not fit into any group. Groups with the most items are likely to be topics you can write about successfully.

Here is brainstorming by student writer Carol Moreno, whose essay on women lifting weights appears in 9b. Moreno grouped the items marked with an asterisk and used them in her third paragraph.

safety with free weights (barbells)*

don't bend at the waist*

don't hold your breath

use leg strength to straighten up*

don't allow a twist*

concentrate on each move

Asking and answering questions

Try exploring your topic by asking questions that journalists use.

- Who?
- What?
- When?

- Why?
- Where?
- How?

This is how Carol Moreno used these questions: *Who* was in my first weight-lifting class? *What* reasons did other women have for taking the class? *Why* did I get interested in weight lifting? *When* did I realize that weight lifting wasn't just an activity for guys? *How* do I feel about weight lifting now?

Here is another useful list of questions.

- What is it?
- How is it the same as other things?
- How is it different from other things?
- Why or how does it happen?
- How is it done?
- What does it look, smell, taste, sound, feel like?

Clustering

Clustering, also called *mapping,* is a visual form of brainstorming. Write your topic in the middle of a sheet and put a circle around it. Now, moving out from the center, use lines and circles to record your ideas, as the example shows. Continue using this method to subdivide and add details. Here is part of Carol Moreno's clustering for the fifth paragraph of her essay in 9b.

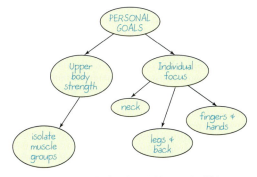

Clustering that became the basis for Carol Moreno's fifth paragraph

BOX 7

 Basic requirements for a thesis statement

1. It states the essay's subject, but it does not repeat the title of the essay.
2. It indicates the essay's PURPOSE but it does not announce it with "The purpose of this essay is. . . ."
3. It conveys the writer's point of view toward the subject.
4. It makes a general statement that leads to a set of main ideas and supporting details; that is, it's much more than a statement of fact that leads nowhere.
5. It uses specific language and avoids vague words.
6. It may give the major subdivisions of the topic.

5h What is a thesis statement?

A **thesis statement** is the central message of an essay. Your thesis statement both reflects the content of your essay and guides your writing. To compose a thesis statement, first write a simple statement that makes an **assertion.** Such a statement names your topic and states your position on it. Writing an assertion focuses your thinking as you progress toward a fully developed thesis statement. As you are writing, if you find that your thesis statement and the content of your essay do not match, revise one or the other—or perhaps both.

Here is student writer Carol Moreno's assertion for her essay about women lifting weights (9b), followed by her progression toward a final version of her thesis statement.

- I think women can pump iron like men. [This assertion is a start.]

- If she is trained well, any woman can pump iron well, just like a man. [This statement is more developed because it mentions training, but the word *well* is used twice and is vague, and the word *any* is inaccurate.]

- Most people think only men can pump iron, but women can also do it successfully with the right training. [This statement is closer to a thesis statement because it is more specific. However, men are not part of Moreno's topic. Also, the concept of building strength, a major aspect of Moreno's final draft, is missing.]

- With the right training, women can "pump iron" to build strength.
  [This final version serves as Moreno's thesis statement, except for one further change: She added a transitional word—*also*—to connect the thesis
  statement to what comes before in her introductory paragraph.]

Moreno's final version fulfills the basic requirements for a thesis
statement, as listed in Box 7.

5i How might outlining help me write?

An **outline** is a structured, sequential list of the contents of an essay.
Some writers always use outlines, while others never do. Some instructors require an outline with an essay, while others don't. You need to
find what works best for you personally as well as what your assignment calls for.

In some writing situations, writers like to outline before they write
their essay. In other situations, writers prefer to outline after they've
written their first draft. In addition, some writers like to outline during
the WRITING PROCESS, especially at two distinct points. They outline
before DRAFTING, to flesh out, pull together, and arrange material. They
also outline while REVISING, to check the logic and flow of thought of the
essay. Outlines are excellent tools for revealing where information is
missing, repeated, or off the topic.

An **informal outline** doesn't follow any of the numbering and let-
tering conventions of a formal outline. It often looks like a BRAINSTORM-
ING list, with ideas jotted down in a somewhat random order. Here is
part of an informal outline for the second paragraph of Carol Moreno's
essay (9b).

SAMPLE INFORMAL OUTLINE

Need the right training

Muscle building

Biology

Hormones and longer muscles

An aerobic exercise

Aerobic workout

A **formal outline** follows long-established conventions for using
numbers and letters to show relationships among ideas (Box 8). A formal outline can be a **topic outline,** composed of words and phrases, or
a **sentence outline,** composed entirely of complete sentences (Box 8
shows both styles). Never mix the two styles in one outline.

Formal outline requirements

FORMAL OUTLINE FORM

<u>Thesis statement</u>

   I. First main idea

      A. First subordinate idea

         1. First reason or example

         2. Second reason or example

            a. First supporting detail

            b. Second supporting detail

      B. Second subordinate idea

  II. Second main idea

SAMPLE OF A FORMAL SENTENCE OUTLINE

This outline goes with the third paragraph of Carol Moreno's essay (9b).

<u>Thesis statement</u>: With the right training, women can also "pump iron" to build strength.

   I. The right training shows women how to use weights safely to prevent injury.

      A. Free weights require special precautions.

         1. Bending at the waist and jerking a barbell up is unsafe.

         2. Squatting and using leg and back muscles to straighten up is safe.

            a. The head is held erect and faces forward.

            b. The neck and back are aligned and held straight.

      B. Weight machines make it easier to lift safely because they force proper body alignment.

TIPS AND GUIDELINES FOR WRITING AN OUTLINE

- Use at least two subdivisions at each level—no I without a II, no A without a B, and so on. If a level has only one subdivision, either integrate it into a higher level or expand it to at least two subdivisions.

- Keep all subdivisions at the same level of generality (do not pair a main idea with a supporting detail).

- Use PARALLELISM for entries on the same level.

6 DRAFTING

6a What strategies can I use to write a first draft?

A first draft is always rough. Its goal is to give you something to improve by REVISING. Here are three suggested alternatives for writing a first draft.

- Put aside all the notes you made to get started. Write a **discovery draft,** which uses FOCUSED FREEWRITING to uncover ideas and make connections that spring to mind during freewriting.

- Or, keep your notes from the techniques described in 5g at hand and write a structured first draft by working your way through your notes.

- Or, combine the two approaches. When your notes can guide you, use them. When you feel stuck about what to say next, switch to a discovery draft.

The direction of drafting is forward: Keep pressing ahead. If you wonder about the spelling of a word or a point in grammar, underline it and check it later. If you can't think of an exact word, use a SYNONYM and mark it to change later. If you're worried about your sentence style or the order in which you present details, jot *Style?* or *Order?* in the margin and return to the issue later. No matter what, keep moving ahead. If you begin to run dry, reread what you have written to propel yourself to write further. Keep writing until you've managed to write a complete first draft. Be careful not to stop in the middle of your drafting so that you can REVISE. Revising comes later, using the process described in Chapter 7.

6b What can I do if I experience writer's block?

Writer's block means the writer can't think of ideas or get words onto paper. Such blocks hit writers whether they're students or experienced writers. Box 9 lists some strategies that experienced writers often use to overcome writer's block.

COMPUTER TIPS: (1) When you draft on a computer and have questions but need to keep moving ahead, insert a symbol. Later, search for the symbols and make your changes. (2) If you print out your first draft, resist the urge to consider it final merely because it looks neatly typed.

BOX 9

 Ways to overcome writer's block

- **Avoid staring at a blank page.** Relax and move your hand across the page or keyboard while you think about your TOPIC.
- **Visualize yourself writing.** Imagine yourself where you usually write, busy at work.
- **Imagine a scene or sound that relates to your topic.** Start writing by describing what you see or hear.
- **Write a letter or an e-mail.** Start with "Dear" using a specific name. Pretend you are writing to that person.
- **Write pretending that you're someone else.** Take on someone else's identity and write from that person's perspective.
- **Start in the middle.** Write from the center of your essay out instead of from beginning to end.

7 REVISING, EDITING, AND PROOFREADING

Once you have finished your first DRAFT, you begin to revise. Then you edit and proofread.

7a What strategies can I use to revise?

When you **revise,** you take a draft from first to final version by evaluating, adding, cutting, replacing, and moving material. In other words, you need to shift from suspending judgment to making judgments.

At the same time that you want to be critical, do not be overly harsh on yourself. Most early drafts provide sufficient raw material for you to revise. Do, however, be systematic in evaluating your draft. Use the questions in Box 10 (p. 30) or guidelines supplied by your instructor. Every time you make a change, evaluate it alone and in the context of the surrounding material. Continue this process until you are satisfied that you have made all the improvements you can and your essay is in its final form.

7b　How do a thesis statement and an essay title help me revise?

Use the THESIS STATEMENT to guide your revision. At the end of every paragraph, ask yourself, "How does this paragraph relate to my thesis statement?" If your thesis statement does not match what your essay says, revise the thesis statement, the essay, or both.

Your essay title can also play an important part in revising, so do not wait until the last minute and merely tack on a title. Create at least a working title during your first draft. Use it as a checkpoint as your essay evolves.

A **direct title** tells exactly what the essay will be about: for example, "Women Can Pump Iron, Too." An **indirect title** hints at an essay's topic: "Why Not Try Pumping Iron?" Indirect titles can be very effective as long as the connection is not too obscure.

ALERT: A title stands alone. Do not open an essay by referring to the title as though its words are in the essay's first sentence. Carol Moreno titled her paper "Women Can Pump Iron, Too." Below is an example of how *not* to open that essay by referring to its title. To see how Carol Moreno's paper actually begins, go to page 47.

　　NO　They certainly can, and I'm living proof.

COMPUTER TIPS: Revising is easy on a computer. You can add, delete, and rearrange anything from a word or a sentence to a paragraph without the agony of retyping your entire essay. (1) If you are undecided about a revision, create several versions of your paper. (2) Experiment by reordering your body paragraphs, splitting or joining paragraphs, or moving your last paragraph to the very beginning. (3) Resist the temptation to revise endlessly. (4) Delete cautiously. If you want to drop material, resist merely deleting it. Instead, save it in a new document so that you can use it later if you change your mind.

7c　How can a revision checklist help me revise?

Use a revision checklist like the one in Box 10 to focus your attention as you evaluate your writing. Do not let a checklist overwhelm you, though. Adjust it to each of your writing situations so that your checklist works for you.

BOX 10

 Revision checklist

If your answer to any question in this checklist is no, you need to revise. The section numbers in parentheses tell you where in this book to look for help.

THE GLOBAL VIEW: WHOLE ESSAY AND PARAGRAPHS

1. Is your essay topic suitable and sufficiently narrow? (5e)
2. Does your thesis statement communicate your topic, focus, and purpose? (5h, Box 7)
3. Does your essay show that you are aware of your audience? (5c, Box 5)
4. Is your essay arranged effectively? (5i)
5. Have you checked for material that strays off the topic? (7c)
6. Does your introduction prepare your reader for the rest of the essay? (8b)
7. Do your body paragraphs express main ideas in topic sentences as needed? (8c) Are your main ideas clearly related to your thesis statement? (5h)
8. Do your body paragraphs provide specific, concrete support for each main idea? (8d, 8f)
9. Do you use transitions and other techniques to connect ideas within and between paragraphs? (8e)
10. Does your conclusion give your essay a sense of completion? (8g)

LOCAL VIEW: SENTENCES AND WORDS

1. Have you eliminated sentence fragments? (Ch. 11) Have you eliminated comma splices and fused sentences? (Ch. 12)
2. Have you eliminated confusing shifts? (Ch. 13)
3. Have you eliminated disjointed sentences? (Ch. 13)
4. Have you eliminated misplaced and dangling modifiers? (Ch. 14)
5. Are your sentences concise? (Ch. 15)
6. Do your sentences show clear relationships among ideas? (Ch. 16)
7. Do you use parallelism, variety, and emphasis correctly and to increase the impact of your writing? (Ch. 17)
8. Have you used exact words? (19b)
9. Is your usage correct and your language appropriate? (Ch. 18, 19d)
10. Have you avoided sexist language? (20b)

Here's part of a paragraph from the informative essay by student Carol Moreno. Using a revision checklist, Moreno made several changes and added more specific, concrete details. For the final draft, see body paragraph 3 of Moreno's essay (9b).

My topic sentence needs work

After safety comes our needs for physical

strength. A well-planned, progressive weight

training program. ~~You begin~~ *begins* with whatever

a person

weight ~~you~~ can lift comfortably and then

^ adds to the base weight as she gets stronger.

gradually ~~add.~~ What builds muscle strength

the lifter does,

is the number of "reps" ~~we do,~~ not necessarily

resistance from adding

an increase in the amount of ~~added~~ weight.

In my class, we ranged from 18 to 43, scrawny

pudgy,   *couch potato*

to ~~fat,~~ and ~~lazy~~ to superstar, and we each

?Start sentence here? Not sure

developed a program that was (OK) for us.

I'm being lazy here

Some women didn't listen to our instructor

try

who urged us not to ~~do~~ more reps or weight than

our first workouts

our programs called for, even if ~~it~~ seemed

too easy. This turned out to be good advice

the next morning

because those of us who didn't listen woke up

feeling as though our bodies had been twisted by

evil forces.

■ BOX 11 ■

 Editing checklist

If an answer to a question in this checklist is no, you need to edit. The section numbers in parentheses tell you where in this book to look for help.

1. Is the grammar correct? (Chs. 39–49)
2. Are the sentences correct? (Chs. 11–14)
3. Are commas used correctly? (Ch. 50)
4. Are all other punctuation marks used correctly? (Chs. 51–56)
5. Are hyphens, capital letters, italics (or underlining), abbreviations, and numbers used correctly? (Chs. 57–61)
6. Are all words spelled correctly? (Ch. 21)

7d What strategies can I use to edit?

Editing means finding and fixing errors you have made in grammar, spelling, punctuation, capitals, numbers, italics, and abbreviations. Some instructors call these *surface-level features*. You're ready to edit when the content and organization of your paper is set—that is, when it's revised. Edit slowly and methodically. Looking up advice and rules in this handbook takes concentration and time. You may also want to ask a friend with a good editing "eye" to read your paper and circle anything that you should check for correctness.

7e How can an editing checklist help me edit?

An editing checklist can help you focus your attention systematically on everything you need to be concerned about during this part of the writing process. Adjust the checklist in Box 11 to each of your different writing situations so that the questions work for you.

On the next page is the introductory paragraph from Carol Moreno's essay showing her edits. (For the final draft, see 9b.)

7f What strategies can I use to proofread?

Proofreading is a careful, line-by-line reading of a final, clean version of your essay. You always proofread before you hand in your paper. Correct any errors you find, but if a page has numerous errors, recopy it or

When my grandmother fell and broke her hip last

summer, I wanted to help take care of her. Because she

was bedridden, she needed to be lifted at times, but I

was shocked to discover than I could not lift her without

my mothers or brothers help. My grandmother does not

weigh much, but she was to much for me. My pride was

hurt, and even important, I began to worry about my plans

to be a nurse specializing in care of elderly people.

What if I was to weak to help my patients get around

When I realized that I could satisfy one of my Physical

Ed requirements by taking a weight—lifting course for

women, I decided to try it. Many people picture only big

macho men wanting to lift weights, but times have

changed. With the right training, women can also "pump

iron" successfully to build strength.

print out a corrected page. A neat, accurate paper conveys your positive
attitude toward your course, your teacher, and yourself.

PROOFREADING STRATEGIES

- Proofread with a ruler so that you can focus on one line at a time.
- Start at the end of a paragraph or the end of your essay and read
  each sentence in reverse order or word by word, to avoid being distracted by the content.
- Read your final draft aloud so that you see and hear errors; look
  carefully for omitted letters and words as well as for repeated
  words.

COMPUTER TIPS: (1) Try editing and proofreading by highlighting a small section of your writing. This separates it visually from the rest of the screen and helps reduce your tendency to read too quickly and overlook errors. (2) Create your personal spell-check or style checker by keeping a file of the errors you have made in the past. Access it each time you revise and edit. If you use a word processing program's spell-check, proofread for words that are misused rather than misspelled (for example, *it's* for *its*) and words that cannot be identified by a spell-check because the errors are real words (for example, *form* for *from*).

8 COMPOSING PARAGRAPHS

8a What is a paragraph?

A **paragraph** is a group of sentences that work together to develop a unit of thought. Paragraphing permits writers to divide material into manageable parts and arrange the parts in a unified whole. Much of the assigned writing you do in college will typically consist of an introductory paragraph, a group of body paragraphs, and a concluding paragraph. (Your instructors may call such writing essays, compositions, themes, reports, or papers.)

8b How can I write effective introductory paragraphs?

An introductory paragraph serves several functions. It prepares the reader for what lies ahead by giving background information or setting the stage in some other way. It also tries to arouse interest so the reader will want to read on. Box 12 suggests some strategies for creating interest.

You may be required to include a THESIS STATEMENT in the introductory paragraph (5h, 7b). Usually, the thesis statement appears in the last sentence or two of the introductory paragraph, as shown in paragraphs 1 and 3 below. (Experienced writers sometimes diverge from this basic pattern, depending on their writing PURPOSE.)

1 Alone one is never lonely, May Sarton says in her essay "The Rewards of Living a Solitary Life." Most people, however, are terrified of living alone. They are used to living with others— children with parents, roommates with roommates, friends with friends, husbands with wives. When the statistics catch up with

BOX 12

 Strategies for writing introductory paragraphs

STRATEGIES FOR INTERESTING YOUR READER

- Provide relevant background information about your topic.
- Relate a brief, interesting anecdote that applies to your topic.
- Give pertinent, perhaps surprising statistics about your topic.
- Ask a provocative question or questions to lead into your topic.
- Use a quotation that relates closely to your topic.
- Draw an analogy to clarify or illustrate your topic.
- Define a key term you use throughout your essay.

STRATEGIES TO AVOID

- Avoid obvious statements about the essay's topic or purpose: Do not say, "I am going to discuss why women can learn to lift weights."
- Avoid apologizing, as in "I am not sure I'm right, but this is my opinion."
- Avoid overworked expressions, such as "Haste really does make waste, as I recently discovered."

them, therefore, they are rarely prepared. Chances are high that most adult men and women will live alone, briefly or longer, at some time.

—Tara Foster, student

8c How do topic sentences work?

A **topic sentence** contains the main idea of a body paragraph. The topic sentence controls what the paragraph can include. Though in student writing, topic sentences come most often at the beginning of a paragraph, putting them at the end or implying them is fine.

Starting with a topic sentence

When a topic sentence starts a paragraph, readers immediately know what topic will be discussed.

The cockroach lore that has been daunting us for years is mostly true. Roaches can live for twenty days without food, fourteen days without water; they can flatten their bodies and crawl

2 through a crack thinner than a dime; they can eat huge doses of carcinogens and still die of old age. They can even survive as much radiation as an oak tree can, says William Bell, the University of Kansas entomologist whose cockroaches appeared in the movie *The Day After*. They'll eat almost anything—regular food, leather, glue, hair, paper, even the starch in book bindings. (The New York Public Library has quite a cockroach problem.) They sense the slightest breeze, and they can react and start running in .05 seconds; they can also remain motionless for days. And if all this isn't creepy enough, they can fly too.

—Jane Goodman, "What's Bugging You"

Ending with a topic sentence

When a topic sentence ends a body paragraph, readers sometimes feel more eager to read on to the next paragraph.

3 When he was ten years old, Lester taught himself to windsurf by hanging around the European and Canadian tourists who rented boards on the beach at Varadero. "If you made friends with them, they would sometimes let you use their equipment," he says. As he grew older and got better at the sport, he found he liked the isolation and freedom of the sea. "Sometimes I would sail for eight hours without stopping, and go very far out," he says. His windsurfing to freedom seemed destined.

—Sam Moses, "A New Dawn"

Implying a topic sentence

Some paragraphs convey a main idea without a specific topic sentence. Writers carefully construct these paragraphs so that details add up in such a way that the main idea is clear even though it is not explicitly stated.

4 Annie was a compact, gray-haired woman whose carriage belied a strength acquired from many years of work. She mounted the hall stairs and opened a door to the left to show me a small, modest one-bedroom apartment. "I clean on Tuesdays and Fridays. Just leave the trash outside in the hall," she said. I liked the soft resonance of her voice. She took my check and gave me the key.

—Bob Akin, "Out of Their Element"

8d How can I use details to develop body paragraphs?

Use specific, concrete details to develop body paragraphs that support the generalization in the TOPIC SENTENCE. What separates most good writing from bad is the writer's ability to move back and forth between gener-

BOX 13

 RENNS = specific, concrete details

R   **R**easons
E   **E**xamples
N   **N**ames
N   **N**umbers
S   **S**enses (sight, sound, smell, taste, touch)

alizations and specific details. To check that you have enough detail, try using **RENNS,** a memory device summarized in Box 13. You don't need to use details in the order of the letters in RENNS. Neither do you need to use all the RENNS. For example, paragraph 5 uses three RENNS. See if you can identify them before you read the analysis after the paragraph.

Whether bad or good, in tune or not, whistling has its practical side. Clifford Pratt is working with a group of speech therapists to develop whistling techniques to help children overcome speech problems through improved breath control and tongue flexibility. People who have a piercing whistle have a clear ad-
5 vantage when it comes to hailing cabs, calling the dog or the children, or indicating approval during a sporting event. And if you want to leave the house and can't remember where you put your keys, there's a key chain on the market now with a beep that can be activated by a whistle: You whistle and the key chain tells you where it is.

—Cassandra Tate, "Whistlers Blow New Life into a Forgotten Art"

Paragraph 5 uses several examples (E) of how whistling can be help-ful: overcoming speech problems, hailing cabs, calling dogs and children, cheering at sporting events, and finding keys. Also, it uses specific names (N): *Clifford Pratt* (not the general term *researcher*), *children* (not the gen-eral term *people*), and *dogs* (not the general term *animals*). In addition, the paragraph uses sensory description (S): the feeling of breath control, tongue flexibility, and the sound of whistles and a beeping key chain.

8e What strategies can I use to create coherent paragraphs?

A paragraph is **coherent** when its sentences are connected in content and relate to each other in form and language. **Coherence** creates a smooth flow of thoughts within each paragraph as well as from one paragraph to

BOX 14

Transitional words and expressions and the relationships they signal

ADDITION	in addition, also, too, besides, equally important, furthermore, moreover
COMPARISON	in the same way, likewise, similarly
CONCESSION	granted, naturally, of course
CONTRAST	in contrast, however, instead, on the contrary, on the other hand, at the same time, despite the fact that, otherwise, nevertheless, still
EMPHASIS	of course, certainly, indeed, in fact
EXAMPLE	for example, for instance, as an illustration, a case in point, namely, specifically
RESULT	as a result, consequently, hence, then, therefore, thus, accordingly
SUMMARY	finally, in conclusion, in short, in summary
TIME SEQUENCE	today, tomorrow, yesterday, once, now, next, then, eventually, meanwhile, subsequently, finally

another. You can use transitional words and expressions, deliberate repetition, and parallelism help to make your writing coherent.

Using transitional words and expressions

Transitional words and expressions help connect ideas within and between paragraphs. They do this by showing relationships, such as addition or contrast or result. Box 14 lists frequently used transitional words and the relationships they show. In paragraph 6, transitional words and expressions are in boldface type.

6   Jaguars, **for example,** were **once** found in the United States from southern Louisiana to California. **Today** they are rare north of the Mexican border, with no confirmed sightings since 1971. They are rare, **too,** in Mexico, where biologist Carl Koford estimated their population at fewer than a thousand in a 1972 survey. Some biologists think the number is even smaller **today.** **Similarly,** jaguars have disappeared from southern Argentina and Paraguay.

—Jeffrey P. Cohen, "Kings of the Wild"

Never overuse transitional expressions.

> NO   **In addition,** they served ice cream **also.**

> YES   **In addition,** they served ice cream.

Equally important, be sure that the transitional word you choose fits your intended meaning. For instance, use *on the other hand* for contrast, never for summary. Also, vary the transitional expressions you use. For example, avoid *for instance* every time you give an example.

👁 **ALERT:** Within a sentence, a transitional expression is usually set off with commas (50h). However, between INDEPENDENT CLAUSES, a semicolon must come before the transitional expression (51b). 👁

Using deliberate repetition and parallelism

You can also achieve coherence through **deliberate repetition** of key words. You can introduce key words in your topic sentence or use them to refer to major details. Use such deliberate repetition sparingly or your writing will become monotonous. Paragraph 7 shows effective use of deliberate repetition. The word *work* is repeated throughout, and within a single sentence, *walking* and *without* are repeated for added coherence.

You can also use **parallelism** to link ideas and achieve coherence. Sentences are parallel when they repeat a grammatical structure. Notice, for example, that in paragraph 7, the middle supporting sentences all open with the same structure: *It was work.* Notice, too, the parallelism within the fourth sentence—*to swing, to tighten,* and *to walk.*

> The world of *work* into which Jacinto and the other seven-year-olds were apprenticed was within sight and sound of the pueblo. **It was *work*** under blazing suns, in rainstorms, in pitch-black nights. **It was *work*** that you were always *walking to* or *walking from, work without wages* and *work without end.*
>
> 7 **It was *work*** that gave you a bone-tired feeling at the end of the day, so you learned **to swing** a machete, **to tighten** a cinch, and **to walk** without lost motion. Between seven and twelve you learned all this, each lesson driven home when your *jefe* said with a scowl: "*Así no, hombre; así.*" And he showed you how.
>
> —Ernesto Galarza, *Barrio Boy*

8f What strategies can I use to develop body paragraphs?

As you develop the supporting body paragraphs in your writing, you can use various rhetorical strategies. **Rhetorical strategies** are patterns and techniques for presenting ideas clearly and effectively. The specific rhetorical strategies that you choose to use depend on what you want to accomplish.

In this section, you'll learn about rhetorical strategies one at a time. When you write, however, no paragraph is isolated, so techniques of rhetorical strategies often overlap in one paragraph. For example, in a paragraph explaining how to prepare a slide to study under a microscope, you would likely use the process pattern along with definition and description.

Composing a narration

Narrative writing tells what is happening or what has happened—it is storytelling. Narration is usually organized chronologically—first this, then that.

> We walked down the path to the well-house, attracted by the fragrance of the honeysuckle with which it was covered. Someone was drawing water and my teacher placed my hand under the spout. As the cool stream gushed over one hand she spelled into the other the word *water,* first slowly, then rapidly. I stood still, my whole attention fixed upon the motions of her fingers.
>
> 8 Suddenly I felt a misty consciousness as of something forgotten—a thrill of returning thought; and somehow the mystery of language was revealed to me. I knew then that "water" meant the wonderful cool something that was flowing over my hand. That living word awakened my soul, gave it light, hope, joy, set it free! There were barriers still, it is true, but barriers that could in time be swept away.
>
> —Helen Keller, *The Story of My Life*

Composing a description

Descriptive writing paints a picture in words. It usually calls on the five senses. It may be organized spatially (from top to bottom, or left to right, or inside to outside, and so on). Paragraph 9 is organized spatially. Description can also be organized from general to specific (presenting a dominant impression followed by details) and from least to most important (arranging information so that it builds to a climax).

9   The old store, lighted only by three fifty-watt bulbs, smelled of coal oil and baking bread. In the middle of the rectangular room, where the oak floor sagged a little, stood an iron stove. To the right was a wooden table with an unfinished game of checkers and a stool made from an apple-tree stump. On shelves around the walls sat earthen jugs with corncob stoppers, a few canned goods, and some of the two thousand old clocks and clockworks Thurmond Watts owned. Only one was ticking; the others he just looked at.

—William Least Heat Moon, *Blue Highways*

Describing a process

Process writing tells how to do something. It gives instruction or advice. Most process writing is organized chronologically because sequence is very important. In fact, not only must you give the steps of the process in order, but you must include all the steps.

10   Carrying loads of equal weight like paint cans and toolboxes is easier if you carry one in each hand. Keep your shoulders back and down so that the weight is balanced on each side of your body, not suspended in front. With this method, you will be able to lift heavier loads and also to walk and stand erect. Your back will not be strained by being pulled to one side.

—John Warde, "Safe Lifting Techniques"

Composing an example or illustration

Writing developed with **examples** provides concrete, specific representations of the main idea. A single extended example is often called an **illustration.** If you use several examples, you can choose to arrange them from least to most important or the other way around—from most to least important. Choose according to your purpose and the meaning and impact you want to deliver.

11   One major value of rain forests is biomedical. The plants and animals of rain forests are the source of many compounds used in today's medicines. A drug that helps treat Parkinson's disease is manufactured from a plant that grows only in South American rain forests. Some plants and insects found in rain forests contain chemicals that relieve certain mental disorders. Discoveries, however, have only begun. Scientists say that rain forests contain over a thousand plants that have great anticancer potential. To destroy life forms in these forests is to deprive the human race of further medical advances.

—Gary Lee Houseman, student

Composing a definition

When you **define** something, you give its meaning. Many writers find that they often use definition with other rhetorical strategies. For instance, if you're explaining how to build a picture frame (process), you'll probably need to define the woodworking term *miter.*

You can also develop an entire paragraph by definition. To do this, you would discuss the meaning of a word or concept in more detail than a dictionary definition. You might, for example, tell what the word you are defining is *not* as well as what it *is,* as in paragraph 12.

> Chemistry is that branch of science which has the task of investigating the materials out of which the universe is made. It is not concerned with the forms into which they may be fashioned. Such objects as chairs, tables, vases, bottles, or wires are of no
> 12 significance in chemistry; but such substances as glass, wool, iron, sulfur, and clay, as the materials out of which they are made, are what it studies. Chemistry is concerned not only with the composition of such substances, but also with their inner structure.
>
> —John Arrend Timm, *General Chemistry*

Composing a comparison and contrast

Writing developed by **comparisons** deals with similarities. Writing developed by **contrasts** deals with differences. Comparison and contrast writing is usually organized in one of two ways. **Point-by-point organization** moves back and forth between the items being compared, as in paragraph 13 (which moves between Mark, Wayne, Mark, and Wayne). **Block organization** discusses one item completely before discussing the next, as in paragraph 14 (sports are discussed completely before anything is said about business).

> My husband and I constantly marvel at the fact that our two sons, born of the same parents and only two years apart in age, are such completely opposite human beings. The most obvious differences became apparent at their births. Our firstborn, **Mark,** was big and bold—his intense, already wise eyes, broad shoulders, huge and heavy hands, and powerful, chunky legs gave us the impression that he could have walked out of the delivery room on his own. Our second son, **Wayne,** was delightfully different. Rather than having the football physique that
> 13 Mark was born with, Wayne came into the world with a long, slim, wiry body more suited to running, jumping, and contorting. Wayne's eyes, rather than being intense like Mark's, were impish

and innocent. When **Mark** was delivered, he cried only momentarily, then seemed to settle into a state of intense concentration, as if trying to absorb everything he could about the strange, new environment he found himself in. Conversely, **Wayne** screamed from the moment he first appeared. There was nothing helpless or pathetic about his cry either—he was darn angry!

—Roseanne Labonte, student

14 **Games** are of limited duration, take place on or in fixed and finite sites and are governed by openly promulgated rules that are enforced on the spot by neutral professionals. Moreover, they are performed by relatively evenly matched teams that are counseled and led through every move by seasoned hands. Scores are kept, and at the end of the game, a winner is declared. **Business** is usually a little different. In fact, if there is anyone out there who can say that the business is of limited duration, takes place on a fixed site, is governed by openly promulgated rules that are enforced on the spot by neutral professionals, competes only on relatively even terms, and performs in a way that can be measured in runs or points, then that person is either extraordinarily lucky or seriously deluded.

—Warren Bennis, "Time to Hang Up the Old Sports Clichés"

Composing an analysis

Analysis examines and discusses separate parts of a whole. For example, paragraph 15 identifies a new type of zoo design and then analyzes why this design has developed, specifying three reasons for "the landscape revolution."

15 The current revolution in zoo design—the landscape revolution—is driven by three kinds of change that have occurred during this century. First are great leaps in animal ecology, veterinary medicine, landscape design, and exhibit technology, making possible unprecedented realism in zoo exhibits. Second, and perhaps most important, is the progressive disappearance of wilderness—the very subject of zoos—from the earth. Third is knowledge derived from market research and from environmental psychology, making possible a sophisticated focus on the zoo-goer.

—Melissa Greene, "No Rms, Jungle Vu"

Composing a classification

Classification groups items according to a shared characteristic. In writing a classification, you want to discuss or clarify each category in turn.

> Many different kinds of signals are used by the coaches. There are flash signals, which are just what the name implies: The coach may flash a hand across his face or chest to indicate a bunt or hit-and-run. There are holding signals, which are held in one position for several seconds. There might be the clenched
> **16** fist, bent elbow, or both hands on knees. Then there are the block signals. These divide the coach's body into different sections, or blocks. Touching a part of his body, rubbing his shirt, or touching his cap indicates a sign. Different players can be keyed to various parts of the block so the coach is actually giving several signals with the same sign.
>
> —Rockwell Stensrud, "Who's on Third?"

Composing an analogy

Analogy is a kind of comparison, identifying similarities between objects or ideas that are not usually associated with each other.

> Casual dress, like casual speech, tends to be loose, relaxed, and colorful. It often contains what might be called "slang words": blue jeans, sneakers, baseball caps, aprons, flowered cotton housedresses, and the like. These garments could not be worn on a formal occasion without causing disapproval, but in ordinary circumstances they pass without remark. "Vulgar words" in dress,
> **17** on the other hand, give emphasis and get immediate attention in almost any circumstances, just as they do in speech. Only the skillful can employ them without some loss of face, and even then they must be used in the right way. A torn, unbuttoned shirt, or wildly uncombed hair can signify strong emotions: passion, grief, rage, despair. They are most effective if people already think of you as being neatly dressed, just as the curses of well-spoken persons count for more than those of the customarily foul-mouthed.
>
> —Alison Lurie, *The Language of Clothes*

Explaining cause and effect

Causes lead to an event or an effect; effects result from causes. Writing that shows **cause and effect** examines outcomes and reasons for outcomes.

Because television is so wonderfully available as child amuser and child defuser, capable of rendering a volatile three-year-old harmless at the flick of a switch, parents grow to depend upon it in the course of their daily lives. And as they continue to utilize television day after day, its importance in their children's lives increases. From a simple source of entertainment provided by 18 parents when they need a break from child care, television gradually changes into a powerful and disruptive presence in family life. But despite their increasing resentment of television's intrusions into their family life, and despite their considerable guilt at not being able to control their children's viewing, parents do not take steps to extricate themselves from television's domination. They can no longer cope without it.

—Marie Winn, *The Plug-In Drug*

8g How can I write effective concluding paragraphs?

BOX 15

 Strategies for writing concluding paragraphs

STRATEGIES FOR INTERESTING YOUR READER

- Use one of the strategies suggested for introductory paragraphs (see Box 12), but not the same one used in the introduction.
- Ask the reader for awareness, action, or a similar outcome.
- Project into the future.
- Summarize the main points if the essay is longer than three pages.

STRATEGIES TO AVOID

- Avoid introducing new ideas or facts that belong in the body of the essay.
- Avoid merely rewording the introduction.
- Avoid announcing what you have done, as in "In this paper, I have explained why women can pump iron safely."
- Avoid making absolute claims, as in "In this essay, I have proved that women can pump iron safely."
- Avoid apologizing, as in "Even though I am not an expert, I feel the points I have made are accurate."

The concluding paragraph of an essay ends the entire essay. Your conclusion needs to follow logically from your THESIS STATEMENT and body paragraphs. Never merely tack on a conclusion. Use it to provide a sense of completion, a finishing touch that enhances the whole essay. The conclusion shown in paragraph 19 poses a challenging question and asks the reader to prepare for the future. (For the introductory paragraph to the same essay, see paragraph 1 on pp. 34-35.) See Box 15 on page 45 for ideas about writing conclusions.

> You need to ask yourself, "If I had to live alone starting tomorrow morning, would I know how?" If the answer is no, you need to become conscious of what living alone calls for. If you face up to life today, you will not have to hide from it later on.
>
> —Tara Foster, student

9 WRITING TO INFORM

To deliver your message most effectively, you want to arrange all elements of your essay for the greatest clarity and impact. No one arrangement fits all essays. But all arrangements are based on the ancient principles of storytelling: that is, every essay should have a beginning, a middle, and an end. In this chapter, you can see how such an arrangement works in INFORMATIVE WRITING by studying the final draft of an essay by student writer Carol Moreno. In Chapter 10 you can find a full discussion of arrangement in PERSUASIVE WRITING.

9a How is an informative essay usually arranged?

1. **Introductory paragraph:** captures the reader's interest and leads into the subject of the essay (8b).

2. **Thesis statement:** states the central message of the essay (5h, 7b). In academic essays the thesis statement usually appears at the end of the introductory paragraph.

3. **Background information:** provides a context for the ideas that will be presented in the essay. Depending on its complexity, background information may be presented in the introductory paragraph or given its own paragraph.

4. **Body paragraphs:** explain and expand on the message of the essay. They form the core of the essay. Body paragraphs usually open with a TOPIC SENTENCE (general statement) and are backed up

by specific details. Generalizations come to life with RENNS (8d). Each paragraph should be unified and coherent (8e).

5. **Concluding paragraph:** ends the essay smoothly and flows logically from the rest of the essay (8g).

9b Final draft of a student's informative essay

Moreno 1

Women Can Pump Iron, Too

When my grandmother fell and broke her hip last summer, I wanted to help take care of her. Because she was bedridden, she needed to be lifted at times, but I was shocked to discover that I could not lift her without my mother's or brother's help. My grandmother does not weigh much, but she was too much for me. My pride was hurt, and even more important, I began to worry about my plans to be a nurse specializing in the care of elderly people. What if I were too weak to help my patients get around? When I realized that I could satisfy one of my physical education requirements by taking a weight-lifting course for women, I decided to try it. Many people think only big, macho men want to lift weights, but times have changed. With the right training, women can also "pump iron" to build strength.

Women who lift weights, I was happy to learn from my course, can easily avoid developing overly masculine muscle mass. Women can rely on their biology to protect them. Women's bodies produce only very small amounts of the hormones that enlarge muscles in men. With normal weight training, women's muscles grow longer rather than bulkier. The

TITLE

INTRODUCTION: Gets reader's attention with personal anecdote

Question to add sentence variety

THESIS STATEMENT: Focus of essay

BODY PARAGRAPH 1: Gives background information

Refutes possible objection

continued ⟶

(Proportions shown in this paper are adjusted to fit space limitations of this book. Follow actual dimensions shown in this book and your instructor's directions.)

Moreno 2

Transition to signal additional point

result is smoother, firmer muscles, not massive bulges. Also, women benefit most when they combine weight lifting, which is a form of anaerobic exercise, with aerobic exercise. Anaero-

Specific details of two types of conditioning

bic exercise strengthens and builds muscles, but it does not make people breathe harder or their hearts beat faster for sustained periods. In contrast, aerobic exercises like running, walking, and swimming build endurance, but not massive muscles, because they force a person to take in more oxygen, which increases lung capacity, improves circulatory health, and tones the entire body. Encouraged by my instructor, I balanced my weight-lifting workouts by swimming laps twice a week.

BODY PARAGRAPH 2: Describes safe use of equipment and lifting techniques

Striving for strength can end in injury unless weight lifters use free weights and weight machines safely. Free weights are barbells, the metal bars that round metal weights can be attached to at each end. To be safe, no matter how little the weight, lifters must never raise a barbell by bending at the waist, grabbing the barbell, and then straightening up.

Transition to show contrast

Instead, they should squat, grasp the barbell, and then use their leg muscles to straighten into a standing position. To avoid a twist that can lead to serious injury, lifters must use this posture: head erect and facing forward, back and neck aligned. The big advantage of weight machines, which use weighted handles and bars hooked to wires and pulleys, is that lifters must use them sitting down. Therefore, machines like the Nautilus and Universal actually force lifters to keep their bodies properly aligned, which drastically reduces the chance of injury.

continued →

Moreno 3

Once a weight lifter understands how to lift safely, she needs a weight-lifting regime personalized to her specific physical needs. Because benefits come from "resistance," which is the stress that lifting any amount of weight puts on a muscle, no one has to be strong to get started. A well-planned progressive weight-training program begins with whatever weight a person can lift comfortably and gradually adds to the base weight as she gets stronger. What builds muscle strength is the number of repetitions, or "reps," the lifter does, not necessarily an increase in the amount of resistance from adding weight. Our instructor helped the women in the class, who ranged in age from eighteen to forty-three, from scrawny to pudgy, and from couch potato to superstar, to develop a program that was right for our individual weights, ages, and overall level of conditioning. Everyone's program differed in how much weight to start out with and how many reps to do for each exercise. Our instructor urged us not to try more weight or reps than our programs called for, even if our first workouts seemed too easy. This turned out to be good advice because those of us who did not listen woke up the next day feeling as though our bodies had been twisted by evil forces.

In addition to fitting a program to her physical capabilities, a weight lifter needs to design an individual routine to fit her personal goals. Most students in my group wanted to improve their upper body strength, so we focused on exercises to strengthen arms, shoulders, abdomens, and chests. Each student learned to use specific exercises to isolate certain muscle groups. Because muscles strengthen and grow when

BODY PARAGRAPH 3: Describes and explains the design and purpose of weight-training programs

Specific details for reader to visualize a class

BODY PARAGRAPH 4: Explains the need for developing a program to fit individual needs

continued ⟶

Moreno 4

they are rested after a workout, our instructor taught us to

**Specific
examples to
add interest** work alternate muscle groups on different days. For example,
a woman might work on her arms and abdomen one day and
then her shoulders and chest the next day. Because I had had
such trouble lifting my grandmother, I added exercises to
strengthen my legs and back. Another student, who had hurt
her neck in a car crash, added neck-strengthening exercises.
Someone else, planning to be a physical therapist, added
finger- and hand-strengthening exercises.

**CONCLUSION:
Reports
writer's
personal
progress** At the end of our ten weeks of weight training, we had
to evaluate our progress. Was I impressed! I felt ready to lift
the world. When I started, I could lift only ten pounds over my
head for three reps. By the end of the course, I could lift ten
pounds over my head for twenty reps, and I could lift eighteen
pounds for three reps. Also, I could swim laps for twenty sustained minutes instead of the ten I had barely managed at
first. I am so proud of my weight-training accomplishments
that I still work out three or four times a week. I am proof that
any woman can benefit from "pumping iron." Not only will she
become stronger and have more stamina, but she will also
feel energetic and confident. After all, there is nothing to lose--
except maybe some flab.

10 WRITING TO ARGUE

10a What is an argument?

A written argument consists of these elements.

- The **claim**, which states the issue and then takes a position on a debatable topic (the taking of a position reads somewhat like a THESIS STATEMENT)
- **Support** for the claim: EVIDENCE, REASONS, and EXAMPLES presented factually and logically

In daily life, you may think of an argument as a personal conflict or disagreement. For ACADEMIC WRITING, however, arguments are ways of demonstrating critical thinking. Arguments involve making and defending a position, proposal, or interpretation on a topic open to debate. So that you can argue your position effectively, you want to examine critically all sides of the topic. Your goal is to persuade an audience to accept your position, which means that your audience's viewpoints and values need to influence your decisions about content, organization, and style.

10b How do I choose a topic and develop a claim for an argument?

When you choose a topic for written argument, be sure that it is open to debate. An essay becomes an argument when it makes a claim—that is, takes a position—on information. An effective way to develop a position on a topic is to ask a question about it or to identify the controversy surrounding it.

FACT	Students at Calhoon College must study a foreign language.
DEBATABLE QUESTION	Should Calhoon College require students to study a foreign language?
ONE SIDE	Calhoon College should not require students to study a foreign language.
OTHER SIDE	Calhoon College should require students to study a foreign language.

Though you need to select one side of a debatable question to defend in your essay, you always want to keep the other side(s) in mind as you develop your argument. So that your readers see that you are well informed and fair-minded, you want to mention viewpoints that are different from your own. For an argument to be effective, you need to present and then refute opposing positions. As you do so, always maintain a respectful tone by avoiding insults, abstaining from exaggerations, and resisting sarcasm.

Often, instructors assign an argument topic, including the claim to make. In such cases, you need to argue in support of that position. Even if you personally disagree with the position, readers expect that you reason logically about it. Indeed, experienced debate teams practice arguing all sides of an issue. In official competitions, judges never announce in advance whether a debate team will have to argue the pro or the con position.

If you can choose your own topic, choose one that is suitable for college writing. Your readers expect you to select a topic of substance and to argue convincingly and reasonably about it. For example, taking a position about "book censorship in public libraries" is worthy of a college-level essay, as is "sending nonviolent criminals to maximum security prisons." Also, so that you choose a claim sufficiently narrow for the practical situation, consider the length and time frame mentioned in your assignment.

Lacie Juris, the student who wrote the argument essay shown in 10h, chose her own topic for her essay assignment. Lacie was thinking about a career as a zookeeper, which led to her interest in issues concerning wild animals. In her career research, especially when she looked for the latest information on the WEB, she discovered a major concern: the problem of private ownership of wild animals. Her curiosity aroused, Lacie read a number of sources and then found that she had a topic appropriate for her assignment to write an argument essay for her first-year English class. Next, she worked on developing a claim about that topic which would then evolve into the THESIS STATEMENT for her essay. Here's how Lacie progressed from topic to thesis statement.

TOPIC Private ownership of wild animals

MY CLAIM I think private ownership of wild animals should not be allowed.

THESIS It is bad for private citizens to own wild animals as pets.
STATEMENT [This is a preliminary thesis statement. It states the writer's
(first draft) position and gives reason for that position, but the word *bad* is

vague, and the writer does not address how to stop private ownership of wild animals.]

THESIS
STATEMENT
(second draft)
To eliminate what few people realize are increasingly dangerous situations for people and animals alike, ownership
of wild animals as pets needs to be made completely
illegal.
[This revised thesis statement of the writer's position is better because it not only states the writer's claim but also a reason for
the position. However, it suffers from lack of CONCISENESS in wording and from the presence of the PASSIVE CONSTRUCTION *needs to
be made.*]

THESIS
STATEMENT
(final draft)
To eliminate dangerous situations for both people and animals alike, policymakers need to ban private ownership of
wild animals as pets.
[This final version of the thesis statement is improved and ready
to use. Not only does it state the writer's claim clearly, but the
language is concise and all verbs are in the ACTIVE VOICE. The
writer now has a thesis statement that is narrow enough for an effective argument and suitable for the time and length given in
her assignment.]

10c   How do I support my argument?

Use evidence, reasons, and examples to support an argument's claim.
Evidence needs to be sufficient, representative, relevant, accurate, and
reasonable (see pp. 175–77 for complete explanations of these terms).
Specifically, evidence consists of facts, statistics, expert testimony, personal experience, and so forth. One good method for developing reasons
for an argument is to ask yourself *why* you believe your claim. When
you respond, "Because . . . ," you offer reasons for your claim. Another
method to find reasons is to list pros and cons about your claim. The
lists usually contain reasons.

If you consult SOURCES to find supporting evidence, reasons, or
examples, be sure to use correct DOCUMENTATION within the text of your
essay and in your bibliography at the end of your paper (Chs. 28–29).
By doing this, you avoid engaging in PLAGIARISM, the adopting of someone else's ideas and trying to pass them off as your own. This is a form
of stealing, sometimes done unintentionally but often done intentionally. Take the time to master the concept and applications of documentation. Today faculty can use Internet sites to scan student writing
for undocumented borrowed material. Instructors almost always

report plagiarism to college administrators who, in turn, take punitive action, often to the extent of asking a plagiarizing student to leave the institution.

10d How do I structure an argument?

No single method is best for organizing an argument, but the two most frequently used structures are classical argument and the Toulmin model for argument. Whatever structure you choose, readers expect your argument essay to have a clear introduction, body, and conclusion.

The ancient Greeks and Romans developed the structure for the **classical argument**. The student essay in 10h uses this structure. Box 16 lists its parts.

BOX 16

Structure of a classical argument

- **Introductory paragraph:** Sets the stage for the position argued in the essay. It gains the reader's interest and respect. In some cases, it provides background information on the topic or problem.

- **Thesis statement:** States the position that the writer wants to argue.

- **Evidence and reasons:** Supports the position that the writer wants to argue. Each piece of evidence or reason usually consists of a general statement backed up with specific details, including examples. Evidence and reasons presented in logical sequences reach audience most successfully. Common sequences include most familiar to least familiar, least important to most important.

- **Rebuttal (objections and responses to them):** Presents the opposition's position and then argues against that position. Writers can position this information in one of three ways: after the introduction, before the conclusion, or in a point-counterpoint format throughout the essay's body.

- **Concluding paragraph:** Wraps up the essay, often with a summary of the argument, an elaboration of the argument's significance, or a call to action for the readers.

The **Toulmin model,** developed by philosopher Stephen Toulmin, is another common argument method. Box 17 presents the elements in Toulmin's system for mounting an argument.

BOX 17

🎯 The Toulmin model for argument

- The CLAIM, which is a variation of a thesis statement. (If needed, the claim is qualified or limited.)
  - Some college students cheat on exams. To reduce cheating on exams, colleges should establish an honor code.
- The SUPPORT of the claim with EVIDENCE and REASONS, moving from broad reasons to specific data and details.
  - The writer gives evidence that some college students cheat on exams, based on SOURCES or personal experience; offers reasons why an honor code should be established; and includes examples of college students cheating on exams, based on sources or personal experience.
- The **warrants** are the writer's underlying assumptions, which are often implied rather than stated. Warrants may also need support (also called *backing*).
  - Enough college students cheat on exams for colleges to need to address the problem.
  - Cheating is a dishonorable activity.
  - If the concept of *honor* is cultivated, college students will take the concept more seriously (and will be less likely to cheat).

10e How do I convince my audience?

The PURPOSE of written argument is to convince your readers, known as your **audience,** either to agree with you or to be open to your position. Therefore, you want to consider the characteristics of your audience. What do your readers already know about your topic? What are their values, viewpoints, and assumptions? Always use this information to develop your strategy for being persuasive in your argument essay.

Do you think that your audience is likely to read your point of view with hostility? If so, you might consider using a **Rogerian argument.** Rogerian argument, based on psychologist Carl Rogers's communication principles, suggests that tension between adversaries eases when people can find **common ground.** In many instances, of course, you can't actually expect to change your reader's mind, which means your goal is to demonstrate that your point of view has its own merit.

An effective argument relies on three types of persuasive appeals: logical appeals, emotional appeals, and ethical appeals. The ancient Greeks called these appeals *logos, pathos,* and *ethos.*

When you use **logical appeals,** also known as *logos,* you allow your readers, whether they agree or disagree with you, to respect your position on the topic. Sound reasoning involves using effective evidence (27b) and reasons, accurate deductive and inductive reasoning (10f), and clear distinctions between fact and opinion. Equally important, you want to avoid using logical fallacies (10f) in your reasoning.

When you use **emotional appeals,** or *pathos,* you try to persuade your readers by appealing to their hearts more than their minds. Note, however, that when you use such appeals in college-level writing, you need to combine it with logical appeals. Emotional appeals can use descriptive language and concrete details or examples to create a mental picture for readers, which is an approach that leads them to feel or understand the importance of your claim. You want to appeal to your audience's values and beliefs through honest examples and description that add a sense of humanity and reality to the issue you are arguing. At all costs, never manipulate your readers with biased, SLANTED LANGUAGE, and never lecture your readers on how they "should" feel. Readers see through such tactics and resent them.

When you use **ethical appeals,** or *ethos,* you establish your personal credibility with your audience. Your readers need to trust and respect you before they can be open to your position. One effective way to make an ethical appeal is to draw on your personal experience, as long as it relates directly to your argument. (Some college instructors don't want students to write in the first person; check with your instructor so that you can adjust your style accordingly.) You can also establish your credibility by demonstrating that you know what you are talking about, showing—not merely claiming—that you are well informed about your topic. Arguing by considering a variety of perspectives and using reliable SOURCES for supporting evidence communicates that you are arguing fairly and honestly. Equally important, when you use a reasonable TONE, you communicate that you are being fair-minded.

10f What are logical fallacies?

Logical fallacies are flaws in reasoning that lead to faulty, illogical statements. Logical fallacies often masquerade as reasonable statements in a written argument, but they represent either a writer's attempt to manipulate readers or errors in the writer's reasoning process.

- **Hasty generalization** occurs when someone draws a conclusion based on inadequate evidence. Stereotyping is a common example of hasty generalization. For example, it is faulty to come to that conclusion that *redheads have hot tempers* based on a few people someone knows who fit that description.

- The **either-or fallacy,** also called *false dilemma,* limits the choices to only two alternatives when more exist. For example, *either go to college or forget about getting a job* falsely implies that a college education is a prerequisite for all jobs.

- **False analogy** claims that two items are alike when actually they are more different than similar. The statement *If we can put a man on the moon, we should be able to find a cure for cancer* is faulty because space science is very different from biological science.

- **False cause** asserts that one event leads to another when, in fact, the two events may only be related. A common type of false cause is called *post hoc, ergo propter hoc,* which in Latin means "after this, therefore because of this." For example, *Because a new weather satellite was launched last week, it has rained every day without stopping* suggests that the weather satellite caused a change in weather patterns.

- **Slippery slope** arguments suggest that an event will cause a "domino effect," a series of uncontrollable consequences. The anti–gun control and pro-choice movements use this fallacy when they say that any limitation of individual rights will inevitably lead to the removal of civil rights.

- **Personal attack,** also known as *ad hominem,* attacks a person's appearance, personal habits, or character instead of dealing with the merits of the individual's argument. The following example is faulty because the writer attacks the person rather than the person's argument: *If Senator Martinez had children of his own, we could take seriously his argument against jailing all child abusers permanently.*

- **Bandwagon,** also known as *ad populum,* implies that something is right because everyone else is doing it. An example is a teenager asking, *Why can't I go to the concert next week? All my friends are going.*

- **False authority** means citing the opinion of an "expert" who has no claim to expertise about the subject at hand. Using celebrities to advertise products unrelated to their careers is a common example of this tactic.

- **Irrelevant argument** is also called *non sequitur* in Latin, which means "It does not follow." This flaw occurs when a conclusion does not follow from the premise: *Ms. Sih is a forceful speaker, so she will be an outstanding mayor.* Ms. Sih's forceful speaking style does not support the claim that she will do an outstanding job as mayor.

- **Red herring** is a fallacy of distraction. Sidetracking an issue by bringing up totally unrelated issues can distract people from the truth. The following question diverts attention from the issue of animal extinction rather than arguing about it: *Why worry about pandas and tigers becoming extinct when we should be concerned about the plight of the homeless?*

- **Begging the question** is also called *circular reasoning*. The supporting reasons only restate the claim. For example in, *Wrestling is a dangerous sport because it is unsafe,* the words *dangerous* and *unsafe* essentially have the same meaning; the reason simply restates the claim rather than supporting it.

- **Emotional appeals,** such as appeals to fear, tradition, or pity, substitute emotions for logical reasoning. These appeals attempt to manipulate readers by reaching their hearts rather than their heads. The following statement attempts to appeal to readers' pity rather than their logic: *This woman has lived in poverty all of her life; she is ill and has four children at home to care for, so she should not be punished for her crimes.*

- **Slanted language** involves biasing the reader by using word choices that have strong positive or negative connotations. Calling a group of people involved in a protest rally a *mob* elicits a negative response, whereas referring to the group as *active citizens* receives a positive response from readers.

10g What guidelines do I use to revise my argument essays?

You revise your argument essay as you would any essay (Boxes 10 and 11). In addition, you want to check the elements listed in Box 18.

BOX 18

✔ Guidelines for revising a written argument

- Does the claim take a position on a debatable topic? (10b)
- Do the evidence and reasons support the claim? (10c)
- Is the evidence sufficient, representative, relevant, and accurate? (27b)
- Is borrowed information cited correctly? (Chs. 28–29)
- Is the argument structured effectively? (10d)
- Does the writer use logical, emotional, and ethical appeals to convince his or her audience? (10e)
- Does the writer reason logically, avoiding logical fallacies? (10e, 10f)

10h Final draft of a student's argument essay

Lacie Juris

Professor Calhoon-Dillahunt

English 101

16 June 2002

Lions, Tigers, and Bears, Oh My!

Fuzzy orange-and-white tiger cubs playfully fight over a chew toy while baby chimps hang precariously in front of the nursery window, looking almost human with their big ears and adorable expressions. They look so cute at the zoo. Would-n't it be exciting to have one for your very own, to play with in your living room and show off to your neighbors? It would be a childhood fantasy come true—and for many people living in the United States, it is true. Tigers, for example, cost the same amount as purebred puppies. Animal rights advocates esti-mate that as many tigers are kept as pets in the United States as exist in the wild worldwide (Boehm). Unfortunately, these exotic dreams come true can turn deadly at any moment. Because regulation of wild animal ownership varies from county to county in the United States, laws are difficult to enforce ("Wild Animals Are Not"). To eliminate dangerous situ-ations for both people and animals alike, policymakers need to ban private ownership of wild animals as pets.

Wild animals are dangerous to humans, both owners and nearby residents. Wild animals have inborn behavior pat-terns and instincts, such as stalking prey, attacking when

continued ⟶

(Proportions shown in this paper are adjusted to fit space limitations of this book. Follow actual dimensions shown in this book and your instructor's directions.)

Juris 2

threatened, and self-defense. Such patterns remain no matter where or how the animals grow up, no matter how well the owners train them for domesticated living. This is what makes the animals truly wild. Humans cannot influence, change, or even predict an animal's wild behaviors. An attack can occur at any time when their wild instincts take over without warning ("Wild Animals Are Not"). In fact, in the past three years, authorities blame pet tigers for at least seven deaths and thirty-one injuries (Davenport). In addition, wild pets can cause tremendous property damage, as illustrated by the case of Stoli, a tiger who caused $20,000 worth of damage to his owner's Mercedes in less than five minutes ("Stoli and Lil").

Many animal owners teach their young exotic pets little games and tricks. Owners don't realize, however, that when the wild animals have grown to three or four times the strength of most people, the "pets" still expect to take part in the same games and tricks. Take, for example, the story of a pet African serval named Kenya. Servals are known as "leaping cats," with the capacity to jump twelve feet straight up and run forty-five miles an hour. Kenya belonged to a woman who purchased him at a pet store. Because Kenya was small, he seemed like the perfect exotic pet. However, no one told the woman about servals' amazing jumping abilities—or about their becoming extremely territorial as adults. At home, the woman taught the baby Kenya to leap onto her shoulder, without realizing that she was actually teaching him to leap onto people in general. In addition, as he grew,

continued →

Juris 3

he became so territorial that he attacked anyone who came to her house ("Kenya").

Another little-realized fact is that wild animals greatly endanger owners and people in the surrounding areas by transmitting diseases. When people purchase exotic animals, no one tells them if the animals are carrying diseases. Wild animals can host internal parasites, such as ascarid worms, tapeworms, flukes, and protozoa, all of which can be debilitating or even fatal to their human caretakers—especially their small children. The animals can also carry external parasites that cause spotted fever and bubonic plague ("Questions," par. 3). In addition, no known vaccination can protect wild animals from rabies ("Rabies").

While the risk to humans of exotic pet ownership is very high, domestication is hazardous to the animals themselves. After all, wild animals need specific and natural environments to survive. Such settings do not include humans, houses, or backyard kennels. Owners of wild animals usually lack the knowledge and funds to re-create the animal's environment or to provide proper nutrition, let alone care for the animals if they become sick or injured (Boehm). Very few professional veterinarians are trained or willing to work on wild animals.

Usually, infant wild animals are stolen from their parents at only a few weeks, or even days, of life. Their capture robs the babies of the chance to learn skills necessary for survival if they are ever abandoned or rereleased into the wild. These animals often develop stress and behavior disorders

continued ⟶

Juris 4

because they have never experienced social interaction with their own species ("Wild Animals Are Not"). Eventually, many owners become frightened or confused by sudden behavior problems with their "little babies," and they decide to leave the animals in remote places to fend for themselves. Sadly, these animals never learned how to survive on their own. As a result, they starve to death, or they seek out human habitation for food, an act that frequently ends in their death at the hands of frightened people ("Wild Animals Do Not").

Some people may argue for the benefits of personal ownership of wild animals. It allows ordinary people to enjoy exotic pets in their own homes. These people insist that they can safety restrict their wild animals' movements to their own property. Further, defenders of the private possession of wild animals argue that owners can help preserve endangered species. Increasingly, however, exotic pet owners' fantasies turn into nightmares as the wild animals become adults controlled by their basic instincts and inbred behaviors. Owners often expect local animal control agencies or animal sanctuaries to deal with their problems, even though such facilities are already over capacity or are staffed by people unequipped to deal with undomesticated animals (Milloy).

Keeping wild animals as pets must be outlawed. Though exotic creatures may look like Simba or Tigger, they are still completely wild, and it is in the wild that they belong. "Wild Animals Are Not Pets" points out, "The only ones who benefit from the practice of sales of exotic animals as pets are

continued ⟶

Juris 5

the breeders and sellers. These people make an enormous
amount of money by exploiting these animals once they are
sold." Poachers also profit when they capture baby wild animals from their native habitats and sell them as pets to the
highest bidder. The best way for humans to see and experience wild animals in safe environments is to visit and support
zoos and wildlife parks that specialize in providing professionally constructed natural habitats for animals. In such settings, people can enjoy the beauty and behaviors of wild
animals without putting humans and the animals at risk.

Works Cited

Boehm, Ted. "A New Local Worry: Exotic Cats--Lion and Tiger
        Prices Fall, and Once Rare Pets Become a Costly Men-
        ace." Wall Street Journal 30 June 2000: B1.

Davenport, Christian. "Fighting the Lure of the Wild: Danger of
        Exotic Animals as Pets Spurs Quest for Regulation."
        Washington Post 11 Mar. 2002: B1.

"Kenya." Cat Tales Zoological Park, 1999. 19 Apr. 2002
        <http://cattales.org/kenya.html>.

Milloy, Ross E. "Banning Lions and Other Large Pets." New
        York Times 10 Dec. 2001: A19.

"Questions and Answers About Captive Exotic and Wild Ani-
        mals as Pets." 2002. Humane Society of the United
        States. 11 June 2002 <http://hsus.org/ace/12055>.

"Rabies and Animal Bites." York County Virginia. 6 June 2002
        <http://www.yorkcounty.gov/fls/ac/rabies.htm>.

Note: works cited always begins on a new page

continued —→

Juris 6

"Stoli and Lil." <u>Cat Tales Zoological Park</u>. 1999. 19 Apr. 2002

        <http://cattales.org/stolilil.html>.

"Wild Animals Are Not Pets." <u>The Wild Animal Orphanage</u>.

        2001. 19 Apr. 2002

        <http://www.wildanimalorphanage.org/wild/html>.

"Wild Animals Do Not Make Good Pets." <u>Cat Tales Zoological</u>

        <u>Park</u>. 1999. 19 Apr. 2002

        <http://cattales.org/notapet.html>.

Sentences

www.prenhall.com/troyka

Sentences

11 SENTENCE FRAGMENTS

11a What is a sentence fragment?

A **sentence fragment** looks like a sentence but isn't one. It tries to look like a sentence by starting with a capital and ending with a period (or question mark or exclamation point). Yet, it's only an imitation of the real thing. A fragment is an error because it's only a part, not a whole sentence. Watch out for errors like these.

- When winter comes early. [fragment]
- Whales in the Arctic Ocean. [fragment]
- Stranded in the Arctic Ocean. [fragment]

11b How can I recognize fragments?

You will find it easier to recognize fragments once you can recognize complete sentences. Get to know the basic pattern of an INDEPENDENT CLAUSE (Box 56, p. 323). Then, when you read your own writing, ask

---

BOX 19

 How to identify sentence fragments

Note: When any answer here is yes, you have a sentence fragment.

- Is a word group that starts with a SUBORDINATING WORD not joined to a complete sentence?

  FRAGMENT **When** winter comes early.

  CORRECT **When winter comes early,** ice sometimes traps whales in the Arctic Ocean.

- Does a word group lack a VERB without being joined to a complete sentence?

  FRAGMENT Whales in the Arctic Ocean.

  CORRECT Whales **live** in the Arctic Ocean.

- Does a word group lack a SUBJECT without being joined to a complete sentence?

  FRAGMENT Trapped in the Arctic Ocean.

  CORRECT **Many whales** were trapped in the Arctic Ocean.

yourself the questions in Box 19 (p. 65). If any answer is yes, you're looking at a sentence fragment. To eliminate the fragment, follow the advice in 11c, 11d, or 11e.

11c How can I correct a fragment that starts with a subordinating word?

Start by recognizing SUBORDINATING CONJUNCTIONS (39h). Then you can choose between two methods to correct a fragment that starts with a subordinating conjunction. You can join the fragment to an independent clause, or you can delete the subordinating conjunction.

FRAGMENT **Because** the ship had to cut a path through the ice.

CORRECT Because the ship had to cut a path through the ice, the rescue effort took time. [Fragment corrected by joining it to an independent clause.]

CORRECT The ship had to cut a path through the ice. [Fragment corrected by deleting the subordinating conjunction.]

Some fragments start with the subordinating words *who* or *which*. Either join such fragments to an independent clause or rewrite the idea in an independent clause.

FRAGMENT The ship's noisy motor worried the **scientists. Who feared the whales would panic.**

CORRECT The ship's noisy motor worried the **scientists, who feared the whales would panic.** [Fragment corrected by joining it to an independent clause.]

CORRECT The ship's noisy motor worried the **scientists. They feared the whales would panic.** [Fragment corrected by rewriting it as an independent clause.]

11d How can I correct a phrase fragment?

To start, learn to recognize a PHRASE (39m). A phrase that begins with a capital letter and ends with a period (or question mark or exclamation point) is a fragment. In the following five examples, the phrase fragments are in bold type.

The crew played classical music. **To calm the whales.** [infinitive phrase fragment]

The crew chose classical music. **Hoping for success.** [*-ing* participle phrase fragment]

The whales began to panic. **Trapped by the ice.** [past-participle phrase fragment]

The ship moved slowly. **Toward the whales.** [prepositional phrase fragment]

An enormously powerful icebreaker. The ship arrived to free the whales. [appositive phrase fragment]

You can choose between two methods to correct a fragment that is a phrase not joined to an independent clause. You can join it to an independent clause or you can rewrite it as an independent clause.

FRAGMENTS JOINED TO AN INDEPENDENT CLAUSE

The crew played classical music **to calm the whales.**

The crew chose classical music, **hoping for success.**

The whales began to panic, **trapped by the ice.**

The ship moved slowly **toward the whales.**

An enormously powerful icebreaker, the ship arrived to free the whales.

FRAGMENTS REWRITTEN AS AN INDEPENDENT CLAUSE

The major concern was how **to calm the whales.**

The crew, **hoping for success,** put classical music on the ship's sound system.

No one knew whether whales **trapped by the ice** would cooperate with a rescue attempt.

The ship moved quietly and slowly **toward the whales.**

An enormously powerful icebreaker arrived to free the whales.

11e How can I correct a fragment that is a part of a compound predicate?

In a complete sentence, a **compound predicate** contains two or more VERBS connected by a COORDINATING CONJUNCTION (*and, but, for, or, nor, yet, so*). The boldface type in the next example shows a fragment that is half of a compound predicate. You can choose between two methods to correct this kind of fragment. You can join it to an independent clause or you can rewrite the sentence without a compound predicate.

FRAGMENT   The ship reached the whales. **And led them to freedom.**

CORRECT   The ship reached the whales **and led them to freedom.**
[Fragment corrected by joining it to an independent clause.]

CORRECT   The crew cheered as the whales swam to freedom. [Fragment corrected by rewriting it without a compound predicate.]

11f   What are intentional fragments?

Professional writers sometimes intentionally use fragments for emphasis and effect. The ability to judge the difference between acceptable and unacceptable sentence fragments comes from much exposure to the works of skilled writers. Many teachers, therefore, consider sentence fragments errors. A few teachers occasionally allow well-placed intentional fragments after a student has shown the consistent ability to write well-constructed complete sentences.

12   COMMA SPLICES AND RUN-ON SENTENCES

12a   What are comma splices and run-on sentences?

Comma splices and run-on sentences are errors that look almost alike. They incorrectly join two INDEPENDENT CLAUSES. A **comma splice** is created when only a comma separates independent clauses. A **run-on sentence** is created when no punctuation at all separates independent clauses (Box 20).

COMMA SPLICE   The hurricane **intensified, it** turned toward land.

RUN-ON SENTENCE   The hurricane **intensified it** turned toward land.

👁 **ALERT:** Occasionally, experienced writers use a comma to join short independent clauses: *Mosquitoes do not **bite, they** stab.* Your teacher may consider this punctuation an error, so check before you use it. 👁

■■■■ **BOX 20** ■■■

How to identify and correct comma splices and run-on sentences

1. Watch out for a second INDEPENDENT CLAUSE that starts with a pronoun.

COMMA SPLICE	Thomas Edison was a productive **inventor, he held** more than 1,300 U.S. and foreign patents.
RUN-ON SENTENCE	Thomas Edison was a productive **inventor he held** more than 1,300 U.S. and foreign patents.
CORRECT	Thomas Edison was a productive **inventor. He held** more than 1,300 U.S. and foreign patents.

2. Watch out for a CONJUNCTIVE ADVERB that joins two sentences.

COMMA SPLICE	Thomas Edison was a brilliant **scientist, however,** he spent only three months in school.
RUN-ON SENTENCE	Thomas Edison was a brilliant **scientist however,** he spent only three months in school.
CORRECT	Thomas Edison was a brilliant **scientist; however,** he spent only three months in school.

3. Watch out for a TRANSITIONAL EXPRESSION that joins two sentences.

COMMA SPLICE	Thomas Edison invented the **microphone, in addition,** he created a superior storage battery.
RUN-ON SENTENCE	Thomas Edison invented the **microphone in addition, he created** a superior storage battery.
CORRECT	Thomas Edison invented the **microphone. In addition, he created** a superior storage battery.

4. Watch out when a second independent clause explains or gives an example of the information in the first independent clause.

COMMA SPLICE	Thomas Edison was the genius behind **many inventions, among** the best known are the phonograph and the incandescent lamp.
RUN-ON SENTENCE	Thomas Edison was the genius behind **many inventions among** the best known are the phonograph and the incandescent lamp.
CORRECT	Thomas Edison was the genius behind many **inventions. Among** the best known are the phonograph and the incandescent lamp.

12b How can I recognize comma splices and run-on sentences?

Watch out for the four major causes of comma splices and run-on sentences.

12c How can I correct comma splices and run-on sentences?

You have many choices for correcting comma splices and run-on sentences. You can use punctuation or a coordinating conjunction, or you can revise an independent clause into a dependent clause.

Using punctuation

You can use a period or a semicolon to separate independent clauses in a comma splice or run-on sentence.

> COMMA SPLICE   A shark's skeleton is all **cartilage, the shark** does not have a bone in its body.

> RUN-ON SENTENCE   A shark's skeleton is all **cartilage the shark** does not have a bone in its body.

> CORRECT   A shark's skeleton is all **cartilage. The shark** does not have a bone in its body.

Using a coordinating conjunction

If the ideas in your independent clauses relate closely in meaning and are grammatically equivalent, you can connect them with a comma followed by a coordinating conjunction (*and, but, for, or, nor, yet, so*).

> COMMA SPLICE   Every living creature gives off a weak electrical charge in **water, special pores** on a shark's skin can detect these signals.

> RUN-ON SENTENCE   Every living creature gives off a weak electrical charge in **water special pores** on a shark's skin can detect these signals.

> CORRECT   Every living creature gives off a weak electrical charge in **water, *and* special pores** on a shark's skin can detect these signals.

Revising an independent clause into a dependent clause

If one of two independent clauses expresses information that can be logically subordinated to the other independent clause, start it with a SUBORDINATING WORD and join it correctly to the independent clause.

COMMA SPLICE	Costa Rica's Cocos Island harbors more sharks than any where on **earth, it is** paradise to underwater filmmakers.
RUN-ON SENTENCE	Costa Rica's Cocos Island harbors more sharks than any where on **earth it is** paradise to underwater filmmakers.
CORRECT	***Because*** Costa Rica's Cocos Island harbors more sharks than anywhere on **earth, it is** paradise to underwater filmmakers. [*Because* makes the first clause dependent.]

COMMA SPLICE	Some sharks have large, triangular **teeth, these** teeth can tear flesh.
RUN-ON SENTENCE	Some sharks have large, triangular **teeth these** teeth can tear flesh.
CORRECT	Some sharks have large, triangular teeth ***that*** can tear flesh. [*That* makes the second clause dependent.]

👁 **ALERT:** When a CONJUNCTIVE ADVERB (such as *however, therefore, also, next, then, thus, furthermore,* and *nevertheless*) or TRANSITIONAL EXPRESSION (such as *for example, for instance,* and other expressions listed in Box 50 (p. 316)) falls between spliced or run-on independent clauses, you must use a period or a SEMICOLON to correct the error. 👁

COMMA SPLICE	Some sharks cannot **bite, for example,** the basking shark can only filter plankton through its small mouth.
RUN-ON SENTENCE	Some sharks cannot **bite for example,** the basking shark can only filter plankton through its small mouth.
CORRECT	Some sharks cannot **bite. For example,** the basking shark can only filter plankton through its small mouth.
CORRECT	Some sharks cannot **bite; for example,** the basking shark can only filter plankton through its small mouth.

13 PROBLEMS WITH SENTENCE SHIFTS

A correct sentence does not "shift." **Shifts** are grammatical changes that lead to mismatched grammatical forms, which are errors. To avoid writing sentence shifts, be consistent in using the grammatical forms covered in 13a–13d.

13a What is being consistent in person and number?

Person tells who or what is acting or being acted upon. **First person** (*I, we*) focuses attention on the writer or speaker: *I see a field of fireflies.* **Second person** (*you*) focuses attention on the reader or listener: *You see a shower of sparks.* **Third person** focuses attention on the subject being discussed: *The physicist sees a cloud of cosmic dust.*

👁 **ALERT:** All NOUNS and many PRONOUNS are always in the third person. 👁

Number refers to singular (one) or plural (more than one). Don't mix singular and plural unless your meaning calls for it.

> NO **I** enjoy reading forecasts of the future, but **you** never know which ones will ever happen. **One** recent prediction claimed that U.S. car buyers will pay twice today's price for a car, but **you** will get twice the gas mileage. [This passage shifts from first to second to third person and back to second, which is confusing.]

> YES Although forecasts of the future make enjoyable reading, it is impossible to know which ones will ever happen. One recent prediction claimed that **U.S. car buyers** will pay twice today's price for a car, but **they** will get twice the gas mileage. [The revisions here use the third-person perspective consistently. To bring first-person or second-person perspectives into focus, you can revise accordingly.]

👁 **ALERTS:** (1) Watch out for shifts from nouns (always third person) to the second-person pronoun *you.*

- By the year 2020, **most people** will live longer, and ~~you~~ they will have to work longer, too.

(2) Watch out for shifts between singular and plural in third person.

- The longer ~~a person stays~~ *people stay* in the work force, the more competition they will face from younger job seekers. 👁

13b What is being consistent in subject, voice, and mood?

Rarely, a shift in SUBJECT within or between sentences is justified by its meaning; most of the time, such shifts show that your writing is drifting out of focus.

To be consistent in subject, VOICE, and MOOD, avoid changing these aspects of your writing within sentences and paragraphs. For example, don't switch between the ACTIVE VOICE and the PASSIVE VOICE.

SHIFT IN SUBJECT AND VOICE People complain about sugary, high-fat foods, but donuts by the millions are eaten for breakfast every day. [The subject shifts from *people* to *donuts*, and the verb voice shifts from active *complain* to passive *are eaten*.]

CORRECT People complain about sugary, high-fat foods, but **they eat** donuts by the millions for breakfast every day.

Similarly, within the same sentence, avoid combining statements (INDICATIVE MOOD), questions (INTERROGATIVE MOOD), and commands (IMPERATIVE MOOD).

SHIFT IN MOOD Breakfast is the most important meal of the day. Eat cereal, not donuts. [The first sentence is a statement, but the second sentence shifts unnecessarily to a command.]

CORRECT Breakfast is the most important meal of the day. Cereal may be a better breakfast choice than donuts.

13c What is being consistent in verb tense?

To be consistent in VERB TENSE, remain in the same tense unless a shift is necessary to show time passing (Box 60, p. 333).

SHIFT IN VERB TENSE The campaign to clean up the movies **began** in the late 1940s when civic and religious groups **try** to ban sex and violence from films. [The tense shifts from past *began* to present *try*, even though the action of both verbs occurred in the past.]

CORRECT   The campaign to clean up the movies **began** in the late
1940s when civic and religious groups **tried** to ban sex and
violence from films. [Both verbs are in the past tense.]

13d What is being consistent in direct and indirect discourse?

Because the grammatical patterns of direct discourse and indirect
discourse differ, writers should not shift between the two. **Direct discourse**
repeats someone's words exactly, with quotation marks enclosing them. **Indirect discourse** reports, rather than repeats exactly,
someone's words without using quotation marks.

SHIFT BETWEEN   He asked did we enjoy the movie. [The verb *asked* is
DIRECT AND   direct discourse, but the needed quotation marks are
INDIRECT DISCOURSE   missing. Conversely, *did we enjoy* is direct discourse.]

CORRECT   He asked, "Did you enjoy the movie?" [The quotation
marks indicate this is direct discourse.]

CORRECT   He asked whether we had enjoyed the movie. [The
statement indicates that words are being reported, not
quoted. The verb *had enjoyed* clarifies the time relationship
between the enjoyment and the asking.]

13e What happens in sentences with mixed parts?

A sentence with mixed parts starts in one direction but goes off in a different
direction. This mixing of parts makes the meaning of the sentence
unclear. To revise such errors, think through exactly what you
want to say.

Avoiding mixed clauses

In a sentence containing a DEPENDENT CLAUSE and an INDEPENDENT
CLAUSE, the clauses are clear when they carry meaning in one direction,
not in two directions.

MIXED   Because television's first transmissions in the late 1940s in-
CLAUSES   cluded **news, programs** were popular. [The dependent
clause talks about the news, but the independent clause goes off

in another direction by talking about the popularity of programs in general.]

CORRECT Television's first transmissions in the late 1940s included **news programs, which** were popular. [Dropping *Because*, putting *news* and *programs* together, and adding *which* solves the problem by keeping the focus on news programs throughout.]

Avoiding mixed phrase-clauses

In a sentence containing a PHRASE and only part of an independent clause, the material makes no sense.

MIXED
PHRASE-
CLAUSE **By doubling the time allotment** to thirty minutes **increased** the prestige of news programs. [This sentence uses the prepositional phrase *By doubling the time allotment*, but what follows does not make sense.]

CORRECT **Doubling** the time allotment to thirty minutes **increased** the prestige of news programs. [Dropping the preposition *By* allows the sentence to make sense.]

CORRECT **By doubling the time allotment** to thirty minutes, **network executives increased** the prestige of news programs. [Inserting a logical subject, *network executives,* allows the sentence to make sense.]

Avoiding faulty predication

Faulty predication results when the subject and PREDICATE of a sentence don't make sense together. You can correct the error by revising one part or the other so that they work together.

FAULTY
PREDICATION The purpose of television was invented to entertain. [The subject of the sentence is *purpose*. The predicate is *was invented to entertain*. Together, they make no sense.]

CORRECT **Television** was invented to entertain. [Revising the subject and keeping the original predicate allows the sentence to make sense.]

CORRECT The purpose of television **was to entertain.** [Revising the predicate and keeping the original subject allows the sentence to make sense.]

13f How do elliptical constructions and comparisons work?

An **elliptical construction** deliberately leaves out, rather than repeats, one or more words that appear earlier in a sentence. Here is a correctly written elliptical sentence.

- I have my book and Joan's. [This means *I have my book and Joan's book.*]

An elliptical sentence is correct only when it contains exactly the same words that are omitted.

- In 1920s Chicago, cornetist Manuel Perez ~~was leading~~ *led* one outstanding jazz group, Tommy and Jimmy Dorsey another.

  [The singular verb *was leading* cannot take the place of *were leading.* *Led* works because it goes with both the singular and plural subjects.]

- The period of the big jazz dance bands began *in* and lasted through World War II. [*Began* must be followed by *in*, not *through*.]

In writing a comparison, you can omit words as long as the reader can clearly tell what the missing words are.

- High achievers make better business executives *than low achievers do*.

  [*Better* implies a comparison, but none was stated, so the revision corrects the problem.]

- Most stockholders value high achievers more than *they value* risk takers.

  [Before the revision, it is not clear who values whom most. The revised sentence makes the meaning clear. An alternative revision, with a different meaning, is *Most stockholders value high achievers more than risk takers do.*]

- A risk taker's ability to manage long-term growth is very different *from that of a high achiever*.

  [Different from what? Both items must be expressed for the comparison to work.]

👁 **ALERT:** When you write *as much as, as . . . as . . . than . . .* (for example, *as pretty as, if not prettier than*), and similar comparisons, be sure to state the second *as*.

- High achievers value success as much, ^as if not more than, high salary. 👁

14 MISPLACED MODIFIERS

A **modifier** describes or limits other words, phrases, or clauses. A modifier can be a word, PHRASE, or CLAUSE. When you write, place modifiers carefully so that your intended meaning is clear.

14a How can I correct misplaced modifiers?

The correct placement for a modifier is almost always next to the word that it modifies. If you place modifiers elsewhere in a sentence, your meaning can easily become confused. (Sometimes, as the example shows, **misplaced modifiers** provide unintended humor.)

MISPLACED MODIFIER   Nicholas Cugnot built the first self-propelled vehicle, determined to travel without horses. [The modifier *determined to travel without horses* is meant to describe *Nicholas Cugnot*. But it is placed next to *vehicle*, so the sentence says that the vehicle was determined to travel without horses.]

CORRECT   Determined to travel without horses, Nicholas Cugnot built the first self-propelled vehicle.

Adverbs such as *only, just, almost, hardly, scarcely*, and *simply* always limit the word that they immediately precede. Their placement in the sentence strongly affects the meaning your sentence delivers. For example, notice how various positions of *only* influence the meaning of the sentence *Professional coaches say that high salaries motivate players*.

- **Only** professional coaches say that high salaries motivate players. [No one else says that.]

- Professional coaches **only** say that high salaries motivate players. [The coaches don't believe it.]

- Professional coaches say that **only** high salaries motivate players. [The coaches think nothing else works.]

- Professional coaches say that high salaries motivate **only** players. [No one else is motivated by high salaries.]

14b How can I correct squinting modifiers?

A **squinting modifier** appears to apply to what comes before it as well as to what comes after it. Revise so that the modifier applies to only one word.

- While Karl Benz watched, the vehicle he had built ~~noisily~~ announced its arrival.
  noisily

  [Before the revision, the car seems to be both noisily built and noisily announcing its arrival.]

14c How can I correct split infinitives?

A **split infinitive** occurs when a modifier of more than one word separates *to* and the verb that completes the infinitive. (*To conclude* is an infinitive. *To **without a doubt** conclude* is a split infinitive.)

SPLIT INFINITIVE	Orson Welles's radio drama *War of the Worlds* managed **to, on October 30, 1938,** convince listeners that they were hearing an invasion by Martians.
CORRECT	On October 30, 1938, Orson Welles's radio drama *War of the Worlds* managed **to convince** listeners that they were hearing an invasion by Martians.

14d How can I keep modifiers from disrupting a sentence?

Avoid writing complex descriptive PHRASES or CLAUSES that separate the subject and verb of a sentence. They make a sentence overly complicated, disturbing its smooth flow.

- ~~The invention of the automobile, if~~ *If* we consider the complete history of many people working independently in different countries, *the invention of the automobile* should probably be credited to Nicholas Cugnot in 1769.

Also, interrupting a VERB PHRASE with modifiers makes a sentence lurch instead of flow. Observe the general rule to put modifiers next to the word they modify.

- Karl Benz has ~~by most automobile historians,~~ been given credit, *by most automobile historians* for the invention of the automobile.

14e How can I correct dangling modifiers?

A **dangling modifier** is an introductory PHRASE that hangs (that is, it dangles) helplessly because the NOUN it modifies isn't the intended subject. Introductory phrases attach their meaning to the first noun after the phrase—indeed, that noun is the sentence's subject. If some other word falls in that position, the result is confusing (and may be humorous).

DANGLING MODIFIER	Reading Faulkner's short story "A Rose for Emily," the ending surprised us. [*The ending* did not read the story.]
CORRECT	Reading Faulkner's short story "A Rose for Emily," **we were surprised** by the ending.
CORRECT	**We read** Faulkner's short story "A Rose for Emily" and were surprised by the ending.
DANGLING MODIFIER	When courting Emily, the townspeople gossiped about Homer Baron. [*The townspeople* were not courting Emily, and they were not gossiping about Homer so much as about Emily.]
YES	**When Homer Baron was courting Emily,** the townspeople gossiped about her.

15 CONCISENESS

Concise writing is direct and to the point. **Wordy writing** uses empty words and phrases that increase the word count, but contribute nothing to meaning. Your goal is to write concisely so that your readers understand your message clearly.

15a How can I write concisely?

You can write concisely by deleting all words not necessary for delivering your message clearly (Box 21). Prune your sentences of deadwood.

- ~~As a matter of fact, the~~ The local television station ~~which was situated in the local area~~ had won ~~a great~~ many awards ~~as a result of~~ for its ~~having been involved in the~~ coverage of ~~all kinds of~~ controversial issues.

■■■■ BOX 21 ■■ ■

🎯 Deleting unneeded words

EMPTY WORDS	WORDY EXAMPLES REVISED
as a matter of fact	*M* ~~As a matter of fact,~~ **many** marriages end in divorce.
at the present time	*now.* The bill is being debated ~~at the present time.~~
because of the fact that, in light of the fact that, due to the fact that	Because ~~of the fact that~~ a special exhibit is scheduled, the museum is open late each day.
by means of	We traveled by ~~means of~~ cars.
factor	The project's final cost was ~~an~~ essential ~~factor~~ to consider.
that exists	The crime rate ~~that exists~~ is unacceptable.
for the purpose of	*to* A work crew arrived ~~for the purpose of~~ fixing the pothole.
have a tendency to	*tended* The mixture ~~had a tendency~~ to evaporate.
in a very real sense	*D* ~~In a very real sense,~~ drainage problems caused the flooding.
in the case of	*T* *angered* ~~In the case of~~ the proposed tax residents . ~~were angry.~~
in the final analysis	*N* ~~In the final analysis,~~ no observer described the accident accurately.
in the event that	*If* ~~In the event that~~ you are late, I will buy our tickets.

CONTINUED ➔

BOX 21

Deleting unneeded words *(continued)*

EMPTY WORDS	WORDY EXAMPLES REVISED
in the process of	We are ~~in the process of~~ reviewing six sites.
it seems that	~~It seems that~~ ^T^ the union struck over wages.
manner	The hikers looked at the snake ~~in a fearful manner.~~ *fearfully.*
nature	The review was ~~of a~~ sarcastic. ~~nature.~~
the point that I am trying to make	~~The point that I am trying to make is that~~ *N* news reporters often invade people's privacy.
what I mean to say	~~What I mean to say is that~~ I expect a bonus.
type of, kind of	Gordon took a relaxing ~~type of~~ vacation.

15b How can I avoid redundant writing?

Redundant writing is repetitious writing, delivering the same message more than once, but in slightly different words. Unlike planned repetition (17d), which can create a powerful rhythmic effect, unplanned repetition reflects sloppy revision.

• ~~People~~ *A* anesthetized ~~for surgery~~ *people* can remain semiconscious during surgery but nevertheless feel no pain.

  [*Surgery* is used twice unnecessarily. The word *anesthetized* carries the concept of surgery. The revision is not redundant.]

• ~~Bringing~~ *Completing* the project ~~to final completion~~ three weeks early, the new manager earned our ~~respectful regard.~~ *respect.*

  [*Completing* carries the idea of *final*. Also, *regard* implies *respect*. The revisions are not redundant.]

• The package, ~~rectangular in shape,~~ *rectangular* lay on the counter.

  [*Rectangular* includes the concept of *shape*. The revision is not redundant.]

15c How can I avoid wordy sentence structures?

The two sentence structures that most frequently lead to wordiness are expletive constructions and use of the passive voice.

Avoiding expletive constructions

An **expletive** construction places *it* or *there* and a form of *be* before the subject of the sentence. To make the sentence more concise, revise it to eliminate the expletive.

- ~~It is necessary for~~ students ~~to~~ fill out both registration forms.
  [handwritten: S above "students", need above "to"]

- ~~There are~~ three ~~majors offered by~~ the computer science department.
  [handwritten: T, offers three majors.]

Using the passive voice appropriately

In general, the PASSIVE VOICE is less lively and concise than the ACTIVE VOICE (40g). Unless your meaning justifies using the passive voice, write in the active voice.

PASSIVE   Volunteer work was done by the students for credit in sociology. [Here the passive voice is unnecessary. *The students*, who are the ones doing the action of volunteer work, should be the subject of this sentence.]

ACTIVE   The students did volunteer work for credit in sociology.

ACTIVE   Volunteer work earned the students credit in sociology. [Here, *volunteer work* performs the action of the verb *earned*, so it is the subject of the sentence.]

15d How can combining sentence elements help me be concise?

Sometimes you can combine sentences to save words. Look at your sentences two at a time to see if a group of words in one sentence can be included in another sentence.

- ~~The Titanic was discovered~~ seventy-three years after being sunk by an iceberg. ~~The~~ ~~liner~~ was located under the water by a team of French and American scientists.
  [handwritten: S, + Titanic, ,The]

Sometimes you can shorten longer structures to become a PHRASE or even a single word.

- The Titanic, ~~which was~~ a huge ocean liner, sank in 1911.

- The scientists who discovered the Titanic held a memorial service
  dead
  for the passengers and crew. ~~members who had died.~~

- ~~Loaded with luxuries,~~ *T luxury* the liner was thought to be unsinkable.

15e How do action verbs improve conciseness?

ACTION VERBS are strong verbs. Weak verbs, especially forms of *to be* and *to have,* usually lead to wordy sentences.

WEAK VERB The plan before the city council **has to do** with tax rebates.

STRONG VERB The plan before the city council **proposes** tax rebates.

ALERT: When you revise, look for phrase patterns such as *be aware of* and *be capable of* and revise them to be more concise. Often such phrases are better stated with one-word verbs: for example, *I envy* [not *am envious of*] *your self-confidence.* Here are a few more examples: Use *appreciate* in place of *be appreciative of*, *illustrate* in place of *be illustrative of*, and *support* in place of *be supportive of.*

When you revise to use strong verbs, look for nouns built from verbs. Turning nouns that end with *-ance, -ment*, and *-tion* into verbs allows you to write more concisely.

NO The accumulation of old newspapers went on for more than thirty years.

YES The old newspapers **accumulated** for more than thirty years.

16 COORDINATION AND SUBORDINATION

Coordination and subordination are sentence structures that help writers communicate the relationships between ideas. Neither structure is superior on its own, but the emphasis that you want your sentence to deliver usually influences your choice. In addition, many experienced writers use both structures to achieve variety in their writing style.

TWO IDEAS   The sky turned brighter.

The wind calmed down.

COORDINATED   The sky turned brighter, **and** the wind calmed down.
VERSION   [Here, the word *and* gives the *sky* and *wind* equal emphasis.]

SUBORDINATED   When the sky turned brighter, the wind calmed down.
VERSIONS   [Here, *the **wind*** is the subject of the INDEPENDENT CLAUSE, so it is the main focus of the sentence.]

As the wind calmed down, the sky turned brighter.
[Here, *the **sky*** is the subject of the INDEPENDENT CLAUSE, so it is the main focus of the sentence.]

16a How does coordination show that ideas are equivalent?

Coordination gives you a grammatical strategy to show that ideas are equal or balanced. A **coordinate sentence,** also called a COMPOUND SENTENCE, has INDEPENDENT CLAUSES joined either by a SEMICOLON or by a coordinating conjunction (*and, but, for, or, nor, yet, so*).

- The sky turned brighter, **and** the wind calmed down.
- The sky turned brighter**;** the wind calmed down.

👁 **ALERT:** Unless you use a semicolon, use a comma before a coordinating conjunction that joins two independent clauses (50c). 👁

16b How can I avoid problems with coordination?

Two problems can occur with coordination. First, you create an illogical sentence if you join unrelated or nonequivalent ideas with a coordinating conjunction.

NO   Computers came into common use in the 1970s, and they sometimes make costly errors. [The statement in each INDEPENDENT CLAUSE is true, but the ideas are not logically connected and therefore should not be coordinated.]

YES   Computers came into common use in the 1970s, and now they are indispensable business tools.

Second, you create unclear, unfocused material if you overuse coordination. Avoid stringing more than two or three sentences together with coordinating conjunctions (*and, but, for, or, nor, yet, so*).

> **NO** Dinosaurs could have disappeared for many reasons, and one theory holds that the climate suddenly became cold, and another suggests that a sudden shower of meteors and asteroids hit the earth, so the impact created a huge dust cloud that caused a false winter. The winter lasted for years, and the dinosaurs died.

> **YES** Dinosaurs could have disappeared for many reasons. One theory holds that the climate suddenly became cold, and another suggests that a sudden shower of meteors and asteroids hit the earth. The impact created a huge dust cloud that caused a false winter. The winter lasted for years, killing the dinosaurs.

16c How does subordination work to express nonequivalent ideas?

Subordination gives you a grammatical strategy to show that one of the ideas in a sentence is more important than another idea. The more important idea goes in an INDEPENDENT CLAUSE; the less important idea goes in a DEPENDENT CLAUSE, also called a subordinate clause. The information you choose to subordinate depends on the meaning you want to deliver.

> **NO** In 1888, two cowboys had to fight a dangerous Colorado snowstorm. They were looking for cattle. They came to a canyon. They saw outlines of buildings through the snow. Survival then seemed certain.

> **YES** In 1888, two cowboys had to fight a dangerous Colorado snowstorm while they were looking for cattle. When they came to a canyon, they saw outlines of buildings through the snow. Survival then seemed certain.

To subordinate ideas successfully, you need a subordinating word to start the dependent clause.

- SUBORDINATING CONJUNCTIONS (Box 22, p. 86,) start ADVERB CLAUSES.

- RELATIVE PRONOUNS (*who, which, that*) and RELATIVE ADVERBS (such as *where* or *why*) start ADJECTIVE CLAUSES.

BOX 22

 Subordination patterns

SENTENCES WITH ADVERB CLAUSES

- **Adverb clause,** independent clause.
  - **After the sky grew dark,** the wind died suddenly.
- Independent clause, **adverb clause.**
  - Birds stopped singing, **as they do during an eclipse.**
- Independent clause, **adverb clause.**
  - The stores closed **before the storm began.**

SENTENCES WITH ADJECTIVE CLAUSES

- Independent clause, restrictive (that is, essential)* **adjective clause.**
  - Weather forecasts warned of a storm **that might bring a thirty-inch snowfall.**
- Independent clause, nonrestrictive (that is, nonessential)* **adjective clause.**
  - Spring is the season for tornadoes, **which may develop wind speeds over 220 miles an hour.**
- Beginning of independent clause, restrictive (essential)* **adjective clause,** end of independent clause.
  - Anyone **who lives through a tornado** remembers the experience.
- Beginning of independent clause, nonrestrictive (nonessential)* **adjective clause,** end of independent clause.
  - The sky, **which had been clear,** turned greenish black.

*To understand restrictive (essential) and nonrestrictive (nonessential) elements, see 50f.

16d How can I avoid problems with subordination?

Two problems can occur with subordination. First, you create an illogical sentence when the subordinating conjunction doesn't communicate a sensible relationship between the independent clause and the dependent clause. (For the relationships subordinating conjunctions express, see Box 22 above.)

> NO Because Beethoven was deaf when he wrote them, his final symphonies were masterpieces [*Because* is illogical. It suggests that the masterpieces resulted from the deafness.]

> **YES** Although Beethoven was deaf when he wrote them, his final symphonies were masterpieces. [*Although* is logical. It suggests that Beethoven wrote masterpieces despite being deaf.]

Second, your readers lose track of your message if you overuse subordination. Avoid crowding too many images or ideas together.

> **NO** A new technique for eye surgery, which is supposed to correct nearsightedness, which previously could be corrected only by glasses, has been developed, although many doctors do not approve of the new technique because it can create unstable vision.

> **YES** A new technique for eye surgery, which is supposed to correct nearsightedness, has been developed. Previously, nearsightedness could be corrected only by glasses. However, many doctors do not approve of the new technique, because it can create unstable vision. [In this revision, one long sentence is broken into three sentences, making the relationships among ideas clearer.]

17 SENTENCE STYLE

To develop your writing style, experiment with the techniques described in this chapter: parallelism, sentence variety, and emphasis.

17a What is parallelism?

When words, phrases, or clauses within a sentence grammatically match, the result is **parallelism.** Parallelism serves to emphasize information or ideas. Also, balance and rhythm in parallel structures add style and grace to your writing.

PARALLEL WORDS Recommended exercise includes running, swimming, and cycling.

PARALLEL PHRASES Exercise helps people maintain healthy bodies and handle mental pressures.

PARALLEL
CLAUSES
Many people exercise because they want to look healthy,

because they need to increase stamina, and

because they hope to live longer.

17b How can I avoid faulty parallelism?

You can avoid faulty parallelism by checking that you always use the same grammatical form for words, PHRASES, or CLAUSES.

NO The strikers had tried shouting, threats, and pleading. [The last three words incorrectly mix-*ing* forms and a plural.]

YES The strikers had tried shouting, threatening, and pleading. [The last three words use the same -*ing* form.]

YES The strikers had tried shouts, threats, and pleas. [The last three words use the plural *s.*]

NO The strikers read the offer, were discussing it, and the unanimous decision was to reject it. [Two of the three items incorrectly mix verb forms, and the third item switches to the PASSIVE VOICE.]

YES The strikers read the offer, discussed it, and unanimously decided to reject it. [All three items use the past tense.]

17c How should I use parallelism with conjunctions?

Words, phrases, or clauses joined with coordinating conjunctions (*and, but, for, or, nor, yet, so*) usually deliver their message most clearly and concisely when put in parallel form.

You come to understand what to expect when you tease a cat, or toss a pebble in a pool, or touch a hot stove.

—Ann E. Berthoff, *Forming, Thinking, and Writing*

In addition, use parallel forms when you link elements of a sentence with CORRELATIVE CONJUNCTIONS (such as *either . . . or* and *not only . . . but also*).

Differing expectations for marriage can lead **not only to** disappointment **but also to** anger.

—Norman DuBois, student

👁 **ALERTS:** (1) A PREPOSITION or a VERB placed immediately *before* the first correlative conjunction (in this case, the word *both*) in a pair carries its meaning to each item in the pair. That is, in the following sentence, the word *in* is carried over from *the encyclopedia* to *the dictionary: Look **in both** the encyclopedia **and** the dictionary*. (2) Conversely, the same preposition or verb placed *after* the first correlative conjunction (in this case, the word *both*) requires that each item in a pair have its own preposition or verb: *Look **both in** the encyclopedia **and in** the dictionary.* ◉

17d How does parallelism strengthen my message?

Parallelism—which calls for deliberate but controlled repetition of word forms, word groups, and sounds—creates a rhythm that can strengthen and intensify a sentence's message.

> You can fool some of the people all of the time, and all of the people some of the time, but you cannot fool all of the people all of the time.
>
> —Abraham Lincoln

Another technique for using parallel structures to intensify ideas is balanced sentences. **Balanced sentences** consist of two short INDEPENDENT CLAUSES that serve to compare or contrast.

> By night, the litter and desperation disappeared as the city's glittering lights came on; by day, the filth and despair reappeared as the sun rose.
>
> —Jennifer Kirk, student

17e What is sentence variety?

Sentence variety results when you vary the length and structure of your sentences in relation to each other. This variety helps you communicate distinctions among ideas and avoid monotonous rhythm in your writing.

Revising strings of short sentences

Sometimes, you can plan several short sentences in a row to create impact. Nevertheless, unplanned strings of many short sentences don't establish relationships among ideas and tend to make reading dull.

> **NO** There is a problem. It is widely known as sick-building syndrome. It comes from indoor air pollution. It causes the suffering of office workers. They have trouble breathing. The workers develop rashes that are painful. Their heads ache badly. Their eyes burn.

YES Widely known as sick-building syndrome, indoor air pollution causes office workers to suffer. They have trouble breathing. They have painful rashes. Their heads ache. Their eyes burn. [Many revisions are possible. This one begins with a long sentence that introduces the interaction of indoor air pollution and its victims. Then a series of short sentences emphasizes each problem the victims suffer. The revised version is also more CONCISE, reducing 42 words to 27.]

Revising for a mix of sentence lengths

You can emphasize one idea among many others by expressing that idea in a sentence noticeably different in length or structure from the sentences surrounding it. The "yes" example above illustrates the graceful impact of one long sentence among many shorter ones. Here is an example of one short sentence among longer ones.

> Today is one of those excellent January partly cloudies in which light chooses an unexpected landscape to trick out in gilt, and then shadow sweeps it away. **You know you are alive.** You take huge steps, trying to feel the planet's roundness arc between your feet.
>
> —Annie Dillard, *Pilgrim at Tinker Creek*

17f How does the subject of a sentence affect emphasis?

Because the SUBJECT of a sentence establishes the sentence's focus, always choose the subject that gives the sentence the emphasis you want to communicate. Each of the following sentences contains the same information, but changing each subject (and VERB, as needed) affects the meaning and emphasis.

- Our study showed that 25 percent of college students' time is spent eating or sleeping. [Focus is on the study.]

- College students eat or sleep 25 percent of the time, according to our study. [Focus is on the students.]

- Eating or sleeping occupies 25 percent of college students' time, according to our study. [Focus is on eating and sleeping.]

- Twenty-five percent of college students' time is spent in eating or sleeping, according to our study. [Focus is on the percentage of time.]

17g How does adding modifiers affect writing style?

You can add richness and variety to your writing with MODIFIERS. How you expand a sentence with modifiers depends on the focus you want to achieve and how the sentence works with surrounding sentences.

BASIC SENTENCE	The river rose.
ADJECTIVE	The **swollen** river rose.
ADVERB	The river rose **dangerously.**
PREPOSITIONAL PHRASE	**In April,** the river rose **above its banks.**
PARTICIPIAL PHRASE	**Swelled by melting snow,** the river rose, **flooding the farmland.**
ABSOLUTE PHRASE	**Trees swirling away in the current,** the river rose.
ADVERB CLAUSE	**Because the snows had been heavy that winter,** the river rose.
ADJECTIVE CLAUSE	The river, **which runs through vital farm land,** rose.

17h How does inverting standard word order affect writing style?

Standard word order in English sentences places the subject before the verb: *The mayor* [subject] *walked* [verb] *into the room*.

Because standard word order is common, variations from it create interest and emphasis. Therefore, inverted word order, used sparingly, produces an interesting writing style. **Inverted word order** places the verb before the subject: *Into the room walked* [verb] *the mayor* [subject].

Words

www.prenhall.com/troyka

Words

18 USAGE GLOSSARY

This usage glossary presents the customary manner of using particular words and phrases. "Customary manner," however, is not as firm in practice as the term implies. Usage standards change. If you think a word's usage might differ from what you read here, consult a dictionary published more recently than this book.

As used here, *informal* and *colloquial* indicate that words or phrases occur commonly in speech but should be avoided in academic writing. *Nonstandard* indicates that words or phrases should not be used in either standard spoken English or writing.

This glossary includes some of the most commonly confused words listed in Box 24 (pp. 121–26). All grammatical terms mentioned below are defined in the Terms Glossary (pp. 467–85).

a, an   Use *a* before words that begin with a consonant (*a dog, a grade, a hole*) or a consonant sound (*a one-day sale, a European*). Use *an* before words or acronyms that begin with a vowel sound or a silent *h* (*an owl, an hour, an MRI*). American English uses *a*, not *an*, before words starting with a pronounced *h: a* [not *an*] *historical event.*

accept, except   The verb *accept* means "agree to, receive." As a preposition, *except* means "leaving out." As a verb, *except* means "exclude, leave out."

- The workers were ready to **accept** [verb] management's offer **except** [preposition] for one detail: They wanted the no-smoking rule **excepted** [verb] from the contract.

adapt, adept, adopt   The verb *adapt* means "to make fit or suitable by changing or adjusting." *Adept,* which can serve as an adjective or a noun, means "to be highly skillful or an expert." The verb *adopt* means "to take into your family legally and then consider to be your own child" and "to draw on an idea or practice as if it is your own."

advice, advise   *Advice,* a noun, means "recommendation." *Advise*, a verb, means "recommend; give advice."

- I **advise** [verb] you to follow your car mechanic's **advice** [noun].

affect, effect   As a verb, *affect* means "cause a change in; influence." (*Affect* also functions as a noun in the discipline of psychology.) As a noun, *effect* means "result or conclusion"; as a verb, it means "bring about."

- Because loud music **affects** people's hearing, many bands have **effected** quieter concerts. Many fans, however, happily ignore the harmful **effects** of high decibel levels.

aggravate, irritate *Aggravate* is used colloquially to mean "irritate." In formal writing, use *aggravate* to mean "intensify; make worse." Use *irritate* to mean "annoy; make impatient."

- The coach was **irritated** by her assistant's impatience, which **aggravated** the team's inability to concentrate.

ain't *Ain't* is a nonstandard contraction. Use *am not, is not*, or *are not* instead.

all ready, already *Already* means "before; by this time." *All ready* means "completely prepared."

- The team was **all ready** to play, and the manager had **already** given the lineup card to the umpire.

all right *All right* should be written as two words, never one (not *alright*).

all together, altogether *All together* means "in a group, in unison." *Altogether* means "entirely, thoroughly."

- The judge decided it was **altogether** absurd to expect the jurors to stay **all together** in one hotel room.

allude, elude *Allude* means "refer to indirectly." *Elude* means "escape notice."

- The detective **alluded** to budget cuts when she said, "Events beyond our control enabled the suspect to **elude** us."

allusion, illusion An *allusion* is an indirect reference to something. An *illusion* is a false impression or idea.

- The applicant's casual **allusions** to many European tourist attractions created the **illusion** that he had seen them himself.

a lot *A lot* is informal for *a great deal* or *a great many;* avoid it in academic writing. Write it as two words (not *alot*) when you do use it.

a.m., p.m. These abbreviations may also be written as A.M., P.M. Use them only with numbers, not as substitutes for *morning, afternoon*, or *evening*.

- We will arrive **in the afternoon** [*not* in the p.m.], and we have to leave no later than **8:00 a.m.**

among, amongst, between Use *among* for three or more items and *between* for two items. American English prefers *among* to *amongst*.

- My roommates and I discussed **among** [*not* between *or* amongst] ourselves the choice **between** staying in school and getting full-time jobs.

amoral, immoral   *Amoral* means "neither moral nor immoral"; it can also mean "not concerned with right or wrong." *Immoral* means "morally wrong."

- Although most people consider card playing an **amoral** issue, some Christians consider it **immoral.**

amount, number   Use *amount* for uncountable things (*wealth, work, corn, happiness*). Use *number* for countable items.

- The **amount** of rice to cook depends on the **number** of dinner guests.

an   See *a, an.*

and/or   This term is appropriate in business and legal writing when either or both of two items can apply: *The process is quicker if you have a modem and/or a fax machine.* In the humanities, writers usually express the alternatives in words: *This process is quicker if you have a modem, a fax machine, or both.*

anymore   Use *anymore* with the meaning "now, any longer" only in negations or questions.

- Hardly anyone knits **anymore.**

In positive statements, use an adverb such as *now.*

- Summers are so hot **now** [*not* anymore] that holding yarn is unbearable.

anyone, any one   *Anyone* is a singular indefinite pronoun meaning "any person at all." *Any one* (two words), an adjective modifying a pronoun, means a member of a group.

- **Anyone** could test-drive **any one** of the display vehicles.

anyplace   *Anyplace* is informal. Use *any place* or *anywhere* instead.

anyways, anywheres   *Anyways* and *anywheres* are nonstandard. Use *anyway* and *anywhere* instead.

apt, likely, liable   *Apt* and *likely* are used interchangeably. Strictly, *apt* indicates a tendency or inclination. *Likely* indicates a reasonable expectation or greater certainty than *apt. Liable* denotes legal responsibility or implies unpleasant consequences.

- Alan is **apt** to leave early on Friday. I will **likely** go with him to the party. Maggy and Gabriel are **liable** to be angry if we do not show up.

as, as if, as though, like   Use *as, as if,* or *as though*, but not *like*, to introduce clauses.

- This hamburger tastes good, **as** [*not* like] a hamburger should. It tastes **as if** [*or* as though *but not* like] it was grilled by a chef.

Both *as* and *like* can function as prepositions in comparisons. Use *as* to indicate equivalence between two nouns or pronouns. Use *like* to indicate similarity but not equivalence.

- Beryl acted **as** [*not* like] the moderator in our panel.

- Mexico, **like** [*not* as] Argentina, belongs to the United Nations.

assure, ensure, insure   *Assure* means "promise, convince." *Ensure* and *insure* both mean "make certain or secure," but *insure* is reserved for financial or legal certainty, as in insurance.

- The agent **assured** me that he could **insure** my roller blades but that only I could **ensure** that my elbows and knees would outlast the skates.

as to   *As to* is nonstandard. Use *about* instead.

awful, awfully   Do not use *awful* or *awfully* in place of *terribly, extremely,* or *very*.

a while, awhile   As two words, *a while* (an article and a noun) can function as a subject or object. As one word, *awhile* is an adverb; it modifies verbs. In a prepositional phrase, the correct form is *a while: for a while, in a while, after a while*.

- The seals basked **awhile** in the sun after they had played for **a while** in the sea.

backup, back up   As a noun, *backup* is a copy of electronic data. *Backup* can also be used as an adjective. *Back up* is a verb phrase.

- Many people recommend that you **back up** even your **backup** files and protect all your **backups** from heat.

bad, badly   *Bad* is an adjective; use it after linking verbs. (Remember that verbs like *feel* and *smell* can function as either linking verbs or action verbs.) *Badly* is an adverb and is nonstandard after linking verbs (43d).

- Farmers feel **bad** because a **bad** drought has **badly** damaged the crops.

been, being   *Been* is the past participle of the verb *be; being* is the present participle of *be*. As main verbs, *being* and *been* must be used with auxiliary verbs.

- You **are being** [*not* You being] silly if you think I believe you **have been** [*not* you been] to Sumatra.

being as, being that   *Being as* and *being that* are nonstandard. Use *because* or *since* instead.

- We forfeited the game **because** [*not* being as *or* being that] our goalie has appendicitis.

beside, besides   *Beside* is a preposition meaning "next to, by the side of."

- She stood **beside** the new car, insisting that she would drive.

As a preposition, *besides* means "other than, in addition to."

- No one **besides** her had a driver's license.

As an adverb, *besides* means "also, moreover."

- **Besides,** she owned the car.

better, had better   Used in place of *had better, better* is informal.

- We **had better** [*not* We better] be careful.

between   See *among, amongst, between*.

breath, breathe   *Breath* is a noun; *breathe* is a verb.

- Don't take a **breath** [noun] or you will **breathe** [verb] diesel fumes.

bring, take   Use *bring* to indicate movement from a distant place to a near place or to the speaker. Use *take* to indicate movement from a near place or from the speaker to a distant place.

- If you **bring** a leash to my house, you can **take** the dog to the vet.

but, however, yet   Use *but, however*, or *yet* alone, not in combination with each other.

- The economy is strong, **but** [*not* but yet *or* but however] unemployment is high.

calculate, figure, reckon   These are regional terms for *estimate, imagine, expect, think*, and similar, more formal words.

can, may   *Can* signifies ability or capacity; *may* requests or grants permission. In negations, however, *can* is acceptable in place of *may*.

- You **can** [*or* **may**] leave after lunch.

can't hardly, can't scarcely   These double negatives are nonstandard (43c).

capitol, capital   *Capitol* means "a building in which state legislators meet." *Capital* means either a city or wealth and resources.

- If they can generate enough **capital,** the residents of the state **capital** will build a new **capitol.**

censor, censure   The verb *censor* means "delete objectionable material; judge." The verb *censure* means "condemn or reprimand officially."

- The town council **censured** the mayor for trying to **censor** a report.

chairman, chairperson, chair   Many writers and speakers prefer the gender-neutral terms *chairperson* and *chair* to *chairman; chair* is more common than *chairperson.*

choose, chose   *Choose* is the simple form of the verb. *Chose* is the past-tense form.

- I **chose** a movie last week, so you **choose** one tonight.

cite, site   The verb *cite* means "quote by way of example, authority, or proof." The noun *site* means a particular place.

- The investigator **cited** evidence he had gathered from both the crime **site** and the defendant's personal Web **site.**

cloth, clothe   *Cloth* is a noun meaning "fabric." *Clothe* is a verb meaning "cover with garments or fabric; dress."

- "**Clothe** me in red velvet," snapped the monarch, and servants scurried forward with **cloth.**

complement, compliment   Both these terms function as both nouns and verbs. As a noun, *complement* means "something that goes well with or completes." As a noun, *compliment* means "praise, flattery." As a verb, *complement* means "bring to perfection, go well with; complete." As a verb, *compliment* means "praise, flatter."

- The president's **compliment** was a fine **complement** to our celebration.
- When the president **complimented** us, her praise **complemented** our joy.

comprise, include   See *include, comprise.*

conscience, conscious   The noun *conscience* means "a sense of right and wrong." The adjective *conscious* means "being aware or awake."

- To live happily, be **conscious** of what your **conscience** tells you.

consensus of opinion   This phrase is redundant; use *consensus* only.

- After bitter disagreement, the jury achieved **consensus** on the nineteenth day.

continual(ly), continuous(ly)   *Continual* means "occurring repeatedly." *Continuous* means "going on without interruption."

- Intravenous fluids were given **continuously** for three days after surgery, so nurses were **continually** hooking up new bottles of saline solution.

could care less   *Could care less* is nonstandard; use *couldn't care less* instead.

could of   *Could of* is nonstandard; use *could have* instead.

couple, a couple of   These terms are nonstandard. Use *a few* or *several* instead.

- Rest for **a few** [*not* a couple *or* a couple of] minutes.

criteria, criterion   A *criterion* is "a standard of judgment." *Criteria* is the plural form of *criterion.*

- Although charisma is an important **criterion** for political candidates to meet, voters must also consider other **criteria.**

data   This is the plural of *datum,* a rarely used word. Informally, *data* is commonly used as a singular noun requiring a singular verb. In academic or professional writing, it is more acceptable to treat *data* as plural.

- The researchers' **data** suggest that some people become addicted to e-mail.

different from, different than   *Different from* is preferred for formal writing, although *different than* is common in speech.

- Please advise the council if your research produces data **different from** past results.

disinterested, uninterested   *Disinterested* means "impartial, unbiased" in its preferred usage and is also used to mean "uninterested, indifferent." Some authorities object to this second usage, so you may want to reserve *disinterested* to convey "impartial" and *uninterested* to convey "indifferent."

- Although jurors must be **disinterested,** attorneys cannot afford for them to be **uninterested.**

don't   *Don't* is a contraction for *do not,* but not for *does not* (use *doesn't*).

- She **doesn't** [*not* She don't] like crowds.

effect   See *affect, effect*.

elicit, illicit   The verb *elicit* means "draw forth or bring out." The adjective *illicit* means "illegal."

- The government's **illicit** conduct **elicited** mass protest.

elude   See *allude, elude*.

emigrate (from), immigrate (to)   *Emigrate* means "leave one country to live in another." *Immigrate* means "enter a country to live there."

- My great-grandmother **emigrated** from Kiev in 1890. After a brief stay in Germany, she **immigrated** to Canada in 1892.

ensure   See *assure, ensure, insure*.

enthused *Enthused* is nonstandard. Use *enthusiastic* instead.

etc. *Etc.* is the abbreviation for the Latin *et cetera*, meaning "and the rest." For writing in the humanities, avoid using *etc.* outside parentheses. Acceptable substitutes are *and the like, and so on,* and *and so forth.*

everyday, every day The adjective *everyday* means "daily." *Every day* is an adjective-noun combination that can function as a subject or an object.

- Being late for work has become an **everyday** occurrence. **Every day** that I am late brings me closer to being fired.

everyone, every one *Everyone* is a singular, indefinite pronoun. *Every one* (two words), an adjective modifying a pronoun, means each member in a group.

- **Everyone** enjoyed **every one** of the variety acts.

everywheres Nonstandard for *everywhere*.

except See *accept, except*.

explicit, implicit *Explicit* means "directly stated or expressed." *Implicit* means "implied, suggested."

- The warning on cigarette packs is **explicit:** "Smoking is dangerous to health." The **implicit** message is "Don't smoke."

farther, further Although many writers reserve *farther* for geographical distances and *further* for all other cases, current usage treats them as interchangeable.

fewer, less Use *fewer* for anything that can be counted (with count nouns): *fewer dollars, fewer fleas, fewer haircuts.* Use *less* with collective or other noncount nouns: *less money, less scratching, less hair.*

finalize Academic audiences prefer *complete* or *make final* instead of *finalize*.

- After intense negotiations, the two nations **completed** [*not* finalized] a treaty.

firstly, secondly, thirdly British English commonly uses *firstly, secondly,* and *thirdly;* formal American English uses *first, second,* and *third.*

former, latter When two items are referred to, *former* signifies the first one and *latter* signifies the second. Avoid using *former* and *latter* when referring to more than two items.

- Brazil and Ecuador are South American countries. Portuguese is the most common language in the **former,** Spanish in the **latter.**

go, say   *Go* is nonstandard when used to mean *say, says*, or *said.*

- After he stepped on my hand, he **said** [*not* he goes], "Your hand was in my way."

gone, went   *Gone* is the past participle of *go; went* is the past tense of *go.*

- They **went** [*not* gone] to the concert after Ira **had gone** [*not* had went] home.

good and   This phrase is a nonstandard intensifier; omit it.

- They were **exhausted** [*not* good and tired].

good, well   *Good* is an adjective. Using it as an adverb is nonstandard. *Well* is the equivalent adverb.

- **Good** maintenance helps cars run **well.**

got, have   *Got* is nonstandard in place of *have.*

- What do we **have** [*not* got] for supper?

hardly   See *can't hardly, can't scarcely.*

have, of   Use *have,* not *of,* after such verbs as *could, should, would, might,* and *must.*

- You **should have** [*not* should of] called first.

have got, have to, have got to   Avoid using *have got* when *have* alone delivers your meaning.

- I **have** [*not* have got] two more sources to read.

Avoid using *have to* or *have got to* for *must.*

- I **must** [*not* have got to] finish this assignment today.

he/she, s/he, his, her   To avoid sexist language, use *he or her* or *his or her.* A less wordy solution is to use plural pronouns and antecedents.

- The **mourners** bowed their heads.
- Everyone bowed **his or her** head. [*Not* Everyone bowed his head.]

historic, historical   The adjective *historic* means "important in history" or "to be highly memorable." The adjective *historical* means "relating to history."

hopefully   An adverb meaning "with hope, in a hopeful manner," *hopefully* can modify a verb, an adjective, or another adverb: *They waited hopefully for the plane to land. Hopefully* is commonly used as a sentence modifier with the meaning "I hope," but you should avoid this usage in academic writing.

- I **hope** [*not* Hopefully] the plane will land safely.

humanity, humankind, humans, mankind   To avoid sexist language, use *humanity, humankind*, or *humans* instead of *mankind*.

- Some people think computers have influenced **humanity** more than any other twentieth-century invention has done.

i.e.   This abbreviation refers to the Latin term *id est*. In formal writing, use the English translation *that is*.

if, whether   At the start of a noun clause, use either *if* or *whether*.

- I don't know **if** [*or* whether] I want to dance with you.

In conditional clauses, use *whether* (or *whether or not*) when alternatives are expressed or implied.

- I will dance with you **whether or not** I like the music. I will dance with you **whether** the next song is fast or slow.

In a conditional clause that does not express or imply alternatives, use *if*.

- **If** you promise not to step on my feet, I will dance with you.

illicit   See *elicit, illicit*.

illusion   See *allusion, illusion*.

immigrate   See *emigrate, immigrate*.

immoral   See *amoral, immoral*.

imply, infer   *Imply* means "hint at or suggest." *Infer* means "draw a conclusion." A writer or speaker implies; a reader or listener infers.

- When the governor **implied** that she would not seek reelection, reporters **inferred** that she was planning to run for vice president.

include, comprise   The verb *include* means "to contain or to regard as part of a whole." The verb *comprise* means "to consist or be composed of."

incredible, incredulous   *Incredible* means "extraordinary; not believable." *Incredulous* means "unable or unwilling to believe."

- Listeners were **incredulous** as the freed hostages described the **incredible** hardships they had experienced.

in regard to, with regard to, as regards, regarding   Replace these wordy phrases with *about, concerning,* or *for*. Avoid the nonstandard *as regards to*.

- **In regard to** [*or* With regard to *or* As regards] your query, we confirm that your payment was received.

inside of, outside of   These phrases are nonstandard when used to mean *inside* or *outside*.

- She waited **outside** [*not* outside of] the dormitory.

In time references, avoid using *inside of* to mean "in less than."

- I changed clothes **in less than** [*not* inside of] ten minutes.

insure   See *assure, ensure, insure*.

irregardless   *Irregardless* is nonstandard. Use *regardless* instead.

is when, is where   Avoid these constructions in giving definitions.

- Defensive driving **requires that** [*not* is when] drivers stay alert.

its, it's   *Its* is a personal pronoun in the possessive case. *It's* is a contraction of *it is*.

- The dog buried **its** bone.
- **It's** a hot day.

kind, sort   Use *this* or *that* with these singular nouns; use *these* or *those* with the plural nouns *kinds* and *sorts*. Also, do not use *a* or *an* after *kind of* or *sort of*.

- Drink **these kinds of** fluids [*not* this kind of fluids] on **this sort of** [*not* this sort of a] day.

kind of, sort of   These phrases are colloquial adverbs. In formal writing, use *somewhat* instead.

- The campers were **somewhat** [*not* kind of] dehydrated after the hike.

later, latter   *Late* means "after some time; subsequently." *Latter* refers to the second of two items.

- The college library stays open **later** than the town library; also, the **latter** is closed on weekends.

lay, lie   *Lay* (*laid, laid, laying*) means "place or put something, usually on something else" and needs a direct object. *Lie* (*lay, lain, lying*), meaning "recline," does not take a direct object (40d). Substituting *lay* for *lie* is nonstandard.

- **Lay** [*not* Lie] the blanket down, and then **lay** the babies on it so they can **lie** [*not* lay] in the shade.

leave, let   *Leave* means "depart"; *let* means "allow, permit." *Leave* is nonstandard for *let*.

- **Let** [*not* Leave] me use your car tonight.

less   See *fewer, less*.

lie   See *lay, lie*.

like   See *as, as if, as though, like.*

likely   See *apt, likely, liable.*

lots, lots of, a lot of   These are colloquial usages. Use *many, much,* or *a great deal* instead.

mankind   See *humanity, humankind, humans, mankind.*

may   See *can, may.*

maybe, may be   *Maybe* is an adverb; *may be* is a verb phrase.

• **Maybe** [adverb] we can win, but our team **may be** [verb phrase] too tired.

may of, might of   *May of* and *might of* are nonstandard. Use *may have* and *might have* instead.

media   This word is the plural of *medium,* but common usage pairs it with a singular verb. In most cases, a more specific word is preferable.

• **Television reporters** offend [*or* The media offend; *not* The media offends] me by shouting personal questions at grief-stricken people.

morale, moral   *Morale* is a noun meaning "a mental state relating to courage, confidence, or enthusiasm." As a noun, *moral* means an "ethical lesson implied or taught by a story or event"; as an adjective, *moral* means "ethical."

• One **moral** to draw from corporate downsizings is that overstressed employees suffer from low **morale.** Unhappy employees with otherwise high **moral** standards may steal from their employers.

most   *Most* is nonstandard for *almost: Almost* [not *Most*] *all the dancers agree. Most* is correct as the superlative form of an adjective (*some, more, most*): *Most dancers agree.* It also makes the superlative form of adverbs and some adjectives: *most suddenly, most important.*

Ms.   A women's title free of reference to marital status, equivalent to *Mr.* for men. For a woman who does not use *Dr.* or another title, use *Ms.* unless she requests *Miss* or *Mrs.*

must of   *Must of* is nonstandard. Use *must have* instead.

nowheres   Nonstandard for *nowhere.*

number   See *amount, number.*

of   Use *have* instead of *of* after the following verbs: *could, may, might, must, should,* and *would.* See *could of; may of, might of; must of; should of;* and *would of.*

off of   *Off of* is nonstandard. Omit the *of*.

- Don't fall **off** [*not* off of] the piano.

OK, O.K., okay   All three forms are acceptable in informal writing. In academic writing, try to express meaning more specifically.

- The weather was **satisfactory** [*not* okay] for the race.

on account of, owing to the fact that   These phrases are wordy. Use *because* or *because of* instead.

- **Because** [*not* Owing to the fact that] humidity was high, paper jammed in the photocopier.
- **Because of** [*not* On account of] the high humidity, paper jammed in the photocopier.

oral, verbal   The adjective *oral* means "spoken or being done by the mouth." The adjective *verbal* means "relating to language" [verbal skills] or to words rather than actions, facts, or ideas.

outside of   See *inside of, outside of.*

percent, percentage   Use *percent* with specific numbers: *two percent, 95 percent.* Use *percentage* to refer to less exact portions of a whole.

- About **47 percent** of the eligible U.S. population votes regularly; but when presidential elections are excluded, the **percentage** [*not* percent] drops sharply.

plus   *Plus* is nonstandard as a substitute for *and, also, in addition*, or *moreover.*

- The band will give three concerts in Hungary, **and** [*not* plus] it will tour Poland for a month. Also [*not* Plus], it may perform once in Vienna.

precede, proceed   *Precede* means "go before." *Proceed* means "advance, go on; undertake; carry on."

- **Preceded** by elephants and tigers, the clowns **proceeded** into the tent.

pretty   *Pretty* is an informal qualifying word; use *rather, quite, somewhat*, or *very* in academic writing.

- The flu epidemic was **quite** [*not* pretty] severe.

principal, principle   *Principle* means "a basic truth or rule." As a noun, *principal* means "chief person; main or original amount"; as an adjective, *principal* means "most important."

- During the assembly, the **principal** said, "A **principal** value in this society is the **principle** of free speech."

proceed   See *precede, proceed.*

quotation, quote   *Quotation* is a noun; *quote* is a verb. Do not use *quote* as a noun.

- The newspaper **quoted** the attorney general, and the **quotations** [*not* quotes] quickly showed up in public health messages.

raise, rise   *Raise* (*raised, raised, raising*) means "lift" and needs a direct object. *Rise* (*rose, risen, rising*) means "go upward" and does not take a direct object. Using these verbs interchangeably is nonstandard.

- If the citizens **rise** [*not* raise], they may **raise** the flag of liberty.

real, really   These are nonstandard intensifiers.

reason is because   This phrase is redundant; use *reason is that* instead.

- One **reason** we moved **is that** [*not* is because] we changed jobs.

reason why   This phrase is redundant; use either *reason* or *why* instead.

- I still do not know the **reason that** [*or* **I still do not know why**, *not* the reason why] they left home.

regarding   See *in regard to, with regard to, as regards, regarding.*

regardless   See *irregardless.*

respective, respectively   The adjective *respective* relates the noun it modifies to two or more individual persons or things. The adverb *respectively* refers to a second set of items in a sequence established by a preceding set of items.

- After the fire drill, Dr. Pan and Dr. Moll returned to their **respective** offices [that is, each to his or her office] on the second and third floors, **respectively.** [Dr. Pan has an office on the second floor; Dr. Moll has an office on the third floor.]

Do not confuse *respective* and *respectively* with *respectful* and *respectfully*, which refer to showing regard for or honor to something or someone.

- The child listened **respectfully** to the lecture about **respectful** behavior.

right   *Right* is a colloquial intensifier; use *quite, very, extremely,* or a similar word for most purposes.

- You did **very** [*not* right] well on the quiz.

rise   See *raise, rise.*

scarcely   See *can't hardly, can't scarcely.*

secondly   See *firstly, secondly, thirdly.*

seen   Past participle of *see* (*see, saw, seen, seeing*), *seen* is a nonstandard substitute for the past-tense form, *saw*. As a verb, *seen* must be used with an auxiliary verb.

- Last night, I **saw** [*not* seen] the show that you **had seen** in Florida.

set, sit   *Set* (*set, set, setting*) means "put in place, position, put down" and must have a direct object. *Sit* (*sat, sat, sitting*) means "be seated." Using these verbs interchangeably is nonstandard.

- Susan **set** [*not* sat] the sandwiches beside the salad, made Spot **sit** [*not* set] down, and then **sat** [*not* set] on the sofa.

shall, will, should   *Shall* was once used with *I* or *we* for future-tense verbs, and *will* was used with all other persons: ***We shall** leave Monday, and **he will** leave Thursday. Will* is commonly used for all persons now.

Similarly, distinctions were once made between *shall* and *should*. *Should* is much more common with all persons now, although *shall* is used about as often as *should* in questions asking what to do: ***Shall*** [or *Should*] *I get your jacket?*

should of   *Should of* is nonstandard. Use *should have* instead.

sit   See *set, sit*.

site   See *cite, site*.

sometime, sometimes, some time   The adverb *sometime* means "at an unspecified time." The adverb *sometimes* means "now and then." *Some time* is an adjective-noun combination meaning "an amount or span of time."

- **Sometime** next year we have to take qualifying exams. I **sometimes** worry about finding **some time** to study for them.

sort of   See *kind of, sort of*.

stationary, stationery   *Stationary* means "not moving." *Stationery* refers to paper and related writing products.

- Immediately after the shelves became **stationary,** Zelda called the earthquake hotline and straightened the **stationery.**

such   *Such* is an informal intensifier; avoid it in academic writing unless it precedes a noun introducing a *that* clause.

- The play got **terrible** [*not* such terrible] reviews. It was **such** a dull drama **that** it closed after one performance.

supposed to, used to   The final *d* is essential in both phrases.

- We were **supposed to** [*not* suppose to] leave early. I **used to** [*not* use to] wake up as soon as the alarm rang.

sure   *Sure* is nonstandard as a substitute for *surely* or *certainly*.

- I was **certainly** [*not* sure] surprised at the results.

sure and, try and   Both phrases are nonstandard. Use *sure to* and *try to* instead.

than, then   *Than* indicates comparison; *then* relates to time.

- Please put on your gloves, and **then** put on your hat. It is colder outside **than** inside.

that there, them there, this here, these here   These phrases are nonstandard. Use *that, them, this*, and *these,* respectively.

that, which   Use *that* with restrictive (essential) clauses only. *Which* can be used with both restrictive and nonrestrictive clauses; many writers, however, use *which* only for nonrestrictive clauses, using *that* for all restrictive clauses (42h, 42j).

- The house **that** [*or* **which**] Jack built is on Beanstalk Street, **which** [*not* that] runs past the reservoir.

their, there, they're   *Their* is a possessive. *There* means "in that place" or is part of an expletive construction (41h). *They're* is a contraction of *they are.*

- **They're** going to **their** accounting class in the building **there** behind the library. **There** are twelve sections of Accounting 101.

theirself, theirselves, themself   These are nonstandard. Use *themselves* instead.

them   Use *them* as an object pronoun only. Do not use *them* in place of the adjective *these* or *those*.

- Buy **those** [*not* them] strawberries.

then   See *than, then*.

thusly   *Thusly* is nonstandard. Use *thus* instead.

till, until   Both are acceptable; except in expressive writing, avoid the contracted form *'til.*

to, too, two   *To* is a preposition. *Too* is an adverb meaning "also; more than enough." *Two* is the number.

- When you go **to** Chicago, visit the Art Institute. Go to Harry Caray's for dinner, **too.** It won't be **too** expensive because **two** people can share an entrée.

toward, towards   Both are acceptable; U.S. writers generally prefer *toward.*

try and, sure and   See *sure and, try and.*

type   *Type* is nonstandard when used to mean *type of.*
- Use that **type of** [*not* type] glue on plastic.

uninterested   See *disinterested, uninterested.*

unique   *Unique* is an absolute adjective; do not combine it with *more, most*, or other qualifiers.
- Solar heating is **uncommon** [*not* somewhat unique] in the Northeast. A **unique** [*not* very unique] heating system in one Vermont home uses hydrogen for fuel.

used to   See *supposed to, used to.*

utilize   Academic writers prefer *use* to *utilize.*
- The team **used** [*not* utilized] all its players to win the game.

verbal, oral   See *oral, verbal.*

wait on   *Wait on* is an informal substitute for *wait for;* it is appropriate in the context of persons giving service to others.
- I had to **wait** half an hour **for** [*not* wait . . . on] that clerk to **wait on** me.

way, ways   When referring to distance, use *way* rather than *ways.*
- He is a long **way** [*not* ways] from home.

well   See *good, well.*

where   *Where* is nonstandard when used for *that* as a subordinating conjunction.
- I read **that** [*not* where] Michael Jordan is the greatest basketball player ever.

where . . . at   The phrase is redundant; drop *at.*
- **Where** is your house? [*not* Where is your house at?]

whether   See *if, whether.*

which   See *that, which.*

who, whom   Use *who* as a subject or a subject complement. Use *whom* as an object (42g).

who's, whose   *Who's* is a contraction of *who is. Whose* is a possessive pronoun.
- **Who's** willing to drive? **Whose** truck should we take?

will   See *shall, will*

-wise   The suffix *-wise* means "in a manner, direction, or position." Be careful not to attach *-wise* indiscriminately to create new words rather than using good words that already exist. When in doubt, check your dictionary to be sure that a *-wise* word you want to use is acceptable.

would of   *Would of* is nonstandard. Use *would have* instead.

your, you're   *Your* is a possessive. *You're* is the contraction of *you are*.

- **You're** generous to volunteer **your** time at the elementary school.

19 WORD MEANINGS AND WORD IMPACT

19a How can I learn about words and their meanings?

A good recently published dictionary tells you about the meaning and use of words. Three fine dictionaries are *Webster's New World Dictionary, Webster's New Collegiate Dictionary,* and the *American Heritage Dictionary of the English Language*. A dictionary's introductory pages describe the types of information found in word entries.

19b How can I choose exact words?

Exact words are words that are precise and accurate for the context in which you use them. Your **diction,** the official term for the use of exact words, affects the clarity and impact of your messages. To use good diction in your writing, you want to be aware of the distinctions between denotation and connotation, as well as between general and specific words.

Distinguishing between denotation and connotation

Denotation is a word's explicit dictionary meaning—its definition. Interestingly, subtle shades of meaning differentiate words with the same general definitions. For example, would you use *famous* or *notorious* to describe a person well known for praiseworthy achievements? *Famous* is correct because it means "much talked about" and "renowned." *Notorious* means "unfavorably known or talked about." George Washington is famous; Timothy McVeigh, the Oklahoma City bomber, is notorious.

   Connotation refers to ideas that a word implies. Connotations convey the associations and emotional overtones we bring to a word from our experiences. For example, the word *home* may evoke more emotion than does its denotation, "a dwelling place," or its synonym *house*. For some people, *home* may connote warmth, security, and the love of family. But for others, *home* may connote painful sights and sounds of institutionalized old or disabled people. As you write, be aware of the denotations and connotations of your words.

Using specific and concrete language

Specific words identify individual items in a group (*Jeep, Honda*). **General words** relate to an overall group (*car*). **Concrete words** identify persons and things that can be perceived by the senses—seen, heard, tasted, felt, smelled (*black padded vinyl dashboard*). **Abstract words** denote qualities, concepts, relationships, acts, conditions, and ideas (*transportation*).

Specific and concrete words bring life to general and abstract words. As you write, try to supply specific, concrete details and examples to illustrate generalizations and abstractions. At the same time, keep in mind that most good writing combines general and specific with abstract and concrete.

GENERAL　　　　SPECIFIC　　　SPECIFIC　　　　　　　SPECIFIC
My **car,** a **220-horsepower Maxi Armo,** accelerates **from 0 to 50**

　　SPECIFIC　　　　SPECIFIC　　　　　　　　SPECIFIC
miles per hour in **6 seconds** but gets only **18 miles per gallon.**

　　　　　　　　.SPECIFIC　　　　　GENERAL
In contrast, the **Gavin Motors' Bobcat** gets **very good** gas mileage,

　　SPECIFIC　　　GENERAL　　　　SPECIFIC　　SPECIFIC
about **35 mpg** in **highway driving** and **30 mpg** in **stop-and-go**

traffic.

19c How can I increase my vocabulary?

All people have an **active vocabulary,** the words that come to mind easily. Everyone also has a **passive vocabulary,** the words people don't use actively yet recognize and understand. The larger your vocabulary, the more you understand what you read and hear—and the more skillfully you can speak and write.

CHOOSING WHAT WORDS TO LEARN

- Move words in your passive vocabulary into your active one. Because you're already familiar with the words you know passively, you can push them into your active vocabulary rather quickly.

- Underline or circle unfamiliar words as you read them and then write them on index cards to study.

- Use context clues to figure out definitions.

- Use **prefixes,** syllables in front of a word that modify its meaning (for example, ***in**tend* and ***pre**tend*).

- Use **suffixes,** syllables added to the end of a word that modify its meaning (for example, *excit**able*** means "able to be excited" and *excite**ment*** means "the state of being excited").

- Listen closely to speakers who know the language well. When you hear a new word, jot it down to look up later in the dictionary.

- Look up the words in a dictionary and then write them on index cards to study.

STUDYING NEW VOCABULARY WORDS

- Select eight to ten words to study each week.

- Write each new word and its meaning on an index card, in a notebook, or on a computer list.

- Set aside time each day to study your selected words. (Carry your cards, notebook, or computer printout to study in spare moments.)

- Try **mnemonics**—memory-jogging techniques—to help you memorize words. (For example, *desert* spelled with one *s* is filled with *s*and; in contrast, *dessert* spelled with two *s*'s could stand for *s*trawberry *s*hortcake, a favorite end-of-the-meal treat.)

- Push yourself to actively use your newly learned vocabulary words in writing and conversation.

19d What is suitable language for writing?

Using appropriate language

When you use **appropriate language,** your word choice suits your AUDIENCE and PURPOSE.* For example, profane and obscene words don't belong in ACADEMIC WRITING. Similarly, technical medical terms don't belong in a magazine for the general public.

---

* Words printed in small capital letters (such as AUDIENCE and PURPOSE) are defined in the Terms Glossary on pages 467–85.

Being aware of levels of formality

The **levels of formality** in English include highly informal, highly formal, and intermediate. The level you choose depends on your audience and purpose. Highly informal language can be suitable for a letter or an e-mail message to a friend. In contrast, highly formal language is suitable for speeches at, or writings for, ceremonial occasions or for official invitations to events such as weddings. The intermediate level of formality uses standard vocabulary (for example, *learn*, not *wise up*) and conventional sentence structure.

- Ya know stars? They're a gas! [highly informal]
- Gas clouds slowly changed into stars. [intermediate]
- Condensations transmogrified a gas cloud into a star. [highly formal]

Using edited American English

Edited American English conforms to established rules of grammar, sentence structure, punctuation, and spelling. Academic writing uses edited American English—the forms of written language that I use in this *handbook*.

Almost everyone has read English that varies from the standard, especially in advertisements. As a writer, never think that because you see sentence fragments and slang in print, you can use them in academic writing. In addition, many people speak or have heard nonedited American English typical of a great variety of groups of people. These language forms, often based on a long history of combining diverse languages, serve legitimately to unify a group and, often, to promote solidarity and comradeship. Even though such language forms serve important purposes for many people, they are rarely acceptable in academic writing.

Using slang, colloquialisms, and regionalisms

Slang consists of new words (*phat* meaning "very good") or existing words that have new meanings (*wired* meaning "nervous"). Slang is appropriate only in very informal situations.

Colloquial language is characteristic of casual conversation and informal writing: *The student flunked* [instead of *failed*] *chemistry*. **Regional** (also called **dialectal**) **language** is specific to a particular geographic area: *They have nary a cent*. Slang, colloquial, and regional language are not substandard or illiterate, but they're usually not appropriate for academic writing.

19e What is figurative language?

Figurative language consists of words that carry other meanings along with their literal meaning. There are various kinds of figurative language.

Analogy: comparing similar traits shared by dissimilar things. You can develop it in one, several, or many sentences.

- A **cheetah sprinting across the dry plains** after its prey, the **base runner dashed** for home plate, cleats kicking up dust.

Irony: using words to suggest the opposite of their usual sense.

- Told that a minor repair would cost $2,000 and take two weeks, she said, "Oh, how nice!"

Metaphor: comparing otherwise dissimilar things. A metaphor doesn't use the words *like* or *as* to make a comparison.

- Rush-hour **traffic** in the city **bled out through major arteries** to the suburbs.

  Avoid **mixed metaphors,** the combining of two or more inconsistent images in one sentence or expression.

- The violence of the hurricane reminded me of a train ride. [A train ride is not violent, stormy, or destructive.]

Personification: assigning a human trait to something not human. (Be careful about not using mixed metaphors.)

- The book begged to be read.

Overstatement (also called *hyperbole*): exaggerating deliberately for emphasis.

- If this paper is late, the professor will kill me.

Simile: comparing dissimilar things. A simile uses the word *like* or *as*.

- Langston Hughes observes that a deferred dream dries up "like a raisin in the sun."

Understatement: emphasizing by using deliberate restraint.

- It feels warm when the temperature reaches 105 degrees.

19f What is a cliché?

A **cliché** is an overused, worn-out expression. Clichés are once-clever phrases that have grown trite from overuse: *dead as a doornail, gentle as a lamb, straight as an arrow*. Such clichés are SIMILES (comparisons using *like* or *as*) that have become corny. Sometimes a cliché is an action or idea, such as "living happily every after." Rephrase a cliché, or delete it.

> **NO** Needing to travel five hundred miles before dark, we left at **the crack of dawn.**

> **YES** Needing to travel five hundred miles before dark, we left at **dawn.**

19g What is the effect of tone in writing?

Tone relates not so much to *what* you say as to *how* you say it. You want to control your choice of words so that they work with your message, not against it. Words carry messages beyond their literal meanings. For example, if you were to write a chatty, informal message to your superiors about safety hazards in your workplace, you would communicate both that you don't take the hazards seriously and that you likely disrespect your peers and your superiors. Similarly, when you report bad news, jokes are in bad taste. In ACADEMIC WRITING, you want to convey a reasonable tone in both content and choice of words. Avoid the misuses of word choice discussed below.

Avoiding slanted language

When you feel strongly about a topic, you might slip into using slanted language. Such language is biased or emotionally loaded. Slanted language doesn't persuade your readers to agree with you. Rather, it ruins your credibility in the reader's mind. For example, suppose you're arguing against the reelection of your senator. If you write "Our senator is a deceitful, crooked thug," you're using slanted language. Less loaded language would be "Our senator has lied to the public and taken bribes."

Avoiding pretentious language

Pretentious language draws attention to itself with big, unusual words and overly complex sentence structures. Such overblown language obscures your message and damages your credibility with your reader.

NO   The raison d'être for my matriculation in this institution of higher learning is the acquisition of an education.

YES   My reason for being in college is to get an education.

Avoiding jargon

Jargon is common in every field—the professions, academic disciplines, business, and sports—because each field has its own specialized vocabulary. Specialized language, including jargon, allows people who share technical vocabularies to understand each other quickly. When your readers are members of the general public, however, they rarely know what you mean. Therefore, if you absolutely can't avoid a special term when writing for such an audience, define or revise it in simpler terms.

Avoiding euphemisms

Euphemisms attempt to avoid unpleasant truths by substituting "tactful" words for more direct, perhaps harsh-sounding words. When the truth is "Our leader tells many lies," you don't want to be overly indirect by writing "Our leader has a wonderfully vivid imagination." Of course, a euphemism is not only acceptable but also expected in certain social situations. When offering condolences, for example, you may use *passed away* instead of *died*.

20 GENDER-NEUTRAL LANGUAGE

20a What is gender in the English language?

Gender is a grammatical classification reflecting masculinity or femininity. Many languages—but not English—assign gender (masculine, feminine, or neuter) to a large variety of words. In English, only a few words have gender-specific meanings: *she, it, him, her, his, hers, its, man, boy, woman, girl, prince, princess*. These words deliver gender information along with other meanings.

20b What is gender-neutral language?

Using **gender-neutral language,** sometimes called *nonsexist language,* means choosing words that don't carry a message of masculinity or femininity. **Sexist language** unfairly discriminates against both sexes. For example, it inaccurately assumes that all nurses and home-makers are female (calling them *she*) and all physicians and car mechanics are male (calling them *he*).

When you write, turn any gender-specific words you have used into gender-neutral words. For example, use *police officer* instead of *policeman, people* or *humans* instead of *mankind, representative* instead of *congressman*, and *salesperson* instead of *salesman* or *saleswoman*. Also eliminate your use of masculine pronouns in gender-neutral cases. Revise the sexist sentence **He** *has lost* **his** *way* to **They** *have lost* **their** *way*.

BOX 23

Avoiding sexist language

- **Avoid using the masculine pronoun to refer to both men and women.**

  Use a pair of pronouns.   • A doctor has little time to read outside
  or her
  his specialty.

  Use the plural.   • A successful doctor knows that he has
  s   *s*   *they have*
  to work hard.

  Omit gender-specific   • Everyone hopes that he will win the
  pronouns.   *to*
  scholarship.

- **Avoid stereotyping jobs and roles by gender.**
  - supervisor [*not* foreman]
  - businessperson, business executive [*not* businessman]
  - poet, actor [*not* poetess, actress]

- **Avoid expressions that exclude one sex.**
  - person [*not* man]
  - humanity, people [*not* mankind]
  - the average person [*not* the common man]
  - superstition [*not* old wives' tale]

- **Avoid demeaning and patronizing labels.**
  - nurse [*not* male nurse]
  - professional, executive, manager [*not* career girl]
  - My administrative assistant will help you *or* Ida Morea will help you [*not* My girl will help you].

Some writers avoid sexist PRONOUNS by using a *he or she* construction rather than only *he* or only *she*. Revising the pronouns into the plural is preferred whenever possible. If you do choose to use *he or she,* remember that it is a singular expression. Never, however, use too many *he or she* constructions in one sentence or in consecutive sentences.

Most writers today use gender-neutral language to avoid demeaning stereotypes such as *Women are bad drivers* or *Men can't cook*. In ACADEMIC WRITING, treat both sexes equally. For example, if you describe a woman by her looks, clothes, age, or marital status, describe a man the same way in the same context. If you use the first name of one person in a partnership, use the first name of the other—and if you use a title for one, such as *Mr., Dr.*, or *Mrs.,* use a title for both.

NO   Mr. Nathaniel Wallace and his wife Lisa are both lawyers.

YES   Nathaniel and Lisa Wallace are both lawyers.

YES   Mr. and Mrs. Wallace are both lawyers.

21   SPELLING

You might be surprised to learn that good spellers don't know how to spell every word they want to use. What they do know is to check if they are not sure of a word's spelling. If your inner voice questions a spelling, do what good spellers do—check your dictionary.

But how do you look up a word when you don't know how to spell it? If you know the first few letters, find them and then browse for the word. If you do not know the first few letters, think of a synonym and look it up in a thesaurus.

COMPUTER TIP: Use all spell-check programs on computers with one caution. Computerized spell-checks are misleading much of the time. For example, if you write *whole* for *hole* or *it's* for *its,* your spell-check program will not catch the mistake. If you write *your,* many spell-check programs will suggest *you're* automatically, without any knowledge of the content of your material.

21a   How are plurals spelled?

- **Adding -s or -es:** Plurals of most words are formed by adding *-s,* including words that end in "hard" *-ch* (sounding like *k*): *leg, legs; shoe, shoes; stomach, stomachs*. Words ending in *-s, -sh, -x, -z,* or "soft" *-ch* (as in *beach*) are formed by adding *-es* to the singular: *lens, lenses; beach, beaches; tax, taxes; coach, coaches.*

- **Words ending in *-o*:** Add *-s* if the *-o* is preceded by a vowel: *radio, radios; cameo, cameos.* Add *-es* if the *-o* is preceded by a consonant: *potato, potatoes.* A few words can be made plural either way: *cargo, volcano, tornado, zero.*

- **Words ending in *-f* or *-fe*:** Some *-f* and *-fe* words are made plural by adding *-s: belief, beliefs.* Others require changing *-f* or *-fe* to *-ves: life, lives; leaf, leaves.* Words ending in *-ff* or *-ffe* simply add *-s: staff, staffs; giraffe, giraffes.*

- **Compound words:** For most compound words, add *-s* or *-es* at the end of the last word: *checkbooks, player-coaches.* In a few cases, the first word is made plural: *sister-in-law, sisters-in-law; mile per hour, miles per hour.* (For hyphenating compound words, see Box 76, p. 417.)

- **Internal changes and endings other than *-s*:** A few words change internally or add endings other than *-s* to become plural: *foot, feet; man, men; mouse, mice; crisis, crises; child, children.*

- **Foreign words:** The best advice is to check your dictionary. In general, though, many Latin words ending in *-um* form the plural by changing *-um* to *-a: curriculum, curricula; datum, data; medium, media; stratum, strata.* Latin words that end in *-us* usually form the plural by changing *-us* to *-i: alumnus, alumni; syllabus, syllabi.* Greek words that end in *-on* usually form the plural by changing *-on* to *-a: criterion, criteria; phenomenon, phenomena.*

- **One-form words:** Some words have the same form in both the singular and plural: *deer, elk, fish, quail.* Additional words indicate which form is meant: *one deer, nine deer; some rice.*

21b　How are suffixes spelled?

A **suffix** is an ending added to a word to change the word's meaning or its grammatical function. For example, adding the suffix *-able* to the verb *depend* creates the adjective *depend**able.***

- **-y words:** If the letter before the final *y* is a consonant, change the *y* to *i* and add the suffix. If, however, the suffix begins with an *i*, keep the *y: fry, fried, frying.* If the letter before the *-y* is a vowel, keep the final *y: employ, employed, employing.* These rules do not apply to irregular verbs (Box 59, p. 328–29).

- **-e words:** Drop a final *e* when the suffix begins with a vowel unless this would cause confusion: *be + ing* does not become *bing,* but *require, requiring; like, liking*. Keep the final *e* when the suffix begins with a consonant: *require, requirement; like, likely*. Exceptions include *argument, judgment*, and *truly*.

- **Words that double a final letter:** If the final letter is a consonant, double it only if it passes all three of these tests: (1) Its last two letters are a vowel followed by a consonant. (2) It has one syllable or is accented on the last syllable. (3) The suffix begins with a vowel: *drop, dropped; begin, beginning; forget, forgetful, forgettable*.

- **-cede, -ceed, -sede words:** Only one word in the English language ends in *-sede: supersede*. Three words end in *-ceed: exceed, proceed, succeed*. All other words with endings that sound like "seed" end in *-cede: concede, intercede, precede*.

- **-ally and -ly words:** The suffixes *-ally* and *-ly* turn words into adverbs. For words ending in *-ic*, add *-ally: logically, statistically*. Otherwise, add *-ly: quickly, sharply*.

21c What is the *ie, ei* rule?

The old rhyme for *ie* and *ei* is usually true:

I before *e* [*believe, field, grief*],
Except after *c* [*ceiling, conceit*],
Or when sounded like "ay"
As in *neighbor* and *weigh* [*eight, vein*].

Unfortunately, many exceptions exist (sorry!), so you need to memorize them.

ie conscience, financier, science, species

ei either, neither, leisure, seize, counterfeit, foreign, forfeit, sleigh, sleight (*as in* sleight of hand), weird

21d How are homonyms and other frequently confused words spelled?

Words that sound exactly like others (*to, too, two; no, know*) are called **homonyms.** They, as well as words that sound almost alike (*accept, except; morning, mourning*), can lead to spelling errors that often "mark" a writer very negatively. Box 24 lists many such words.

BOX 24

 Homonyms and other commonly confused words

ACCEPT	to receive
EXCEPT	with the exclusion of
ADVICE	recommendation
ADVISE	to recommend
AFFECT	to influence [VERB]; emotion [NOUN]
EFFECT	result [NOUN]; to bring about or cause [VERB]
AISLE	space between rows
ISLE	island
ALLUDE	to make indirect reference to
ELUDE	to avoid
ALLUSION	indirect reference
ILLUSION	false idea, misleading appearance
ALREADY	by this time
ALL READY	fully prepared
ALTAR	sacred platform or place
ALTER	to change
ALTOGETHER	thoroughly
ALL TOGETHER	everyone or everything in one place
ARE	PLURAL form of *to be*
HOUR	sixty minutes
OUR	PLURAL form of *my*
ASCENT	the act of rising or climbing
ASSENT	consent [NOUN]; to consent [VERB]
ASSISTANCE	help
ASSISTANTS	helpers
BARE	nude, unadorned
BEAR	to carry; an animal
BOARD	piece of wood
BORED	uninterested
BRAKE	device for stopping
BREAK	to destroy, make into pieces

CONTINUED →

BOX 24

 Homonyms and other commonly confused words *(continued)*

BREATH	air taken in
BREATHE	to take in air
BUY	to purchase
BY	next to, through the agency of
CAPITAL	major city; money
CAPITOL	government building
CHOOSE	to pick
CHOSE	PAST TENSE of *choose*
CITE	to point out
SIGHT	vision
SITE	a place
CLOTHES	garments
CLOTHS	pieces of fabric
COARSE	rough
COURSE	path; series of lectures
COMPLEMENT	something that completes
COMPLIMENT	praise, flattery
CONSCIENCE	sense of morality
CONSCIOUS	awake, aware
COUNCIL	governing body
COUNSEL	advice [NOUN]; to advise [VERB]
DAIRY	place associated with milk production
DIARY	personal journal
DESCENT	downward movement
DISSENT	disagreement
DESERT	to abandon [VERB]; dry, usually sandy area [NOUN]
DESSERT	final, sweet course in a meal
DEVICE	a plan; an implement
DEVISE	to create
DIE	to lose life (dying) [VERB]; one of a pair of dice [NOUN]
DYE	to change the color of something (dyeing)

CONTINUED →

BOX 24

 Homonyms and other commonly confused words *(continued)*

DOMINANT	commanding, controlling
DOMINATE	to control
ELICIT	to draw out
ILLICIT	illegal
EMINENT	prominent
IMMANENT	living within; inherent
IMMINENT	about to happen
ENVELOP	to surround
ENVELOPE	container for a letter or other papers
FAIR	light-skinned; just, honest
FARE	money for transportation; food
FORMALLY	conventionally, with ceremony
FORMERLY	previously
FORTH	forward
FOURTH	number four in a series
GORILLA	animal in ape family
GUERRILLA	soldier conducting surprise attacks
HEAR	to sense sound by ear
HERE	in this place
HOLE	opening
WHOLE	complete; an entire thing
HUMAN	relating to the species *Homo sapiens*
HUMANE	compassionate
INSURE	buy or give insurance
ENSURE	guarantee, protect
ITS	POSSESSIVE form of *it*
IT'S	contraction for *it is*
KNOW	to comprehend
NO	negative
LATER	after a time
LATTER	second one of two things

CONTINUED ⟶

BOX 24

 Homonyms and other commonly confused words *(continued)*

LEAD	heavy metal substance [NOUN]; to guide [VERB]
LED	PAST TENSE of *lead*
LIGHTNING	storm-related electricity
LIGHTENING	making lighter
LOOSE	unbound, not tightly fastened
LOSE	to misplace
MAYBE	perhaps [ADVERB]
MAY BE	might be [VERB]
MEAT	animal flesh
MEET	to encounter
MINER	a person who works in a mine
MINOR	underage
MORAL	distinguishing right from wrong; the lesson of a fable, story, or event
MORALE	attitude or outlook, usually of a group
OF	PREPOSITION indicating origin
OFF	away from, not on
PASSED	PAST TENSE of *pass*
PAST	at a previous time
PATIENCE	forbearance
PATIENTS	people under medical care
PEACE	absence of fighting
PIECE	part of a whole; musical arrangement
PERSONAL	intimate
PERSONNEL	employees
PLAIN	simple, unadorned
PLANE	to shave wood; aircraft
PRECEDE	to come before
PROCEED	to continue
PRESENCE	being at hand; attendance at a place or in something
PRESENTS	gifts

CONTINUED ➝

■ BOX 24 ■ ■

◉ Homonyms and other commonly confused words *(continued)*

PRINCIPAL	foremost [ADJECTIVE]; school head [NOUN]
PRINCIPLE	moral conviction, basic truth
QUIET	silent, calm
QUITE	very
RAIN	water that falls to earth [NOUN]; to fall like rain [VERB]
REIGN	to rule
REIN	strap to guide or control an animal [NOUN]; to guide or control [VERB]
RAISE	to lift up
RAZE	to tear down
RESPECTFULLY	with respect
RESPECTIVELY	in that order
RIGHT	correct; opposite of *left*
RITE	ritual
WRITE	to put words on paper
ROAD	path
RODE	PAST TENSE of *ride*
SCENE	place of an action; segment of a play
SEEN	viewed
SENSE	perception, understanding
SINCE	measurement of past time; because
STATIONARY	standing still
STATIONERY	writing paper
THAN	in comparison with; besides
THEN	at that time; next; therefore
THEIR	POSSESSIVE form of *they*
THERE	in that place
THEY'RE	contraction for *they are*
THROUGH	finished; into and out of
THREW	PAST TENSE of *throw*
THOROUGH	complete

CONTINUED ⟶

■ **BOX 24** ■

⊙ **Homonyms and other commonly confused words** *(continued)*

TO	toward
TOO	also; indicates degree (*too much*)
TWO	number following *one*
WAIST	midsection of the body
WASTE	discarded material [NOUN]; to squander, to fail to use up [VERB]
WEAK	not strong
WEEK	seven days
WEATHER	climatic condition
WHETHER	if, when alternatives are expressed or implied
WHERE	in which place
WERE	PAST TENSE of *be*
WHICH	one of a group
WITCH	female sorcerer
WHOSE	POSSESSIVE form of *who*
WHO'S	contraction for *who is*
YOUR	POSSESSIVE form of *you*
YOU'RE	contraction for *you are*
YORE	long past

21e What else leads to spelling errors?

"Swallowed" pronunciation—not pronouncing a letter or letters at the end of a word—can also cause misspellings. For example, the *-ed* endings in *used to* and *prejudiced* are often swallowed and pronounced as *use to* and *prejudice*. If you write what you hear, your spelling will be incorrect.

In addition, some misspellings result from writing one word instead of two. The most common errors of this kind are *all right* (not *alright*) and *a lot* (not *alot*).

Research

www.prenhall.com/troyka

Research

22 STARTING A RESEARCH PROJECT

22a What is research writing?

Every research project involves three processes: conducting research, understanding the results of your research, and writing an accurately documented paper based on your research. For some students, information comes from **primary sources**—from interviewing, reading diaries, and directly observing, measuring, or interpreting physical phenomena or social interactions. For most students, especially when writing college research papers, information comes from **secondary sources**—from reading, analyzing, discussing, and reviewing what people with respected academic and professional credentials have written.

Research writing can seem very intimidating, but if you follow a research plan (22e) the process is manageable. Keep in mind that the goal of every research project is to *attempt* to answer a question. Your first step is to choose a suitable research topic (22b). Because assignments rarely are phrased as questions, your next, crucial step is to think about, search for, and develop a research question (22c) that is suitable for a college-level research paper.

22b How do I choose a research topic?

Some instructors assign a specific topic for research (for example, "the feasibility of making robots that act like humans"). Others assign a general subject ("artificial intelligence") and expect you to narrow it to a manageable topic. Still other instructors expect you to choose a topic on your own ("Write a research paper on a topic of current importance").

A good research topic is narrow enough so that you can research and write about it within the time and length allowed in the assignment. Make sure that enough material has been published on the topic to offer you a sufficient number of sources and perspectives to answer your research question and write your paper.

A good topic generally allows you to demonstrate your critical thinking abilities. There are two broad ways of doing so. First, you might choose a topic on which intelligent people have formed different opinions. Then you might analyze your sources to decide which position appears most reasonable. Your paper might take the form of an argument that shows readers you have considered the various positions and reached a reasonable conclusion.

Second, you might choose to write an informative paper in which you *synthesize* several sources related to a complex subject. Writing a SYNTHESIS* means pulling together extensive information in an attempt to explain the essential points involved in a topic. For example, after you have read a dozen articles on the topic of artificial intelligence, you might try to identify three or four key points and then organize information from your reading around those points. Your goal is to clarify complicated or scattered information for your readers.

Finally, a good research topic is one that your readers will perceive as significant and worthwhile. That is, the topic is important or timely, your insights are fresh, or your synthesis is particularly clear and skillful.

To summarize, keep the following points in mind as you choose your topic.

- Select a topic that interests you. It will be your companion for quite a while, perhaps most of a semester.

- Choose a sufficiently narrow topic. Avoid topics that are too broad, such as "emotions." A well-narrowed topic is "how people perceive and respond to anger in others."

- Choose a topic that is worth researching. Avoid trivial topics that prevent you from doing what is expected of a student researcher: investigating ideas, analyzing them critically, and creating a synthesis of complex concepts.

> **NO** Types of cars that are popular among teenagers.

> **YES** The effect of SUV's on the environment.

The freedom to choose any topic you want can sometimes lead to what is called "research topic block." Don't panic. Instead, use some of these strategies for generating ideas.

- Browse through some textbooks in your area of interest. Read the table of contents and major headings. Scan the text for material that catches your eye. As you narrow your focus, note the names of important books and experts, often mentioned in reference lists at the end of chapters or at the back of the book.

- Talk briefly with an instructor or another expert in your area of interest. Ask for the names of major books and authorities on the subject and for advice about subcategories related to your area of

---

* Words printed in small capital letters (such as SYNTHESIS) are defined in the Terms Glossary on pages 467–85.

interest. Ask what issues currently seem important or "hot" to them.

- Read an encyclopedia article about your area of interest and its subcategories. Never, however, stop with the encyclopedia—it is too basic for college-level research, which demands a thorough search of a variety of sources.

- Browse through books and periodicals. Stroll through the open stacks of your library, if available, to find subjects that interest you, or spend some time in a good bookstore. Look at books as well as periodicals. Browse academic journals in fields that interest you. Thumb through more popular magazines as well.

- Browse the Internet. Many Web search engines provide a list of general categories on their opening screens (25b). Click on a general category to get subcategories. Browsing increasingly specific subcategories can turn up an interesting topic.

22c What is a research question?

A **research question** controls and drives your research. Without such a question, your research writing can become an aimless search for a haphazard collection of facts and opinions. Consider the difference between a paper on the topic of "artificial intelligence" and a paper on the question "What role does emotion play in creating artificial intelligence?" The question provides a clear focus for your research and a goal for your writing process. Depending on your question, you may write a successful paper even if your attempt to answer your research question is unsuccessful.

Attempt is an important word in research. Some research questions can lead to a final, definitive answer (for example, "How does penicillin destroy bacteria?"). Other research questions cannot (for example, "Is the U.S. Congress more responsible than the Supreme Court for setting social policy?"). When a question concerns a very recent or highly debatable topic, your answer calls for you to present a convincing, informed opinion. This means that you need to use sources that represent various viewpoints, and that your own position must take those viewpoints into account. In fact, all answers to research questions, whether definitive or not, need to be supported by thorough research that is based on (or supported by) reliable scholarly and expert sources.

As is true of the writing process for all essays and papers, your research writing often moves forward, loops back, and jumps ahead as you ask and refine your research question, read source material, take notes, SYNTHESIZE your findings, and support your findings with

QUOTATIONS, PARAPHRASES, and SUMMARIES of your source materials. Consider the following example of refining a research question.

1. What is the future of computers?
2. Is it possible to create artificial intelligence?
3. What problems need to be solved in creating artificial intelligence?
4. Do computers need emotions to be considered intelligent?

From the first, very broad question, a succession of more specific questions emerges. The last one focuses on one issue out of many possible ones. Even this question is quite complicated, but at least it provides a clear direction for your writing.

The answer to your research question usually, but not always, appears in your thesis statement. Sometimes the thesis statement simply alludes to your answer, especially when the answer is long or complicated. Chandra Johnson's MLA research paper (30b) attempts to answer research question 4 above.

Research is an absorbing, creative activity. Developing a research question, gathering information about it, and creating a synthesis of what you've learned lets you come to know a subject deeply. It leads you to fresh insights. The entire process, especially when repeated in a number of college courses, helps to shape you into a self-reliant learner with the discipline to pursue new and unfamiliar topics.

22d What is a research log?

A **research log** is a diary of your research process. Create a new file or folder on the computer for this log, or use a separate notebook. Use your research log to

- Record each step in your search for information. Enter the date; your search strategies; the gist of the information you discovered; the name, location, and other details of exactly where you found it; and exactly where you filed your detailed notes—for example, the file or folder name.
- Note the next step you think you should take when you return to your research.
- Decide when you're ready to move away from gathering material to organizing it or writing about it.
- Write down your thoughts and insights as you move through the research and writing processes.

Although much of what you write in your research log will never find its way into your paper, whatever you read and reread in the log will greatly increase your efficiency as a researcher.

EXCERPT FROM CHANDRA JOHNSON'S RESEARCH LOG

October 16: Went online to find sources for "artificial intelligence" and was overwhelmed by the number of hits in Yahoo. Gave up. Logged onto the college library's Web site and searched some databases there. PsycINFO turned up lots of promising stuff. Chose several citations and e-mailed full records to myself to check out later. *Readers' Guide Abstracts* also had articles, and some were available as full text. Printed out three of the best ones. Need to start taking notes on them. Will go to library tomorrow to look at possible PsycINFO sources.

22e How do I plan a research project?

If you feel overwhelmed by the prospect of research writing, you are not alone. The best approach is to divide your project into a series of steps, which makes the process far less intimidating. Research projects take time, so plan your schedule realistically using the checklist in Box 25. Then add about 10 percent more time to your plan as a safety margin.

BOX 25

✔ Sample research project plan

Assignment received (date) _____ **Finish by (date)** _____

STARTING A RESEARCH PROJECT
✔ Set up my research log.   _____
✔ Choose a suitable topic.   _____
✔ Draft my research question.   _____

FINDING AND EVALUATING SOURCES
✔ Decide what documentation style to use.   _____
✔ Decide the kinds of research I need to do.   _____
  • Field research   yes/no
  • Library sources   yes/no
  • Online sources   yes/no

CONTINUED ➜

> ╺━ BOX 25 ━╸
>
> ✔ **Sample research project plan** *(continued)*
>
> ✔ Locate and evaluate sources. _____
> ✔ Take notes. _____
> ✔ Draft a preliminary thesis statement. _____
> ✔ Outline, as required. _____
>
> **WRITING THE RESEARCH PAPER**
> ✔ Draft my paper. _____
> ✔ Document correctly. _____
> ✔ Revise the paper. _____
> ✔ Edit and proofread the paper. _____
>
> Assignment due (date) _____

23 DEVELOPING A SEARCH STRATEGY

23a What is a search strategy?

A **search strategy** is an organized procedure for locating and assembling information for your research. A wealth of source material is available to researchers (23b). To find material that helps to answer your specific RESEARCH QUESTION, you need to search systematically and thoroughly. Using a search strategy guarantees that you'll work systematically rather than haphazardly and, you'll find what you're looking for more quickly. For example, if you start your search with books, you might collect a list of them before you move on to periodicals or the Internet. You use what you learn from books to focus your search through periodicals and the Internet.

Following are three frequently used search strategies. If no single strategy meets your requirements, you can create one of your own. As you work through useful sources, you can switch or combine strategies.

EXPERT METHOD Useful when your topic is specific and narrow. Start with articles or books by an expert in the field. You might want to interview an expert on the topic. If your topic calls for FIELD RESEARCH, such as direct observation, a survey, or personal visits to museums or events, build it into your plan.

CHAINING METHOD   Useful when your topic is a general one. Start with reference books and bibliographies in current articles or Web sites; use them to link to additional sources. Keep following the links until you reach increasingly expert sources. Alternatively, talk with people who have some general knowledge of your topic, and ask them to refer you to experts they might know.

LAYERING METHOD   Useful when you need to find your own topic. Start with general sources and gather layers of information that lead to increasingly specific topics and sources. If you need to conduct field research, such as interviews or observations, try to relate the information you gather to other studies or to scholarly sources on the same subject.

Start and complete your search as soon as possible after you get your assignment. Early in your process you may discover sources that take time to obtain (for example, through an interlibrary loan) or are hard to locate (for example, a business document or government information that is available only through the Freedom of Information Act).

One more piece of advice: Avoid getting too far along in your search until you're reasonably certain you're going in a useful direction. Rather than spend endless hours simply gathering sources, read and analyze some of your materials to make sure your topic is a good one. Your RESEARCH LOG can be useful for this purpose.

23b What is a source?

A **source** can be a **secondary source** such as a book, an article in a periodical or essay collection, a World Wide Web site, or a CD-ROM, videotape, DVD, or another electronic data storage medium. These sources are called secondary sources because their information comes to researchers secondhand, as reported or analyzed by an expert on the subject. Many student researchers, especially in college English courses, depend heavily on secondary sources. In contrast, information that researchers gain firsthand through interviews, performances, original art works, experiments, observation, or surveys is referred to as a **primary source.** Your decision to use primary or secondary sources depends on your RESEARCH QUESTION. Neither type of source is superior to the other.

As you locate, assemble, and evaluate sources related to your topic, expect to accumulate much more information than you will actually use. Indeed, the quality of your paper depends partly on your ability to eliminate inadequate or repetitive sources and recognize what is valuable material.

23c What is field research?

Field research is one type of PRIMARY RESEARCH. Because it involves going into real-life situations to survey people, interview experts, or observe or participate firsthand in an activity, field research yields original data. Allow extra time to conduct field research. Plan carefully to assure yourself enough time to conduct your survey, interviews, or observations and to gather, ANALYZE, and SYNTHESIZE the information you collect.

A research assignment may state or imply that you need to do field research, or it may say that the decision is yours. If you have a choice, ask yourself whether field research on your topic would add useful information to your paper. If you're unsure, ask your instructor.

If you want to interview an expert on your topic, first schedule an appointment at the person's convenience. Then write, reflect on, and perhaps revise the questions you want to ask so that you feel confident about getting the information you seek. Perhaps the best way to find an expert on a topic is to consult the faculty at your college. Your teachers are also scholars and researchers, who not only may provide information and insights but also may suggest additional resources. Other experts might come from the public arena: businesspeople, government officials, church leaders, or heads of local organizations and clubs. For a paper on astronomy, for example, you might interview a local amateur astronomer. You can conduct interviews by telephone as well as in person.

If you want to survey a group of people on an issue related to your topic, first write out your questions in full sentences. Then test your questionnaire on a few people who will not be in the group you intend to survey. Revise any questions that do not work well.

If you intend to observe an event such as a concert or a play, get tickets as soon as you receive your assignment. If you need to visit a museum, go as soon as possible to allow time for a follow-up visit if you need one.

Your success in doing field research depends on effective notetaking. Here are some guidelines to follow for interviews and observations.

NOTETAKING GUIDELINES FOR INTERVIEWS

- Use a large notebook or standard 8½ × 11 inch paper so that you have room to write.

- Bring extra pens (in case yours runs out of ink) or pencils (in case yours break).

- Before you go for the interview, practice asking your questions without reading them (perhaps highlight the key words in red).

- During the interview, look your interviewee in the eye. If you are interviewing over the telephone, be organized and precise.

- Create shortcut symbols or letters for key terms you expect to hear during the interview, so that you don't have to look away from the interviewee.

- Take careful notes, listening especially for key names, book titles, or other print or online sources.

- Don't depend on tape-recording an interview. Many people are reluctant to permit recording. If you want to record, ask permission when you schedule the interview, and ask again in person when you arrive for the interview. Never imply that a recording is essential to you or your research, however. Some interviewees will cancel the appointment on the spot if a tape recording is even mentioned.

NOTETAKING GUIDELINES FOR OBSERVATIONS

- Follow the guidelines for an interview.

- For observations of behavior (for example, of an audience at a sporting event or schoolchildren at play), plan to take notes during the activity. Permission to videotape is hard to get because of privacy concerns. If conditions make notetaking impossible, write detailed notes immediately afterward. Review and fill in your notes while your memory is fresh.

23d Where do I locate secondary sources?

The two best places to locate SECONDARY SOURCES are the library and the Internet. Your main goal in conducting **library research** is to identify source materials that exist in print: books, magazines, journals, microfilm, and so on. Some print sources exist also in electronic versions, on CD-ROMs, on Web sites, or in databases, although few books are available electronically. For detailed, practical strategies for finding and evaluating library sources, see Chapter 24.

Researchers find the Internet a valuable resource in addition to the library. For detailed, practical strategies for finding and evaluating online sources, on the World Wide Web or in the larger universe of the Internet, see Chapter 25.

23e What documentation style should I use?

A **documentation style** is a system for providing information about each source you have used in your research paper. Determine the documentation style you need to follow when you're developing your SEARCH

STRATEGY (23a). Doing so helps to guarantee that you'll write down the exact details you need to document your sources.

If you're doing field research, decide what you must document before you begin. Your instructor may have special requirements for such documentation, so be sure to ask for guidelines. Because your observations, questionnaires, surveys, or interviews produce primary data on your research topic, your instructor may expect you to submit them with your research paper.

Documentation styles vary from one academic discipline to another. MLA (Modern Language Association) style is often used in the humanities (Chs. 28–30). APA (American Psychological Association) style is used frequently in the social sciences (Chs. 31–33). CM (Chicago Manual) style is used in various disciplines in the humanities, including English and history (Ch. 34). CSE (Council of Science Editors) style is used in the biological and other sciences (Ch. 35). Finally, COS (Columbia Online) style includes format elements that are unique to electronic publications (Ch. 36). If you don't know which style to use, ask your instructor. Never mix documentation styles; use only one style in each piece of writing.

23f What is a working bibliography?

A **working bibliography** is a preliminary list of the PRIMARY and SECONDARY SOURCES you gather in your research. Begin your working bibliography as soon as you start identifying sources. Compiling a working bibliography will help you find out what is available on a particular subject before you do extensive reading and notetaking. If your search turns up very few sources, you may want to change your topic. If it reveals a vast number of sources, you definitely want to narrow your topic or even choose a different one. Expect to add and drop sources as you refine your RESEARCH QUESTION and locate other sources.

You can record your working bibliography on 3 × 5 inch note cards or on a computer. Note cards have the advantage of being easy to sift through and rearrange when you're adding or discarding sources. You can also carry them with you when you do library research. At the end of your writing process, you can easily sort and alphabetize them to prepare your final bibliography. Write only one source on each card.

On the other hand, putting your working bibliography on a computer saves you from having to type your list of sources later. If you use a computer for this purpose, clearly separate one entry from another. You can organize the list alphabetically, by author, or group the entries according to your subtopics.

Whichever method you use, when you come across a source you think you might be able to use, write a card or computer entry for it immediately, while the source is in front of you. Record the information exactly as you need it to fulfill the requirements of the DOCUMENTATION STYLE your instructor prefers. Spending a few extra moments at this stage can save you hours of work and frustration later on. Few things are as aggravating as having to return to the library merely to check the volume or page numbers of a source you recorded weeks earlier. (Besides, the book you need might not be available when you return.)

As a rough estimate, your working bibliography needs to be about twice as long as the list of sources you end up using. If your assignment asks for ten to twelve sources, then at a minimum you want your working bibliography to contain twenty to twenty-five entries.

24 FINDING, EVALUATING, AND USING LIBRARY SOURCES

24a What is library research?

Library research uses sources that are stored in the library or cataloged by librarians. Before the Internet, library research involved print sources (books, periodicals, microfiche) and portable electronic sources (CD-ROMs), which students could access by going to the library in person.

Now that the Internet has come into widespread use, some—but not nearly all—of what used to be located in a library building is available online. Similarly, researchers can now find many—but not all—library sources using computer-based searches, both inside and outside the library. The distinguishing characteristic of library research is that professional librarians or scholars have gathered, organized, and made available the sources. If you ever feel confused about how to find what you're looking for, ask a reference librarian. These professionals enjoy helping students master the art and science of research both in libraries and online.

24b What is a library search strategy?

A library search strategy leads you from general to specific sources to answer your RESEARCH QUESTION (22c). Libraries contain several kinds of sources, including books, general reference works, specialized reference works, periodicals, and government documents. Each type of source is cataloged in a particular way, so you need to know how to identify and use the index or database appropriate to your topic and each type of source.

24c How do I find books on my topic?

A library's **book catalog** lists all the holdings in its entire collection. The catalog exists in the form of a computer database in almost every modern library. You can access it from computer terminals inside the library, and sometimes from outside the library, through the Internet. You find a book by searching the catalog for the book's author, title, or subject or for a related KEYWORD. When you search the book catalog, some computer programs ask which of these four categories you would like to search. For instance, try searching the Library of Congress Online Catalog.

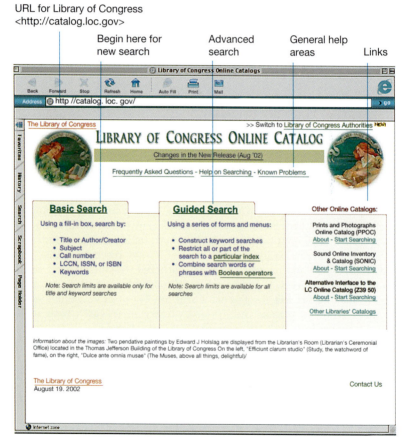

Search categories in the Library of Congress Online Catalog

Suppose you want to find a book by Antonio Damasio, but you don't know its title. You can search the catalog for books by this author. In the space for "author" on the computer screen, you type in "Damasio, Antonio." (Usually you enter the last name first, but check to see how your library's system works.) If your library owns any books by Antonio Damasio, the computer will show you their titles and other information (24e). Among the books you might find are *The Feeling of What Happens: Body and Emotion in the Making of Consciousness* (New York: Harcourt Brace, 1999). Or suppose you know this title and want to see if your library owns the book. In the space for "title" you type in *Feeling of What Happens*. (Usually you don't need to include words like *the* or *a*.)

Often you don't know a title or author's name. Instead, you have a research topic and need to find sources. In this case you need to search by subject, using the terms listed in the *Library of Congress Subject Headings (LCSH)*. The *LCSH* is a multivolume catalog available, as of this handbook's publication, only in book form in the reference section of the library. The *LCSH* lists only subject headings, which are organized from most general to most narrow. Suppose you are researching the topic of "consciousness," for example. If you enter that term in the space for subject searches, *The Feeling of What Happens: Body and Emotion in the Making of Consciousness* by Antonio Damasio will be listed—if your library owns that book. Finally, you may wish to search by KEYWORD.

24d What is a keyword?

Keywords are the main words that appear in a source's title, or that the author or editor has identified as central to that source. Keywords are sometimes called *descriptors* or *identifiers*. *LCSH* entries can serve as keywords, as can the important terms in your working THESIS STATEMENT or RESEARCH QUESTION. Keywords can help you search not only most book catalogs but also periodical indexes (24i) and Web sites (25d). You could find Damasio's book, mentioned above in the last paragraph, using the keywords "feeling," "body," "emotion," "consciousness," "intelligence," "mind," and so on.

In using keywords to search for sources, chances are you'll come up with a large or even overwhelming number of sources. Soon you'll discover that much of what turns up isn't relevant to your topic. You need to figure out which words best generate the sources you find helpful. Expect to use a "try and see" approach. Keep a record of helpful and unhelpful keywords in your research log so you don't have to retrace your steps. Don't get discouraged. If you're stumped, ask a research librarian for help.

24e What does a catalog entry tell me about a book?

Each entry in the book catalog contains a great deal of invaluable information. Some libraries allow you to print out the entry, and some even let you send it to your e-mail account or download it to a disk. Whether you use any of these options or choose to copy the information directly into your working bibliography, be sure to record the call number exactly as it appears, with all its numbers, letters, and decimal points.

The call number tells where the book is located in the stacks (rows of storage shelves). If you're working in a library with open stacks (that is, if you can go where the books are shelved), the call number leads you to the area where all the books on your subject can be found. Simply looking at the books shelved next to the ones you have identified may yield some useful sources. But keep in mind that in physically browsing the stacks, you're not seeing those sources that other students have checked out, or that librarians are holding at the reserve desk.

The call number is especially crucial if you are working in a library with closed stacks (that is, one where you fill out a call slip, hand it in at the call desk, and wait for the book to arrive). In such libraries you aren't permitted to browse the stacks, so you have to rely entirely on the book catalog. If you fill in an incorrect or incomplete number on the call slip, your wait will be in vain.

24f What are general reference works?

General reference works include encyclopedias, almanacs, yearbooks, fact books, atlases, dictionaries, biographical reference works, and bibliographies. A reference is general if it provides limited information on a vast number of subjects.

Reference books and the CD-ROM reference collection are the starting point for many researchers—but only the starting point. Reference works summarize, so they are too general for use in academic research. Still, because general reference works give you an overall picture, they're one of the best places to find useful subject headings and keywords for online catalog searches. In addition, general reference works are excellent sources for examples and facts. Most widely used reference works are available in electronic versions, usually on CD-ROMs. Some can even be accessed on the Internet, either at the publisher's Web site (for example, the *Encyclopaedia Britannica* site can be found at <http://www.britannica.com>) or through an online database.

Using general encyclopedias

Articles in multivolume general encyclopedias, such as the *Encyclopaedia Britannica,* summarize information on a wide variety of subjects. The articles give helpful background information and the names of major figures and experts in many fields. Best of all, many articles end with a brief bibliography of major works on the subject. Remain aware that general encyclopedias don't include information on recent events or current research, although they sometimes cover ongoing controversies in a field up to the date of publication.

To locate information in a multivolume encyclopedia, start with the index volume, which lists the volume and page numbers for your topic. Be on the alert for the letters *bib* at the end of each entry. They indicate that the article contains a bibliography, which could be helpful in finding additional sources. If you can't locate an entry on your topic, try alternative keywords.

Using almanacs, yearbooks, and fact books

Almanacs, yearbooks, and fact books are huge compilations of facts in many subject areas. These books often appear both in print and online. They are excellent sources for verifying information from other sources, and in some cases, for finding supporting facts and figures on a subject. Almanacs, such as *The World Almanac,* present capsule accounts of a year's events along with data on government, politics, economics, science and technology, sports, and many other topics. *Facts on File* covers world events in both a weekly digest and an annual one-volume yearbook; it is indexed online by LEXIS-NEXIS. The annual *Statistical Abstract of the United States* contains a wealth of data on the United States. *Demographic Yearbook* and the *United Nations Statistical Yearbook* carry worldwide data.

Using atlases and gazetteers

Atlases contain maps of our planet's continents, seas, and skies—and whatever experts currently know about other planets. An example is the *Times Atlas of the World.* Gazetteers provide comprehensive geographical information on topography, climates, populations, migrations, natural resources, crops, and so on. An example is *The Columbia Gazetteer of the World.*

Using dictionaries

Dictionaries define words and terms. Unabridged dictionaries are complete, containing hundreds of thousands of words. Abridged dictionaries are less complete but still contain tens of thousands of words. Cheap paperback dictionaries often can be useful for college-level work. Two good college editions are *Merriam-Webster's Collegiate Dictionary* and *The American Heritage Dictionary*. In addition to general dictionaries, you might want to consult specialized dictionaries, which define words and phrases specific to a particular academic discipline.

Using biographical reference works

Biographical reference books give brief factual information about famous people, including their accomplishments and pertinent events and dates in their lives. Biographical references include the *Who's Who* series, *The Dictionary of American Biography,* and many others. In most college libraries, you can find specialized biographical reference books about people in various fields. Because you have access to so many different biographical sources, you may want to ask a reference librarian which volumes might help you most.

Using bibliographies

Bibliographies, available both in print and online, list books, articles, documents, films, and other resources with their publication information. Some bibliographies are comprehensive and list sources on a wide range of topics. For example, the database WorldCat, available through FirstSearch, lists all the book holdings in most libraries in the United States and throughout the world. These listings don't describe a book's contents, but they do list the subject headings assigned to the book by librarians. Other bibliographies are specialized and list only sources on a particular subject. These bibliographies can be very helpful in your research process. Annotated or critical bibliographies describe and evaluate the works they list.

24g What are specialized reference works?

Specialized reference works provide more authoritative and specific information than general reference works. Specialized reference works are usually appropriate for college-level research. The information they contain is more advanced and detailed than what you find in general reference works. Box 26 lists some specialized reference works in several subject areas.

Some students mistakenly overlook specialized encyclopedias, moving from general references directly to books and articles. However, specialized encyclopedias are invaluable for accumulating a list of experts on your topic or discovering the controversies and keywords in a subject area. Those names and keywords are useful in searching book and periodical catalogs and online resources.

BOX 26

 Some specialized reference works

Encyclopedia of Banking and Finance

Handbook of Modern Marketing

New Grove Dictionary of Music and Musicians

Oxford Companion to Art

Dictionary of American Biography

An Encyclopedia of World History

Dictionary of Literary Biography

MLA International Bxibliography of Books and Articles on the Modern Languages and Literature

Encyclopedia of Philosophy

Encyclopedia of Religion

Political Handbook and Atlas of the World

Political Science Bibliographies

Encyclopedia of Chemistry

Encyclopedia of the Biological Sciences

Dictionary of Anthropology

Encyclopedia of Psychology

International Encyclopedia of Film

Oxford Companion to the Theatre

ALERT: Hundreds of one-volume works are highly specific (for example, in the social sciences, *Encyclopedia of Divorce, Encyclopedia of Aging,* and *Encyclopedic Dictionary of Psychology*). Check to see what one-volume specialized reference books your college library has available. You can use the general call number for your subject area to browse the reference collection and to see whether new special reference works have arrived.

24h How do I use electronic databases?

Databases are indexes that contain electronic records of articles, reports, and books. Most databases exist online; you access them through the World Wide Web. Some databases exist on CD-ROMs. Each entry in a database contains bibliographic information: title, author, date of publication, and publisher (for books or reports) or periodical (for articles). The entry might also provide an abstract or summary of the material. However, you need the full source for research purposes.

Once you locate an entry that seems promising, you want to track down the source itself. Some databases, including ERIC (Educational Resources Information Center), provide the full text of articles on microfiche. With this type of system, each citation contains an abstract as well as a catalog number (for example, ERIC ED 139 580), which allows you to look up the microfiche that contains the article (ask a librarian where it is stored). ERIC is available online at <http://www.eric.ed.gov>. Some databases allow you to purchase full copies of the sources you find.

You will find both general databases and specialized ones concentrating on a single discipline or topic. Choose which databases will be most helpful before you begin to search, and restrict your search to one database at a time. Box 27 lists a few specialized databases, some of which charge a fee to users.

If you provide a specific description of your research, a reference librarian can help you choose the databases best suited to your topic. Electronic databases are generally available in the library through a service like EBSCO, FirstSearch, or IBIS, or less frequently, on a CD-ROM. Online databases require the library to pay a subscription fee, so your library may charge you when you use the system. Find out whether the service is free to students, and if not, what the charge is.

 Some specialized databases*

Academic Search Elite: <http://search.epnet.com>

America History and Life: <http://serials.abc-clio.com>

Children's Literature Comprehensive: <http://clcd.odyssi.com>

Family Index Data: <http://www.famindx.com>

LEXIS-NEXIS: <http://www.lexis-nexis.com>

Medline: <http://medline.cos.com>

Worldnews Connection: <http://wnc.fedworld.gov>

* Libraries subscribe to these sites, which are all fee-based.

Narrowing your search first with KEYWORDS (24d) can help you to avoid paying for a list of useless sources.

24i   How do I find periodicals for research?

Periodicals are newspapers, magazines, and journals that are published at set intervals during the year. To use periodicals efficiently, consult an index to periodicals. These indexes allow you to search by subject and author. They're updated frequently and are often available online as well as in print. Most databases also index periodicals.

👁 **ALERT:** Use the correct index for your research topic. If you're using the wrong index, you may miss some of the best sources for your paper. 👁

Using general indexes to periodicals

General indexes to periodicals list articles in journals, magazines, and newspapers that are published for general, nonexpert readers. Headings and keywords vary from one index to another, so think of every possible way to look up the information you seek. Large libraries have many general indexes.

• The *New York Times Index* catalogs all articles printed in the *New York Times* since 1851.

• *NewsBank* covers more than five hundred U.S. newspapers. It offers full-text coverage from 1993. Reproductions of articles printed from 1980–1992 are stored on microfiche.

• *The Readers' Guide to Periodical Literature* includes more than a hundred magazines and journals for general (rather than specialized) readers. Because this index doesn't include scholarly journals, its value in college-level research is limited. Nevertheless, you can use it to find topics, get a broad overview, and narrow a subject.

Using specialized indexes to periodicals

Specialized indexes list articles in journals that are published for expert, academic, or professional readers. Each profession and field (and many subfields) has several specialized periodicals that are more appropriate for college-level research than general ones. Many specialized indexes print an abstract, or summary, at the beginning of each article. Box 28 on the next page lists some specialized indexes.

Prior to the 1990s, specialized indexes appeared only in print; during the 1990s, many appeared on CD-ROM. Since the end of that

BOX 28

 ## Some specialized indexes to periodicals

Art Index

Art Abstracts (also has online database)

Business Periodicals Index

Education Index

Education Abstracts (also has online database)

General Science Index

General Science Abstracts (also has online database)

Humanities Index (also has online database)

MLA International Bibliography of Books and Articles in the Modern
   Languages and Literatures (also has online database)

Music Index

Music Index Online

Psychological Abstracts

PsycINFO (also has online database)

Social Science Index

Social Sciences Abstracts (also has online database)

decade, a great many indexes have gone online. You can access them through your library's computer or at a Web site on the Internet (24h). Check to see if your library has print, CD-ROM, or online versions of the indexes you wish to use.

Acquiring articles from periodicals

Indexes help you to identify specific articles on your topic. Once you have done so, how do you get your hands on an article? Sometimes you will find an online version of the article to read, download, or print. Frequently you will need to find a print copy of the periodical.

Most libraries include information about periodicals in their online catalogs, though many list periodicals separately. In either case, search for the periodical's name (for example, *American Literature* or *The Economist*), not the title of the article or the name of the author who wrote it. If your library subscribes to that periodical, you can use its call number to find its location in the library. The citation you found in the index will then get you the article you want.

24j How do I use government documents?

U.S. government publications are available in astounding variety. You can find information on laws and legal decisions, regulations, population, weather patterns, agriculture, national parks, education, and health, to name just a few topics. Print collections of government documents are available in many large reference libraries. Since the mid-1990s, however, most government documents have become available on the World Wide Web. The Government Printing Office (GPO) maintains an online catalog at <http://www.access.gpo.gov/su_docslocators/cgp>. This site has a searchable database. Information about legislation is also available at the Web site *Thomas,* <http://thomas.loc.gov/>. *Thomas* is a service of the Library of Congress. The direct site for the Library of Congress is now <http://catalog.loc.gov>.

24k What if my library doesn't have a source I need?

Almost no library owns every book or subscribes to every periodical on every topic. However, many libraries are connected electronically to other libraries, giving you access to additional holdings. Some states link their public and private colleges and universities in one system, and some libraries use the Internet to connect to colleges and universities outside their state. Librarians can request materials from other libraries through interlibrary loan, which is generally free of charge. Often, you can request articles you have found in a periodical index through an interlibrary loan. Alternatively, you may be able to use a different document delivery system (generally at some cost to you).

24l How should I evaluate print sources?

Sources are rarely of equal value. How do you know which are useful and reliable and which are not? First, decide whether the information in the source relates to your topic in more than a vague, general way. Check the table of contents, the introduction or preface, and as you narrow your search, the index for specific subtopics. Ask yourself how a source might help you to answer your research question. Finally, evaluate each source with a cold, critical eye, using your critical thinking skills and the criteria listed in Box 29 on the next page.

Checklist for evaluating print sources

✓ **Is the source authoritative?** Generally, encyclopedias, textbooks, academic journals (such as *Physics Reports* or *Journal of Counseling and Development*), and bibliographies are authoritative. Books published by university presses (such as Northwestern University Press) and by publishers that specialize in scholarly books are also trustworthy. Material in newspapers, general-readership magazines (*Newsweek, Time*), and books published by large commercial publishers (such as Prentice Hall) may be reliable, but you should apply the other criteria in this box carefully, cross-checking names and facts whenever possible. If the same information appears in different sources, it is likely reliable.

✓ **Is the author an expert?** Biographical material in the article or book may tell you whether the author is an expert on the topic. Look up the author in a biographical dictionary (24f). Check to see if the author has an academic degree in the field and works at a respected academic institution, research center, laboratory, institute, or business. If other professionals in the field mention someone as an expert, you can assume that the person is indeed a reliable source.

✓ **Is the source current?** How recent is the publication date? Because research is ongoing in most fields, old information is often modified or replaced by new findings. Check library catalogs (24c), online subject directories (24h), and indexes to periodicals (24i) to see if newer sources are available.

✓ **Does the source support its information sufficiently?** If the author expresses a point of view but offers little evidence to support that position or relies on logical fallacies (10f), reject the source.

✓ **Is the author's tone balanced?** If the author's TONE (19g) is even-handed, the language unbiased, and the reasoning logical, the source is probably useful.

24m **How do I extract information from library sources?**

Taking good notes is essential to using SOURCE materials. The following guidelines suggest ways to make sure your notes are useful.

• Decide whether the source is reliable by using the checklist for evaluating print sources (Box 29).

- Decide whether to quote from, paraphrase, or summarize the source. On every note card or in every note in your computer file, do one of three things: (1) copy the exact words of the source in a QUOTATION, enclosing it in quotation marks (26f); (2) write a PARAPHRASE of the source (26g); or (3) write a SUMMARY of the source in your own words (26h). Record the page number(s) of the source that each of your notes refers to. Even if a source does not seem useful, record its title and location in your research log, along with a note about why you rejected it. What seems useless now might become useful as you revise.

- Decide what to put in your notes. Knowing how to select material for your notes comes with experience. Sort major points from minor points as they relate to your topic; leave out unimportant details. If you have only a general sense of your topic when you begin, read and take notes widely, but stay alert for ways to narrow your topic. Once you have narrowed your topic, focus your notetaking accordingly.

- Decide how to differentiate your sources' ideas from your own ideas and opinions as you read and think critically (Chs. 1–2). Doing so will help you avoid PLAGIARISM and put the information from your sources into a more useful form. Because your own ideas tend to pop in and out of mind during research, catch them on paper right away. You can use your research log to keep track of your thoughts on the direction and progress of your research. You might also record your own thoughts in a different color ink, on the back of your note cards, or in boldface type, if you are using a computer.

25 FINDING, EVALUATING, AND USING ONLINE SOURCES

25a What is online research?

Online research uses sources that exist in electronic form and are available through the Internet. This chapter focuses on the sources available on one part of the Internet, the World Wide Web (often called the Web). The Web is organized around pages (called Web pages) that are linked together electronically. A group of pages that an individual or organization has created and linked together is called a Web site. The main page in a Web site, called the home page, acts as a table of contents.

25b How do I search the Web?

The principles for an online search strategy are very much like those for a library search (Ch. 24). You start with a broad subject and narrow it to arrive at a suitable topic for an academic research paper. To search the Web for sites that will help you answer your research question, you use a browser, a software program that gives you access to the Web and the search engines located there. Netscape Navigator and Microsoft Internet Explorer are two popular browsers. Once you're on the Web, you can find a site by entering its address, called a URL (for Universal Resource Locator), or by using a search engine.

Using URLs

To reach a particular URL, type it into the locator box at the top of your screen.

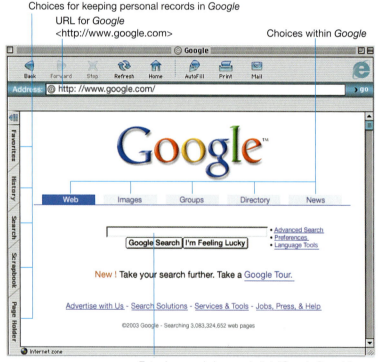

Opening page of the online search engine *Google*

👁 **PUNCTUATION ALERT:** When you write (or type) a URL in your research paper, the MLA and APA suggest that you surround a URL with angle brackets. For example, <http://www.prenhall.com/troyka> is the URL for the Web site about this handbook. The angle brackets separate the URL from other sentence punctuation, which could be mistaken for part of the URL. Never add angle brackets when you type a URL into the locator box at the top of your computer screen, however. 👁

Using search engines

Search engines are programs designed to hunt the Web for sources on specific topics that you identify. When you start a search engine, you generally have two ways to access materials.

- You see one or more **subject directories** on the home page. Subject directories are lists of topics ("Education," "Computing," "Entertainment," and so on) or resources and services ("Shopping," "Travel," and so on), with links to Web sites on those topics and resources (25c).

- You see a search box or space for entering keywords (25d). After you type a word or words into the box, you click on the "search" or "enter" button. The engine lists Web sites that match your topic.

Once you finish a search using one search engine, you might want to try another. Amazingly, different search engines yield somewhat—or even entirely—different lists of Web sites. This fact reflects the enormous range of choices on the World Wide Web. Try various search engines until you find the most useful sources. Some Web sites listed by search engines charge a fee. Often you can find similar information for free. Box 30 lists leading search engines.

BOX 30

🎯 **Leading online search engines and their addresses**

ALTA VISTA <http://altavista.com>
ASK JEEVES <http://www.ask.com>
EXCITE <http://www.excite.com>
GOOGLE <http://www.google.com>
INFOSEEK <http://guide.infoseek.com>
LYCOS <http://www.lycos.com>
METACRAWLER <http://www.metacrawler.com>
YAHOO! <http://www.yahoo.com>

⌨ **COMPUTER TIP:** *Metasearch* engines examine other search engines for you. In other words, instead of using one search engine at a time to look for sources, you can use a metasearch engine such as Google to run simultaneous searches on several search engines. This lets you see at a glance which search engines returned the best results. ⌨

25c How do I narrow my online search?

Because the Web has billions of pages, a search on even a moderately common topic may produce thousands of **hits**—sites listed or visited in a search. Not every hit will be what you are looking for. To help the search engine find the most relevant sites, you want to narrow your search as much as possible. Subject directories and keyword searches (25d) are good ways to begin narrowing your search.

Using a subject directory

A subject directory lists categories of information, with links to related Web sites. In this way, directories are similar to subject catalogs for print sources, like the Library of Congress Subject Headings (24c). Box 31 lists the Internet addresses of some useful subject directories.

One useful directory is the Librarians' Index to the Internet. If you type its URL <http://lii.org> into the search box, the first screen you'll see is the home page with an alphabetical list of topics. When you click on a subject that interests you, you get a list divided into categories. From there you can narrow down your choices to a list of subject head-

---

■ BOX 31 ■

◉ **Some online subject directories and their addresses**

AskERIC	<http://ericir.syr.edu>
INFOMINE	<http://infomine.ucr.edu/>
INTERNET PUBLIC LIBRARY	<http://www.ipl.org>
LIBRARIANS' INDEX TO THE INTERNET	<http://lii.org>
LIBRARY OF CONGRESS	<http://catalog.loc.gov>
VIRTUAL INFORMATION CENTER	<http://www.lib.berkeley.edu>
VIRTUAL DESK REFERENCE	<http://www.refdesk.com>
VIRTUAL REFERENCE COLLECTION	<http://www.lib.uci.edu>

URL for *Yahoo!*
<http://www.yahoo.com>

Topic accessed in four clicks
(Home is first; artificial intelligence is fourth)

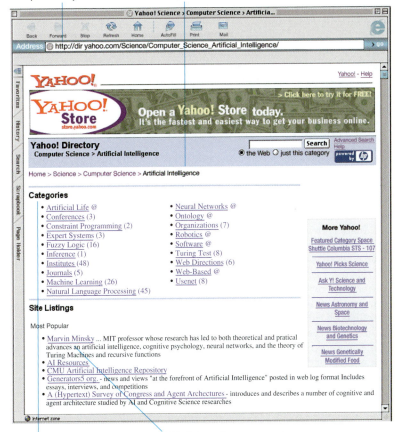

Search to find information

This list continues on next page

The *Yahoo!* Artificial Intelligence directory

Source: Reproduced with permission of Yahoo! Inc. © 2003 by Yahoo! Inc. YAHOO and the YAHOO! logo are trademarks of Yahoo! Inc. *Microsoft®* *Internet Explorer* reprinted by permission from Microsoft® Corporation.

ings and site links you can use for future research on that topic. In this way, subject directories let you browse subjects and start narrowing your topic.

Many search engine home pages have a subject directory that lists categories such as "Government," "Health," "News," "Science," and so forth. Clicking on a general category will take you to lists of increasingly specific categories. Eventually, you'll get a list of Web pages on the most specific subtopic you select. These search engines also allow you to click on a category and enter keywords to search that category. For example, suppose that you are using Yahoo to search for information on "artificial intelligence." You would first go to Yahoo's general category "Science." Under "Science" you would find the category "Computer science," which contains a link to "Artificial intelligence," a page that lists many sources.

25d How do I conduct a keyword search?

To conduct a keyword search, go to a search engine (Box 30, p. 151) and type your topic into the search box on the opening page. The engine then scans Web pages for your word(s) and lists Web sites that contain them. Very general terms may appear on thousands of Web sites. If a search engine produces thousands of hits for your keyword, do not give up. Instead, try more specific keywords. For example, a google.com keyword search for "intelligence" yielded more than seven million hits to Web sites containing that word. A search for the more specific keywords *"artificial intelligence"* yielded more than one million hits. An even narrower search for the keywords "Artificial intelligence computers emotion" yielded 16,300 hits. Finally, a search for the keywords "artificial intelligence computers emotion robots" yielded 4,130 hits.

As you become more adept at using keywords, your searches will become more directed and less time-consuming. The further you are in the process of drafting a thesis statement or assertion, the more specific your searches become. In fact, the keywords in your thesis statement are likely to be good keywords for your searches. Most keyword search engines permit you to request very specific searches using Boolean expressions, quotation marks, and truncation.

Using Boolean expressions

Some search engines let you create keyword combinations that narrow and refine your search. These searches use **Boolean expressions**—the words AND, OR, NOT, and NEAR, or symbols that represent those words. You can also use parentheses to group expressions just as you would group mathematical functions. When you use Boolean expressions between keywords, you are telling the search engine to list Web sites with your keyword specifications and ignore others. When you group terms in parentheses, you direct or "force" the engine to look first at the grouped words and then at either the ungrouped or grouped words that follow.

To see how Boolean expressions work, we can use a keyword search on the subject of "artificial intelligence" as an example. Without Boolean expressions, the keywords "intelligence computers emotions" would yield pages that include any of those words—and not necessarily in that order. Note the amount of weeding out that Boolean expressions allow.

- **AND** narrows the focus of your search to pages that contain both keywords. If you want to find information on the role of emotions in artificial intelligence, try the expression "artificial AND intelligence AND emotion." Some search engines, such as Google, do not require you to type "AND" between your terms. Instead, the search engine assumes that two or more terms are connected by AND.

- **NOT** narrows your search by excluding texts that contain the specified word or phrase. If you want to eliminate "robots" from your search, type "artificial AND intelligence AND emotion NOT robots." Sometimes you need to use NOT with another expression, such as AND—for example, "artificial AND intelligence AND emotion AND NOT robots."

- **OR** expands a search to include more than one keyword. To expand your search to sources about artificial intelligence in either computers or robots, try the expression "artificial AND intelligence AND emotion AND computers OR robots." Pages mentioning "artificial AND intelligence AND emotion" in connection with "computers OR robots" will be returned.

- **NEAR** indicates that the keywords may be found close to each other or on either side of each other. However, depending on which search engine you are using, NEAR may produce hits that are found either in the same sentence or on the same site.

- **Parentheses ( )** groups more than two expressions. For example, a search for (artificial intelligence AND emotions) AND (Turing test OR Chinese room) would find documents about artificial intelligence and emotions and either the Turing test or the Chinese room test. (These two tests are ways of judging whether a computer can be regarded as intelligent.)

These examples aren't meant to be all-inclusive. Always review a search engine's search tips, since engines differ in the way they handle expressions and formats. For example, some search engines are case sensitive, which means that they look for keywords exactly as you type them, including capitals and lowercase letters.

Finally, many search engines have "advanced search" pages, which prompt you to enter search phrases in various spaces that function as Boolean expressions. Many allow you to restrict sources to those created or updated within a specified period—for example, the last six months.

Using quotation marks for online searches

Enclosing your keywords in quotation marks directs the search engine to match your exact word order. For example, a search on Lycos for "robots that think," nets only 165 hits, each containing the title or phrase *robots that think*. This approach is helpful when you are searching for a name. If you search for the name *James Joyce* without using quotation marks, most engines will return pages containing the names *James* and *Joyce* anywhere in the document. A search using the keyword "James Joyce" will bring you closer to finding Web sites about the Irish author.

Using truncation

Truncation, sometimes called *wildcarding*, allows you to look for sites by listing only the first few letters of a keyword. You can also direct the search engine to search for variants of a keyword by using the wildcard symbol * in place of either the word ending or some of the letters in the word. For example, a truncated search for "wom*n" (or, in some cases, "wom#n") would return hits for both *woman* and *women*. This approach is helpful when you do not want to exclude the plural form of a noun or when a term comes in varying forms. Suppose you wanted to search for both *cognitive* and *cognition*. The search for "cogni*" would turn up both forms. Most search engines recognize the symbol * for truncation, but a few use other symbols. As always, check the Help screen of the engine you are using for specific details.

Box 32 offers some additional guidelines for using search engines.

25e How can I avoid plagiarizing from online sources?

Easy access to Web sources can be a tremendous help in your research. However, it can also cause problems if you aren't careful. Because downloading material from the Web is usually effortless, it is easy to PLAGIARIZE, or misrepresent the words of others as your own. Be very careful to avoid plagiarism while using online sources. Chapter 26 discusses plagiarism and its consequences. The special risks of using online sources demand that you take the precautions described in 26c.

BOX 32

⊙ Guidelines for using search engines

- Use keyword searches only when you have chosen a specific, narrow topic with unique keywords. If you enter a general topic in most search engines, you'll be overwhelmed by thousands of returns. If this happens, switch to a subject directory like those available on Yahoo.com or see if you can restrict the number of hits by using additional keywords or Boolean expressions.

- Try using more than one search engine or do a metasearch. Different search engines will yield different results for the same search.

- Check the Help screen in the search engine you use; as with the rest of the Web, search engines add or change features frequently.

- Ask the search engine to list results by "ranking." If you do not, the search results will be returned in random order, and the most important source may be last.

- If possible, limit the date range. For example, you might ask to see only pages that have been updated in the past six to twelve months.

- When you find a useful site, add it to your bookmarks or favorites list (click on "Bookmark" or "Favorites," and then "Add") so you can return to it later.

- Use the History or Go function to track the sites you visit, in case you want to revisit one later. If you want to, you can move a site from History to Bookmark.

25f How do I evaluate online sources?

The unregulated nature of the Web creates special responsibilities for online researchers. You need to evaluate Web sources carefully, for two reasons. First, since anyone can post anything on the Web, some sources you find may well be plagiarized. Second, many sources on the Web are written by individuals who are posing as experts and giving out false or misleading information.

You are always accountable for the sources you choose. To evaluate an online source, use the checklist in Box 33. These criteria can

Checklist for evaluating an online site

RELIABLE SITES ARE . . .

✔ **from educational, not-for-profit, or government organizations.** One good sign is an Internet address ending in *.edu, .org, .gov,* or a country abbreviation such as *.us* or *.uk.* These organizations should list their sources, however. If they fail to, don't use them. And be careful: Many colleges now host student Web sites, which also end in *.edu.*

✔ **from expert authors.** Experts have degrees or credentials that you can check. See if their names appear in other reliable sources, in bibliographies on your topic, or in reference books in your college library. Check whether the site's author gives an e-mail address for questions or comments.

✔ **from reliable print sources.** Online versions of the *New York Times, Time* magazine, and so on, which are produced by the publisher or that appear in a full text index, are just as reliable as the print versions.

✔ **supported by evidence and presented in a balanced, unbiased fashion.**

✔ **current or recently updated.**

QUESTIONABLE SITES ARE . . .

✔ **sponsored by commercial organizations.** The addresses of these sites end in *.com.* This category includes online advertisements, personal pages, and junk mail. Such sites may or may not list their sources. If they don't, you should not use them. If they do, check that the sources are legitimate, not a front for a commercial enterprise.

✔ **written by anonymous authors or authors who lack identifiable credentials.** Chat rooms, Usenet news groups, discussion groups, bulletin boards, and similar sites are questionable for this reason.

✔ **supported by secondhand excerpts and quotations.** Materials that appear on a site that is not the publisher's official site (such as a quotation taken from the *New York Times*) may have been edited or abridged in a biased or inaccurate manner.

✔ **unsupported or biased.** These sites carry declarations and assertions that have little or no supporting evidence.

✔ **old—that is, they have not been updated for a long time.**

help you separate sources that are worth a closer look from those that are not. Most reputable sites contain material that will help you to assess their credibility, such as a bibliography, links to the author or editor, or a description of the sponsoring organization. You want to discard sites that do not contain such information, however useful they may seem. To err on the side of caution is far better than to use a corrupt source.

An important question to ask about any Web site is why the information was put on the Internet. Be sure to question the motives of the site's author, especially if you are being asked to take a specific action.

For more help in evaluating online sources, try these Web sites.

- *Thinking Critically About World Wide Web Resources* <http://www.library.ucla.edu/libraries/college/help/critical/index.htm>

- *Thinking Critically About Discipline-Based World Wide Web Resources* <http://www.library.ucla.edu/libraries/college/help/critical/ discipline.htm>

- *Evaluating Web Resources* <http://www2.widener.edu/Wolfgram-Memorial-Library/ webevaluation/webeval.htm>

25g How do I extract information from online sources?

You need to take notes from online sources just as you do from library sources (24m). You may take notes on cards or enter them in a carefully organized computer file. Be sure to record the exact source with each note. Each source should have an entry in your WORKING BIBLIOGRAPHY.

Because Web pages can change and servers can go down, you want to bookmark good online sources, print them out, or copy them onto your own computer. These steps (which parallel photocopying articles from a periodical) will ensure that you have ready access to the sources you need. However, the crucial work of moving from gathering sources to writing with sources requires that you take notes from the materials you have found. Unless you QUOTE (26f), PARAPHRASE (26g), or SUMMARIZE (26h) your sources, writing a good SYNTHESIS will be very difficult. Not only do you risk plagiarism (26a, 26c); you also risk compiling a choppy and ineffective paste-up of sources. The process of taking notes from your materials allows you to understand the sources better and begin seeing connections among them. Box 34 offers some guidelines for working with online sources.

BOX 34

◉ Guidelines for using online sources

- Once you've narrowed your research focus, immediately print out or download those sources that relate to your topic. Keep your sources in separate files from your paper to avoid the risk of PLAGIARISM.

- Make sure each note shows (1) the URL, (2) the name of the source, and (3) the date you accessed the source and printed or downloaded it.

- Check the documentation style you are required to use to see exactly what details you'll need to list the source in your in-text citations and final bibliography.

- Write down the exact reason you chose to print or download each source. Underline or highlight particular sections you think will be useful to you, and note why.

---

26 USING SOURCES AND AVOIDING PLAGIARISM

To use sources well, you need to learn three skills. First, you need to incorporate others' words or ideas into your own papers accurately. Second, you need to do so effectively. And third, you need to do so honestly. This last skill is especially important, so that you avoid plagiarism.

26a What is plagiarism?

Plagiarism is presenting another person's words or ideas as if they were your own. Plagiarizing, like stealing, is a form of academic dishonesty or cheating. It's a serious offense that can be grounds for a failing grade or expulsion from a college. Beyond that, you're hurting yourself. If you're plagiarizing, you're not learning.

You're most definitely plagiarizing if you turn in a paper that someone else has written. This is true whether the paper comes from a friend, another student, the library, the Internet, or elsewhere. You're plagiarizing whether someone has "given" you the paper, you've found it in a file or on the Internet, or you've bought it. Furthermore, changing

BOX 35

 Types of plagiarism

You're plagiarizing if you . . .

- Buy a paper from an Internet site, another student or writer, or any other source.
- Turn in any paper that someone else has written, whether the person has given it to you, you have downloaded it from the Internet, or you have copied it from any other source.
- Copy or paste into your paper any *key terms, phrases, sentences, or longer passages* from another source without using QUOTATION MARKS and correctly citing that source (that is, without indicating precisely what you have used and listing the source on your Works Cited page).
- Use *ideas* from another source without correctly citing and documenting that source, even if you put the ideas into your own words.
- Combine ideas from many sources and pass them off as your own without correctly citing and documenting the sources.

parts of an existing paper doesn't make it your work. Box 35 lists the major types of plagiarism.

Never assume that your instructor can't detect plagiarism. Instructors have a keen eye for writing styles that are different from those of students in general, and you in particular. Instructors can access Web sites that check your work against that of all online paper providers. Furthermore, some Internet sites allow instructors to check your writing against hundreds of thousands of papers on the World Wide Web and the Internet. When instructors receive papers that they suspect contain plagiarized passages, they can also check with other professors who may have seen the paper.

26b How do I avoid plagiarism?

The first step in avoiding plagiarism is to learn the techniques of QUOTING (26f), PARAPHRASING (26g), and SUMMARIZING (26h) source materials. The second step is to master how to DOCUMENT sources correctly, according to the DOCUMENTATION STYLE you're required to use. To do this, take advantage of the learning opportunities your instructor may build into research assignments. Many instructors require students to hand in a

BOX 36

 Guidelines for avoiding plagiarism

- Acknowledge when you're using the ideas or words of others. Always document the sources.

- Become thoroughly familiar with the documentation style your instructor requires you to use (Chs. 28–36). Then make a master list of the information you must provide when you QUOTE, PARAPHRASE, or SUMMARIZE a source.

- Write down all the facts that you need to document a source the first time you consult it or you risk not finding it again.

- Follow a consistent notetaking system. Use different colors of ink, or some other coding system, to distinguish three different types of material.
  - Quotations from a source
  - Material you have paraphrased or summarized from a source
  - Your own thoughts, triggered by what you have read or experienced

- Write clear, even oversized quotation marks when you are quoting a passage directly. Make them stand out so that you can't miss them later.

- Consult your instructor if you're unsure about any phase of the documentation process.

WORKING BIBLIOGRAPHY (23f) or **annotated bibliography** (a list of sources that contains a brief summary of or commentary on each source). Your instructor may ask to see your RESEARCH LOG (22d), your working notes, copies of your sources, or working drafts of your paper. Not only do such practices help you to avoid plagiarism; they also help you to plan your research project (22e) and move through the writing process. Box 36 suggests some practical steps you can take to avoid plagiarism.

26c How do I work with the Internet to avoid plagiarism?

As Chapter 25 explains, the Internet can both greatly help researchers and create potential problems. One of those problems is plagiarism. You might be tempted to download a paper from the Internet. Don't. That kind of intellectual dishonesty can get you into real trouble. Box 37 suggests some ways you can avoid plagiarism when you are working on the Internet.

Guidelines for avoiding plagiarism on the Internet

- Never cut material from an online source and paste it directly into your paper. You can too easily lose track of which language is your own and which comes from a source.

- Keep material that you downloaded or printed from the Internet separate from your own writing, whether you intend to QUOTE, SUMMARIZE, or PARAPHRASE the material. Be careful how you manage those copied files. When you know the exact place in your paper where you will use each passage, record that location clearly using another color or a much larger font. Just as important, make sure that you write down all the information you need to identify each source, according to the documentation style you need to use.

- Copy or paste downloaded or printed material into your paper only when you intend to use it as a direct quotation. Immediately place quotation marks around the material, or set off a long passage as a block quotation. Be sure to document the source at the same time as you copy or paste the quotation into your paper. If you put off documenting the passage until later, you may forget to do it or use the wrong source.

- SUMMARIZE or PARAPHRASE materials *before* you include them in your paper. If you have printed or downloaded Internet sources to separate files, don't copy directly from those files into your paper. Summarize or paraphrase the sources in a different file, and then paste the summaries or paraphrases into your paper. Document the source of each passage at the same time you insert it in your paper. If you put off this task until later, you may forget to do it or get it wrong.

- Use an Internet service to check a passage you're not sure about. If you're concerned that you may have plagiarized by mistake, try submitting one or two sentences that concern you to <http://www.yahoo.com>. To do so, you must place quotation marks around the sentences when you type them into the search window. You might also submit your paper to one of the for-profit plagiarism-detection services. These services charge a fee for checking your work and they keep a copy of your paper in their databases.

26d What don't I have to document?

You don't have to document common knowledge or your own thinking. Common knowledge is information that most educated people know, although they might need to remind themselves of certain facts by looking them up in a reference book. For example, you would not need to document that

- Bill Clinton was the U.S. president before George W. Bush.
- Mercury is the planet closest to the sun.
- The normal human body temperature is 98.6° F.
- All the oceans on our planet contain salt water.

Your own thinking is what you have concluded by building on what you already know. It consists of your analysis and interpretation of new material as you read or observe it. These thoughts of yours help you to formulate a thesis statement and organize your research paper. For example, suppose you're drawing on an article about the connections between emotions and logic in humans. While reading the article, you come to your own personal conclusion that computers don't have emotions. You don't need to find a source that supports this thought, although such a source might strengthen your assertion.

What *should* you document? Everything that you learn from a source, including ideas as well as specific language. Expressing the ideas of others in your own words doesn't release you from the obligation to tell exactly where you got those ideas using correct documentation. Consider the following example.

SOURCE

Searle, John R. "I Married a Computer." Rev. of *The Age of Spiritual Machines* by Ray Kurzweil. *New York Review of Books* 8 Apr. 1999: 34+. [This source information is arranged in MLA documentation style.]

ORIGINAL MATERIAL

We are now in the midst of a technological revolution that is full of surprises. No one thirty years ago was aware that one day household computers would become as common as dishwashers. And those of us who used the old Arpanet of twenty years ago had no idea that it would evolve into the Internet. (37) [These are Searle's exact words.]

PLAGIARISM

- The current technological revolution is surprising. Thirty years ago no one expected computers to be as common today as air conditioners. What once was the Arpanet has evolved into the Internet, and no one expected that. [Searle's ideas appear without documentation.]

Note that even though the writer has changed some of Searle's wording, the ideas are virtually the same. Therefore, the writer is required to document Searle's review as the source.

CORRECT

- John Searle states that we are in a surprising technological revolution in which computers have "become as common as dishwashers" (37). Twenty years ago no one could have predicted that the Arpanet would become the Internet (Searle 37). [The writer uses quotation, paraphrase, and documentation correctly.]

In this revision, the writer has properly cited Searle's ideas through a combination of quotation and paraphrase. Sections 26e–26h explain exactly how to use sources effectively and document them correctly.

26e How should I integrate sources into my writing?

Before trying to integrate sources into your writing, you need to analyze and synthesize your material (1b). ANALYSIS is the process of breaking ideas down into their component parts, so that you can think them through separately. Do this while reading and reviewing your notes. SYNTHESIS is the process of making connections among different ideas, seeking relationships that tie them together.

Your research paper can be successful only if it reflects your personal synthesis of the ideas you are dealing with. The major requirement of a research paper is to demonstrate your ability to think well. Never simply list or summarize separate ideas. Use QUOTATION (26f), PARAPHRASE (26g), and SUMMARY (26h) to present your synthesis of the material you have read.

26f How can I use quotations effectively?

A **quotation** is the exact words of a source enclosed in QUOTATION MARKS (54a–54b). You face conflicting demands when you add quotations to your writing. Although quotations provide support, you can lose control of your paper if you add too many. You want your writing to be coherent and readable, so use quotations sparingly. If more than a quarter of your paper consists of quotations, you've probably written what some people call a "scotch-tape special," merely stringing together a bunch of quotations. Depending too heavily on quotations gives your readers—including your instructor—the impression that you haven't bothered to develop your own thinking and that you're letting other people do your talking.

GUIDELINES FOR USING QUOTATIONS

1. Use quotations from authorities on your subject to support or refute what you have written.

2. Never use a quotation to present your THESIS STATEMENT or a TOPIC SENTENCE.

3. Select quotations that fit your message. Choose a quotation only for these reasons.
   a. Its language is particularly appropriate or distinctive.
   b. Its idea is particularly hard to paraphrase accurately.
   c. The source's authority is especially important to support your thesis or main point in a paragraph.
   d. The source's words are open to interpretation.

4. Never use quotations in more than a quarter of your paper. Instead, rely on PARAPHRASE (26g) and SUMMARY (26h).

5. Quote accurately. Always check a quotation against the original source—and then recheck it.

6. Integrate quotations smoothly into your writing.

7. Avoid PLAGIARISM (26a–26c).

8. Document quotations carefully, just as you do for a paraphrase or summary.

Making quotations fit smoothly with your sentences

When you use quotations, the greatest risk you take is that you'll end up with incoherent, choppy sentences. You can avoid this problem by making the words you quote fit smoothly with three aspects of your writing: grammar, style, and logic. After writing a sentence that contains a quotation, read it aloud to hear whether the language flows smoothly and gracefully. If it doesn't, revise the sentence. Here are some examples of sentences that don't mesh well with quotations, followed by revised versions.

SOURCE

Goleman, Daniel. *Emotional Intelligence*. New York: Bantam, 1995. 9.
[This source information is arranged in MLA documentation style.]

ORIGINAL MATERIAL

These two minds, the emotional and the rational, operate in tight harmony for the most part, intertwining their very different ways of knowing to guide us through the world. [These are Goleman's exact words.]

INCOHERENT GRAMMAR

• Goleman explains how the emotional and rational minds "intertwining their very different ways of knowing to guide us through the world" (9).

INCOHERENT STYLE—INVERTED WORD ORDER

• Goleman explains how "intertwining their very different ways of knowing to guide us through the world," the emotional and rational minds work together (9).

INCOHERENT LOGIC

• Goleman explains how the emotional and rational minds work together by "their very different ways of knowing to guide us through the world" (9).

REVISED FOR COHERENCE

• Goleman explains how the emotional and rational minds work together by "intertwining their very different ways of knowing to guide us through the world" (9).

What do you do when a quotation doesn't fit smoothly with your writing? You can add a word or two to the quotation, in BRACKETS (56c), so that it fits seamlessly with the rest of your sentence. Make sure, however, that your bracketed additions don't distort the meaning of the quotation.

Another way to fit a quotation smoothly into your sentence is to delete the part of the quotation that seems to be causing the problem by using an ELLIPSIS (56d). When you use an ellipsis to delete troublesome words, make sure that the remaining words accurately reflect the source's meaning, and that your sentence still flows smoothly. For example, suppose you want to quote from the following source.

SOURCE

Goleman, Daniel. *Emotional Intelligence*. New York: Bantam, 1995. 9.
[This source information is arranged in MLA documentation style.]

ORIGINAL MATERIAL

But when passions surge, the balance tips: it is the emotional mind that captures the upper hand, swamping the rational mind. [These are Goleman's exact words.]

QUOTATION USING ELLIPSIS

• Goleman contends that "when passions surge, . . . the emotional mind . . . captures the upper hand" (9).

Integrating author names, source titles, and other information

Another strategy for working quotations smoothly into your paper is to integrate the author's name, the source title, or other information into your paper. You can prepare your reader for a quotation using one of these methods.

- Mention in your sentence (before or after the quotation) the name of the author you're quoting.
- Mention in your sentence the title of the work you're quoting from.
- If the author of a quotation is a noteworthy figure, refer in your sentence to his or her credentials.
- Add your own introductory analysis to the quotation, along with the name of the author, the title of the source, and/or the author's credentials.

Here are some examples of effective integration of an author's name, source title, and credentials, along with an introductory analysis.

SOURCE

Binkley, Sue. *The Clockwork Sparrow: Time, Clocks, and Calendars in Biological Organisms*. Englewood Cliffs: Prentice, 1990. [This source information is arranged in MLA documentation style.]

ORIGINAL MATERIAL

Artificial lighting, jet travel, and space exploration permit sudden disruptions of natural temporal sequences (4). [These are Binkley's exact words.]

AUTHOR'S NAME

- **Sue Binkley explains that** "artificial lighting, jet travel, and space exploration permit sudden disruptions of natural temporal sequences" (4).

AUTHOR'S NAME AND SOURCE TITLE

- **Sue Binkley explains in The Clockwork Sparrow that** "artificial lighting, jet travel, and space exploration permit sudden disruptions of natural temporal sequences" (4).

AUTHOR'S NAME, CREDENTIALS, AND SOURCE TITLE

- **Sue Binkley, who has researched circadian rhythms for twenty years, explains in The Clockwork Sparrow that** "artificial lighting, jet travel, and space exploration permit sudden disruptions of natural temporal sequences" (4).

AUTHOR'S NAME WITH STUDENT'S INTRODUCTORY ANALYSIS

- **Sue Binkley, a leading researcher in circadian rhythms who has found that modern life interferes with our biological clocks, explains that** "artificial lighting, jet travel, and space exploration permit sudden disruptions of natural temporal sequences" (4).

26g How can I write good paraphrases?

A **paraphrase** precisely restates in your own words the written or spoken words of someone else. Select for paraphrase only those passages that carry ideas you need to reproduce in detail. Because paraphrasing calls for a very close approximation of a source, avoid trying to paraphrase a whole chapter—or even a whole page.

GUIDELINES FOR WRITING PARAPHRASES

- Paraphrase the words of authorities on your subject to support or counter what you write in your paper.
- Never write a paraphrase to present your thesis statement or topic sentences.
- Say what the source says, but no more.
- Reproduce the source's emphases and order of ideas.
- Use your own words, phrasing, and sentence structure to restate the material. If some technical words in the original have only awkward synonyms, you may quote the original words—but do so very sparingly. For example, you may use the term *circadian rhythms* if you're paraphrasing the original source by Sue Binkley in 26f.
- Read your sentences over to make sure they don't distort the source's meaning.
- Expect your material to be as long as, or even longer than, the original.
- Integrate your paraphrase into your writing so that it fits smoothly.
- Avoid PLAGIARISM (26a–26c).
- Document your paraphrase carefully, just as you do for QUOTATIONS (26f) and SUMMARIES (26h). Otherwise, you'll be plagiarizing.

Here is a passage that Chandra Johnson came across while researching her MLA-style research paper (30b). Read the passage and then study the two paraphrases that follow it. The first paraphrase is unacceptable because the underlined words have been plagiarized. The second paraphrase is acceptable.

SOURCE

Goleman, Daniel. *Emotional Intelligence*. New York: Bantam, 1995. 9.
[This source information is arranged in MLA documentation style.]

ORIGINAL MATERIAL

These two minds, the emotional and the rational, operate in tight harmony for the most part, intertwining their very different ways of knowing to guide us through the world. Ordinarily there is a balance between emotional and rational minds, with emotion feeding into and informing the operations of the rational mind, and the rational mind refining and sometimes vetoing the inputs of the emotions. Still, the emotional and rational minds are semi-independent faculties, each, as we shall see, reflecting the operation of distinct, but interconnected circuitry of the brain.

In many or most moments, these minds are exquisitely coordinated; feelings are essential to thought, thought to feeling. But when passions surge, the balance tips: it is the emotional mind that captures the upper hand, swamping the rational mind. [These are Goleman's exact words.]

UNACCEPTABLE PARAPHRASE

- The emotional and the rational parts of our mind operate in tight harmony for the most part as they help us make our way through our lives. Usually the two minds are balanced, with emotion feeding into and informing the operations of the rational mind, and the rational mind refining and sometimes overruling what the emotions desire. Still, the emotional and rational minds are semi-independent faculties, for as research shows, although they function separately, they are linked in the brain.

  Most of the time our two minds work together, with feelings necessary for thinking and thinking necessary for feeling. Nevertheless, if strong emotions develop, it is the emotional mind that captures the upper hand, swamping the rational mind (Goleman 9). [Underlined words are plagiarized.]

ACCEPTABLE PARAPHRASE

- According to Goleman, the emotional and rational parts of our mind work together to help us make our way through our lives. Usually, the two minds have equal input. The emotional mind provides information to the logical mind, and the logical mind processes the data and sometimes overrules emotional desires. Nevertheless, while the two minds show a biological connection in the brain, each can assert some independence. Most of the time our two minds work together, with feelings necessary for thinking and thinking necessary for feeling. Still, if strong emotions develop, passions overrule logical thinking (9).

The first attempt to paraphrase is unacceptable because the writer has simply changed a few words. What remains is plagiarized: it retains most of the original language, has the same sentence structure as the original, and uses no quotation marks. The documentation is correct, but its accuracy doesn't make up for the unacceptable paraphrasing.

The second paraphrase is acceptable. It captures the meaning of the original in the student's own words.

26h How can I write good summaries?

A **summary** differs from a PARAPHRASE (26g) in one important way: While a paraphrase restates the original material completely, a summary provides only the main point of the original source. As a result, a summary is much shorter than a paraphrase. Summarizing is the technique you will probably use most frequently in writing research papers, both for taking notes and for integrating what you have learned into your own writing.

GUIDELINES FOR WRITING SUMMARIES

- Summarize the work of authorities on your subject to support or refute what you write in your paper.
- Identify the main points you want to summarize and condense them in your own words, taking care not to lose the meaning of the original source.
- Never use a summary to present your thesis statement or a topic sentence.
- Keep your summary short.
- Integrate your summary smoothly into your writing.
- Avoid PLAGIARISM (26a–26c).
- Document your sources carefully, just as you do for QUOTATIONS (26f) and PARAPHRASES (26g). Otherwise, you'll be plagiarizing.

As you summarize a passage in a source, don't be tempted to include your personal interpretation or judgment along with the author's thoughts. Your own opinions don't belong in a summary. This doesn't mean that your opinions and ideas have no value. On the contrary: Jot them down immediately, so you can use them in a different paragraph. Always take notes in a way that distinguishes your own opinions or ideas from your summary. If you handwrite your notes, use a different color ink for your own ideas. If you take notes on a computer, use a double underline, boldface, highlighting, or a different color or font to mark your own thoughts.

Here are two summaries of the same passage. The first one is unacceptable because it mixes the writer's words with those of the source.

SOURCE

Coleman, Richard. *Wide Awake at 3:00 A.M.: By Choice or By Chance?* New York: Freeman, 1986. 69. [This source information is arranged in MLA documentation style.]

ORIGINAL MATERIAL

An important variable in determining the degree of jet lag is the direction of travel, not whether the flight is outgoing or homecoming. When traveling in a westbound direction, New York to Los Angeles, for example, we must set our wristwatches and biological clocks back by 3 hours because our day has been extended. (If you normally keep to a bedtime of 11:00 p.m. to 7:00 a.m. and upon arrival in Los Angeles, you also stay up till 11:00 p.m. local time, you will experience a 27-hour day. Traveling eastbound, Los Angeles to New York, requires setting your watch ahead by 3 hours, or shortening the day to 21 hours.)

Because our internal biological clock naturally gravitates to a 25-hour day, it makes sense that we can more easily adjust to westbound travel, which extends the day. In a series of studies of jet lag, volunteers have been flown back and forth between Europe and the United States (six time zones) to measure cognitive-motor performance, body temperature, and fatigue ratings. When performance before and after the six-time-zone flight was assessed, it was found that the travelers reached their peak performance within two to four days following westbound flight, but required nine days following eastbound travel. [These are Coleman's exact words.]

UNACCEPTABLE SUMMARY

- The degree of jet lag is related to the <u>direction of travel</u>, westbound travel lengthening the day, which is easier for biological clocks <u>to adjust to</u>, and <u>eastbound travel shortening it</u>, which is harder on biological clocks (Coleman 69). [The underlined words are plagiarized.]

■■■ **BOX 38** ■■

 ## Verbs useful for integrating quotations, paraphrases, and summaries

agrees	concludes	estimates	notes	sees
analyzes	confirms	explains	observes	shows
argues	considers	finds	offers	signals
asks	contends	grants	points out	speculates
asserts	declares	illustrates	recommends	states
believes	demonstrates	implies	refutes	suggests
claims	denies	informs	remarks	supposes
comments	describes	insists	reports	thinks
complains	discusses	maintains	reveals	wishes
concedes	emphasizes	negates	says	writes

ACCEPTABLE SUMMARY

- Eastbound travelers find it harder than westbound travelers to adjust because traveling east shortens the day unnaturally (Coleman 69).

👁 **ALERT:** Never confuse summarizing with SYNTHESIZING. For a full explanation of the differences, see 4a and 4b. In writing a research paper, you want to summarize your sources' ideas and information, but your summaries are only the foundation on which to build your synthesis. A research paper that merely offers summaries doesn't demonstrate your ability to make the connections among ideas that synthesis demands. 👁

26i Which verbs can help me weave source material into my sentences?

Use the verbs in Box 38 appropriately according to their meanings in your sentences.

27 DRAFTING AND REVISING A RESEARCH PAPER

Drafting and revising a research paper is much like drafting and revising any piece of writing (Chs. 6–7). Yet you need to do much more. To write a research paper, you need extra time for planning, drafting, thinking, redrafting, rethinking, and creating a final draft. This is so because in a research paper, you need to demonstrate that

- You've followed the steps of the research process presented in Chapters 22–26.
- You understand the information that you've located during your research.
- You have not PLAGIARIZED your material from someone else (26a–26c).
- You've used SOURCES well in your writing, correctly employing QUOTATIONS, PARAPHRASES, and SUMMARIES (26f–26h).
- You've moved beyond SUMMARY to SYNTHESIS so that your sources are interwoven with each other and with your own thinking, not merely listed one by one (4a–4b).
- You've used DOCUMENTATION accurately (For MLA STYLE, see Chs. 28–30; for APA STYLE, see Chs. 31–33; for other documentation styles, see Chs. 34–36.)

Expect to write several drafts of your research paper. The first draft is your first chance to discover new insights and fresh connections. Only the act of writing makes such breakthroughs possible.

27a How do I draft a research paper?

Here are some ways to write a first draft of a research paper.

- Some researchers work with their notes at hand. They organize the notes into broad categories by making a separate pile of note cards (or printouts of their notes) for each category of information. As patterns begin to emerge, these writers might move material from one category to another. Each category becomes a section of the first draft. This method not only assures researchers that their first draft will include all the material from their research, but reveals any gaps in information that call for additional research. Of course, you may discover that some of your research does not fit your topic and thesis. Just put it aside; it might be useful in a later draft.

- Some researchers finish their research and then slowly review half the information they've gathered. Next, setting aside that information, they write a partial first draft by drawing on the information they remember from their reading. Then they use the same process with the second half of the information that they've gathered. Finally, with their two partial drafts and all their research notes in front of them, they write a complete first draft. Researchers who use this method say it gives them a broad overview of their material quickly and identifies any gaps in information that they need to fill in with further research.

- Some researchers stop at various points during their research and use FREEWRITING to get their ideas into words. Researchers who use this method say that it helps them to recognize when they need to adjust their RESEARCH QUESTION or change the emphasis of their search. After a number of rounds of researching and freewriting, these researchers find that they can write their complete first draft relatively easily.

- Some writers review their sources and create an outline before drafting. Some find a formal outline helpful, while others use a less formal approach.

27b How do I revise a research paper?

Before you write your second draft, read your first one with a sharp eye. Assess all the features listed in Box 39 at the end of this section, as well as in Box 10 (p. 30). For best results, take a break of a few days (or at least a few hours) before beginning this process. This gives you distance from your material, and a clearer vision of what you need to REVISE. For a more objective point of view, consider asking a few people you respect to read and react to your first, or perhaps your second, draft.

One key to revising any research paper is to carefully examine the evidence you have included. **Evidence** consists of facts, statistics, expert studies and opinions, examples, and stories. As a reader, you expect writers to provide solid evidence to back up their claims and conclusions. Similarly, when you write, your readers expect you to provide evidence that clearly supports your claims and conclusions. Identify each of the points you have made in your paper, including your thesis and all your subpoints. Then ask the following questions.

- **Is the evidence sufficient?** To be sufficient, evidence cannot be thin or trivial. As a rule, the more evidence you present, the more convincing your thesis will be to readers.

- **Is the evidence representative?** Representative evidence is customary and normal, not based on exceptions. When evidence is representative, it provides a view of the issue that reflects the usual circumstances rather than rare ones.

- **Is the evidence relevant?** Relevant evidence relates directly to your thesis or topic sentence. It illustrates your reasons in a

Revision checklist for a research paper

If the answer to a question in this checklist is no, you need to revise. The section numbers in parentheses tell you where to find helpful information.

WRITING

✔ Have you met the basic requirements for a written thesis statement? (7b)

✔ Does your introductory paragraph lead effectively into the material? (8b)

✔ Do you stay on the topic of each paragraph? (8c)

✔ Have you discussed the topic of each paragraph fully, using RENNS? (8d)

✔ Do your ideas follow sensibly and logically within each paragraph and from one paragraph to the next? (8e)

✔ Does the concluding paragraph end your paper effectively? (8g)

RESEARCH

✔ Does your thesis statement allude to, or directly address, your research question? (22c)

✔ Does the content of your paper address your research question? (22c)

✔ Have you integrated your source material well without plagiarizing? (26e)

✔ Have you written good quotations, paraphrases, and summaries? (26f–26h)

✔ Have you included appropriate and effective evidence? (27b)

✔ Have you deleted irrelevant or insignificant evidence? (27b)

FORMAT AND DOCUMENTATION

✔ Have you used the correct format in your parenthetical references? (28b, 31b)

✔ Does each of your parenthetical references tie into an item in your WORKS CITED list (MLA STYLE) or REFERENCES list (APA STYLE) at the end of your paper? (29b, 32b)

✔ Does your paper follow the format you've been assigned to use? Check the margins, spacing, title, headings, page numbers, and so on. (30a; 31a, 31e)

straightforward way and is never unrelated to your main point. Only if your evidence is important and central to your point will readers accept your thesis.

- **Is the evidence accurate?** Accurate evidence is correct, complete, and up to date. It comes from a reliable SOURCE (24l, 25f). Equally important, you present it honestly, without distorting or misrepresenting it.

- **Is the evidence reasonable?** Reasonable evidence is not phrased in extreme language, such as *all, never*, or *certainly*. Reasonable evidence is well thought out and free of logical fallacies (10f).

As you reread and revise, pay attention to any uneasy feelings you may develop that hint at the need to rethink or rework your material. Most students find that research papers are their most demanding assignments. They know that no amount of careful research and good writing can make up for an incorrectly presented or sloppy paper. Be sure, therefore, to allow lots of time for rewriting, revising, EDITING, and PROOFREADING. **Experienced student writers know that writing is really rewriting.**

For an example of a student research paper in MLA documentation style, see 30b. For an example of a student research paper in APA documentation style, see Chapter 33.

MLA

Documentation

www.prenhall.com/troyka

MLA Documentation

28 MLA IN-TEXT CITATIONS

The most frequently used documentation style in the humanities has been developed by the Modern Language Association (MLA). In MLA style, you're expected to document your sources in two separate, equally important ways.

1. Within the body of the paper, use in-text citations, as described in this chapter.
2. At the end of the paper, provide a list of sources you used in your paper. Title this list Works Cited, as described in Chapter 29.

28a What are MLA in-text citations?

In-text citations are information included in the sentences or in parenthetical references within the paper. They both signal material used from outside sources and enable readers to locate the original sources.

In most in-text citations, a name or a title usually identifies a source, and page numbers usually show the exact location in that source. In general, put page number information in parentheses at the end of a quotation, paraphrase, or summary. Try to introduce names of authors and titles of sources in your own sentences, where they become part of the flow of your writing. If that isn't possible, put the information in parentheses at the end of a quotation, paraphrase, or summary. For advice on incorporating names, titles, and other information in your sentences to establish the authority of your sources, see 26e.

CITATIONS OF PARAPHRASES

- People from the Mediterranean prefer an elbow-to-shoulder distance from each other (Morris 131). [name and page number cited in parentheses]
- Desmond Morris notes that people from the Mediterranean prefer an elbow-to-shoulder distance from each other (131). [name cited in text, page number cited in parentheses]

A parenthetical reference belongs at the end of the material it refers to, usually at the end of a sentence. If you're citing a quotation enclosed in quotation marks, place the parentheses after the closing quotation mark but before sentence-ending punctuation.

- Binkley claims that artificial light reduced SAD-related "depression in 87 percent of patients . . . within a few days; relapses followed" (203–04) when light treatment ended. [The ellipsis (three spaced periods) indicates words omitted by the writer.]

- Research shows that "the number, rate, and direction of time-zone changes are the critical factors in determining the extent and degree of jet lag symptoms" (Coleman 67).

Place a parenthetical reference for a long quotation, (one you set off from your own sentences with indentation—54b) outside the punctuation ending the last sentence; for an example, see page 220 in Chandra Johnson's research paper in 30b.

28b What are MLA guidelines for in-text citations?

The directory below corresponds to the numbered examples that follow the list. The examples show you how to handle various types of citations in the body of your paper. Many of these examples show parenthetical citations, but remember that you usually can—and want to—give names and titles of your sources in your own sentences.

DIRECTORY—MLA IN-TEXT CITATIONS

1. One Author—MLA
2. Two or Three Authors—MLA
3. More Than Three Authors—MLA
4. More Than One Source by an Author—MLA
5. Two or More Authors with the Same Last Name—MLA
6. Group or Corporate Author—MLA
7. Work Cited by Title—MLA
8. Multivolume Work—MLA
9. Novel, Play, or Poem—MLA
10. Work in an Anthology or Other Collection—MLA
11. Indirect Source—MLA
12. Two or More Sources in One Reference—MLA
13. An Entire Work—MLA
14. The Bible—MLA
15. An Electronic Source with a Name or Title and Page Numbers—MLA
16. An Electronic Source with Paragraph, Screen, or Section Numbers—MLA
17. An Electronic Source without Page or Other Numbers—MLA

MLA MLA MLA MLA MLA MLA MLA MLA

1. One Author—MLA

All the examples in 28a show citations of works by one author. Notice that no punctuation separates the author's name from the page number in parenthetical citations.

2. Two or Three Authors—MLA

Give authors' names (order and spelling) as they appear on the book (title page) or article. Spell out the word *and*.

- As children get older, they become more aware of standards for personal space (Worchel and Cooper 536).

3. More Than Three Authors—MLA

For a book by more than three authors, you can name all authors, or you can use the first author's name only, followed by *et al.,* either in a parenthetical reference or in your sentence.

- Fisher et al. have found that personal space gets larger or smaller depending on the circumstances of the social interaction (158).

- Personal space gets larger or smaller depending on the circumstances of the social interaction (Fisher et al. 158).

4. More Than One Source by an Author—MLA

When you use two or more sources by the same author, include the relevant title in each citation. In parenthetical citations, use a shortened version of the title. For a paper using as sources Edward T. Hall's *The Hidden Dimension* and "Learning the Arabs' Silent Language," parenthetical citations would be *Hidden* and "Learning." Shorten the titles as much as you can without making them ambiguous to readers, and start with the word by which the work is alphabetized in Works Cited. Separate the name and title with a comma, but don't use punctuation between the title and page number.

- Most people are unaware that interpersonal distances exist and contribute to people's reactions to one another (Hall, Hidden 109).

- Arabs know the practicality of close conversational distances (Hall, "Learning" 41).

When you incorporate the title into your own sentences, you can omit a subtitle, but do not shorten more than that on first mention.

5. Two or More Authors with the Same Last Name—MLA

Use each author's first initial and full last name in each parenthetical citation. In your sentences, you can use either the first initial or the full first name. If both authors have the same first initial, use the full name in all instances.

- According to British zoologist Desmond Morris, conversational distances vary between people from different countries (131). If an American backs away from an Arab, the American is considered cold, the Arab pushy (C. Morris 516).

6. Group or Corporate Author—MLA

When a corporation or other group is named as the author of a source you want to cite, use the corporate name just as you would an individual's name.

- In a five-year study, the Boston Women's Health Collective reported that these tests are usually unreliable (11).

- A five-year study shows that these tests are usually unreliable (Boston Women's Health Collective 11).

7. Work Cited by Title—MLA

If no author is named, use only the title. If the title is long, shorten it. Here's an in-text citation to an article titled "Are You a Day or Night Person?"

- The "morning lark" and "night owl" descriptions typically are used to categorize the human extremes ("Are You" 11).

8. Multivolume Work—MLA

If you use more than one volume of a multivolume work, include the relevant volume number in each citation. Separate the volume number and page number with a colon followed by a space.

- Although Amazon forest dwellers had been exposed to these viruses by 1900 (Rand 3: 202), Borneo forest dwellers escaped them until the 1960s (Rand 1: 543).

9. Novel, Play, or Poem—MLA

Often when you cite literary works, you can give location information that is more useful than page numbers. Part, chapter, act, scene, canto, stanza, or line numbers generally don't change no matter where the work appears. Unless your instructor tells you differently, use arabic numerals for these references. Do this even if the literary work uses roman numerals (except for lowercase roman numerals used for pages of a preface or other front matter in a book). If a novel has parts and/or chapters, give these after the page numbers. Use a semicolon after the page number but a comma to separate a part from a chapter.

- Flannery O'Connor describes one character in <u>The Violent Bear It Away</u> as "[seeing] himself divided in two--a violent and a rational self" (139; pt. 2, ch. 6).

For plays, give act, scene, and/or line numbers if they are used. Use periods between these numbers.

- Among the most quoted of Shakespeare's lines is Hamlet's soliloquy beginning "To be, or not to be: that is the question" (3.1.56).

For poems and songs, give canto, stanza, and/or line numbers. Use periods between these numbers.

- In "To Autumn," Keats's most melancholy image occurs in the lines "Then in a wailful choir the small gnats mourn / Among the river swallows" (3.27-28).

10. Work in an Anthology or Other Collection—MLA

You may want to cite a work you have read in a book that contains many works by various authors and that was compiled, written, or edited by someone other than the person you are citing. For example, suppose you want to cite "When in Rome" by Mari Evans, which you have read in a literature text by Pamela Annas and Robert Rosen. Use Evans's name and the title of her work in the in-text citation.

- In "When in Rome," Mari Evans uses parentheses to enclose lines expressing the houseworker's thoughts as her employer offers lunch, as in the first stanza's "(an egg / or soup / . . . there ain't no meat)" (688-89).

11. Indirect Source—MLA

When you want to quote words that you found quoted in someone else's work, put the name of the person whose words you are quoting into your own sentence. Indicate the work where you found the quotation either in your sentence or in a parenthetical citation beginning with *qtd. in.*

- Martin Scorsese acknowledges the link between himself and his films: "I realize that all my life, I've been an outsider. I splatter bits of myself all over the screen" (qtd. in Giannetti and Eyman 397).

- Giannetti and Eyman quote Martin Scorsese as acknowledging the link between himself and his films: "I realize that all my life, I've been an outsider. I splatter bits of myself all over the screen" (397).

12. Two or More Sources in One Reference—MLA

If more than one source has contributed to an idea, opinion, or fact in your paper, cite them all. In a parenthetical citation, separate each block of information with a semicolon. You can also use a footnote or an endnote to cite several sources (28c).

- Once researchers agreed that these cultural "distance zones" existed, their next step was to try to measure or define them (Hall 110-20; Henley 32-33; Fisher, Bell, and Baum 153).

13. An Entire Work—MLA

References to an entire work usually fit best into your own sentences.

- In <u>The Clockwork Sparrow</u>, Sue Binkley analyzes studies of circadian rhythms undertaken between 1967 and 1989.

14. The Bible—MLA

When citing the Bible in MLA style, you need to give the version of the Bible cited, the book (often abbreviated), and the chapter and verse numbers. For the first biblical citation, give the version you're using (*New Revised Standard Version, New International Version,* etc.) In your subsequent in-text citations from the same text, you don't need to repeat the version.

- Joseph's interpretation of Pharaoh's dream as meaning "Seven years of great abundance" and "seven years of famine" was a pivotal event affecting Joseph's destiny (<u>The Holy Bible: New International Version</u>, Gen. 41.29-30).

When using MLA style, separate Bible chapters from verses with a period. While a colon is more commonly used today for this purpose, the sixth edition of the *MLA Handbook* permits only the use of the period. You might check with your instructor to see which punctuation you need to use.

- Paul's letter to the Galatians declaring that in Christianity there is "Neither Jew nor Greek, slave nor free, male nor female" was a revolutionary statement of equality for his time (Gal. 3.28).

Biblical citations in the form shown above are valid for Old and New Testament verses. MLA does not differentiate between the two. When citing from the Old Testament book of Psalms, each individual psalm is referred to in the singular form. Thus, we have Psalm 121, not Psalms 121.

- In this time of global strife and political confusion, one can find solace in many different ways. Some find comfort in religion, such as the psalmist of the Old Testament did when he looked upon the mountains knowing that all help was a gift of the Lord (Ps. 121.1-2).

15. An Electronic Source with a Name or Title and Page Numbers—MLA

The principles that govern in-text citations of electronic sources are exactly the same as the ones that apply to books, articles, letters, interviews, or any other information source. When an electronically accessed source identifies its author, use the author's name for in-text citations. If no author is named, use the title of the source. When an electronic source has page numbers, use them exactly as you would the page numbers of a print source.

16. An Electronic Source with Paragraph, Screen, or Section Numbers—MLA

When an electronic source has numbered paragraphs, screens, or sections instead of page numbers, use them for in-text citations as you would page numbers, with these differences: (1) Use a comma followed by one space after the name or title; (2) use the abbreviation *par.* for a reference to one paragraph or *pars.* for a reference to more than one paragraph followed by the paragraph number(s); (3) use *screen* or *screens*; and (4) use *sec.* or *secs.* for section(s).

- Coleman worried that psychoanalysis might destroy his musical creativity (Francis, pars. 3-7).

- The renovation cost $25 million, according to Conklin (screen 5).

17. An Electronic Source without Page or Other Numbers—MLA

Many online sources do not number pages, paragraphs, screens, or sections.

- From March to April in 2000, violations of this important environmental regulation increased 123 percent (Procope).

28c What are MLA guidelines for content or bibliographic notes?

In MLA style, footnotes or endnotes serve two specific purposes: (1) You can use them for commentary that does not fit into your paper but is still worth relating, and (2) you can use them for extensive bibliographic information that would intrude if you were to include it in your text. See 30a for advice about formatting notes.

TEXT OF PAPER

- Eudora Welty's literary biography, One Writer's Beginnings, shows us how both the inner world of self and the outer world of family and place form a writer's imagination.[1]

COMMENTARY ENDNOTE

- [1] Welty, who valued her privacy, resisted investigation of her life. However, at the age of 74, she chose to present her own autobiographical reflections in a series of lectures at Harvard University.

TEXT OF PAPER

- Barbara Randolph believes that enthusiasm is contagious (65).[1] Many psychologists have found that panic, fear, and rage spread more quickly in crowds than positive emotions do, however.

BIBLIOGRAPHIC ENDNOTE

- [1] Others agree with Randolph. See Thurman 21, 84, 155; Kelley 421-25; and Brookes 65-76.

29 MLA WORKS CITED LIST

In MLA documentation, the Works Cited list includes only the sources from which you quote or paraphrase or summarize. Never include sources that you consulted but don't refer to in the paper. Box 40 gives general information about a Works Cited list. The rest of this chapter gives models of many specific kinds of Works Cited entries.

29a What are MLA guidelines for a Works Cited list?

BOX 40

 Guidelines for an MLA-style Works Cited list

TITLE
Works Cited

PLACEMENT OF LIST
Start a new page numbered sequentially with the rest of the paper, after Notes pages, if any.

CONTENTS AND FORMAT
Include all sources quoted from, paraphrased, or summarized in your paper. Start each entry on a new line and at the regular left margin. If the entry uses more than one line, indent the second and all other lines

CONTINUED ⟶

BOX 40

 Guidelines for an MLA-style Works Cited list *(continued)*

five spaces (or one-half inch) from the left margin. Double-space all lines.

SPACING AFTER PUNCTUATION

Computer type fonts have influenced many users of MLA style to leave one space rather than two spaces after punctuation at the ends of sentences. The *MLA Handbook* uses one space, as does this book. Either style is acceptable, although current practice tends strongly toward one space. Use whichever style your instructor prefers. Always put only one space after a comma or a colon.

ARRANGEMENT OF ENTRIES

Alphabetize by author's last name. If no author is named, alphabetize by the title's first significant word (*not* A, An, *or* The).

AUTHORS' NAMES

Use first names and middle names or middle initials, if any, as given in the source. Do not reduce to initials any name that is given in full. For one author or the first-named author in multiauthor works, give the last name first. Use the word *and* with two or more authors. List multiple authors in the order given in the source. Use a comma between the first author's last and first names and after each complete author name except the last, which ends with a period. After the last author name, use a period: Fein, Ethel Andrea, Bert Griggs, and Delaware Rogash.

   Include *Jr., Sr., II, III,* but no other titles and degrees before or after a name. For example, an entry for a work by Edward Meep III, M.D., and Sir Feeney Bolton would start like this: Meep Edward, III, and Feeney Bolton.

CAPITALIZATION OF TITLES

Capitalize all major words in titles.

SPECIAL TREATMENT OF TITLES

Use quotation marks around titles of shorter works (poems, short stories, essays, articles). The *MLA Handbook for Writers of Research Papers* (6th ed., 2003) states that although computers can create italic type, underlined roman type in student papers may be more exact. Check which style your instructor prefers.

   Underline titles of longer works (books, names of newspapers or journals containing cited articles). For underlining, use an unbroken

CONTINUED →

BOX 40

 Guidelines for an MLA-style Works Cited list *(continued)*

line like this (unless your software underlines only with a broken line like this).

When a book title includes the title of another work that is usually underlined (such as a novel, play, or long poem), the preferred MLA style is not to underline the incorporated title: *Decoding* Jane Eyre. For a second style MLA accepts, see item 20, p. 198.

If the incorporated title is usually enclosed in quotation marks (such as a short story or short poem), keep the quotation marks and underline the complete title of the book (do not underline the period): Theme and Form in "I Shall Laugh Purely." Drop *A, An,* or *The* as the first word of a periodical title.

PLACE OF PUBLICATION

If several cities are listed for the place of publication, give only the first. For an unfamiliar city outside the United States, include an abbreviated country name or an abbreviated Canadian province name.

PUBLISHER

Use shortened names as long as they are clear: *Prentice* for *Prentice Hall, Simon* for *Simon & Schuster.* For university presses, use the capital letters *U* and *P* (without periods): Oxford UP; U of Chicago P.

PUBLICATION MONTH ABBREVIATIONS

Abbreviate all publication months except *May, June,* and *July.* Use the first three letters followed by a period (see any standard dictionary: Dec., Feb.)

PARAGRAPH AND SCREEN NUMBERS IN ELECTRONIC SOURCES

For electronic sources that number paragraphs instead of pages, at the end of the publication information give the total number of paragraphs followed by the abbreviation *pars.*: 77 pars. If screens are numbered, give the total number of screens as the final information in the entry. For in-text citations, use paragraph and screen numbers for reference as you use page numbers.

PAGE RANGES

Give the page range—the starting page number and the ending page number, connected by a hyphen—of any paginated electronic source and any paginated print source that is part of a longer work (for example, a chapter in a book, an article in a journal). A range indicates that

CONTINUED →

BOX 40

 Guidelines for an MLA-style Works Cited list *(continued)*

the cited work is on those pages and all pages in between. If that is not the case, use the style shown next for discontinuous pages. In either case, use numerals only, without the word *page* or *pages* or the abbreviation *p.* or *pp.*

Use the full second number through 99. Above that, use only the last two digits for the second number unless it would be unclear: *103–04* is clear, but *567–602* requires full numbers.

DISCONTINUOUS PAGES
Use the starting page number followed by a plus sign (+): 32+.

WORKS CITED ENTRIES: BOOKS
Citations for books have three main parts: author, title, and publication information (place of publication, publisher, and date of publication).

AUTHOR   TITLE   PUBLICATION INFORMATION
Didion, Joan. <u>Salvador</u>. New York: Simon, 1983.

WORKS CITED ENTRIES: PRINT ARTICLES
Citations for periodical articles contain three major parts: author, title of article, and publication information (usually periodical title, volume number, year of publication, and page range).

AUTHOR   ARTICLE TITLE
Shuter, Robert. "A Field Study of Nonverbal Communication in Germany, Italy,

                                    JOURNAL TITLE   PUBLICATION INFORMATION
and the United States." <u>Communication Monographs</u> 44 (1977): 298-305.

ARTICLE TITLE   JOURNAL TITLE   PUBLICATION INFORMATION
"A Start." <u>New Republic</u> 2 May 1994: 7+.

WORKS CITED ENTRIES: ONLINE SOURCES
To document sources reached by entering a URL or Internet address (including World Wide Web, FTP, and Gopher sites), list as much of the following information as you can find: author, title, publication information about a print version if there is one, publication information about the online source, the date you accessed the material, and the

CONTINUED →

BOX 40

Guidelines for an MLA-style Works Cited list *(continued)*

URL (electronic address). For these sources, the URL is required in the Works Cited entry, enclosed in angle brackets <like these>, after the access date and before the period at the end of the entry. Here's an entry for an article in a scientific news journal that appears only on the Web.

ARTICLE
AUTHOR | ARTICLE TITLE

Lewis, Ricki. "Chronobiology Researchers Say Their Field's Time Has Come."

PUBLICATION | PUBLICATION | ACCESS
TITLE | INFORMATION | DATE

Scientist | 9.24 (1995):14. | 02 Sep. 2002

URL

<http://www.the-scientist.library.upenn.edu/yr1995/dec/chrono_951211.html>.

WORKS CITED ENTRIES: PORTABLE AND ONLINE SOURCES WITHOUT URLS

Citations for electronic sources that do not have URLs contain at least six major parts: author, publication information, title of database, publication medium, name of vendor or computer service, and electronic publication date (add access date if different). Electronic versions of sources that also appear in print start with information about the print version. Here is an entry for a journal article accessed through a computer service; it also has a print version. This entry includes a keyword (see item 51, p. 204).

PUBLICATION | ELECTRONIC
ARTICLE | TITLE OF | INFORMATION FOR | PUBLICATION | ONLINE
TITLE | PRINT JOURNAL | PRINT JOURNAL | MEDIUM | SERVICE

"A Start." New Republic (2 May 1994): n. pag. Online. America Online.

ACCESS DATE | KEYWORD

21 Apr. 2002. Keyword: new republic.

Here is an entry for an article from a CD-ROM encyclopedia.

ARTICLE
AUTHOR | ARTICLE TITLE | CD-ROM TITLE

Regan, Robert. "Poe, Edgar Allan." Academic American Encyclopedia.

ELECTRONIC
PUBLICATION MEDIUM | CD-ROM PUBLICATION INFORMATION

CD-ROM. | Danbury, CT: Grolier Electronic Publishing. 1993.

29b What are MLA guidelines for sources in a Works Cited list?

The directory below corresponds to the numbered examples that follow it. Not every possible documentation model is here. You may find that you have to combine features of models to document a particular source. You will also find information in the *MLA Handbook for Writers of Research Papers* (6th edition, 2003), by Joseph Gibaldi, and at <http://www.mla.org/style/style_index.asp?mode=section>.

Directory—MLA Style

PRINT SOURCES

PRINT SOURCES

1. Book by One Author—MLA

Welty, Eudora. One Writer's Beginnings. Cambridge: Harvard UP, 1984.

2. Book by Two or Three Authors—MLA

Leghorn, Lisa, and Katherine Parker. Woman's Worth. Boston: Routledge, 1981.

Kelly, Alfred H., Winfred A. Harbison, and Herman Belz. The American Constitution: Its Origins and Development. New York: Norton, 1983.

3. Book by More Than Three Authors—MLA

Moore, Mark H., et al. Dangerous Offenders: The Elusive Target of Justice. Cambridge: Harvard UP, 1984.

Give only the first author's name, followed by a comma and the phrase *et al.* ("and others"), or list all names in full in the order in which they appear on the title page.

4. Two or More Works by the Same Author(s)—MLA

Gardner, Howard. <u>Intelligence Reframed: Multiple Intelligences for the 21st Century</u>. New York: Basic, 1999.

---. <u>Multiple Intelligences: The Theory in Practice</u>. New York: Basic, 1993.

Give author name(s) in the first entry only. In the second and subsequent entries, use three hyphens and a period to stand for exactly the same name(s). If the person served as editor or translator, put a comma and the appropriate abbreviation (*ed.* or *trans.*) following the three hyphens. Arrange the works in alphabetical (not chronological) order according to book title, ignoring labels such as *ed.* or *trans.*

5. Book by Group or Corporate Author—MLA

American Psychological Association. <u>Publication Manual of the American Psychological Association</u>. 5th ed. Washington: APA, 2001.

Cite the full name of the corporate author first. When a corporate author is also the publisher, use a shortened form of the corporate name at the publisher position.

6. Book with No Author Named—MLA

<u>The Chicago Manual of Style</u>. 14th ed. Chicago: U of Chicago P, 1993.

If there is no author's name on the title page, begin the citation with the title. Alphabetize the entry according to the first significant word of the title (*Chicago*, not *The*).

7. Book with an Author and an Editor—MLA

If your paper refers to the work of the book's author, put the author's name first. If your paper refers to the work of the editor, put the editor's name first.

Brontë, Emily. <u>Wuthering Heights</u>. Ed. David Daiches. London: Penguin, 1985.

Daiches, David, ed. <u>Wuthering Heights</u>. By Emily Brontë. London: Penguin, 1985.

8. Translation—MLA

Kundera, Milan. <u>The Unbearable Lightness of Being</u>. Trans. Michael Henry Heim. New York: HarperPerennial, 1999.

9. Work in Several Volumes or Parts—MLA

Jones, Ernest. <u>The Last Phase</u>. New York: Basic, 1957. Vol. 3 of <u>The Life and Work of Sigmund Freud</u>. 3 vols.

Randall, John Herman, Jr. The Career of Philosophy. Vol. 1. New York: Columbia UP, 1962. 2 vols.

If you are citing only one volume, put the volume number before the publication information. If you wish, you can give the total number of volumes at the end of the entry.

MLA recommends using arabic numerals, even if the source uses roman numerals (*Vol. 6* for *Vol. VI*).

10. One Selection from an Anthology or an Edited Book—MLA

Galarza, Ernest. "The Roots of Migration." Aztlan: An Anthology of Mexican American Literature. Ed. Luis Valdez and Stan Steiner. New York: Knopf, 1972. 127-32.

Give the author and title of the selection first and then the full title of the anthology. Information about the editor starts with *Ed.* (for "Edited by"), so do not use *Eds.* when there is more than one editor. Give the name(s) of the editor(s) in normal order rather than reversing first and last names.

11. More Than One Selection from the Same Anthology or Edited Book—MLA

Gilbert, Sandra M., and Susan Gubar, eds. The Norton Anthology of Literature by Women. New York: Norton, 1985.

Kingston, Maxine Hong. "No Name Woman." Gilbert and Gubar 2337-47.

Welty, Eudora. "The Wild Net." Gilbert and Gubar 2544-61.

If you cite more than one selection from the same anthology, you can list the anthology as a separate entry with all the publication information. Then list each selection from the anthology by author and title of the selection, but give only the name of the editor(s) of the anthology and the page number(s) of the selection. Here, *ed.* stands for "editor," so use *eds.* if more than one editor is named.

12. Signed Article in a Reference Book—MLA

Burnbam, John C. "Freud, Sigmund." The Encyclopedia of Psychiatry, Psychology, and Psychoanalysis. Ed. Benjamin B. Wolman. New York: Holt, 1996.

If the articles in the book are alphabetically arranged, you do not need to give volume and page numbers.

13. Unsigned Article in a Reference Book—MLA

"Ireland." Encyclopaedia Britannica. 1998 ed.

If you are citing a widely used reference work, do not give full publication information. Instead, give only the edition and year of publication.

14. Second or Subsequent Edition—MLA

Gibaldi, Joseph. MLA Handbook for Writers of Research Papers. 6th ed. New
    York: MLA, 2003.

If a book is not a first edition, the edition number is on the title page. Place the abbreviated information (2nd ed., 3rd ed., etc.) between the title and the publication information. Give only the latest copyright date for the edition you are using.

15. Anthology or Edited Book—MLA

Valdez, Luis, and Stan Steiner, eds. Aztlan: An Anthology of Mexican American
    Literature. New York: Knopf, 1972.

Here, *ed.* stands for "editor," so use *eds.* when more than one editor is named; also see items 10 and 11.

16. Introduction, Preface, Foreword, or Afterword—MLA

Angeli, Primo. Foreword. Shopping Bag Design 2: Creative Promotional
    Graphics. By Judi Radice. New York: Library of Applied Design-PBC
    International, 1991. 8.

Give first the name of the writer of the part you are citing, then the name of the cited part, capitalized but not underlined or in quotation marks. After the book title, put *By* and the book author's full name, if different from the writer of the cited material. If the writer of the cited material is the same as the book author, use only the last name after *By*. After the publication information, give inclusive page numbers for the cited part, using roman or arabic numerals as the source does.

Fox-Genovese, Elizabeth. "Mothers and Daughters: The Ties That Bind."
    Foreword. Southern Mothers. Ed. Nagueyalti Warren and Sally Wolff.
    Baton Rouge: Louisiana State UP, 1999.

But if the introduction, preface, foreword, or afterword has a title, include that title in the citation, placing it before the section name.

17. Unpublished Dissertation or Essay—MLA

Geissinger, Shirley Burry. "Openness versus Secrecy in Adoptive Parenthood."
    Diss. U of North Carolina at Greensboro, 1984.

State the author's name first, then the title in quotation marks (not underlined), then a descriptive label (such as *Diss.* or *Unpublished essay*), then the degree-granting institution (for dissertations), and finally the date.

18. Republished Book—MLA

Hurston, Zora Neale. Their Eyes Were Watching God. 1937. Urbana: U of Illinois P, 1978.

Republishing information can be found on the copyright page. Give the date of the original version before the publication information for the version you are citing.

19. Book in a Series—MLA

Goldman, Dorothy J. Women Writers and World War I. Literature and Society Ser. New York: Macmillan, 1995.

Mukherjee, Meenakshi. Jane Austen. Women Writers Ser. New York: St. Martin's, 1991.

20. Book with a Title within a Title—MLA

The MLA recognizes two distinct styles for handling normally independent titles when they appear within an underlined title. In the MLA's preferred style, the embedded title should not be underlined or set within quotation marks:

Lumiansky, Robert M., and Herschel Baker, eds. Critical Approaches to Six Major English Works: Beowulf Through Paradise Lost. Philadelphia: U of Pennsylvania P, 1968.

However, the MLA now accepts a second style for handling such embedded titles. In this alternative style, the normally independent titles should be set within quotation marks, and they should be underlined:

Lumiansky, Robert M., and Herschel Baker, eds. Critical Approaches to Six Major English Works: "Beowulf" Through "Paradise Lost." Philadelphia: U of Pennsylvania P, 1968.

Use whichever style your instructor prefers.

21. The Bible—MLA

The Holy Bible: New International Version. New York: Harper, 1983.

Holy Bible: New Testament. Grand Rapids: Zondervan, 2002.

22. Government Publication—MLA

United States. Cong. House. Subcommittee on Technology of the Committee on
    Science. Y2K: What Every Consumer Should Know to Prepare for the Year
    2000 Problem. Washington: GPO, 1998.

United States. Cong. Senate. Special Committee on Aging. The Risk of
    Malnutrition in Nursing Homes. Washington: GPO, 1998.

For government publications that name no author, start with the name
of the government or government body. Then name the government
agency. *GPO* is a standard abbreviation for *Government Printing Office*,
the publisher of most U.S. government publications.

23. Published Proceedings of a Conference—MLA

Harris, Diana, and Laurie Nelson-Heern, eds. Proceedings of NECC 1981:
    National Education Computing Conference. 17-19 June 1981. Iowa City:
    Weeg Computing Center, U of Iowa, 1981.

24. Signed Article from a Daily Newspaper—MLA

Wyatt, Edward. "A High School Without a Home." New York Times 3 Dec. 1999:
    B1+.

"Fire Delays School Election." Patriot Ledger [Quincy, MA] 14 June 1994: A1.

Omit *A* or *The* as the first word in a newspaper title. If the city of publication is not part of the title, put it in square brackets after the title,
not underlined. Give the day, month, and year of the issue. If sections
are designated, give the section letter as well as the page number. If an
article runs on nonconsecutive pages, give the starting page number
followed by a plus sign (for example, *23+* for an article that starts on p.
23 and continues on p. 42).

25. Unsigned Article from a Daily Newspaper—MLA

"A Crusade to Revitalize the City Opera." New York Times 25 Jan. 2001, late ed.: B6.

26. Editorial, Letter to the Editor, or Review—MLA

Didion, Joan. "The Day Was Hot and Still. . . ." Rev. of Dutch: A Memoir of Ronald
    Reagan, by Edmund Morris. New York Review of Books 4 Nov. 1999: 4-6.

"Mr. Gorbachev's Role." Editorial. New York Times 10 Nov. 1999: A22.

Wolfe, Cheryl. Letter. Newsweek 22 Nov. 1999: 22.

27. Signed Article from a Weekly or Biweekly Periodical—MLA

Greenfield, Karl Taro. "Giving Away the E-Store." Time 22 Nov. 1999: 58-60.

28. Signed Article in a Monthly or Bimonthly Periodical—MLA

Bonner, John Tyler. "The Evolution of Evolution." Natural History May 1999: 20-21.

29. Unsigned Article from a Weekly, Biweekly, Monthly, or Bimonthly Periodical—MLA

"A Salute to Everyday Heroes." Time 10 July 1989: 46+.

30. Article from a Collection of Reprinted Articles—MLA

Brumberg, Abraham. "Russia After Perestroika." New York Review of Books 27 June 1991: 53-62. Rpt. in Russian and Soviet History. Ed. Alexander Dallin. Vol. 14 of The Gorbachev Era. New York: Garland, 1992. 300-20.

31. Article from a SIRS Collection of Reprinted Articles—MLA

Curver, Phillip C. "Lighting in the 21st Century." Futurist Jan./Feb. 1989: 29-34. Ed. Eleanor Goldstein. Vol. 4. Boca Raton: SIRS, 1990. Art. 84.

Give the citation for the original publication first, followed by the citation for the collection.

32. Article in a Journal with Continuous Pagination—MLA

Tyson, Phyllis. "The Psychology of Women." Journal of the American Psychoanalytic Association 46 (1998): 361-64.

(If the first issue of a journal with continuous pagination ends on p. 228, the second issue starts with p. 229.) Give only the volume number before the year. Use arabic numerals for all numbers.

33. Article in a Journal That Pages Each Issue Separately—MLA

Hogarty, Thomas F. "Gasoline: Still Powering Cars in 2050?" Futurist 33.3 (1999): 51-55.

When each issue begins with page 1, give both the volume number (33) and the issue number (3), separated by a period.

34. Abstract from a Collection of Abstracts—MLA

To cite an abstract, first give information for the full work: the author's name, the title of the article, and publication information about the full article. If a reader could not know that the cited material is an abstract, write the word *Abstract,* not underlined, followed by a period. Give publication information about the collection of abstracts. For abstracts identified by item numbers rather than page numbers, use the word *item* before the item number.

Marcus, Hazel R., and Shinobu Kitayamo. "Culture and the Self: Implications for Cognition, Emotion, and Motivation." Psychological Review 88 (1991): 224–53. Psychological Abstracts 78 (1991): item 23878.

35. Published and Unpublished Letters—MLA

Sand, George. Letter to her mother. 31 May 1831. Letters Home: Celebrated Authors Write to Their Mothers. Ed. Reid Sherline. New York: Timkin, 1993. 17-20.

Brown, Theodore. Letter to the author. 7 Jan. 2000.

36. Map or Chart—MLA

The Caribbean and South America. Map. Falls Church: AAA, 1992.

NONPRINT SOURCES
37. Interview—MLA

Friedman, Randi. Telephone interview. 30 June 1997.

For a face-to-face interview, use *Personal interview* in place of *Telephone interview.*

38. Lecture, Speech, or Address—MLA

Kennedy, John Fitzgerald. Address. Greater Houston Ministerial Assn. Houston. 12 Sept. 1960.

39. Film, Videotape, or DVD—MLA

Shakespeare in Love. Screenplay by Marc Norman and Tom Stoppard. Dir. John Maddon. Prod. David Parfitt, Donna Gigliotta, Harvey Weinstein, Edward Zwick, and Mark Norman. Perf. Gwyneth Paltrow, Joseph Fiennes, and Judi Dench. Videocassette. Miramax/Universal, 1999.

It Happened One Night. Screenplay by Robert Riskin. Dir. and prod. Frank Capra. Perf. Clark Gable and Claudette Colbert. 1934. Videocassette. Columbia, 1999.

Give the title first, and include the director, the distributor, and the year. For older films that were subsequently released on videocassettes or DVDs provide the original release date of the movie *before* the name of the distributor. Other information (writer, producer, major actors) is optional but helpful. Put first names first.

40. Musical Recording—MLA

Smetana, Bedrich. My Country. Cond. Karel Anserl. Czech Philharmonic Orch.
    LP. Vanguard, 1975.

Springsteen, Bruce. "Local Hero." Lucky Town. Columbia, 1992.

Put first the name most relevant to what you discuss in your paper (performer, conductor, the work performed, etc.). Include the recording's title, the medium for any recording other than a CD (e.g., *LP, Audiocassette*), the name of the issuer (e.g., *Vanguard*), and the year.

41. Live Performance—MLA

Via Dolorosa. By David Hare. Dir. Steven Daldry. Perf. David Hare. Lincoln
    Center Theater, New York. 11 Apr. 1999.

42. Work of Art, Photograph, or Musical Composition—MLA

Cassatt, Mary. La Toilette. Art Institute of Chicago.

Mydans, Carl. General Douglas MacArthur Landing at Luzon, 1945. Soho Triad
    Fine Art Gallery, New York. 21 Oct.-28 Nov. 1999.

Schubert, Franz. Symphony no. 8 in B minor.

Schubert, Franz. Unfinished Symphony.

Do not underline or put in quotation marks music identified only by form, number, and key, but do underline any work that has a title, such as an opera, ballet, or a named symphony.

43. Radio or Television Program—MLA

Not for Ourselves Alone: The Story of Elizabeth Cady Stanton and Susan B.
    Anthony. Writ. Ken Burns. Perf. Julie Harris, Ronnie Gilbert, and Sally
    Kellerman. Prod. Paul Barnes and Ken Burns. PBS. WNET, New York.
    8 Nov. 1999.

Include at least the title of the program (underlined), the network, the local station and its city, and the date(s) of the broadcast. For a series, also supply the title of the specific episode (in quotation marks) before the title of the program (underlined) and the title of the series (neither underlined nor in quotation marks).

44. Microfiche Collection of Articles—MLA

Wenzell, Ron. "Businesses Prepare for a More Diverse Work Force." St. Louis Post
  Dispatch 3 Feb. 1990. NewsBank: Employment 27 (1990): fiche 2, grid D12.

PORTABLE ELECTRONIC SOURCES

The following basic blocks of information are used to document a
portable electronic source (such as a CD-ROM or a diskette) in MLA
style. A period ends each block.

1. Documentation information about the print version, if any. (Many
   sources accessed electronically also exist in published print versions. Others exist only in electronic form.) Follow the models in directory items 1–36 above for print sources. You may not find all the
   details about a print version in an electronic version, but provide
   as much information as you can. Information about a print version usually is given at the beginning or the end of an electronic
   document.

2. Author (if any) and title (underlined) of the electronic source or
   database. If there is no print version, start your Works Cited entry
   with this information.

3. Electronic medium, such as *CD-ROM, Diskette,* or *Magnetic tape.*

4. Name of the producer.

5. Publication date.

45. CD-ROM Database: Abstract with a Print Version—MLA

Marcus, Hazel R., and Shinobu Kitayamo. "Culture and the Self: Implications
  for Cognition, Emotion, and Motivation." Psychological Abstracts 78
  (1991): item 23878. PsycLIT. CD-ROM. SilverPlatter. Sept. 1991.

All the information through *item 23878* is for the print version of this
source. The volume number is 78, and the abstract's number is 23878.
All the information from *PsycLIT* to the end of the entry is for the electronic version of the source. *PsycLIT* is the name of the CD-ROM database, and *SilverPlatter* is the name of the producer of the CD-ROM. The
CD-ROM was issued in September 1991.

46. CD-ROM: Article from a Periodical with a Print Version—MLA

"The Price Is Right." Time. 20 Jan. 1992: 38. Time Man of the Year. CD-ROM. New
  York: Compact, 1993.

Information for the print version ends with the article's page number,
38. The title of the CD-ROM is *Time Man of the Year,* its producer is the

publisher Compact, and its copyright year is 1993. Both the title of the print publication and the title of the CD-ROM are underlined.

47. CD-ROM: Selection from a Book with a Print Version—MLA

"Prehistoric Humans: Earliest Homo sapiens." The Guinness Book of Records
1994. London: Guinness Publishing, Ltd., 1994. The Guinness Multimedia
Disk of Records. CD-ROM. Version 2.0. Danbury: Grolier Electronic
Publishing, 1994.

Version 2.0 signals that this CD-ROM is updated periodically; the producer changes version numbers rather than giving update dates.

48. CD-ROM: Material with No Print Version—MLA

"Spanish Dance." Encarta 2000. CD-ROM. Redmond: Microsoft, 1999.

Encarta 2000 is a CD-ROM encyclopedia with no print version. "Spanish Dance" is the title of an article in *Encarta 2000*.

49. Work in More Than One Publication Medium—MLA

Clarke, David James. Novell's CNE Study Guide. Book. Network Support
Encyclopedia. CD-ROM. Alameda: Sybex, 1994.

This book and CD-ROM come together. Each has its own title, but the publication information—*Alameda: Sybex, 1994*—applies to both.

ONLINE SOURCES: NO URL

Online sources fall into two categories: (1) those you access through an online service, such as America Online or at a library; and (2) those you access by entering a specific URL (Internet address). For source material reached through an online service, give the name of the service, and if you used a keyword, give it after the access date. Items 50–52 show how to document such sources.

50. Online Service Access: Abstract with a Print Version—MLA

Bolam, Bruce and Judith Sixsmith. "An Exploratory Study of the Perceptions
and Experiences of Further Education Amongst Young Long-term
Unemployed." Journal of Community and Applied Social Psychology 12
(2002). PsychINFO. 12 Nov. 2002.

This entry notes PsychINFO, the online database used to obtain this abstract. 12 Nov. 2002 is the date that the abstract was accessed.

51. Online Service Access: Material with No Print Version—MLA

Siemens, Raymond G. "A New Computer-assisted Literary Criticism?" Computers and the Humanities 36 (Aug. 2002). America Online. 12 Nov. 2002.

52. Online Service Access with a Keyword: Article from a Periodical with a Print Version—MLA

Kapor, Mitchell, and Jerry Berman. "A Superhighway Through the Wasteland?"
<u>New York Times</u> 24 Nov. 1993: Op-ed page. <u>New York Times Online</u>.
America Online. 5 May 1995. Keyword: nytimes.

Information applying to the print version of this article in the *New York Times* ends with *Op-ed page,* and information about the online version starts with the title of the database, *New York Times Online.* America Online is the service through which the database was accessed, and 5 May 1995 is the access date. The keyword *nytimes* was used to access *New York Times Online,* as noted after the access date.

53. Online Service Access Showing a Path—MLA

When you access a source by choosing a series of keywords, menus, or topics, end the entry with the "path" of words you used. Use semicolons between items in the path, and put a period at the end.

Futrelle, David. "A Smashing Success." <u>Money.com</u> 23 Dec. 1999. America Online. 26 Dec. 1999. Path: Personal Finance; Business News; Business Publications; Money.com.

54. Online Service Access at a Library—MLA

For a source accessed through a library's online service, first give information about the source. Then give the name of the service, the name of the library, and the access date. Give the URL of the online service's home page, if you know it, after the access date. Use angle brackets to enclose this URL, and put a period after the closing bracket.

Dutton, Gail. "Greener Pigs." <u>Popular Science</u> Aug. 1999: 38-39. ProQuest Direct. Public Lib., Teaneck. 7 Dec. 1999 <http://proquest.umi.com>.

URL-ACCESSED ONLINE SOURCES

In this section, you will find models for online sources accessed when you enter a URL or specific Internet address. These guidelines cover Web sites, FTP and Gopher sites, listservs, discussion groups, and other online sources. For such sources, provide as much of the following information as you can.

1. The author's name, if given.

2. In quotation marks, the title of a short work (poem, short story, essay, article, posted message); or underlined, the title of a book.

3. The underlined title of a scholarly project or reference database. (If the site has no title, describe it: e.g., *Home page.*)

4. The name of an editor, translator, or compiler, if any, with an abbreviation such as *Ed., Trans.,* or *Comp.* before the name. If there's more than one such person, don't add an *s.*

5. The date of electronic publication (including a version number, if any), or posting, or the most recent update.

6. The name of a sponsoring organization, if any.

7. The date you accessed the material.

8. The URL in angle brackets (< >), with a period after the closing bracket.

55. URL Access: Book—MLA

Chopin, Kate. The Awakening. 1899. 13 Nov. 2002 <http://www.pbs.org/
    katechopin/library/awakening>.

56. URL Access: Book in a Scholarly Project—MLA

Herodotus. The History of Herodotus. Trans. George Rawlinson. The Internet
    Classics Archive. Ed. Daniel C. Stevenson. 11 Jan. 1998. Massachusetts
    Institute of Technology. 4 Dec. 1999 <http://classics.mit.edu/Herodotus/
    history.sum.html>.

57. URL Access: Government-Published Books—MLA

United States. Cong. Research Service. Space Stations. By Marcia S. Smith.
    12 Dec. 1996. 13 Nov. 2002 <http://fas.org/spp/civil/crs/93-017.htm>.

United States. Dept. of Justice. Natl. Inst. of Justice. Comparing the Criminal
    Behavior of Youth Gangs and At-Risk Youths. By C. Ronald Hoff. Oct.
    1998. 13 Nov. 2002 <http://www.ncjrs.org/txtfiles/172852.txt>.

For government publications that name no author, start with the name of the government or government body, and then name the government agency. For a government text, the title is followed by the writer of the publication, if available.

58. URL Access: Articles in Online Periodicals—MLA

Didion, Joan. "The Day Was Hot and Still. . . ." Rev. of Dutch: A Memoir of Ronald
    Reagan, by Edmund Morris. New York Review of Books 4 Nov. 1999. 5 Dec.
    1999 <http://nybooks.com/nyrev/www.archdisplay.cgi?19991104004R>.

Gold, David. "Ulysses: A Case Study in the Problems of Hypertextualization of
    Complex Documents." Computers, Writing, Rhetoric and Literature 3.1
    (1997): 37 pars. 4 Dec. 1999 <http://www.cwrl.utexas.edu/~cwrl/v3n1/dgold/
    title.htm>.

Keegan, Paul. "Culture Quake." <u>Mother Jones</u> Nov.-Dec. 1999. 13 Nov. 2002
  <http://www.mojones.com/mother_jones/ND99/quake.html>.

Eisenberg, Anne. "The Kind of Noise That Keeps a Body on Balance." <u>New York
  Times on the Web</u> 13 Nov. 2002. 13 Nov. 2002 <http://www.nytimes.com/
  2002/11/14/technology/circuits/14next.html>.

When you cite online periodicals, give the following information.

1. The author's name, if given.

2. In quotation marks, the title of the article or editorial.

3. A description of the cited material as a review, an editorial, or a letter unless the title gives that information.

4. The underlined title of the periodical.

5. Volume and issue numbers, if any.

6. The date of publication.

7. The total number of pages, paragraphs, or other numbered sections,
   if any.

8. The date you accessed the material.

9. The URL in angle brackets (< >), with a period after the closing
   bracket.

59. URL Access: Professional Home Page—MLA

<u>Project Zero</u>. Home page. Harvard Graduate School of Education. 13 Nov. 2002
  <http://pzweb.harvard.edu/default.htm>.

60. URL Access: Personal Home Page—MLA

Roche, Jessica. Home page. June 2001. 13 Nov. 2002 <http://www.lehigh.edu/
  ~ineng/jbr2/jbr2-personalpage.html>.

For home pages, include as much of the following information as you
can find.

1. If available, the name of the person who created or put up the home
   page. If first and last names are given, reverse the order of the first
   author's name.

2. The title, underlined. If there is no title, add the description *Home
   page,* not underlined, followed by a period.

3. For a professional home page, give the name of the sponsoring
   organization.

4. The date you accessed the material.

5. The URL in angle brackets (< >), with a period after the closing
   bracket.

61. URL Access: Government or Institutional Web Site—MLA

Home Education and Private Tutoring. Home page. Pennsylvania Department of Education. 17 Oct. 2002 <http://www.pde.state.pa.us/home_education/site/default.asp>.

62. URL Access: Poem—MLA

Browning, Elizabeth Barrett. "Past and Future." The Women's Studies Database Reading Room. U of Maryland. 17 Oct. 2002 <http://www.mith2.umd.edu/WomensStudies/ReadingRoom/Poetry/>.

63. URL Access: Work of Art—MLA

Van Gogh, Vincent. The Olive Trees, 1889. Museum of Modern Art, New York. 5 Dec. 2001 <http://www.moma.org/docs/collection/paintsculpt/recent/c463.htm>.

64. URL Access: Interview—MLA

Plaxco, Jim. Interview. Planetary Studies Foundation. Oct. 1992. 5 Dec. 2001 <http://www.planets.org/>.

65. URL Access: Film or Film Clip—MLA

Columbus, Chris, dir. Harry Potter and the Sorcerer's Stone. Trailer. Warner Brothers, 2001. 5 Dec. 2001 <http://hollywood.com>.

66. URL Access: Cartoon—MLA

Bell, Darrin. "Rudy Park." Cartoon. New York Times on the Web 5 Dec. 2001. <http://www2.uclick.com/client/nyt/rk/>.

67. URL Access: TV or Radio Program—MLA

Chayes, Sarah. "Concorde." All Things Considered. Natl. Public Radio. 26 July 2000. 7 Dec. 2001 <http://www.npr.com/programs/atc/archives>.

68. URL Access: Academic Department Home Page—MLA

English. Dept. home page. Rutgers U. 26 Feb. 2003 <http://english.rutgers.edu/dmain.htm>.

OTHER ONLINE SOURCES
69. Online Posting—MLA

Woodbury, Chuck. "Free RV Campgrounds." Online posting. 4 Dec. 1999. The RV Home Page Bulletin Board. 13 Nov. 2002 <http://www.rvhome.com/wwwboard/messages/4598.html>.

Be cautious about using online postings as sources. Some postings contain cutting-edge information from experts, but some contain trash. Unfortunately, there is no way to know whether people online are who they claim to be. To cite an online message, give the author name (if any), the title of the message in quotation marks, and then *Online posting*. Give the date of the posting and the name of the bulletin board, if any. Then give the access date and, in angle brackets, the URL.

70. Synchronous Communication—MLA

Bleck, Bradley. Online discussion of "Virtual First Year Composition: Distance
    Education, the Internet, and the World Wide Web." 8 June 1997. DaMOO.
    27 Feb. 1999 <http://DaMOO.csun.edu/CW/brad.html>.

Give the name of the speaker, a title for the event ("Virtual First Year Composition: Distance Education, the Internet, and the World Wide Web"), the forum (DaMOO), date, access date, and URL.

71. E-mail Message—MLA

Thompson, Jim. "Bob Martin's Address." E-mail to June Cain. 11 Nov. 2002.

Start with the name of the person who wrote the e-mail message. Give the title or subject line in quotation marks. Then describe the source (*e-mail*) and identify the recipient. End with the date.

30 A STUDENT'S MLA RESEARCH PAPER

30a What are MLA format guidelines for research papers?

Check whether your instructor has special instructions for the final draft of your research paper. If there are no special instructions, you can use the MLA guidelines here. The student paper in 30b was prepared according to MLA guidelines.

General instructions—MLA

Use 8½ × 11 inch white paper. Double-space throughout, whether the paper is typed or prepared on a computer. Set a 1-inch margin on the left, and leave no less than 1 inch on the right and at the bottom. If you are using a computer, do not justify the type.

Drop down 1/2 inch from the top edge of the paper to the name-and-page-number line described below. Then drop down another 1/2 inch to the first line, whether that is a heading, a title, or a line of the text of your paper. For an example, see page 214.

If you are typing, paragraph indents and indents in Notes and Works Cited are five characters. The indent for a set-off quotation (see p. 211) is ten characters. If you are preparing your paper on a computer, paragraph indents and indents in Notes and Works Cited are 1/2 inch, and the indent for a set-off quotation is 1 inch.

Order of parts—MLA

Use this order for the parts of your paper: body of the paper; endnotes, if any; Works Cited list; attachments, if any (such as questionnaires, data sheets, or any other material your instructor tells you to include). Number all pages consecutively.

Name-and-page-number line for all pages—MLA

Use a name-and-page-number line on every page of your paper. Drop down 1/2 inch from the top edge of the sheet of paper. Type your last name, then a one-character space and the page number. Align the typed line about an inch from the right edge of the paper.

First page—MLA

Use a name-and-page-number line. If your instructor does not require a cover sheet, use a four-line heading at the top of the first page. Drop down 1 inch from the top edge of the paper. Starting each line at the left margin, include the following information.

Your name (first line)

Your instructor's name (second line)

Your course name and section (third line)

The date you hand in your paper (fourth line)

For the submission date, MLA style uses day-month-year form: *26 November 2002.*

On the line below this heading, center the title of your paper. Do not underline the title or enclose it in quotation marks. On the line below the title, start your paper.

⊚ **CAPITALIZATION ALERTS:** (1) Use a capital letter for the first word of your title and the first word of a subtitle, if you use one. Start every NOUN, PRONOUN, VERB, ADVERB, ADJECTIVE, and SUBORDINATING CONJUNC-

TION with a capital letter. Capitalize the last word of your title, no matter what part of speech it is. In a hyphenated compound word (two or more words used together to express one idea), capitalize each word after a hyphen: Father-in-Law. (2) Do not capitalize an article (*a, an, the*) unless one of the preceding capitalization rules applies to it. Do not capitalize any PREPOSITIONS, no matter how many letters they contain. Do not capitalize COORDINATING CONJUNCTIONS. Do not capitalize the word *to* used in an INFINITIVE. ☉

Set-off quotations—MLA

Set off quotations of more than four lines from your words. Start a new line for the quoted words, indenting each line of the double-spaced quotation ten spaces (or 1 inch) from the left margin. Do not enclose the quoted words in quotation marks.

If you are quoting part of a paragraph or one complete paragraph, do not indent the first line of quoted words more than ten spaces. But if you quote more than one paragraph, indent the first line of each paragraph after the first an additional three spaces (thirteen spaces in all).

When the quotation is finished, leave a space after the sentence-ending punctuation, and then give the parenthetical citation. Begin a new line to resume your own words. (For examples of set-off quotations in MLA style, see 54b and Chandra Johnson's paper in 30b.)

Notes—MLA

If you use a note in your paper (28c), try to structure the sentence so that the note number falls at the end. The ideal place for a note number is after the sentence-ending punctuation. Do not leave a space before the number, but raise the number slightly above the line of words, if possible. Leave one space after the note number.

Put your notes on a separate page after the last page of the body of your paper and before the Works Cited list. Use a name-and-page-number line; then drop down 1 inch from the top edge of the paper and center the word *Notes*; do not underline it or put it in quotation marks.

On the next line, start your first note. Indent 5 characters (or 1/2 inch). Raise the note number slightly, if possible. After the number, type one space, and then start the words of your note. Do not indent any lines except the first. Use double spacing for each note and between notes.

Number the notes consecutively throughout the paper, except for notes referring to tables or figures.

Place table or figure notes below the table or illustration. Instead of note numbers, use lowercase letters (*a, b, c*).

Works Cited list—MLA

Starting a new page, type a name-and-page-number line. Then, 1 inch below the top edge of the paper, type the words Works Cited. Do not underline them or put them in quotation marks.

On the next line, start the first entry in your Works Cited list at the left margin. If an entry takes more than one line, indent each line after the first five characters (or 1/2 inch). Use double spacing for each entry and between entries.

30b A Student's MLA research paper

Chandra Johnson, a first-year college student, wrote the following research paper in MLA documentation style for her freshman English course. Her instructor asked students to research a current topic that interested them. Chandra panicked a little at the open-endedness of the assignment, but she followed the suggestions in Chapter 22 to identify a topic. She had always been fascinated by robots in movies and television, so she decided to explore how close their depictions were to reality. Then she narrowed this broad topic to one that focused more on the role of emotions in artificial intelligence.

She began her research by looking in online databases available through her college library. She searched both popular periodicals and more scientific ones. Because she found so much information, she decided to focus on sources published in the past five years. References in some of those articles led her to scholarly books. She wanted to avoid information that was relatively old so that her material would be as up-to-date as possible. New advances in artificial intelligence were being announced almost weekly. At the same time, she decided that she had to establish a reasonable cut-off date for her information.

Chandra preferred to draft both the outline and paper at the same time, using each document to refine the other. Her outline helped her assure a logical flow to her presentation, and her first draft of the paper helped her discover how she could organize her information.

Here is the outline of Chandra's paper, followed by the paper itself.

Outline

I. Introduction

    A. Example from the movie A.I.

    B. Thesis: An unsolved problem is whether computers need emotions for scientists to consider them intelligent.

II. Definitions of intelligence

    A. General definitions

    B. Artificial intelligence (AI)

        1. Qualities of AI

        2. Scientists' opinions of how close we are to AI

        3. Turing test

        4. Chess room argument

III. Types of intelligence

    A. Gardner's eight intelligences

    B. Emotional intelligence

        1. Goleman's research

        2. Damasio's research

IV. Emotion and artificial intelligence

    A. Believers' and doubters' positions on emotion

    B. The role of recognizing and conveying emotions

        1. Children's learning

        2. Applying Disney's techniques to robots

V. Conclusion

    A. The remaining controversy

    B. No emotions in computers any time soon

continued ⟶

Johnson 1   1

2

Use ½-inch top margin,
1-inch bottom and side
margins; double-space
throughout.

Put identifying
information in
upper left
corner; double-
space.

Chandra Johnson

Professor Gregor

English 101

18 November 2002

Center title one
double space
below
identifying
information.

The Role of Emotions in Artificial Intelligence

Start first line of
paper one
double space
below title.

The movie A.I. Artificial Intelligence portrays a future in
which distinguishing robots from peope is almost impossible.
The robots look human and can produce actions that appear to
be human. Still, one important distinction exists: Robots lack
true emotions. In the film, released in 2001, scientists create an
experimental robotic boy who can deeply love the woman who
owns him and can believe that she is his mother. Computer
scientists, psychologists, and philosophers today disagree
whether creating artificial beings like this boy should be the
ultimate goal of research in artificial intelligence. Indeed, an   3
unsolved problem is whether computers need emotion for
scientists to consider them intelligent.

In MLA style,
put author and
page number in
parentheses
when author is
not named in
the sentence.

Defining human intelligence is a major focus of cognitive   4
science, a broad field that studies the mind (Pfeifer 5). Members   5
of this field include psychologists, biologists, linguists, and
computer scientists, among others. Cognitive scientists agree
that human intelligence includes several broad abilities. These
consist of the abilities to think abstractly, to learn, to adapt to
new situations in life, and to profit from experience (7).
Intelligence calls for more than the ability to recall information
or perform set routines. It involves using past knowledge,
intuition, creativity, and experience in new, unfamiliar
situations, and learning from them. It also requires

continued ⟶

(Proportions shown in this paper are adjusted to fit space limitations of this book.
Follow actual dimensions shown in this book and your instructor's directions.)

Commentary

1. 🖳 **COMPUTER TIP:** Following MLA style, Chandra used her name and the page number as a running header throughout the paper. She used the "header" command in her word processing program to automatically insert the proper information on each page. 🖳

2. **Introductory strategy.** Chandra attracts the reader's interest by referring to a recent popular movie. From that specific example, she moves to introducing the topic more broadly. Because the movie *A.I.* gave her the idea for her paper topic, the introduction came fairly easily to her.

3. **Thesis.** The last sentence of Chandra's introductory paragraph is her THESIS STATEMENT. In it she tries to prepare readers for the main message of the paper.

4. 👁 **PROCESS NOTE:** Paragraph 2 begins to define intelligence. In an early draft, Chandra started with attempts to create artificial intelligence in robots. Later she decided that it made more sense to talk generally about intelligence in humans and then discuss computers and robots. 👁

5. **Summarizing a source.** For much of her initial definition of intelligence, Chandra drew on a scholarly book. She decided to summarize concepts from that book rather than paraphrase or quote them. Note that she took care to include page citations.

In MLA style, header has student's last name and page number.

using intuition and creativity (Pfeifer 10). For example, when college student Joshua Vrana, who worked part time in a store, was asked to develop a Web site for the store, he created it from his knowledge of Web design, the store, and its customers. In so doing, he creatively drew upon his knowledge and experience, thereby using all aspects of human intelligence.

6

Cognitive scientists disagree on a definition of artificial intelligence. At one extreme are those who regard it as the ability of a machine to perform every intelligent act that a human can perform. Table 1 lists some of those acts. This is a very high standard. At the other extreme, scientists define artificial intelligence as the ability to perform even a small act that requires human intelligence. For example, the American Association for Artificial Intelligence believes that artificial intelligence already exists in machines as simple as postal machines that can sort handwritten postcards. This is a very low standard.

7

8

Table number, title, and format in MLA style.

Table 1

Some Qualities of Artificial Intelligence

9

Category	Examples
Problem solving	Using informed search methods to solve problems; game playing
Logical behavior	Planning for practical action; acting appropriately for a given situation
Knowledge and reasoning	Using memory; dealing with uncertainty; reasoning using probability; making simple and complex decisions

(continued)

continued ⟶

Commentary

6. **Example from experience.** Chandra decided the point about intuition and creativity would be clearer if she gave an example. She remembered a conversation with her friend Joshua Vrana about a project he had completed at his job, and she realized it would illustrate the point effectively.

7. **Elaborating a key issue from the thesis.** Chandra's topic sentence in this paragraph signals the reader that she is about to explain the disagreement between scientists over the proper measure of artificial intelligence. By starting one sentence with "At one extreme" and another sentence with "At the other extreme," she hoped to contrast and clarify the two positions. She had to write several drafts to state the distinctions clearly and concisely.

8. **Reference to a table.** Although she did not want to interrupt her paragraph, Chandra felt her readers would benefit from a reference to Table 1, which would soon follow.

9. **Table.** Chandra faced a length restriction in this paper, but she needed to present a good deal of information. She decided the most effective way to summarize much of that information would be to include a table. Developing the table also helped her to clarify the ideas it contained.

   As she formatted her paper's final draft, Chandra discovered that the table would not fit on one page. She had two choices: (1) put the table (and any other tables she might create) into an appendix to be placed before her Works Cited list; (2) divide the table between two pages so that it would fall exactly where she wanted her readers to see it. She chose the second option after checking with her instructor.

MLA MLA MLA MLA MLA MLA MLA MLA

Johnson 3

Table 1   *(continued)*

Some Qualities of Artificial Intelligence

Category	Examples
Learning	Learning from observations and experience
Communicating, perceiving, acting	Using language with people; becoming aware of surroundings through the senses; interacting with the environment

Table source note in MLA style.

Source: Adapted from Rolf Pfeifer and Christian Scheier, "Topics in Classical AI," in Understanding Intelligence (Cambridge, MA: MIT P, 2000) 46.

While the dream of creating robots with human   10
intelligence has existed almost a century, scientists disagree how close we have come to realizing that dream. Perhaps the most famous example occurred when computer engineers

In MLA style, put author and page number in parentheses when author is not named in text.

developed IBM's Deep Blue computer, which beat chess grandmaster Garry Kasparov in 1997 (Hayden 46). However, Murray Campbell, one of Deep Blue's creators has conceded that the computer "did not exhibit human qualities and   11
therefore was not 'intelligent' " (qtd. in Stix). Some computer

Square brackets show words added or changed to make a quotation flow.

scientists take a much different position. For example, Hans   12
Moravec believes that "robot computers [will] achieve human intelligence . . . around 2040" (qtd. in Minerd 9). Ray Kurzweil is even more optimistic in that he believes that Moravec's prediction will come true as early as 2029 and that by the end of the twenty-first century, machine-based intelligences will rightfully claim to be human (21).

continued ⟶

Commentary

10. ◉ **PROCESS NOTE:** Chandra revised this paragraph several times because it covers several different opinions (note the number of sources cited in a relatively short space). The example of Deep Blue illustrates efforts to create intelligent computers. The quotation from one of Deep Blue's creators was particularly effective because he takes a position opposite the one we might expect. ◉

11. **Key transition within a paragraph.** Because she was summarizing two very different positions in this paragraph, Chandra needed a strong sentence to signal a contrast between scientists who doubt the possibility of artificial intelligence and those who think we are close to achieving it. In an early draft she had divided this material into two paragraphs, but she later decided it would work better as a single paragraph.

12. **Modified quotation.** To make the quotation from Moravec fit the flow of the sentence, Johnson had to add the word *will*. She enclosed the word in brackets to signal that it was not part of the original quotation. (The original source was written in the hypothetical future and simply said that "computers achieve human intelligence.") Chandra also omitted some words from the source, indicating the omission with an ELLIPSIS.

Johnson 4

The Turing test, developed in 1950 by British mathematician Alan Turing, is one commonly accepted measure of artificial intelligence (McCarthy). A researcher sits in one room, another person in a second room, and a computer in a third room. The researcher does not know whether a person or a computer is in each room. Communicating only through a keyboard and screen, the researcher asks the same questions of both the person and the machine. If the computer answers and the researcher cannot tell whether the response comes from a machine, the computer passes the test.

13

World Wide Web source has no page numbers.

However, some people dispute the Turing test. Prominent philosopher John Searle argues that the appearance of proper answers does not prove the existence of intelligence. He offers "the chess room argument."

Use 1-inch block-indent for a quotation longer than four lines.

> Imagine that a man who does not know how to play chess is locked inside a room, and there he is given a set of, to him, meaningless symbols. Unknown to him, these represent positions on a chessboard. He looks up in a book what he is supposed to do, and he passes back more meaningless symbols. We can suppose that if the rule book . . . is skillfully written, he will win chess games. People outside the room will say, "This man understands chess, and in fact he is a good chess player because he wins." They will be totally mistaken. The man understands nothing of chess, he is just a computer. (qtd. in Allen 30)

14

The ellipsis indicates words omitted from a quotation.

In MLA style, parenthetical information follows the period in a block quotation.

The disagreements about defining artificial intelligence result partly from how complicated the idea of human

continued ⟶

Commentary

13. **Example of summary.** Chandra compressed a lengthy description of the Turing test into a brief summary. 👁 **PROCESS NOTE:** The first time that Chandra wrote about the Turing test, she needed three full paragraphs to present all the information. She was determined to revise and condense it. She deleted sentences, which she kept in a separate document, in case she wanted to reinstate some information. She ended up with a "nutshell" version in her final draft. 👁

14. **Block-indented quotation.** Chandra was unable to produce a satisfactory summary or paraphrase of Searle's "chess room argument." She decided instead to quote the entire passage. Because the passage was longer than four lines, Chandra needed to indent it. She reviewed the MLA guidelines for the format of block quotations and the exact position of the parenthetical citation.

MLA
MLA
MLA
MLA
MLA
MLA
MLA
MLA

intelligence has become. Between 1980 and 1996, the well-respected Howard Gardner, a researcher in psychology at Harvard University, defined seven distinctive categories of human intelligence. Those categories are linguistic, mathematical, spatial, kinesthetic, musical, interpersonal, and intrapersonal intelligence (Goleman 38). In 1996, Gardner added an eighth intelligence: naturalistic. He calls this eight-item list of abilities "multiple intelligences." Gardner believes that every person is born possessing a combination of all eight intelligences (qtd. in Hoerr).

Daniel Goleman, another highly regarded researcher in psychology, groups the concepts of intrapersonal and interpersonal intelligence under the label "emotional intelligence." Goleman says that emotional intelligence involves more than having traditional feelings of anger, sadness, fear, enjoyment, love, surprise, disgust, or shame (289-90). It determines how well people do in life (28). A study of high school valedictorians, for example, shows that they frequently have less successful careers than classmates who excel at interpersonal or emotional skills (35). Goleman assigns five aspects to emotional intelligence: "knowing one's emotions," "managing emotions," "motivating oneself," "handling relationships," and "recognizing emotions in others" (43). The last of these is crucial in the context of artificial intelligence because it determines how people respond to other people and, in turn, how the other people respond back.

Neurologist Antonio Damasio explains that scientists and philosophers historically dismissed the significance of

15

16

17

18

In MLA style, put only page number in parentheses when author is named in text.

Quotation marks around phrases show they appeared separately in the source.

continued ⟶

Commentary

15. ◉ **PROCESS NOTE:** In her first draft, Chandra wrote two or three sentences about each of the eight types of human intelligence. Later she decided that writing so much about the topic would draw attention away from the main topic of her paper, artificial intelligence. In a second draft she simply listed the eight types of intelligence, leaving extra space for emotional intelligence, the most important type for the purpose of her paper. Although she was frustrated at having to omit so much of her work from the final draft, she realized her paper was stronger as a result. ◉

16. **Expert source.** When Chandra first began reading about intelligence, she came across the name of Howard Gardner in several sources. When she realized that Gardner is a leading expert on multiple intelligences, she knew she could depend on the quality of his work.

17. **Elaborating a key point.** Since emotion is a key concept in her paper, Chandra discusses it at some length in this paragraph. Early in her search process, she had used the keywords "emotions" and "intelligence" to search her library's book catalog. Goleman's book came up through that search; so did the book by Pfeifer and Scheier, which refers extensively to Goleman's work.

18. **Example.** To illustrate the point that success in life does not depend only on verbal and quantitative intelligence, the kinds of intelligence typically associated with schools, Johnson gave the example of some high school valedictorians.

Johnson 6

emotions (38). Traditionally, they associated logic and reason with intelligence. Early scientists and philosophers believed emotion belonged to the body, not the mind (39).

The character of Mr. Spock in the original <u>Star Trek</u> television series represents this belief. Incapable of emotion, Spock is flawlessly logical. Certainly, everyone would agree that he is intelligent. **19**

However, Damasio would be unconvinced by the claim that Spock was intelligent--and not just because Spock is a Vulcan. Damasio conducted numerous experiments with people who lost various emotions through brain injuries. These people otherwise seemed to possess all their reasoning and logical abilities, but they had trouble making logical decisions. The experiments led Damasio to conclude that "emotion is integral to the process of reasoning and decision making" (41). He tells of a patient, David, who suffered a disease that destroyed parts of his brain and left him unable to learn any new fact, to recognize any new person, or to remember recent events or people he had just met. Damasio and his colleagues performed an experiment in which one person treated David rudely and another person treated him well for a period of five days. Although David could not remember details of how these people treated him, he behaved differently in the presence of the two people. Clearly, he had learned on an emotional level, which made him respond sensibly (43-47). **20** **21**

Introductory phrase smoothly leads into direct quotation.

Paragraph summarizes several pages of source material, as parenthetical citation shows.

The strongest believers in artificial intelligence mostly downplay the role of emotions, maintaining that only logic **22**

continued ⟶

Commentary

19. **Example from popular culture.** Chandra hesitated to give Mr. Spock as an example of intelligence without emotion. The original *Star Trek* series is nearly four decades old, and she worried the reference might be dated. However, she decided that Mr. Spock was enough a part of popular culture that even people who weren't directly familiar with the show would understand the reference. She checked with several friends just to be sure.

20. **Evaluating a source.** The central issue of Chandra's paper is whether emotion is a necessary part of intelligence. In two of the sources she found early in her research, she had seen references to Antonio Damasio's work, and she wondered if it would help her to make connections between emotions and reasoning. It did, so she drew heavily on Damasio's book in this section. First, however, she checked his credentials. When she discovered that he was an award-winning researcher and head of the neurological sciences department at a major medical school, she was satisfied that he was a reliable source.

21. **Example.** Without the example of Damasio's patient David, this paragraph was extremely thin. Chandra had to summarize several pages of the case study into just a few sentences.

22. 👁 **PROCESS NOTE:** In the course of her research, Chandra encountered many different opinions, both on the achievability of artificial intelligence and on the role of emotions in intelligence. She found it very difficult to synthesize all this material in a manner that read smoothly. Finally, she recognized that believers and doubters of the possibility of artificial intelligence differed in terms of the importance they assigned to emotions. This discovery gave her a way to organize this paragraph. 👁

and reason define intelligence. Others give a qualified yes to "the provocative question whether robots will in fact need to have emotions, similar to the way humans have emotions" (Pfeifer 642). Doubters, on the other hand, point to emotions, feelings, and intuition as the main barriers to artificial intelligence. The ability to write fiction, for example, depends on feelings that computers can never experience. One skeptic even asserts that computers have "inner lives on a par with rocks" (Bringsjord 33). Programmers design computer programs to be efficient and to sort problems into separate steps, ignoring everything that is not part of those steps. In contrast, part of being human is getting bored, angry, or off the subject. John Searle believes that cognitive scientists make a terrible mistake when they imagine that the brain works the same way that computers do (qtd. in Allen 30).

23

Recognizing that the brain does not function through logic alone, some researchers are now studying how humans learn and are trying to incorporate their discoveries into computers. For example, children learn mainly by interacting in social situations with others. Emotions play a large role in those situations ("Sociable" 1). As an illustration, a baby learns that smiling causes adults to pay more attention to her, so she smiles a lot. In contrast, a two-year-old learns to recognize when someone is angry and to avoid that person. A child's growth in emotional intelligence would be hard to build into a computer.

24

Cite part of title when source lists no author.

Programming robots so that they can express as well as sense emotions is important, because people's abilities to convey

25

continued ⟶

Commentary

23. **Colorful quotation.** Bringsjord's statement that computers have "inner lives on a par with rocks" is not a particularly important or well-reasoned assertion. However, Chandra thought it added color to her paper and helped to make her point, so she included it here.

24. **Popular-press source.** Here Chandra's information comes from a popular source, the newspaper *USA Today*. She realized that in comparison to the many scholarly sources cited in her paper, this one might seem insignificant. However, other things she had read convinced her that the position given in the article was accurate. Because she planned to include the example of Kismet, a robot described in the article, later in her paper, she decided to keep the reference to *USA Today* here. Note that no author was listed for the article, so Johnson referred instead to the first word of the title in her parenthetical citation.

25. 👁 **PROCESS NOTE:** Chandra's research made clear that there are two main challenges in creating emotional intelligence in computers: getting computers to recognize emotions and getting them to convey emotions. She revised this topic sentence more than any other in her paper so that it would effectively signal those challenges. 👁

MLA

MLA

MLA

MLA

MLA

MLA

MLA

MLA

Johnson 8

emotions affect the responses that they get from others. To try to learn how inanimate objects suggest emotions, scientists have studied some unlikely sources. One group of researchers analyzed how Disney animators created "the illusion of life" by seeming to give cartoon characters emotions (Bates 122). Using Disney techniques, scientists created computer "creatures" that seemed to display emotions in response to simple situations (123). Further work led to robots that appeared more humanlike. For example, scientists gave a robot named Kismet appealing, childlike features. Kismet's "features, behavior, and 'emotions' " seem to allow the robot to "interact with humans in an intuitive natural way" ("Sociable" 1). Nevertheless, creating the appearance of emotions is much different from creating the existence of emotions.

26

Put quotation marks around even short phrases or key terms taken directly from a source and give source at end of sentence.

Do computers need emotions for scientists to consider them intelligent? This question remains unanswered.

27

Concluding paragraph summarizes paper.

Computers can indeed do some things that resemble a few kinds of intelligence that humans possess, and that is enough to satisfy some scientists. However, Gardner, Goleman, Damasio, Pfeifer, and others regard emotions as a crucial part of human intelligence. At present, computers lack anything like the kinds of emotions found in human beings, and scholars like John Searle doubt that computers will ever have them. Clearly, robots like the little boy in A.I. exist only in movies. The possibility of creating real robots similar to him remains only in the very distant future, if at all.

28

29

continued ⟶

Commentary

26. **Using a technical source.** The article by Bates, from a scientific journal, was fairly difficult to understand. Chandra focused on the theories, findings, and implications of the article rather than on the methodologies, which were harder to follow. This was the oldest source that Chandra consulted for her paper. However, as the reference to the robot Kismet (later in the paragraph) makes clear, the Bates study is still pertinent to current research.

27. **Research question.** Chandra's research question appears at the start of her last paragraph. Often, the research question doesn't directly appear at all in a paper, but Chandra thought it would be a good way to signal her conclusion.

28. **Summary of positions.** Chandra summarizes both positions on the question to show that she has weighed her evidence. By choosing to summarize Searle's argument last, she shows that she agrees more with his position, that emotions are an important part of artificial intelligence, than with the others.

29. **Forceful conclusion.** In her last two sentences, Chandra returned to the movie example she used at the beginning of her paper. She thought this put a pleasing frame around the paper and made it seem complete.

MLA
MLA
MLA
MLA
MLA
MLA
MLA

Johnson 9

Works Cited   30

In MLA style,
the list of
sources, called
Works Cited,
begins a new
page. Double-
space
throughout.

Allen, Frederick E. "The Myth of Artificial Intelligence."

American Heritage 52.1 (Feb./Mar. 2001): 28-30.

American Association for Artificial Intelligence. "The AI   31

Effect" 13 Sept. 2001. <http://www.aaai.org>.

Bates, Joseph. "The Role of Emotion in Believable Agents."

List sources in
alphabetical
order.

Communications of the ACM 37.7 (July 1994): 122-25.

Bringsjord, Selmer. "Just Imagine: What Computers Can't Do."

Education Digest 66.6 (Feb. 2001): 31-33.

Damasio, Antonio. The Feeling of What Happens: Body and

Emotion in the Making of Consciousness. New York:

Harcourt, 1999.

Gardner, Howard. Frames of Mind: The Theory of Multiple

Intelligences. New York: Basic, 1994.

Goleman, Daniel. Emotional Intelligence. New York: Bantam,

1995.

Hayden, Thomas. "The Age of Robots." U.S. News and World

Report 130.16 (23 Apr. 2001): 44-50.

Hoerr, Thomas. "The Naturalistic Intelligence." Building Tool

Divide a URL
only after a
slash.

Room. 20 Sept. 2002 <http://www.mewhorizons.org/   32

trm_hoerrmi.html>.

Kurzweil, Ray. "Spiritual Machines: The Merging of Man and

Machine." Futurist 33.9 (Nov. 1999): 16-21.

McCarthy, John. "What Is Artificial Intelligence?" 20 July 2002.

16 Sept. 2002 <http://www-formal.stanford.edu/jmc/

whatisai.html>.

Minerd, Jeff. "Robots: Our Evolutionary Heirs." Futurist 33.2

(Feb. 1999): 8-9.

continued ⟶

Commentary

30. **Search strategy.** Chandra developed a working bibliography that was nearly three times as long as the list of sources she finally used. Initially, she went online to see what sources she could find on the Internet. However, she was overwhelmed by the number of references to "artificial intelligence." After some effort, she identified a few key sources. Library resources were more useful. The library's book catalog revealed many useful volumes, and the databases she searched turned up both scholarly and popular sources. *PsychINFO* and *Computer Database* were the two most useful databases.

31. **Credible Internet source.** Chandra checked that this professional organization of scientists and professors would be a reliable source of information.

32. 🖥 **COMPUTER TIP:** Including a long and complicated URL in a Works Cited page is often tricky. Copying the URL from the browser window and pasting it directly into the Works Cited page reduces the chance of error. Be sure to divide a URL only after a slash, the rule in MLA style. 🖥

Johnson 10

Pfeifer, Rolf. <u>Understanding Intelligence</u>. Cambridge, MA: 33

    MIT 2000.

"'Sociable Machine' Interacts with Humans," <u>USA Today</u>

    129.2673 (June 2001): 1-2. 11 Sept. 2002.

    WilsonSelectPlus_FT BRDG01031317.

Stix, Gary. "2001: A Scorecard." <u>Scientific American</u> 284.1 (Jan.   34

    2001): 36.

Single quotation marks inside double quotation marks indicate words that were in quotation marks in the source.

Commentary

33. **Full text online.** Although this source initially appeared in one issue of the newspaper *USA Today* and old issues were not stocked at her college library, Chandra found a complete copy of the article online, through a database in the library. Because she used the online version, she cited its source.

34. **Proofreading the Works Cited page.** In proofreading her paper, Chandra made sure this list contained all the works she cited in her paper—and only those works.

MLA

MLA

MLA

MLA

MLA

MLA

MLA

MLA

APA, CM, CSE, and COS Documentation

www.prenhall.com/troyka

APA, CM, CSE, AND COS DOCUMENTATION

31 APA IN-TEXT CITATIONS

The American Psychological Association (APA) has developed a documentation style used often in the social sciences and in other disciplines. APA in-text citations, described in this chapter, alert readers to material used from outside sources.

31a What are APA in-text citations?

IN-TEXT CITATIONS identify a source by a name (usually an author's name) and a year (for print sources, usually the copyright year). You can often incorporate the relevant name, and sometimes the year, into your sentence. Otherwise, put this information in parentheses, placing the parenthetical reference close by so that a reader knows exactly what it refers to. The APA *Publication Manual* (5th edition, 2001) recommends that if you refer to a work more than once in a paragraph, you give the author's name and the date at the first mention and then give only the name after that. (Exception: If you're citing two or more works by the same author or if two or more of your sources have the same name, each citation must include the date so that a reader knows which work is being cited.)

APA style requires page numbers for quotations and recommends them for paraphrases and summaries. Many instructors, however, require page references for all sources. Find out your instructor's preference before you start drafting.

Put page numbers in parentheses, using the abbreviation *p.* before a single page number and *pp.* before two or more pages. For a direct quotation from an electronic source that numbers paragraphs, give a paragraph number (or numbers). Handle paragraph numbers as you do page numbers, but omit *p.* or *pp.*

CITATIONS FOR PARAPHRASES

- People from the Mediterranean prefer an elbow-to-shoulder distance from each other (Morris, 1977). [name and date cited in parentheses]

- Desmond Morris notes that people from the Mediterranean prefer an elbow-to-shoulder distance from each other (1977, p. 131). [name cited in text, date and page cited in parentheses]

CITATIONS FOR QUOTATIONS

- A recent report of reductions in SAD-related "depression in 87 percent of patients" (Binkley, 1990, p. 203) reverses the findings of earlier studies. [name, date, and page reference in parentheses immediately following the quotation]

- Binkley reports reductions in SAD-related "depression in 87 percent of patients" (1990, p. 203). [name incorporated into the words introducing the quotation, and date and page number in parentheses immediately following the quotation]

Formatting quotations

Incorporate a direct quotation of fewer than forty words into your own sentence(s) and enclose it in quotation marks. Place the parenthetical citation after the closing quotation mark and, if the quotation falls at the end of the sentence, before the sentence-ending punctuation.

When you use a quotation of forty words or longer, set it off from your words. Start it on a new line and indent each line of the quotation five spaces (1/2 inch) from the left margin. Don't enclose it in quotation marks, and double-space throughout. Place the parenthetical citation one space after the end punctuation of the last sentence. Start a new line for your own words following the quotation.

DISPLAYED QUOTATION

Jet lag, with its characteristic fatigue and irregular sleep patterns, is a common problem among those who travel great distances by jet airplane to different time zones:

> Jet lag syndrome is the inability of the internal body rhythm to rapidly resynchronize after sudden shifts in the timing. For a variety of reasons, the system attempts to maintain stability and resist temporal change. Consequently, complete adjustment can often be delayed for several days--sometimes for a week--after arrival at one's destination. (Bonner, 1991, p. 72)

Interestingly, this research shows that the number of flying hours is not the cause of jet lag.

31b What are APA guidelines for in-text citations?

The directory on the next page corresponds to the numbered examples that follow it. The examples show how to cite various kinds of sources in the body of your paper. Remember, you often can introduce source names, including titles when necessary, and sometimes even publication years, in your own sentences rather than in parenthetical citations.

DIRECTORY—APA IN-TEXT CITATIONS

1. One Author—APA
2. Two or More Authors—APA
3. Authors with Two or More Works in the Same Year—APA
4. Two or More Authors with the Same Last Name—APA
5. Group or Corporate Author—APA
6. Works Cited by Title—APA
7. The Bible—APA
8. Reference to More Than One Source—APA
9. Reference to an Entire Online Source—APA
10. Other References to Retrievable Online Sources—APA
11. E-mail/References to Nonretrievable Online Sources—APA
12. Source Lines for Graphics and Table Data—APA

1. One Author—APA

All the examples in 31a show citations of works by one author. Notice that in a parenthetical reference, a comma and a space separate a name from a year and a year from a page reference.

2. Two or More Authors—APA

If a work has two authors, give both names in each citation.

- One report describes 2,123 occurrences (Worchel & Cooper, 1994).

- The results Worchel and Cooper (1994) report would not support the conclusions Davis and Shebilske draw in their review of the literature (1992).

For three, four, or five authors, use all the authors' last names in the first reference; in all subsequent references, use only the first author's last name followed by et al.

FIRST REFERENCE

- In one anthology, 35 percent of the selections had not been anthologized before (Elliott, Kerber, Litz, & Martin, 1992).

SUBSEQUENT REFERENCE

- Elliott et al. (1992) include 17 authors whose work had never before been anthologized.

For six or more authors, use the name of the first author followed by et al. for all in-text references, including the first. (See Box 41, p. 245, for the format for six or more authors in the References list.)

For any work by more than one author, use an ampersand (&) between the last two names in a parenthetical citation. If you work the information into your own sentence, use the word *and* instead.

3. Author(s) with Two or More Works in the Same Year—APA

If you use more than one source written in the same year by the same author(s), alphabetize the works by their titles for the References list, and assign letters in alphabetical order to the years: *(1996a), (1996b), (1996c)*. Use this year-letter combination in in-text citations. Note that if two or more of such works are listed in the same citation, the years appear in alphabetical order:. *1996a, 1996b*.

- Most recently, Jones (1996c) draws new conclusions from the results of 17 sets of experiments (1996a, 1996b).

4. Two or More Authors with the Same Last Name—APA

Use first- or first- and middle-name initials for every in-text citation of authors who share a last name.

- R. A. Smith (1997) and C. Smith (1989) both confirm these results.

- These results have been confirmed independently (C. Smith, 1989; R. A. Smith, 1997).

5. Group or Corporate Author—APA

For a source in which the "author" is the name of a corporation, agency, or group, an in-text citation gives that name as author. Use the full name in each citation unless an abbreviated version of the name is likely to be familiar to your audience. In that case, use the full name and give its abbreviation at the first citation; then use the abbreviation for subsequent citations.

FIRST CITATION

- This exploration will continue into the twenty-first century (National Aeronautics and Space Administration [NASA], 2000).

SECOND CITATION

- The program will cost $3 billion (NASA, 2000).

6. Works Cited by Title—APA

If no author is named, use a shortened form of the title in citations. Ignoring *A, An,* or *The*, alphabetize by the first word in the References list. The following citation is to an article fully titled "Are You a Day or Night Person?"

- The morning lark and night owl connotations typically are used to categorize the human extremes ("Are You," 1989).

7. The Bible—APA

To cite the Bible, follow the guidelines for in-text citations of any major classical work (including ancient Greek and Roman works). You need to state the books, chapters, verses, and lines, rather than the page numbers, for the words you're quoting or paraphrasing. For the first biblical citation, give the version you're using (*New Revised Standard Version, New International Version*, etc.) In your subsequent in-text citations from the same text, you don't need to repeat the version. In addition, APA doesn't require that citations of major classical works appear in your References list. The in-text citations suffice.

- In this time of global strife and political confusion, people can find solace in many different ways. Some find comfort in religion, such as the psalmist of the Old Testament did when he looked upon the mountains knowing that all help was a gift of the Lord (Psalm 121:1-2, *New International Version*).

When citing from the Old Testament book of Pslams, each individual psalm is referred to in the singular form. Thus, we have *Psalm 121*, not *Psalms 121*.

- Paul's letter to the Galatians declaring that in Christianity there is "Neither Jew nor Greek, slave nor free, male nor female" (Galatians 3:28) was a revolutionary statement of equality for his time.

Biblical citations in the form shown above are valid for Old and New Testament verses. APA does not differentiate between the two.

8. Reference to More Than One Source—APA

If more than one source has contributed to an idea or opinion in your paper, cite the sources alphabetically in a single reference; separate each block of information with a semicolon.

- Conceptions of personal space vary among cultures (Morris, 1977; Worchel & Cooper, 1983).

9. Reference to an Entire Online Source—APA

If an online source does not provide page numbers, use the paragraph number preceded by the abbreviation *para*. If you cannot decipher the page number or the paragraph, cite the heading and the number of the paragraph following it.

- (Migueis, 2003, para. 14)
- (Anderson, 2002, Introduction, para. 1)

10. Other References to Retrievable Online Sources—APA

When you quote, paraphrase, or summarize an online source that is available to others, include the work in your References list, and cite the author (if any) or title and the date as you would for a print source.

11. E-mail/References to Nonretrievable Online Sources—APA

When you quote, paraphrase, or summarize an online source not available to others, treat it as a personal communication. Do not include the work in your References list, and in your paper include the parenthetical description *personal communication* and the date. Cite an e-mail message sent to you, for example, like this:

- John LeBlanc (personal communication, June 6, 2000) expects the experiment to run for 18 months to 2 years.

12. Source Lines for Graphics and Table Data—APA

If you use a graphic from another source or create a table using data from another source, give a note in the text at the bottom of the table or graphic crediting the original author and the copyright holder. Here are examples of two source lines, one for a graphic from an article, the other for a graphic from a book.

GRAPHIC FROM AN ARTICLE—APA

- *Note.* From "Bridge over troubled waters? Connecting research and pedagogy in composition and business/technical communication," by J. Allen, 1992, *Technical Communication Quarterly, 1*(4), p. 9. Copyright 1992 by the Association of Teachers of Technical Writing.

GRAPHIC FROM A BOOK—APA

- *Note.* From *How to lower your fat thermostat: The no-diet reprogramming plan for lifelong weight control* (p. 74), by D. Remington, A. G. Fisher, and E. Parent, 1983, Provo: Vitality House International. Copyright 1983 by Vitality House International.

31c How do I write an abstract for an APA paper?

You may be asked to include an abstract at the start of a paper you prepare in APA style. As the APA *Publication Manual* explains, "an abstract is a brief, comprehensive summary" (p. 12) of a longer piece of writing. Make a summary accurate, objective, and exact. You may be familiar with effective abstracts, for many disciplines have online abstracts of longer sources. See 31e for guidelines on formatting the Abstract page. Here's an abstract prepared for a paper on biological clocks.

- Circadian rhythms, which greatly affect human lives, often suffer disruptions in technological societies, resulting in such disorders as jet lag syndrome and seasonal affective disorder (SAD). With growing scientific awareness both of natural circadian cycles and the effects of disturbances of these cycles, individuals are learning how to control some negative effects.

31d What are APA guidelines for content notes?

Content notes can be used in APA-style papers for additional relevant information that cannot be worked effectively into a text discussion. Use consecutive arabic numerals for note numbers, both within your paper and on a separate page following the last text page of your paper. See 31e for instructions on formatting the Notes page.

31e What are APA format guidelines for research papers?

Ask whether your instructor has instructions for preparing a final draft. If not, you can use the APA guidelines here.

General instructions—APA

Use 8½ × 11 inch white bond paper. Double-space throughout, whether the paper is typed or prepared on a computer (the APA *Publication Manual* recommends double-spacing a final manuscript like a research paper but suggests that heading, titles, captions, and quotations longer than forty words may be easier to read if they are single-spaced). Set at least a 1-inch margin on the left (1½ inches if you submit your paper in a binder) and leave no less than 1 inch on the right and at the bottom.

Drop down 1/2 inch from the top edge of the paper to the title-and-page-number line, described on page 243. Then drop down another 1/2 inch to 1 inch from the top edge of the paper for the next line on the page, whether that is a heading (like "Abstract") or a line of your paper.

If you are typing, use five- to seven-character indents wherever indents are called for. If you are preparing your paper on a computer, use 1/2-inch indents. Indent the first line of paragraphs five characters (1/2 inch) except in an abstract, the first line of which is flush to the left margin. Do not justify the right margin.

Order of parts—APA

Use this order for the parts of your paper: title page; abstract (if required); body of the paper; References; Footnotes, if any; attachments, if any (such as questionnaires, data sheets, or other material your instructor tells you to include). Number all pages consecutively.

Title-and-page-number line for all pages—APA

Use a title-and-page-number line on all pages of your paper. Drop down 1/2 inch from the top edge of the paper. Type the title (use a shortened version if necessary), leave a five-character space, and then type the page number. End the title-and-page-number line 1 inch from the right edge of the paper. Ask whether your instructor wants you to include your last name in this title-and-page-number line.

Title page—APA

Use a separate title page. On it, begin with the title-and-page-number line described above, using the numeral 1 for this first page. Then center the complete title vertically and horizontally on the page. Use two or more double-spaced lines if the title is long. Do not underline the title or enclose it in quotation marks. On the next line, center your name, and below that center the course title and section.

👁 **CAPITALIZATION ALERTS:** (1) Use the guidelines here for capitalizing the title of your own paper and for capitalizing titles you mention in the body of your paper. But see Box 41, (p. 245) for capitalizing titles in a References list, where different rules apply. (2) Use a capital letter for the first word of your title and the first word of a subtitle, if any. Start every NOUN, PRONOUN, VERB, ADVERB, and ADJECTIVE with a capital letter. Capitalize all major words in a hyphenated COMPOUND WORD (two or more words used together to express one idea): *Father-in-Law*. Capitalize the word after a colon or a dash. (3) Do not capitalize articles (*a, an, the*) unless one of the preceding capitalization rules applies to it. Do not capitalize PREPOSITIONS and CONJUNCTIONS unless they are four or more letters long. Do not capitalize the word *to* in an INFINITIVE. 👁

Abstract—APA

See 31c for advice about what to include in an abstract of your paper. Type the abstract on a separate page, using the numeral 2 in the title-and-page-number line. Drop down 1 inch from the top of the paper and center the word *Abstract*. Double-space once below this title, and then start your abstract, double-spacing it. Do not indent the first line, and do not exceed 120 words.

Set-off quotations—APA

Set off quotations of forty words or more from your text. Start a new line for the quoted words, indenting each line of the (double-spaced) quotation five spaces from the left margin. Do not enclose the quoted words in quotation marks.

If you are quoting part of a paragraph or one complete paragraph, do not indent the first line more than five spaces. But if you quote two or more paragraphs, indent the first line of the second and subsequent paragraphs ten spaces.

When the quotation is finished, leave a space after the sentence-ending punctuation, and then give the parenthetical citation. Begin a new line to resume your own words.

References list—APA

Start a new page for your References list immediately after the end of the body of your paper. Use a title-and-page-number line. Drop down 1 inch from the top of the paper and center the word *References*. Do not underline it or put it in quotation marks. Double-space below it. The first line of each entry in your References list is flush to the left margin. If an entry takes more than one line, indent any line after the first five character spaces (or 1/2 inch). This is called the hanging indent style. Double-space within each entry and between entries.

Notes—APA

Whenever you use a content note in your paper (31d), try to arrange your sentence so that the note number falls at the end. The ideal place for a note number is after the sentence-ending punctuation. Use a numeral raised slightly above the line of words and immediately after the sentence-ending punctuation mark.

Put your notes on a separate page after the last page of your References list. Use a title-and-page-number line. Then, drop down 1 inch from the top of the paper and center the word *Footnotes*. Do not underline it or put it in quotation marks.

On the next line, start your first note, indenting five characters spaces (or 1/2 inch) from the left margin. Raise the note number slightly, and then start the words of your note. Do not leave a space between the numeral and the content note. If the note uses more than one typed line, do not indent any lines except the first. Double-space throughout.

32 APA REFERENCES LIST

The References list provides information for readers who may want to access the sources you cite in your paper.

32a What are APA guidelines for a References list?

Include in References all the sources you quote (26f), paraphrase (26g), or summarize (26h) in your paper so that any other person could find these sources with reasonable effort. Do not include any source not generally available to others; see, for example, item 34 (p. 255) about personal interviews. Also, see Box 41 below.

■ BOX 41 ■ ■

 ### Guidelines for an APA-style References list

TITLE
References

PLACEMENT OF LIST
Start a new page, numbered sequentially with the rest of the paper, immediately after the end of the text.

CONTENTS AND FORMAT
Include all quoted, paraphrased, or summarized sources in your paper that are not personal communications, unless your instructor tells you to include all the references you have consulted, not just those you have referred to. Start each entry on a new line, and double-space all lines.

In the 2001 *Publication Manual* (5th ed.) and at its Web site (http://www.apa.style.org/elecref.html) the APA establishes the hanging indent style as standard. The first line of each entry is full width, with other lines indented. This hanging indent style makes source names and dates prominent. Type the first line of each entry full width and indent subsequent lines five to seven spaces (1/2 inch or one tab).

Shuter, R. (1977). A field study of nonverbal communication in Germany, Italy, and the United States. *Communication Monographs, 44,* 298-305.

CONTINUED ⟶

◉ **Guidelines for an APA-style References list** *(continued)*

SPACING AFTER PUNCTUATION

The 2001 APA manual calls for one space after most punctuation marks.

ARRANGEMENT OF ENTRIES

Alphabetize by the author's last name. If no author is named, alphabetize by the first significant word (*not* A, An, *or* The) in the title of the work.

AUTHORS' NAMES

Use last names, first initials, and middle initials, if any. Reverse the order for all authors' names, and use an ampersand (&) between the second-to-last and last authors: Mills, J. F., & Holahan, R. H.

Give names in the order in which they appear on the work (on the title page of a book; usually under the title of an article or other printed work). Use a comma between the first author's last name and first initial and after each complete name except the last. After the last author's name, use a period. Name the first six authors of a source; substitute et al. for seven or more authors.

DATES

Put date information after name information, enclosing it in parentheses and using a period followed by one space after the closing parenthesis.

For books, articles in journals that have volume numbers, and many other print and nonprint sources, the year of publication or production is the date to use. For articles from most magazines and newspapers, use the year followed by a comma and then the exact date appearing on the issue. Individual entries in 32b show how much information to give for various sources.

CAPITALIZATION OF TITLES

For books, capitalize the first word, the first word after a colon between a title and subtitle, and any proper nouns. For names of journals and proceedings of meetings, capitalize the first word, all nouns and adjectives, and any other words five or more letters long.

SPECIAL TREATMENT OF TITLES

Use no special treatment for titles of shorter works (poems, short stories, essays, articles). Italicize titles of longer works (books, names of newspapers or journals containing cited articles). Underlining is permitted if italic typeface is difficult to produce. When underlining,

CONTINUED ⟶

BOX 41

 Guidelines for an APA-style References list *(continued)*

use an unbroken line if possible. Underline needs to include any punctuation. Check with your instructor before using underlining in place of italic type. Do not drop *A, An*, or *The* from the titles of periodicals (such as newspapers, magazines, and journals).

PUBLISHERS

Use the full name of the publisher, but drop *Co., Inc., Publishers*, and the like. Retain *Books* or *Press*.

PLACE OF PUBLICATION

For publishers in the United States, give the city and add the state (use the two-letter postal abbreviations. Don't add the state to these U.S. cities: Baltimore, Boston, Chicago, Los Angeles, New York, Philadelphia, and San Francisco. Also, if the state is mentioned in the publisher's name, omit it after the name of the city.

PUBLICATION MONTH ABBREVIATIONS

Do not abbreviate publication months.

PAGE NUMBERS

Use all digits, omitting none. *Only* for references to parts of books or material in newspapers, use *p.* and *pp.* before page numbers. List all discontinuous pages, with numbers separated by commas: pp. 32, 44-45, 47-49, 53.

REFERENCES ENTRIES: BOOKS

Citations for books have four main parts: author, date, title, and publication information (place of publication and publisher).

AUTHOR   DATE   TITLE   PUBLICATION INFORMATION

Didion, J. (1977). *A book of common prayer.* New York: Simon & Schuster.

REFERENCES ENTRIES: ARTICLES

Citations for periodical articles contain four major parts: author, date, title of article, and publication information (usually, the periodical title, volume number, and page numbers).

AUTHOR   DATE   ARTICLE TITLE

Shuter, R. (1977). A field study of nonverbal communication in Germany, Italy,

                                           VOLUME   PAGE
                        PERIODICAL TITLE   NUMBER   NUMBERS

and the United States. *Communication Monographs,*   44,   298-305.

CONTINUED ⟶

BOX 41

Guidelines for an APA-style References list *(continued)*

REFERENCES ENTRIES: ELECTRONIC AND ONLINE SOURCES

Style for documenting electric and online* sources have been changing. The 2001 APA *Publication Manual* (pp. 268–281) and the APA Web page (http://www.apastyle.org/elecref.html) are the best sources of up-to-date advice on these formats. Here are two example entries. The first is for an abstract on CD-ROM, a searchable "aggregated database" (i.e., a compilation of resources grouped for directed or simplified access). You are not required to document how you accessed the database—via portable CD-ROM, on a library server, or via a supplier Web site—but a "retrieval statement" that accurately names the source (in this case, the database) and lists the date of retrieval is required. (If you include an item or accession number, place it in parentheses.)

AUTHORS   DATE   ARTICLE TITLE

Marcus, H. F., & Kitayamo, S. (1991). Culture and the self: Implications for

JOURNAL TITLE AND PUBLICATION INFORMATION

cognition, emotion, and motivation. *Psychological Abstracts, 78.*

RETRIEVAL INFORMATION

Retrieved October 2, 2001, from PsycLIT database (Item 23873).

The second example is for an article in a newspaper on the World Wide Web. The "Retrieved from" statement gives the access date and the URL.

AUTHOR   DATE OF PUBLICATION ON THE WEB   TITLE OF ARTICLE

Lewis, R. (1995, December 24). Chronobiology researchers say their field's

TITLE AND VOLUME OF ONLINE NEWSPAPER   PAGE NUMBER   RETRIEVAL INFORMATION

time has come. *The Scientist, 9,*   p. 14.   Retrieved December 30, 1997,

from http://www.the-scientist.library.upenn.edu/yr1995/dec/
chrono_951211.html

Notice that the only punctuation in the URL is part of the address. Do not add a period after a URL.

* The word *online* is hyphenated in APA style, but not in MLA style or the style of this handbook.

32b What are APA guidelines for sources in a References list?

The directory below corresponds to the numbered examples that follow it. Not every possible documentation model is here. You may find that you have to combine features of models to document a particular source. You will also find more information in the *Publication Manual of the American Psychological Association* (5th edition, 2001) and at the APA Web site (http://www.apastyle.org/elecref.html).

Directory—APA Style

PRINT SOURCES

APA
APA
APA
APA
APA
APA
APA
APA

PRINT SOURCES

1. Book by One Author—APA

Welty, E. (1984). *One writer's beginnings.* Cambridge: Harvard University Press.

2. Book by Two Authors—APA

Leghorn, L., & Parker, K. (1981). *Woman's worth*. Boston: Routledge & Kegan Paul.

3. Book by Three or More Authors—APA

Moore, M. H., Estrich, S., McGillis, D., & Spelman, W. (1984). *Dangerous offenders: The elusive target of justice*. Cambridge: Harvard University Press.

4. Two or More Books by the Same Author(s)—APA

Gardner, H. (1993). *Multiple intelligences: The theory in practice*. New York: Basic Books.

Gardner, H. (1999). *Intelligence reframed: Multiple intelligences for the 21st century*. New York: Basic Books.

References by the same author are arranged chronologically, with the earlier date of publication listed first.

5. Book by Group or Corporate Author—APA

American Psychological Association. (2001). *Publication manual of the American Psychological Association* (5th ed.). Washington, DC: Author.

Cite the full name of the corporate author first. If the author is also the publisher, use the word *Author* as the name of the publisher.

6. Book with No Author Named—APA

The Chicago manual of style (14th ed.). (1993). Chicago: University of Chicago Press.

7. Book with an Author and an Editor—APA

Brontë, E. (1985). *Wuthering Heights* (D. Daiches, Ed.). London: Penguin.

8. Translation—APA

Kundera, M. (1999). *The unbearable lightness of being* (M. H. Heim, Trans.). New York: HarperPerennial.

9. Work in Several Volumes or Parts—APA

Randall, J. H., Jr. (1962). *The career of philosophy* (Vols. 1-2). New York: Columbia University Press.

APA

APA

APA

APA

APA

APA

APA

APA

10. One Selection from an Anthology or an Edited Book—APA

Galarza, E. (1972). The roots of migration. In L. Valdez & S. Steiner (Eds.), *Aztlan: An anthology of Mexican American literature* (pp. 127-132). New York: Knopf.

Give the author of the selection first. The word *In* introduces the larger work from which the selection is taken.

11. Two Selections from One Anthology or an Edited Book—APA

Gilbert, S., & Gubar, S. (Eds.). (1985). *The Norton anthology of literature by women.* New York: Norton.

Kingston, M. H. (1985). No name woman. In S. Gilbert & S. Gubar (Eds.), *The Norton anthology of literature by women* (pp. 2337-2347). New York: Norton.

Provide full reference information for each selection cited from an anthology (or collection), using *In* to show the larger work from which the selection is taken.

12. Signed Article in a Reference Book—APA

Burnbam, J. C. (1996). Freud, Sigmund. In B. B. Wolman (Ed.), *The encyclopedia of psychiatry, psychology, and psychoanalysis* (p. 220). New York: Holt.

Use *In* before the title of the larger work from which the selection is taken.

13. Unsigned Article in a Reference Book—APA

Ireland. (1997). In *Encyclopaedia Britannica.*

14. Edition—APA

Janson, A. F. (1997). *History of Art* (5th ed., rev.). New York: Abrams.

When a book is not the first edition, the edition number appears on the title page. Place this information after the title and in parentheses. Use the year of the edition you are citing.

15. Anthology or Edited Book—APA

Valdez, L., & Steiner, S. (Eds.). (1972). *Aztlan: An anthology of Mexican American literature.* New York: Knopf.

16. Introduction, Preface, Foreword, or Afterword—APA

Fox-Genovese, E. (1999). Foreword. In N. Warren & S. Wolff (Eds.), *Southern mothers.* Baton Rouge: Louisiana State University Press.

If you are citing an introduction, preface, foreword, or afterword, give its author's name first. After the year, give the name of the part cited. If the writer of the material you are citing is not the author of the book, use the word *In* and the author's name before the title of the book.

17. Unpublished Dissertation or Essay—APA

Geissinger, S. B. (1984). *Openness versus secrecy in adoptive parenthood*. Unpublished dissertation, University of North Carolina at Greensboro.

18. Reprint of an Older Book—APA

Hurston, Z. N. (1978). *Their eyes were watching God*. Urbana: University of Illinois Press. (Original work published 1937)

Republishing information appears on the copyright page.

19. Book in a Series—APA

Goldman, D. J. (1995). *Women writers and World War I*. New York: Macmillan.

Give the title of the book, but not of the whole series.

20. Book with a Title Within a Title—APA

Lumiansky, R. M., & Baker, H. (Eds.). (1968). *Critical approaches to six major English works*: Beowulf *through* Paradise Lost. Philadelphia: University of Pennsylvania Press.

Do not use italics for an incorporated title, even if it would be italicized by itself.

21. Government Publication—APA

U.S. Congress. House Subcommittee on Health and Environment of the Committee on Commerce. (1999). *The nursing home resident protection amendments of 1999*. Washington, DC: U.S. Government Printing Office.

U.S. Congressional Subcommittee on Technology of the Committee on Science. (1998). *Y2K: What every consumer should know to prepare for the year 2000 program*. Washington, DC: U.S. Government Printing Office.

U.S. Senate Special Committee on Aging. (1998). *The risk of malnutrition in nursing homes*. Washington, DC: U.S. Government Printing Office.

United States Senate Special Committee on the Year 2K Technical Problem. (1999). *Y2K and H_2O: Safeguarding our most vital resources*. Washington, DC: U.S. Government Printing Office.

Use the complete name of a government agency as author when no specific person is named.

22. Published Proceedings of a Conference—APA

Harris, D., & Nelson-Heern, L. (Eds.). (1981). *Proceedings of NECC 1981: National Education Computing Conference*. Iowa City: Weeg Computing Center, University of Iowa.

23. Article from a Daily Newspaper—APA

Wyatt, E. (1999, December 3). A high school without a home. *The New York Times*, pp. B1, B7.

24. Editorial, Letter to the Editor, or Review—APA

Didion, J. (1999, November 4). The day was hot and still . . . [Review of the book *Dutch: A memoir of Ronald Reagan*]. *The New York Review of Books*, 4-6.

Mr. Gorbachev's role [Editorial]. (1999, November 10). *The New York Times*, p. A22.

Wolfe, C. [Letter to the editor]. (1999, November 22). *Newsweek*, 22.

25. Unsigned Article from a Daily Newspaper—APA

Female cadets gaining sway at the Coast Guard. (1999, November 15). *The New York Times*, p. B6.

A hostess, a candidate, and a first lady fully booked. (1999, December 5). *The New York Times*, p. 29.

26. Article from a Weekly or Biweekly Periodical—APA

Greenfield, K. T. (1999, November 22). Giving away the e-store. *Time*, 58-60.

Use the abbreviation *p.* (or *pp.* for more than one page) for newspapers. Do not use this abbreviation for magazines or journals. Give year, month, and day-date for a periodical published every week or every two weeks.

27. Article from a Monthly or Bimonthly Periodical—APA

Bonner, J. T. (1999). The evolution of evolution. *Natural History, 108*(3), 20-21.

Give the year and month(s) for a periodical published every month or every other month.

28. Unsigned Article from a Weekly or Monthly Periodical—APA

A salute to everyday heroes. (1989, July 10). *Time*, 46-51, 54-56, 58-60, 63-64, 66.

29. Article from a SIRS Collection of Reprinted Articles—APA

Curver, P. C. (1990). Lighting in the 21st century. In *Social issues resources series. Energy* (Vol. 4, Article 84). Boca Raton, FL: Social Issues Resources.

When citing an article in a collection of reprinted articles, you do not have to cite the original source of publication. Cite only the reprinted publication.

30. Article in a Journal with Continuous Pagination—APA

Tyson, P. (1998). The psychology of women. *Journal of the American Psychoanalytic Association, 46,* 361-364.

Give only the volume number after the journal title and italicize the volume number.

31. Article in a Journal That Pages Each Issue Separately—APA

Zeleza, P. T. (1997). Visions of freedom and democracy in postcolonial African literature. *Women's Studies Quarterly, 25*(3-4), 10-31.

Give the volume number, italicized with the journal title. Give the issue number in parentheses; do not italicize it.

32. Published and Unpublished Letters—APA

Sand, G. (1993). Letter to her mother. In Reid Sherline (Ed.), *Letters home: Celebrated authors write to their mothers* (pp. 17-20). New York: Timkin.

In the APA system, unpublished letters are considered personal communication inaccessible to general readers, so they do not appear in the References list. Personal communications do not provide recoverable data and so are cited only in the body of the paper, as shown in item 34 on this page.

33. Map or Chart—APA

The Caribbean and South America [Map]. (1992). Falls Church, VA: American Automobile Association.

NONPRINT SOURCES

34. Interview—APA

In APA style, a personal interview is considered personal correspondence and is not included in the References list. Cite the interview in the text with a parenthetical notation that it is a personal communication.

Randi Friedman (personal communication, June 30, 1993) endorses this view.

35. Lecture, Speech, or Address—APA

Kennedy, J. F. (1960, September 12). Address. Speech presented to the Greater Houston Ministerial Association, Houston, TX.

36. Film, Videotape, or DVD—APA

Capra, F. (Director & Producer). (1934). *It happened one night*. United States: Columbia Pictures.

Capra, F. (Director & Producer). (1999). *It happened one night* [Videocassette].

Madden, J. (Director), Parfitt, D., Gigliotti, D., Weinstein, H., Zwick, E., & Norman, M. (Producers). (1999). *Shakespeare in Love* [DVD].

37. Musical recording—APA

Smetana, B. (1975). *My country* [With K. Anserl conducting the Czech Philharmonic Orchestra]. [Record]. London: Vanguard Records.

Springsteen, B. (Performer). (1992). Local hero. On *Lucky town* [CD]. New York: Columbia Records.

38. Live Performance—APA

Hare, D. (Author), Daldry, S. (Director), & Hare, D. (Performer). (1999, April 11). *Via dolorosa* [Live performance]. New York: Lincoln Center Theater.

39. Work of Art, Photograph, or Musical Composition—APA

Cassatt, M. *La toilette* [Artwork]. Chicago: Art Institute of Chicago.

Handel, G. F. *Water music* [Musical composition].

Mydans, C. (1999, October 21-November 28). *General Douglas MacArthur landing at Luzon*. 1945 [Photograph]. New York: Soho Triad Fine Art Gallery.

40. Radio or Television Program—APA

Burns, K. (1999, Nov. 7-8). In Barnes, P., & Burns, K. (Producers), *Not for ourselves alone: The story of Elizabeth Cady Stanton and Susan B. Anthony* [Television broadcast]. New York and Washington, DC: Public Broadcasting Service.

41. Information Services: ERIC and NewsBank—APA

Chiang, L. H. (1993). *Beyond the language: Native Americans' nonverbal communication*. (ERIC Document Reproduction Service No. ED 368 540).

Wenzell, R. (1990). *Businesses prepare for a more diverse work force*. (News-
Bank Document Reproduction Service No. EMP 27:DIZ).

ELECTRONIC AND ONLINE SOURCES

Information from online sources that your readers probably cannot
retrieve for themselves—many e-mail messages and discussion list
communications, for example—should be treated as personal communications. Identify the material in your paper, but do not include it in
your References list.

The APA system for documenting electronic and online sources in a
References list has been evolving. (Refer to the 2001 *Publication Manual* or log on to [http://apastyle.org/elecref.html] when you have a question
not answered here.) In general, APA recommends giving author, title,
and publication information as for a print source. This information is
followed by a "retrieval statement" showing when each source was accessed and naming the source and/or giving its correct URL (online address).

42. Article from an Encyclopedia on CD-ROM—APA

Spanish dance. (2000). *Encarta 2000*. Retrieved May 20, 2001, from Encarta database.

The retrieval statement gives the full date the information was ob-
tained and names the database. Note that the entry ends with a period.

43. Books Retrieved from Databases on the Web—APA

Adams, H. (1918). *The education of Henry Adams*. New York: Houghton Mifflin.
Retrieved December 4, 2002, from Project Bartleby database http://
www.columbia.edu/acis/bartleby/159/index/html

The first information is for the printed version of *The Education of
Henry Adams*. The retrieval statement gives the access date, the name
of the database, and the URL, with no final punctuation added.

Chopin, K. (1899). *The awakening*. Retrieved December 12, 1999 from PBS database http://www.pbs.org/katechopin/library/awakening

44. Article from a Periodical on the Web—APA

Parrott, A. C. (1999). Does cigarette smoking cause stress? *American Psychologist, 54*, 817-820. Retrieved December 7, 2002, from http://www.apa.org/
journals/amp/amp5410817.html

45. Personal or Professional Site on the Web—APA

Williams, R. W. (2002, November). Neurogenetics at UT Health Science Center. Retrieved November 11, 2002, from http://nervenet.org

46. File Transfer Protocol (FTP), Telnet, or Gopher Site—APA

Taine, H. A. (2001, April). *The French Revolution Volume II*. Retrieved October 21, 2002, from ftp://ibiblio.org/pub/docs/books/gutenberg

After the retrieval date, supply the FTP, telnet, or gopher search path.

47. Sychronous Communications (MOO, MUD, IRC)—APA

Give the name of the speaker, a title for the event, the date of the event or posting, the access date, and the URL.

Bleck, B. (1997, June 8). Online discussion of virtual first year composition: Distance education, the Internet and the World Wide Web. Retrieved February 27, 1999, from http://DaMOO.csun.edu/CW/brad.html

48. Web Discussion Forum—APA

Higa, S. (2002, June 26). A potential bookmark [Msg. 483]. Message posted to http://groups.yahoo.com/group/Modern_Era/messages/483

49. Listserv (Electronic Mailing List)—APA

Caruso, T. (2002, June 30). CFP: Flannery O'Connor and feminism. Message posted to Calls for Papers electronic mailing list, archived at http://www.english.upenn.edu/CFP/archive/American/0421.html

50. Newsgroup—APA

Boyle, F. (2002, October 11). Psyche: Cemi field theory: The hard problem made easy [Msg 1]. Message posted to news://sci.psychology.consciousness

33 A STUDENT'S APA RESEARCH PAPER

Carlos Velez wrote the following research paper in response to an assignment calling for a research paper about an unconscious process in humans. [APA papers start with an abstract. For guidelines see 31c on page 241.]

Biological Clocks   1

Biological Clocks:

The Body's Internal Timepieces

Life in modern technological societies is built around timepieces. People set clocks on radios, microwave ovens, VCRs, and much more. Students respond to bells that start and end the school day in kindergarten through twelfth grades. While carefully managing the minutes and hours each day, individuals are often forced by styles of family and work life to violate another kind of time: their body's time. Biological clocks, also known as circadian cycles, are a significant feature of human design that greatly affect people personally and professionally.

The Body's Natural Cycles

The term *circadian*, which is Latin for "about a day," describes the rhythms of people's internal biological clocks. Circadian cycles are in tune with external time cycles such as the 24-hour period of the earth's daily rotation as signaled by the rising and setting of the sun. In fact, according to William Schwartz, professor of neurobiology and a researcher in the field of chronobiology (the study of circadian rhythm), "'All such biological clocks are adaptations to life on a rotating world'" (Lewis, 1995, p. 14). Usually, humans set their biological clocks by seeing these cycles of daylight and darkness. Studies conducted in caves or similar environments that allow researchers to control light and darkness have shown that most people not exposed to natural cycles of day and night create cycles slightly over 24 hours (Czeisler et al.,

APA STYLE: 1" margins; double-space throughout

INTRODUCTION: Gets reader's attention

THESIS STATEMENT: Gives paper's focus

FIRST HEADING

PARAGRAPH 2: First body paragraph gives background information

Single quotation marks inside double quotation marks indicate statement by Schwartz is in article by Lewis

In APA style, summary of two sources separated by semicolon

continued ⟶

(Proportions shown in this paper are adjusted to fit space limitations of this book. Follow actual dimensions shown in this book and your instructor's directions.)

In APA style, header has shortened title and page number

1999; Recer, 1999). Human perception of the external day-night cycle affects the production and release of a brain hormone, melatonin, which is important in initiating and regulating the

No page numbers for paraphrases and summaries

sleep-wake cycle, as Alfred Lewy and other scientists at the National Institutes of Health in Bethesda, Maryland, have found (Winfree, 1987).

Each individual's lifestyle reflects that person's own circadian cycle. Scientists group people as "larks" or "owls"

PARAGRAPH 3: Defines larks and owls

on the basis of whether individuals are more efficient in the morning or at night. The idea behind the labels is that "in nature certain animals are diurnal, active during the light

Partial title used because source does not give an author

period; others are nocturnal, active at night. The 'morning lark' and the 'night owl' connotations typically are used to categorize the human extremes" ("Are You," 1989, p. 11).

Disruptions of Natural Cycles

SECOND HEADING

PARAGRAPH 4: Applies terms to jet lag

"Larks" who must stay up late at night and "owls" who must awaken early in the morning experience mild versions of "jet lag," the disturbances from which time-zone travelers often suffer. Jet lag, which is characterized by fatigue and irregular sleep patterns, results from disruption of circadian rhythms in most people who fly in jets to different time zones:

In APA style, block-indented paragraph for quotations over 40 words. Indent five spaces or ½″

Jet lag syndrome is the inability of the internal body rhythm to rapidly resynchronize after sudden shifts in the timing. For a variety of reasons, the system attempts to maintain stability and resist temporal change.

Quotations require page number with *p.* or *pp.* for more than one page

Consequently, complete adjustment can often be delayed for several days--sometimes for a week--after arrival at one's destination. (Bonner, 1991, p. 72)

continued ⟶

Biological Clocks   3

According to Richard Coleman (1986), "the number, rate, and direction of time-zone changes are the critical factors in determining the extent and degree of jet lag symptoms" (p. 67). In general, eastbound travelers find it harder than westbound travelers to adjust.

Proof of this theory can be found in the national pastime, baseball. Three researchers analyzed win-loss records to discover whether jet lag affected baseball players' performance (Recht, Lew, & Schwartz, 1995). The study focused on the records of teams in the eastern and western United States over a period of 3 years. If a visiting team did not have to travel through any time zones, it lost 54% of the time. If the visiting team had traveled from west to east, it lost 56.2% of the time. But if they had traveled from east to west, the visitors lost only 37.1% of the time.

Another group that suffers greatly from biological-clock disruptions consists of people whose livelihoods depend on erratic schedules. This situation affects 20 to 30 million U.S. workers whose work schedules differ from the usual morning starting time and afternoon or early evening ending time (Weiss, 1989). Sue Binkley (1990) reports that Charles Czeisler, director of the Center for Circadian and Sleep Disorders at Brigham and Women's Hospital in Boston, found that 27% of the U.S. work force does shift work. Shift work can mean, for example, working from 7:00 a.m. to 3:00 p.m. for six weeks, from 3:00 p.m. to 11:00 p.m. for six weeks, and from 11:00 p.m. to 7:00 a.m. for six weeks. Many shift workers endure stomach and intestinal-tract disorders, and, on average, they have three

PARAGRAPH 5: Additional specific support for previous paragraph

Statistics illustrate example

PARAGRAPH 6: New example describes problem as it affects another group, shift workers

Specific details to illustrate example

continued →

Biological Clocks   4

times as much risk of heart disease as non-shift workers (Bingham, 1989). In a 1989 report to the American Association for the Advancement of Science, Czeisler states that "'police officers, [medical] interns, and many others who work nights perform poorly and are involved in more on-the-job accidents than their daytime counterparts'" (Binkley, 1990, p. 26).

PARAGRAPH 7:
Additional
specific support
Other researchers confirm that safety is at risk during late-shift hours. In a study of 28 medical interns observed during late-night shifts over a 1-year period, 25% admitted to falling asleep while talking on the phone, and 34% had had at least one accident or near-accident during that period (Weiss, 1989, p. 37). Investigations into the *Challenger* space shuttle explosion and the nuclear-reactor disasters at Three Mile Island and Chernobyl reveal critical errors made by people undergoing the combined stresses of lack of sleep and unusual work schedules (Toufexis, 1989).

PARAGRAPH 8:
One group's
response to
information on
biological
clocks
Emergency room physicians experience these two stresses all the time. Their professional group, the American College of Emergency Physicians (ACEP), after investigating circadian rhythms and shift work, drafted a formal policy statement, approved by ACEP's board of directors in 1994. The

Ellipsis
indicates words
have been
omitted within a
direct quotation
policy calls for "shifts . . . consistent with circadian principles" to prevent burnout and keep emergency physicians from changing their medical specialty. Also, such a policy would provide the best care for patients (Thomas, 1996).

PARAGRAPH 9:
Applies problem
to a medical
condition
If jet lag and circadian disruptions caused by shift work are obvious ways to upset a biological clock, a less obvious disruption is increasingly recognized as a medical problem:

continued ⟶

Biological Clocks   5

the disorder known as seasonal affective disorder (SAD). Table
1 lists some of the major symptoms of SAD.

Table 1

Common Symptoms of Seasonal Affective Disorder (SAD)   Table title

---

Sadness	Later waking
Anxiety	Increased sleep time
Decreased physical activity	Interrupted, unrefreshing sleep
Irritability	Daytime drowsiness
Increased appetite	Decreased sexual drive
Craving for carbohydrates	Menstrual problems
Weight gain	Work problems
Earlier onset of sleep	Interpersonal problems

Table lists items efficiently, making them easy to find

Note. From *The Clockwork Sparrow* (p. 204), by S. Binkley, 1990,
Englewood Cliffs, NJ: Prentice Hall. Copyright 1990 by Prentice
Hall.   Note below table provides source

Ways to Help People Affected by Cycle Disruptions   THIRD HEADING

SAD appears to be related to the short daylight   PARAGRAPH 10: Solution to problem
(photoperiod) of winter in the temperate zones of the northern
and southern hemispheres. Michael Terman, a clinical
psychologist at Columbia Presbyterian Medical Center's New
York State Psychiatric Institute, has studied SAD patients for
many years. He has observed their inability to function at
home or at work from fall to spring (Caldwell, 1999). The   Author's name and year in parentheses when not included in text
phenomenon of SAD not only illustrates the important role of
circadian rhythms but also dramatically proves that an
understanding of circadian principles can help scientists

continued ⟶

Biological Clocks 6

improve the lives of people who experience disruptions of
their biological clocks. Binkley (1990) claims that exposure to
bright light for periods of up to two hours a day during the

Specific method for reducing SAD

short-photoperiod days of winter reduces SAD-related
"depression in 87 percent of patients . . . within a few days;
relapses followed" (pp. 203-204) when light treatment ended.

Lengthening a person's exposure to bright light can also
help combat the effects of jet lag and shift work. Specific

PARAGRAPH 11: Applies solution in previous paragraph

suggestions for using light to help reset a jet traveler's
biological clock include "a late-afternoon golf game or early-
morning walk" or, for night-shift workers, staying in the dark
during the day and during the night being in artificial light
that mimics daylight (Mayo Clinic, 1997).

Establishing work schedules more sensitive to biological
clocks can increase a sense of well-being and reduce certain

PARAGRAPH 12: Specific system to reduce time- shift problems

safety hazards. A group of police officers in Philadelphia were
studied while on modified shift schedules (Locitzer, 1989;
Toufexis, 1989). The officers were changed between day shifts
and night shifts less frequently than they had been on former
shift schedules. Also, they rotated forward rather than
backward in time, and they worked four rather than six
consecutive days. The officers reported 40% fewer patrol car
accidents and decreased use of drugs or alcohol to get to sleep.
Overall, the police officers preferred the modified shift
schedules. Charles Czeisler, who conducted the study,
summarizes the importance of these results: "When schedules
are introduced that take into account the properties of the
human circadian system, subjective estimates of work schedule

continued ⟶

Biological Clocks 7

satisfaction and health improve, personnel turnover decreases, and work productivity increases" (Locitzer, 1989, p. 66).

Conclusion

Scientists like Charles Czeisler are guiding individuals to live harmoniously with their biological clocks. The growing awareness of the negative effects of shift work and travel across time zones has led to significant advances in reducing problems caused by disruptions of people's natural cycles. The use of light to manipulate the body's sense of time has also helped. As more of us realize how circadian rhythms can affect our lifestyles, we might learn to control our biological clocks instead of our biological clocks controlling us.

CONCLUSION:
Points to future

continued ⟶

Biological Clocks   8

References

Are you a day or night person? (1989, March 4). *USA Today*, p. 11.

Bingham, R. (Writer & Director). (1989, June 10). *The time of our lives* [Television broadcast]. Los Angeles: KCET Public Television of Southern California.

Binkley, S. (1990). *The clockwork sparrow*. Englewood Cliffs, NJ: Prentice Hall.

Bonner, P. (1991, July). Travel rhythms. *Sky Magazine*, 72-73, 76-77.

Caldwell, M. (1999, July). Mind over time. *Discover, 20,* 52. Retrieved October 2, 1999, from General Reference Gold database (Article A55030836).

Coleman, R. (1986). *Wide awake at 3:00 a.m.: By choice or by chance?* New York: Freeman.

Czeisler, C., et al. (1999, June 25). Stability, precision, and near-24-hour period of the human circadian pacemaker. *Science*, 2177-2181.

Lewis, R. (1995, December 24). Chronobiology researchers say their field's time has come. *The Scientist, 9,* p. 14. Retrieved September 6, 2002, from http://www.the-scientist.library.upenn.edu/yr1995/dec/chrono_951211.html

Locitzer, K. (1989, July/August). Are you out of sync with each other? *Psychology Today,* 66.

Mayo Clinic. (1997, December 30). Tricks to try when you're out of sync. *Mayo Health Oasis* [On-line newsletter]. (Original work published in *Mayo Clinic Health Letter,* March 1995). Retrieved October 16, 1999 from http://www.mayohealth.org/mayo/9503/htm/sync_sb.htm

Begin References on new page

Double-space throughout

List References in alphabetical order

See page 244 for advice about formatting an APA-style References list in "flush left" or "hanging indent" style

Example of source by a corporate author

continued ⟶

Biological Clocks 9

Recer, P. (June 25, 1999). Study gives a new reason for insomnia
among elderly. *Philadelphia Inquirer*. Retrieved October 3, 1999, from SIRS Researcher database (Item
101619).

Recht, L., Lew, R., & Schwartz, W. (1995, October 19). Baseball
teams beaten by jet lag [Letter]. *Nature, 377*, 583.

Thomas H. A. (1996). Circadian rhythms and shift work. ACEP
Online. Retrieved August 28, 2002, from
http://www.acep.org/POLICY/PR004166.HTM

Toufexis, A. (1989, June 5). The times of your life. *Time*, 66-67.

Weiss, R. (1989, January 21). Safety gets short shrift on long
night shift. *Science News*, 37.

Winfree, A. (1987). *The timing of biological clocks*. New York:
Freeman.

Source is a
letter appearing
in *Nature*
publication

34 CM-STYLE DOCUMENTATION

The University of Chicago Press endorses two styles of documentation. One is a name-date style similar to the MLA and APA systems of in-text information; it directs readers to a bibliographic list. The other, described in this chapter, is a note system often used in the disciplines of English, humanities, and history.

34a What should I know about CM documentation with bibliographic notes?

The CM (for *Chicago Manual*) note system gives complete bibliographic information within a footnote or endnote the first time a source is cited.

If the source is cited again, the note gives less information. A separate bibliography is unnecessary because each first-citation note contains all the information a reader needs to identify the source. (As *The Chicago Manual of Style* points out, a separate bibliography is a convenience for readers of long works citing many sources.)

In CM style, the notes are either at the end of a paper (endnotes) or at the foot of the page on which a citation falls (footnotes).

TEXT   Welty also makes this point.[3]

NOTE   3. Eudora Welty, <u>One Writer's Beginnings</u> (Cambridge: Harvard University Press, 1984).

Endnotes may be easier for you to format than footnotes, especially if you are using a typewriter for your paper. Most word processing programs facilitate either system.

BOX 42

 Guidelines for CM-style bibliographic notes

TITLE

For endnotes, Notes, on a new page numbered sequentially with the rest of the paper, after the last text page of the paper. (Footnotes appear at the bottom of the page where the relevant citation occurs.)

CONTENTS AND FORMAT

Include a note every time you use a source. Place endnotes after the text of your paper, on a separate page titled *Notes*. Center the word

CONTINUED ⟶

Guidelines for CM-style bibliographic notes *(continued)*

Notes, neither underlined nor in quotation marks, about an inch from the top of the page, and double-space after it. Single-space the notes themselves. Indent each note's first line three characters (or one tab space in your word processing program), but do not indent the note's subsequent lines.

In the body of your paper, use raised (superscript) arabic numerals for the note numbers. Position note numbers after any punctuation marks except the dash, preferably at the end of a sentence. On the Notes page, make note numbers the same type size as the notes, and position them on, not above, the line, followed by a period. (Not all word processing programs allow you to observe these guidelines. Adapt these guidelines if necessary, using a consistent style throughout your paper.)

SPACING AFTER PUNCTUATION

No specific requirements.

ARRANGEMENT

Use sequential numerical order throughout the paper. Even if you use footnotes, do not start with 1 on each page.

AUTHORS' NAMES

Give the names in standard (first name first) order, with names and initials as in the original source. Use *and* before the last author's name.

CAPITALIZATION OF TITLES

Capitalize the first word and all major words.

SPECIAL TREATMENT OF TITLES

Underline the titles of long works, and use quotation marks around the titles of shorter works. Don't underline punctuation unless it's a quotation mark.

Omit *A, An,* and *The* from the titles of newspapers and periodicals. In parentheses, give the city (and state, if the city is not well known) for an unfamiliar newspaper title: (*Newark, N.J.*) *Star-Ledger,* for example. Note that CM style uses state name abbreviations, which can be found in dictionaries, different from the two-letter postal abbreviations.

PUBLICATION INFORMATION

Enclose in parentheses. Use a colon and one space after the city of publication. Give complete publishers' names or abbreviate them according to standard abbreviations in *Books in Print*. Omit *Co., Inc.,* and the like.

CONTINUED →

BOX 42

 Guidelines for CM-style bibliographic notes *(continued)*

You can use *Univ.* for *University*; spell out *Press.* Do not abbreviate publication months.

PAGE NUMBERS

In inclusive page numbers, give the full second number for 2 through 99. For 100 and beyond, give the full second number only if a shortened version is ambiguous: *243–47, 202–6, 300–304.*

List all discontinuous page numbers; see the model at, "First Citation: Book," below.

Use a comma to separate parenthetical publication information from the page numbers that follow it. Use the abbreviations *p.* and *pp.* with page numbers only for material from newspapers or from journals that do not use volume numbers and to avoid ambiguity.

CONTENT NOTES

Try to avoid using content notes. If you must use them, make footnotes, and use symbols rather than numbers: an asterisk (*) for the first note on a page and a dagger (†) for a second note on that page.

FIRST CITATION: BOOK

Citations for books include the author, title, publication information, and page numbers if applicable.

1. Eudora Welty, One Writer's Beginnings (Cambridge: Harvard University Press, 1984), 25-26, 30, 43-51, 208.

FIRST CITATION: ARTICLE

Citations for articles include the author, article title, journal title, volume number, year, and page numbers.

35. D. D. Cochran, W. Daniel Hale, and Christine P. Hissam, "Personal Space Requirements in Indoor versus Outdoor Locations," Journal of Psychology 117 (1984): 132-33.

34b What are CM-style guidelines for bibliographic notes?

The directory below corresponds to the sample bibliographic notes forms that follow it. Not every possible documentation model is here. *The Chicago Manual of Style,* 14th edition, gives note and reference-list forms for most sources. If you cannot find the information you need in this section, consult the *Chicago Manual*.

DIRECTORY—CM STYLE

1. Book by One Author—CM
2. Book by Two or Three Authors—CM
3. Book by More Than Three Authors—CM
4. Multiple Citations of a Source—CM
5. Book by a Group or Corporate Author—CM
6. Book with No Author Named—CM
7. Book with an Author and an Editor—CM
8. Translation—CM
9. Work in Several Volumes or Parts—CM
10. One Selection from an Anthology or an Edited Book—CM
11. Two Selections from an Anthology or an Edited Book—CM
12. Signed Article in a Reference Book—CM
13. Unsigned Article in a Reference Book—CM
14. Edition—CM
15. Anthology or Edited Book—CM
16. Introduction, Preface, Foreword, or Afterword—CM
17. Unpublished Dissertation or Essay—CM
18. Reprint of an Older Book—CM
19. Book in a Series—CM
20. Book with a Title Within a Title—CM
21. Government Publication—CM
22. Published Proceedings of a Conference—CM
23. Article from a Daily Newspaper—CM
24. Editorial, Letter to the Editor, or Review—CM
25. Unsigned Article from a Daily Newspaper—CM
26. Article from a Weekly or Biweekly Magazine or Newspaper—CM
27. Article from a Monthly or Bimonthly Periodical—CM
28. Unsigned Article from a Weekly or Monthly Periodical—CM
29. Article from a Collection of Reprinted Articles—CM
30. Article in a Journal with Continuous Pagination—CM
31. Article in a Journal That Pages Each Issue Separately—CM

32. Personal Interview—CM
33. Published and Unpublished Letters—CM
34. Film, Videotape, or DVD—CM
35. Recording—CM
36. Computer Software—CM
37. ERIC Information Service—CM
38. Electronic Documents—CM
39. Secondary Source—CM

1. Book by One Author—CM

1. Eudora Welty, One Writer's Beginnings (Cambridge: Harvard University Press, 1984).

CM style can combine notes with a bibliography (34a). Here is the bibliographic entry for note 1.

Welty, Eudora. One Writer's Beginnings. Cambridge: Harvard University Press, 1984.

2. Book by Two or Three Authors—CM

2. Lisa Leghorn and Katherine Parker, Woman's Worth (Boston: Routledge, 1981).

3. Alfred H. Kelly, Winfred A. Harbison, and Herman Belz, The American Constitution: Its Origins and Development (New York: W. W. Norton, 1983).

If you are using a bibliography as well as notes, invert only the first name listed.

Kelly, Alfred H., Winfred A. Harbison, and Herman Belz. The American Constitution: Its Origins and Development. New York: W. W. Norton, 1983.

3. Book by More Than Three Authors—CM

4. Mark H. Moore et al., Dangerous Offenders: The Elusive Target of Justice (Cambridge: Harvard University Press, 1984).

Give the name of the author listed first on the title page, and then put either *et al.* or *and others,* using no punctuation after the author's name.

4. Multiple Citations of a Source—CM

For subsequent references to a work you have already cited, give the last name of the author followed by a comma and the page number. Note 5 shows the form for a subsequent reference to the work fully described in note 1.

5. Welty, 25.

If you cite more than one work by the same author, give the title between the name and the page number. If the title is long, you may shorten it.

> 6. Welty, One Writer's Beginnings, 25.

If you cite two or more authors with the same last name, include first names or initials in each note.

> 7. Eudora Welty, 25.

If you cite the same source as the source immediately preceding, you may use *Ibid.* followed by a comma and the page number rather than repeating the author's name.

> 8. Ibid., 25.

5. Book by a Group or Corporate Author—CM

> 9. Boston Women's Health Collective, Our Bodies, Ourselves (New York: Simon and Schuster, 1986).

> 10. American Psychological Association, Publication Manual of the American Psychological Association, 5th ed. (Washington, D.C.: American Psychological Association, 2001).

If a work issued by an organization has no author listed on the title page, cite the name of the organization as the author of the work. The organization may also be the publisher of the work.

6. Book with No Author Named—CM

> 11. The Chicago Manual of Style, 14th ed. (Chicago: University of Chicago Press, 1993).

Begin the citation with the name of the book.

7. Book with an Author and an Editor—CM

> 12. Emily Brontë, Wuthering Heights, ed. David Daiches (London: Penguin, 1985).

In this position, the abbreviation *ed.* stands for "edited by," not "editor." Therefore, *ed.* is correct whether a work has one or more than one editor. (Also see items 10 and 15.)

8. Translation—CM

> 13. Milan Kundera, The Unbearable Lightness of Being, trans. Michael Henry Heim (New York: HarperPerennial Library, 1999).

The abbreviation *trans.* stands for "translated by," not "translator."

CM

CM

CM

CM

CM

CM

CM

CM

CM
CM
CM
CM
CM
CM
CM
CM

9. Work in Several Volumes or Parts—CM

The two notes numbered 14 show ways to give bibliographic information for a specific place in *one* volume of a multivolume work. Use whichever you prefer, being consistent throughout a paper. If you are writing about the volume as a whole (as opposed to citing specific pages), end the note with the publication information.

14. Ernest Jones, The Last Phase, vol. 3 of The Life and Work of Sigmund Freud (New York: Basic Books, 1957), 97.

14. Ernest Jones, The Life and Works of Sigmund Freud, vol. 3, The Last Phase (New York: Basic Books, 1957), 97.

If you are citing an entire work in two or more volumes, use the form shown in note 15.

15. John Herman Randall, Jr., The Career of Philosophy, 2 vols. (New York: Columbia University Press, 1962).

10. One Selection from an Anthology or an Edited Book—CM

16. Ernest Galarza, "The Roots of Migration," in Aztlan: An Anthology of Mexican American Literature, ed. Luis Valdez and Stan Steiner (New York: Alfred A. Knopf, 1972), 127-32.

Give page numbers for the cited work.

11. Two Selections from an Anthology or an Edited Book—CM

If you cite selections from an anthology or edited book, give complete bibliographical information in each citation.

12. Signed Article in a Reference Book—CM

17. John C. Burnbam, "Freud, Sigmund," in The Encyclopedia of Psychiatry, Psychology, and Psychoanalysis, ed. Benjamin B. Wolman (New York: Henry Holt and Company, 1996), 220.

13. Unsigned Article in a Reference Book—CM

18. Encyclopaedia Britannica, 15th ed., s.v. "Ireland."

The abbreviation *s.v.* stands for *sub verbo*, meaning "under the word." Capitalize the heading of the entry only if it is a proper noun. Omit publication information except for the edition number.

14. Edition—CM

19. Anthony F. Janson, History of Art, 5th ed. (New York: Harry N. Abrams, 1997).

Here the abbreviation *ed.* stands for "edition," not "edited by" (see item 7). Give the copyright date for the edition you are citing.

15. Anthology or Edited Book—CM

20. Luis Valdez and Stan Steiner, eds., <u>Aztlan: An Anthology of Mexican American Literature</u> (New York: Alfred A. Knopf, 1972).

16. Introduction, Preface, Foreword, or Afterword—CM

21. Elizabeth Fox-Genovese, foreword to <u>Southern Mothers</u>, by Nagueyalti Warren and Sally Wolff, eds. (Baton Rouge: Louisiana State University Press, 1999).

If the author of the book is different from the author of the cited part, give the name of the book's author after the title of the book.

17. Unpublished Dissertation or Essay—CM

22. Shirley Burry Geissinger, "Openness versus Secrecy in Adoptive Parenthood" (Ph.D. diss., University of North Carolina at Greensboro, 1984), 45-56.

List the author's name first, then the title in quotation marks (not underlined), a descriptive label (such as *Ph.D. diss.* or *master's thesis*), the degree-granting institution, the date, and finally the page numbers.

23. Kimberli M. Stafford, "Trapped in Death and Enchantment: The Liminal Space of Women in Three Classical Ballets" (paper presented at the annual meeting of the American Comparative Literature Association Graduate Student Conference, Riverside, Calif., April 1993).

To cite a paper read at a meeting, give the name of the meeting in parentheses, along with the location and the date.

18. Reprint of an Older Book—CM

24. Zora Neale Hurston, <u>Their Eyes Were Watching God</u> (1937; reprint, Urbana: University of Illinois Press, 1978).

Republishing information is located on the copyright page. List the original date of publication first, followed by the publication information for the reprint.

19. Book in a Series—CM

25. Dorothy J. Goldman, <u>Women Writers and World War I</u>, Literature and Society Series (New York: Macmillan Publishing Company, 1995).

If the series numbers its volumes and the volume number is not part of the title, include the volume number after the series title. Separate the volume number from the title with a comma.

20. Book with a Title Within a Title—CM

26. Aljean Harmetz, <u>The Making of "The Wizard of Oz"</u> (New York: Hyperion, 1998).

If the name of a work that is usually underlined appears in a title, add quotation marks around it. If the name of a work that is usually in quotation marks appears in a title, keep it in quotation marks and underline it.

21. Government Publication—CM

27. House, <u>Coastal Heritage Trail Route in New Jersey</u>, 106th Cong., 1st sess., 1999, H. Rept. 16.

If a government department, bureau, agency, or committee produces a document, cite that group as the author.

22. Published Proceedings of a Conference—CM

28. Arnold Eskin, "Some Properties of the System Controlling the Circadian Activity Rhythm of Sparrows," in <u>Biochronometry</u>, ed. Michael Menaker (Washington, D.C.: National Academy of Sciences, 1971), 55-80.

Treat published conference proceedings as you would a chapter in a book.

23. Article from a Daily Newspaper—CM

29. Edward Wyatt, "A High School Without a Home," <u>New York Times</u>, 3 December 1999, sec. B, p. 1.

If a large paper prints more than one edition a day (such as a morning edition and a final edition), identify the specific edition; make this the last information in the entry, preceded by a comma. For a paper that specifies sections, use *sec.* before the page number. If a paper gives column numbers, use *col.* after the page number. Separate all items with commas.

24. Editorial, Letter to the Editor, or Review—CM

30. "Mr. Gorbachev's Role," editorial, <u>New York Times</u>, 10 November 1999, sec. A, p. 22.

31. Cheryl Wolfe, letter, <u>Newsweek</u>, 22 November 1999, 22.

32. Joan Didion, "The Day Was Hot and Still . . . ," review of <u>Dutch: A Memoir of Ronald Reagan</u>, by Edmund Morris, <u>New York Review of Books</u>, 4 November 1999, 4-6.

Before page numbers, use a comma for popular magazines and a colon for journals.

25. Unsigned Article from a Daily Newspaper—CM

33. "Female Cadets Gaining Sway at the Coast Guard," <u>New York Times</u>, 15 November 1999, sec. B, p. 6.

26. Article from a Weekly or Biweekly Magazine or Newspaper—CM

34. Karl Taro Greenfield, "Giving Away the E-Store," Time, 22 November 1999, 58-60.

For general-readership weekly or biweekly magazines or newspapers, give the day-date, month, and year of publication. Separate page numbers from the year with a comma.

27. Article from a Monthly or Bimonthly Periodical—CM

35. John Tyler Bonner, "The Evolution of Evolution," Natural History, April 1999, 20-21.

For general-readership monthly or bimonthly magazines, give the month and year of publication. Separate page numbers from the year with a comma.

28. Unsigned Article from a Weekly or Monthly Periodical—CM

36. "A Salute to Everyday Heroes," Time, 10 July 1989, 46-51, 54-56, 58-60, 63-64, 66.

If the article is printed on discontinuous pages, give all pages in the note.

29. Article from a Collection of Reprinted Articles—CM

37. Phillip C. Curver, "Lighting in the 21st Century," Energy, Social Issues Resources Series, vol. 4 (Boca Raton, Fla.: Social Issues Resources, 1990).

Cite only the publication actually consulted, not the original source. If you use a bibliography, in it cite both the reprinted publication you consulted and the publication where the article first appeared.

30. Article in a Journal with Continuous Pagination—CM

38. Phyllis Tyson, "The Psychology of Women," Journal of the American Psychoanalytic Association 46 (1997): 361-64.

31. Article in a Journal That Pages Each Issue Separately—CM

39. Thomas F. Hogarty, "Gasoline: Still Powering Cars in 2050?" The Futurist 33, no. 3 (1999): 51-55.

The issue number of a journal is required only if each issue of the journal starts with page 1. In this example, the volume number is 33 and the issue number, abbreviated as *no.*, is 3.

32. Personal Interview—CM

40. Randi Friedman, interview by author, Ames, Iowa, 30 June 2002.

For an unpublished interview, give the name of the interviewee and the interviewer, the location of the interview, and the date of the interview.

33. Published and Unpublished Letters—CM

41. George Sand to her mother, 31 May 1831, Letters Home: Celebrated Authors Write to Their Mothers, ed. Reid Sherline (New York: Timkin Publishers, 1993), 17-20.

42. Theodore Brown, letter to author, 7 December 1999.

For an unpublished letter, give the name of the author, the name of the recipient, and the date the letter was written.

34. Film, Videotape, or DVD—CM

43. Marc Norman, Shakespeare in Love (New York: Miramax Films/Universal Pictures, 1999), videocassette.

44. Robert Riskin, It Happened One Night (Hollywood: Columbia Pictures, 1999), videocassette.

45. Robert Riskin, It Happened One Night (Hollywood: Columbia Pictures, 1934), filmstrip.

35. Recording—CM

46. Bedrich Smetana, My Country, Czech Philharmonic, Karel Anserl, Vanguard SV-9/10.

Bedrich Smetana is the composer and Karel Anserl is the conductor.

47. Bruce Springsteen, "Local Hero," on Lucky Town, Columbia CK 53001.

36. Computer Software—CM

48. Microsoft Word Ver. 8.0, Microsoft, Seattle, Wash.

Place the version or release number, abbreviated *Ver.* or *Rel.*, directly after the name of the software. Then list the company that owns the rights to the software, followed by that company's location.

37. ERIC Information Service—CM

49. Hunter M. Breland, Assessing Writing Skills (New York: College Entrance Examination Board, 1987), ERIC, ED 286920.

ERIC stands for *Educational Resources Information Center*.

38. Electronic Documents—CM

The Chicago Manual of Style (14th ed., 1993) describes electronic sources as an "exceedingly complex, fluid, and rapidly expanding field of source material" (634). The *Chicago Manual* shows several samples of acceptable documentation of electronic sources. The note below shows CM style for documenting a newsgroup posting. CM style for electronic sources is based on the International Standards Organization (ISO) documentation system. If you are using CM style and do not find enough information in this book to help you document your electronic sources, consult the ISO guidelines. Your college library should have a copy of ISO recommendations. Otherwise, consult your instructor.

50. Dan S. Wallach, "FAQ: Typing Injuries (2/5): General Info.," in typing-injury-faq/general.Z [electronic bulletin board], 1993-; [cited 14 November 1993], available from mail-server@rtfm.mit.edu; INTERNET.

39. Secondary Source—CM

51. Mary Wollstonecraft, A Vindication of the Rights of Woman (1792), 90, quoted in Caroline Shrodes, Harry Finestone, and Michael Shugrue, The Conscious Reader, 4th ed. (New York: Macmillan Publishing Company, 1988), 282.

When you quote one person's words, having found them in another person's work, give information as fully as you can about both sources. Note 51 shows the form when the point of your citation is Mary Wollstonecraft's words. If your point is what Shrodes, Finestone, and Shugrue have to say about Wollstonecraft's words, handle the information as in note 52.

52. Caroline Shrodes, Harry Finestone, and Michael Shugrue, The Conscious Reader, 4th ed. (New York: Macmillan Publishing Company, 1988), 282, quoting Mary Wollstonecraft, A Vindication of the Rights of Woman (1792), 90.

Using and Citing Graphics—CM

Place the credit line for a table or illustration from another source next to the reproduced material. (If you intend to publish your paper, you must receive permission to reprint copyrighted material from a source.) Spell out the terms *map*, *plate*, and *table*, but abbreviate *figure* as *fig.*

Reprinted, by permission, from Dennis Remington, A. Garth Fisher, and Edward Parent, How to Lower Your Fat Thermostat: The No-Diet Reprogramming Plan for Lifelong Weight Control (Provo, Utah: Vitality House International, 1983), 74, fig. A2-1.

35 CSE-STYLE DOCUMENTATION

In its style manual, *Scientific Style and Format*, the Council of Science Editors (CSE) endorses two documentation systems widely used in mathematics and the physical and life sciences.

35a What should I know about CSE documentation?

The first system endorsed by CSE uses name-year parenthetical citations in the text of a paper, together with an alphabetically arranged References list that gives full bibliographic information for each source. The second system uses numbers to mark citations in the text of a paper that correlate with a numerically arranged References list. This chapter focuses on this numbered reference system. Here is the way it works.

1. The first time you cite each source in your paper, assign it a number in sequence, starting with 1.

2. Mark each subsequent reference to that source with the assigned number.

3. For your References list, number each entry in the order of its appearance in your paper, starting with the first. Do not list sources alphabetically.

CSE recommends using superscript numbers for source citations in your paper, although numbers in parentheses are also acceptable.

IN-TEXT CITATIONS   Sybesma[1] insists that this behavior occurs periodically, but Crowder[2] claims never to have observed it.

REFERENCES LIST   1. Sybesma C. An introduction to biophysics. New York: Academic Press; 1977. 648 p.

2. Crowder W. Seashore life between the tides. New York: Dodd, Mead; 1931. New York: Dover Reprint; 1975. 372p.

Thereafter, each citation of Sybesma's *Introduction to Biophysics* would be followed by a superscript 1, each citation of Crowder's *Seashore Life* by a superscript 2.

BOX 43

 Guidelines for a CSE-style list of references

TITLE
References *or* Cited References

PLACEMENT OF LIST
Start a new page numbered sequentially with the rest of the paper.

CONTINUED →

BOX 43

 Guidelines for a CSE-style list of references *(continued)*

CONTENTS AND FORMAT

Include all sources quoted from, paraphrased, or summarized in your paper. Center the title about an inch from the top of the page. Start each entry on a new line. Put the number, followed by a period and a space at the left margin. If an entry takes more than one line, use a "hanging indent" for all other lines. Double-space each entry and between entries.

SPACING AFTER PUNCTUATION

Follow the spacing in the models.

ARRANGEMENT OF ENTRIES

Arrange the entries in the sequence in which each is first cited in the text.

AUTHORS' NAMES

Invert all authors' names, giving the last name first. You can give first names, or use only initials, or first and middle names. If you use initials, do not use a period or a space between first and middle initials, and separate the names of multiple authors with a comma. If you use full first names, separate the names of multiple authors with a semicolon. With multiple authors, do not use & or *and*. Place a period after the last author's name.

TREATMENT OF TITLES

Capitalize a newspaper title's major words, dropping a first word of *A, An*, or *The*. Capitalize the titles of academic journals. If a journal title is one word, give it in full; otherwise, abbreviate it according to *American National Standard for Abbreviations of Titles of Periodicals* recommendations. Do not underline titles or enclose them in quotation marks.

PLACE OF PUBLICATION

Use a colon after the city of publication. Add a state postal abbreviation, in parentheses, or a country name to a city whose name by itself might be ambiguous or unfamiliar (see the example in item 3 on p. 284).

PUBLISHERS

Give publishers' names, omitting *Co., Press, Ltd.*, and so on. Place a semicolon after the publisher's name.

CONTINUED →

Guidelines for a CSE-style list of references *(continued)*

PUBLICATION MONTH ABBREVIATIONS

Abbreviate publication months to their first three letters. Do not use a period at the end.

INCLUSIVE PAGE NUMBERS

Shorten the second number as much as possible while keeping the number unambiguous (*233–4* for *233 to 234*, *233–44* for *233 to 244*, *233–304*). Where *p* is used, do not follow it with a period unless it is the last item in the entry. Follow the guidelines in the models.

DISCONTINOUS PAGE NUMBERS

List all discontinous pages, shortening inclusive page numbers.

TOTAL PAGE NUMBERS

When citing an entire book, for the last information unit give the total number of pages followed by the abbreviation *p* and a period to end the information unit.

REFERENCES ENTRY: BOOK

Citations for books usually have four main parts: author(s), title, publication information, and pages (either total pages for citing an entire book or inclusive pages for citing part of a book). A period ends each information unit.

1. Stacy RW, Williams DT, Worden RE, McMorris RO. Essentials of biological and medical sciences. New York: McGraw-Hill; 1955. 747 p.

REFERENCES ENTRY: ARTICLE

Citations for articles usually have four main parts: author(s), article title, journal name, and publication information. The first two sections end with a period. In the example below, *Sci Am* is the abbreviated form of *Scientific American*. Note that there is no space between elements after the year. The volume number is 269, and the issue number is 3.

1. Weissmann IL, Cooper MD. How the immune system develops. Sci Am 1993; 269(3):65-71.

CSE
CSE
CSE
CSE
CSE
CSE
CSE
CSE

35b What are CSE guidelines for sources in a list of references?

The directory below corresponds to the sample references that follow it. Not every possible documentation model is here. For guidance in citing other sources, consult CSE's *Scientific Style and Format* (6th ed., 1994) or a journal in the discipline in which you are writing.

DIRECTORY—CSE STYLE

1. Book by One Author—CSE
2. Book by More Than One Author—CSE
3. Book by Group or Corporate Author—CSE
4. Anthology or Edited Book—CSE
5. One Selection or Chapter from an Anthology or Edited Book—CSE
6. Translation—CSE
7. Reprint of an Older Book—CSE
8. All Volumes of a Multivolume Work—CSE
9. Unpublished Dissertation or Thesis—CSE
10. Published Article from Conference Proceedings—CSE
11. Signed Newspaper Article—CSE
12. Unsigned Newspaper Article—CSE
13. Article in a Journal with Continuous Pagination—CSE
14. Article in a Journal That Pages Each Issue Separately—CSE
15. Journal Article on Discontinuous Pages—CSE
16. Article with Author Affiliation—CSE
17. Entire Issue of a Journal—CSE
18. Article with No Identifiable Author—CSE
19. Map—CSE
20. Unpublished Letter—CSE
21. Filmstrip—CSE
22. Videorecording—CSE
23. Slide Set—CSE
24. Electronic Sources—CSE

1. Book by One Author—CSE

1. Hawking SW. Black holes and baby universes and other essays. New York: Bantam Books; 1993. 320 p.

Use one space but no punctuation between an author's last name and the initial of the first name. Do not put punctuation or a space between a first and middle initial. Do, however, keep the hyphen in a hyphenated first and middle name. See item 2, where *Gille J-C* represents *Jean-Claude Gille*.

2. Book by More Than One Author—CSE

1. Wegzyn S, Gille J-C, Vidal P. Developmental systems: at the crossroads of system theory, computer science, and genetic engineering. New York: Springer-Verlag; 1990. 595 p.

3. Book by Group or Corporate Author—CSE

1. Chemical Rubber Company. Handbook of laboratory safety. 3rd ed. Boca Raton (FL): CRC; 1990. 1352 p.

4. Anthology or Edited Book—CSE

1. Heerman B, Hummel S., editors. Ancient DNA: recovery and analysis of genetic material from paleontological, archeological, museum, medical, and forensic specimens. New York: Springer-Verlag; 1994. 1020 p.

5. One Selection or Chapter from an Anthology or Edited Book—CSE

1. Basov NG, Feoktistov LP, Senatsky YV. Laser driver for inertial confinement fusion. In: Bureckner KA, editor. Research trends in physics: inertial confinement fusion. New York: American Institute of Physics; 1992. p 24–37.

6. Translation—CSE

1. Magris C. A different sea. Spurr MS, translator. London: Harvill; 1993. 194 p. Translation of: Un mare differente.

7. Reprint of an Older Book—CSE

1. Carson R. The sea around us. New York: Oxford University; 1951. New York: Limited Editions Club Reprint; 1980. 220 p.

8. All Volumes of a Multivolume Work—CSE

1. Crane FL, Moore DJ, Low HE, editors. Oxidoreduction at the plasma membrane: relation to growth and transport. Boca Raton (FL): Chemical Rubber Company; 1991. 2 vol.

9. Unpublished Dissertation or Thesis—CSE

1. Baykul MC. Using ballistic electron emission microscopy to investigate the metal-vacuum interface [dissertation]. Orem (UT): Polytechnic University; 1993. 111 p.

10. Published Article from Conference Proceedings—CSE

1. Tsang CP, Bellgard MI. Sequence generation using a network of Boltzmann machines. In: Tsang CP, editor. Proceedings of the 4th Australian Joint Conference on Artificial Intelligence; 1990 Nov 8–11; Perth, Australia. Singapore: World Scientific; 1990. p no. 224-33.

11. Signed Newspaper Article—CSE

1. Hoke F. Gene therapy: Clinical gains yield a wealth of research opportunities. Scientist 1993 Oct 4;Sect A:1, 5, 7.

Sect stands for *Section*.

12. Unsigned Newspaper Article—CSE

1. [Anonymous]. Irish urge postgame caution. USA Today 1993 Nov 12;Sect C:2.

13. Article in a Journal with Continuous Pagination—CSE

1. Scott ML, Fredrickson RJ, Moorhead BB. Characteristics of old-growth forests associated with northern spotted owls in Olympic National Park. J Wildlf Mgt 1993;57:315-21.

Give only the volume number, not an issue number, before the page numbers.

14. Article in a Journal That Pages Each Issue Separately—CSE

1. Weissman IL, Cooper MD. How the immune system develops. Sci Am 1993; 269(3):65-71.

Give both the volume number and the issue number (here, *269* is the volume number and *3* is the issue number).

15. Journal Article on Discontinuous Pages—CSE

1. Richards FM. The protein folding problem. Sci Am 1991 Nov;246(1):54-7, 60-6.

16. Article with Author Affiliation—CSE

1. DeMoll E, Auffenberg T (Dept. of Microbiology, Univ. of Kentucky). Purine metabolism in Methanococcus vannielii. J Bacteriol 1993;175:5754-61.

17. Entire Issue of a Journal—CSE

1. Whales in a modern world: a symposium held in London, November 1988. Mamm Rev 1990 Jan;20(9).

November 1988, the date of the symposium, is part of the title of this issue.

18. Article with No Identifiable Author—CSE

1. [Anonymous]. Cruelty to animals linked to murders of humans. AWI Q 1993 Aug;42(3):16.

19. Map—CSE

1. Russia and Post-Soviet Republics [political map]. Moscow: Mapping Production Association; 1992. Conical equidistant projection; 40 X 48 in.; color, scale 1:8,000,000.

20. Unpublished Letter—CSE

1. Darwin C. [Letter to Mr. Clerke, 1861]. Located at: University of Iowa Library, Iowa City, IA.

21. Filmstrip—CSE

1. Volcano: the eruption and healing of Mount St. Helens [filmstrip]. Westminster (MD): Random House; 1988. 114 frames: color; 35 mm. Accompanied by: cassette tape; 22 min.

After the title and description of the filmstrip, give the author, producer, and year. Then give other descriptive information.

22. Videorecording—CSE

1. The discovery of the pulsar: the ultimate ignorance [videocassette]. London: BBC; 1983. 1 cassette: 48 min, sound, color.

23. Slide Set—CSE

1. Human parasitology [slides]. Chicago (IL): American Society of Clinical Pathologists; 1990. Color. Accompanied by: 1 guide.

24. Electronic Sources—CSE

In general, the CSE manual advises that you cite electronic sources by starting with a statement of the type of document, then giving the information you would give for a print version. Next, give information that would help a reader to locate the electronic source. End with a date: your access date for online sources or the date of the update you used for CD-ROM databases that are updated periodically.

For more information, see CSE's website http://www.nlm.nih.gov/pubs/formats/internet.pdf.

36 COS DOCUMENTATION

For electronic publications, *The Columbia Guide to Online Style* (COS or CO style) by Janice R. Walker and Todd Taylor (Columbia UP, 1998) provides an alternative to other documentation styles.

36a What should I know about COS documentation?

COS uses many of the same citation elements that are present in predominantly print documentation styles such as MLA and APA. However, COS includes new format elements unique to electronic publications. COS for the humanities is similar to MLA style, while COS for the sciences shares elements of APA style. Be sure to find out from your instructor which style to use.

Citing sources in the body of a paper in COS

In print publications, in-text or PARENTHETICAL REFERENCES include elements such as the author's last name and the page number of the reference. Many electronic sources lack such elements, and COS allows for these differences. If an author's name is unknown, refer to the material by its title. Since most electronic sources are not numbered, page references may be irrelevant. Commonly, COS parenthetical citations use only the author's name for humanities style and the author's name and date of publication for scientific style.

👁 **COS CITATION ALERT:** If page numbers, sections, or other navigational aids are available, separate them with a comma and include them in the parenthetical citation as well. 👁

HUMANITIES STYLE

According to the survey, over 80% of the students waited until the night before an exam to begin studying (Jani).

👁 **COS CITATION ALERT:** When the author's name is included in the sentence, the IN-TEXT CITATION is unnecessary. If there is more than one work by the author, use the work's title. 👁

SCIENTIFIC STYLE

The research proved conclusively that individuals deprived of sleep were as dangerous as those driving under the influence of drugs or alcohol (Rezik, 2000).

 COS CITATION ALERT: If the publication date is unavailable, use the date of access (in day-month-year format). ◉

Creating COS bibliographic citations

Box 44 gives guidelines for a COS Works Cited list.

■ BOX 44 ■

◉ Guidelines for a COS Works Cited list

TITLE

Works Cited should be centered, 1 inch below the top of your bibliography page, in upper- and lowercase letters. The title should not be enclosed in quotation marks or be boldfaced, italicized, or underlined.

PLACEMENT OF LIST

If you are producing a print document, begin the Works Cited on a new page, numbered sequentially with the rest of the paper. If your document is a HYPERTEXT publication, you may use a separate file and a link to this page in the table of contents.

CONTENT AND FORMAT

See MLA guidelines in Box 40 (pp. 187–91).

ARRANGEMENT OF ENTRIES

See MLA guidelines in Box 40 (pp. 187–91).

AUTHORS' NAMES

Finding the author of a source may not be simple. Often, online writers use an alias. List your source by these alternate names when they are the only ones you find. If an author's name cannot be identified, cite the source by its title.

In humanities style, give the author's full last name and first and middle names (if available); in scientific style, give the author's full last name and first and middle initials (if applicable). List any additional authors by first name (humanities) or first initial (scientific), followed by the full last name.

CONTINUED ——▶

Guidelines for a COS Works Cited list *(continued)*

CAPITALIZATION AND SPECIAL TREATMENT OF TITLES

Use italics rather than underlining for the titles of complete works. Since hypertext links are underlined online, an underlined title may confuse your readers.

In humanities style, enclose titles of articles and excerpts from longer works in quotation marks, and capitalize all major words. In scientific style, do not distinguish titles of articles and excerpts of longer works in any way, and capitalize only the first word of the title and proper nouns. (If a title is unavailable, use the file name.)

PLACE OF PUBLICATION, PUBLISHER, AND ELECTRONIC ADDRESS

When citing electronic sources available in fixed formats, such as software and certain electronic publications, a publisher and city are usually listed and should be cited.

In online publishing, the city of publication and publisher often are not relevant to Web sites and other open-format electronic sources. In those cases, provide the URL, which is a source's entire electronic address. For long addresses that exceed a line, follow MLA style: Break only after slashes and do not hyphenate.

VERSION OR FILE NUMBER

When applicable, provide the specific file number or version of a program for your reference.

DOCUMENT PUBLICATION OR LAST REVISION DATE

Include a page's publication date or the date of its last revision, unless it is identical to the access date. For humanities style, abbreviate all month names longer than three letters to their first three letters, followed by a period. For scientific style, do not abbreviate names of months.

DATE OF ACCESS

With the constant updates of online material, readers may have a difficult time finding the same content in a source you cite. Always provide the date of access for an online source because it specifies the version of the page you have cited. For humanities and scientific styles, abbreviate month names to three letters, followed by a period.

CONTINUED ➝

BOX 44

Guidelines for a COS Works Cited list *(continued)*

NAVIGATION POINTS

On the World Wide Web, a given site usually occupies one page, regardless of its length. When available, list any helpful navigational aids, such as page references, paragraph numbers, or sections or parts, in your citation. Keep in mind that often these aids are not available.

BIBLIOGRAPHIC CITATION: HUMANITIES

Follow this form as closely as possible in your citations:

Author's Last Name, First Name. "Title of Document." *Title of Complete Work* [if applicable]. Version or File Number [if applicable]. Document date or date of last revision [if known and if different from access date]. Protocol and address, access path or directories (date of access).

BIBLIOGRAPHIC CITATION: SCIENCES

Follow this form as closely as possible in your citations.

Author's Last Name, Initial(s). (Date of document [if known and if different from date accessed]). Title of document. *Title of complete work* [if applicable]. Version or File number [if applicable]. (Edition or revision [if applicable]). Protocol and address, access path or directories (date of access or visit; or date of message).

36b What are COS guidelines for sources in a Works Cited list?

The directory below corresponds to the sample bibliographic forms that follow. COS distinguishes between humanities style and scientific style in creating a bibliography, so you will find all the models given twice, once in each style, to help you be consistent and correct when formatting your references.

DIRECTORY—COS GUIDELINES

1. Site on the World Wide Web—COS
2. Modified or Revised Site—COS
3. Maintained or Compiled Site—COS
4. Article from a Periodical—COS
5. Article in an Online Journal—COS

6. Work by a Group or Organization—COS
7. Corporate Home Pages and Information—COS
8. Government Information and Sites—COS
9. Book Accessed Online—COS
10. Graphic, Video, or Audio File on the Page—COS
11. Personal Electronic Mail (E-mail)—COS
12. Posting to a Discussion List—COS
13. Posting to a Newsgroup or Forum—COS
14. Archived Posting—COS
15. Online Reference Sources—COS
16. Computer Information Services and Online Databases—COS
17. Gopher Site—COS
18. FTP Site—COS
19. Telnet Site—COS
20. Synchronous Communication—COS
21. Software—COS

1. Site on the World Wide Web—COS

H:*   Blackmon, Samantha. *Cows in the Classroom?: MOOs and MUDs and MUSHes . . . Oh My!* 24 Aug. 2000. http://www.sla.purdue.edu/people/engl/blackmon/moo/index.html (11 Mar. 2001).

S: Blackmon, S. (2000, August 24). Cows in the classroom? MOOs and MUDs and MUSHes . . . oh my!!! http://www.sla.purdue.edu/people/engl/blackmon/moo/index.html (11 Mar. 2001).

2. Modified or Revised Site—COS

H: Grant, William E., and Ken Dvorak. *The American 1890s: A Chronology.* Mod. Spring 2000. http://www.bgsu.edu/departments/acs/1890s/america.html (22 Nov. 2000).

S: Grant, W. E., and K. Dvorak. (2000). The American 1890s: A chronology. (Mod. Spring 2000). http://www.bgsu.edu/departments/acs/1890s/america.html (22 Nov. 2000).

If the site is revised, use the abbreviation *Rev.* in place of *Mod.*

* H = Humanities Style; S = Scientific Style

3. Maintained or Compiled Site—COS

H: *E-Zine-List.* Maint. John Labovitz. 8 Mar. 2000. http://www.meer.net/
     ~johnl/e-zine-list (15 Sep. 2000).

S: E-zine-list. (2000, March 8). (John Labovitz, Maint.),
     http://www.meer.net/~johnl/e-zine-list (15 Sep. 2000).

If the site is compiled, use the abbreviation *Comp.* in place of *Maint.*

4. Article from a Periodical—COS

H: Kaplan, Carl S. "Suit Considers Computer Files." *New York Times* (28
     Sep. 2000). http://www.nytimes.com/2000/09/28/technology/
     29CYBERLAW.html (13 Oct. 2000).

S: Kaplan, C. S. (2000, September 28). Suit considers computer files. *The
     New York Times.* http://www.nytimes.com/2000/09/28/technology/
     29CYBERLAW.html (13 Oct. 2000).

5. Article in an Online Journal—COS

H: Winickoff, Jonathan P., et al. "Verve and Jolt: Deadly New Internet
     Drugs." *Pediatrics* 106.4 (Oct. 2000). http://www.pediatrics.org/cgi/
     content/abstract/106/4/829 (10 May 2000).

S: Winickoff, J. P., et al. (2000, October). Verve and jolt: Deadly new
     Internet drugs. *Pediatrics, 106*(4). http://www.pediatrics.org/cgi/
     content/abstract/106/4/829 (10 May 2000).

6. Work by a Group or Organization—COS

H: Environmental Protection Agency. "Browner Lauds Hill Action to
     Protect Everglades, Beaches. Urges House of Representatives to
     Finalize Everglades Plan." 28 Sep. 2000.
     http://www.epa.gov/epahome/headline_0928.htm (29 Nov. 2000).

S: Environmental Protection Agency. (2000, September 28). Browner
     lauds hill action to protect Everglades, beaches. Urges House of
     Representatives to finalize Everglades plan. http://www.epa.gov/
     epahome/headline_0928.htm (29 Nov. 2000).

7. Corporate Home Pages and Information—COS

H: Pearson PLC. "Pearson Home Page." 1999.
     http://www.pearson.com (12 Apr. 2001).

S: Pearson PLC. (1999). Pearson home page.
     http://www.pearson.com (12 Apr. 2001).

8. Government Information and Sites—COS

H: Central Intelligence Agency. "Speeches and Testimony." 6 Oct. 2000.
      http://www.cia.gov/cia/public_affairs/speeches/speeches.html
      (18 Dec. 2000).

S: Central Intelligence Agency. (2000, October 6). Speeches and
      testimony. http://www.cia.gov/cia/public_affairs/speeches/
      speeches.html (18 Dec. 2000).

9. Book Accessed Online—COS

BOOK PUBLISHED FIRST IN PRINT VERSION

H: Brontë, Charlotte. *Jane Eyre*. London: Service & Paton, 1887. 1999.
      University of Maryland Reading Room.
      http://www.inform.umd.edu/EdRes/Reading Room/Fiction/
      Cbronte/JaneEyre/ (15 Sep. 2000).

S: Brontë, C. (1887). *Jane Eyre*. London: Service & Paton. (1999). *University
      of Maryland Reading Room*. http://www.inform.umd.edu/EdRes/
      ReadingRoom/Fiction/Cbronte/JaneEyre/ (15 Sep. 2000).

BOOK PUBLISHED ONLINE

H: Shires, Bob. *CPR (Cardiopulmonary Resuscitation) Guide*. 17 Jan. 2000.
      http://www.memoware.com/
      Category=Medicine_ResultSet=1.htm (17 Apr. 2000).

S: Shires, B. (2000, January 17). *CPR (cardiopulmonary resuscitation)
      guide*. http://www.memoware.com/
      Category=Medicine_ResultSet=1.htm (17 Apr. 2000).

10. Graphic, Video, or Audio File on the Page—COS

H: owl.gif. 2000. "Original free clipart." *Clipart.com*. http://
      www.free-clip-art.net/index4.shtml (27 Oct. 2000).

S: owl.gif [graphic file] (2000). Original free clipart. *Clipart.com*.
      http://www.free-clip-art.net/index4.shtml (27 Oct. 2000).

11. Personal Electronic Mail (E-mail)—COS

H: Torres, Elizabeth. "Re: Puerto Rican Baseball History." Personal
      e-mail (11 Sep. 2000).

S: Torres, E. Re: Puerto Rican baseball history. [Personal e-mail].
      (11 Sep. 2000).

12. Posting to a Discussion List—COS

H: Sheldon, Amy. "Re: Request for Help on Sexism Inscription." 2 Jan.
     2000. *FLING List for Feminists in Linguistics*.
     http://listserv.linguistlist.org (14 Nov. 2000).

S: Sheldon, A. (2000, January 2). Re: Request for help on sexism
     inscription. *FLING List for Feminists in Linguistics*.
     http://listserv.linguistlist.org (14 Nov. 2000).

13. Posting to a Newsgroup or Forum—COS

H: Markowitz, Al. "The Changing Face of Work: A Look at the Way We
     Work." 28 Sep. 2000. http://yourturn.npr.org/cgi-bin/
     WebX?50@121.HjNGardZdaj^0@.ee7a9aa (8 Jan. 2001).

S: Markowitz, A. (2000, September 28). The changing face of work: A look
     at the way we work. http://yourturn.npr.org/cgi-bin/
     WebX?50@121.HjNGardZdaj^0@.ee7a9aa (8 Jan. 2001).

14. Archived Posting—COS

H: Radev, Dragomir R. "Natural Language Processing FAQ." 16 Sep.
     1999. *Institute of Information and Computing Sciences*. http://
     www.cs.ruu.nl/wais/html/na-dir/
     natural-lang-processing-faq.html (27 Jan. 1999).

S: Radev, D. R. (1999, September 16). Natural language processing FAQ.
     Institute of Information and Computing Sciences.
     http://www.cs.ruu.nl/wais/html/na-dir/
     natural-lang-processing-faq.html (27 Jan. 1999).

15. Online Reference Sources—COS

Reference sources such as online encyclopedias, dictionaries, thesaur-
uses, style manuals, bibliographies, or other forms of factual material
can be cited using this model.

H: Nordenberg, Tamar. 2000. "Make No Mistake! Medical Errors Can Be
     Deadly Serious." *Britannica.com*. Ebsco Publishing. http://
     britannica.com/bcom/original/article/0,5744,12430,00.html
     (12 Dec. 2000).

S: Nordenberg, T. (2000). Make no mistake! Medical errors can be deadly
     serious. *Britannica.com*. Ebsco Publishing. http://britannica.com/
     bcom/original/article/0,5744,12430,00.html (12 Dec. 2000).

16. Computer Information Services and Online Databases—COS

H: Raintree Nutrition, Inc. "Pata de Vaca." Jun. 2000. *Raintree Tropical Plant Database*. http://www.rain-tree.com/patadevaca.htm (9 Sep. 2000).

S: Raintree Nutrition Inc. (2000, June). Pata de Vaca. *Raintree Tropical Plant Database*. http://www.rain-tree.com/patadevaca.htm (9 Sep. 2000).

17. Gopher Site—COS

H: "Elections." May 1996. gopher://israel-info.gov.il/00/facts/state/ st4 (27 Dec. 2000).

S: Elections. (1996, May). gopher://israel-info.gov.il/00/facts/state/ st4 (27 Dec. 2000).

18. FTP Site—COS

H: Project Gutenberg. 2000, Mar. 26. *Ibiblio.org*. ftp://metalab.unc.edu/ pub/docs/books/gutenberg (12 Aug. 2000).

S: Project Gutenberg. (2000, March 26). *Ibiblio.org*. ftp://metalab.unc.edu/ pub/docs/books/gutenberg (12 Aug. 2000).

19. Telnet Site—COS

H: Schweller, Kenneth G. "How to Design a Bot." *Collegetown MOO*. 28 May 1999. telnet://galaxy.bvu.edu:7777 (16 Nov. 2000).

S: Schweller, K. G. (1999, May 28). How to design a bot. *Collegetown MOO*. telnet://galaxy.bvu.edu:7777 (16 Nov. 2000).

20. Synchronous Communication—COS

H: Dominguez, Jose. "Interchange." *Daedalus Online*. http://daedalus.pearsoned.com (11 Mar. 2001).

S: Dominguez, J. Interchange. *Daedalus Online*. http://daedalus.pearsoned.com (11 Mar. 2001).

21. Software—COS

H: Wresch, William. *Writer's Helper* Vers. 4.0. Upper Saddle River: Prentice Hall, 1998.

S: Wresch, W. (1998). *Writer's Helper* Vers. 4.0. Upper Saddle River: Prentice Hall.

Document
and Web Design

www.prenhall.com/troyka

Document and Web Design

37 DOCUMENT DESIGN

37a What is document design?

Document design refers to the **layout**, also called the *format*, of print and any accompanying GRAPHICS* on each page of your essays, papers, and Web pages. First impressions count. When readers see your document, they immediately form opinions about you and your information. A well-designed document influences readers positively because it reflects your respect for the assignment and the effort you made to master the required format.

Today, few college instructors accept handwritten essays and research papers, so check before you submit your work. If you don't own a computer, use one at your college's computer lab. Always find out whether you need to sign up in advance or can use the computers on a "first come, first served" basis. Give yourself sufficient time to get there, wait your turn, and go back repeatedly as needed. Use your computer time efficiently by taking your final handwritten draft with you.

37b What is the document design process?

The process of designing documents involves the same steps as the WRITING PROCESS (Chs. 5–7), with a few added considerations.

Plan ahead by finding out the specific page layout and other features your instructor requires, so you can avoid last-minute confusion. If you're going to use GRAPHICS, plan their form, content, and size from the beginning of your project.

As you revise, integrate the layout and other design features as you go along. One decision you need to make is whether to put all your graphics in an appendix (recommended in MLA STYLE) or insert them as they come up (fitting them exactly where you want them can be difficult). Check whether your instructor has a preference. As you revise, check that the content of your graphics matches what you say about them in the revised text of your paper. You might need to revise a graphic to match your text or your wording to match a graphic.

---

* Words printed in small capital letters (such as GRAPHICS) are defined in the Terms Glossary on pages 467–85.

37c What are some general guidelines for designing documents?

If your instructor gives you specific layout or format instructions, use them. Otherwise, follow these guidelines.

- **Margins:** Margins are the blank areas not only on the sides of each page but also at the top and bottom. In ACADEMIC WRITING, always use at least an inch on all sides.

- **Spacing of lines:** For college essays and research papers, double spacing is standard. The extra space gives you, your peers, and your instructors room to write comments in response to your writing. In contrast, business writing usually calls for single-spaced lines in BLOCK STYLE, with double spaces between paragraphs (Ch. 63).

- **Font:** A font is the typeface you use. Select a standard font such as Times Roman, Bookman Old Style, or New Century Schoolbook. Avoid sans-serif fonts such as Helvetica, Arial, Gothic, and Univers, as well as fancy fonts such as MS Comic Sans and handwriting typefaces. As called for by your content, use ITALICS (or underlining) and boldface type in the same font as the rest of the document. For size, select the standard 12-point (easiest to read) and 10-point fonts.

- **Paragraph style:** College essays and research papers call for paragraphs with indented first lines and double spacing throughout the paper. Leave no extra space between paragraphs. BUSINESS WRITING calls for unindented first lines, single spacing of paragraphs, and double spacing between paragraphs (unless your instructor specifies otherwise), a format called *block style*. Never mix these two paragraph styles.

- **Title:** Never underline the title or enclose it in quotation marks. For college essays and research papers, place the title at the top of the first page of a document—unless your instructor tells you to use a **title page**, which calls for the title, your name, and the course name and number on one page (Chs. 30, 33).

37d How do I format each type of document?

Throughout this book, you can find examples of specific formats for many types of documents.

- Essays to inform and to argue (Chs. 9, 10)
- MLA-style research papers (Chs. 10, 30).

- APA-style research paper (Ch. 33)
- Web page structures and hyperlinks (Ch. 38)
- Essay about literature (Ch. 62)
- Business letters and memos (Ch. 63)
- Résumés and job application letters (Ch. 63)

Most word processing software doesn't provide the standard formats for college essays or research papers, so you need to follow your instructor's guidelines or the guidelines in this book. However, most word processing programs do provide page layouts for letters, envelopes, and memos in the form of **templates** ("fill-in-the-blank" forms) or **wizards** (questions about what you want to do).

37e How do I use headings in my writing?

Headings, like newspaper and magazine headlines, guide your reader through your document. Write headings that are brief and informative so your readers can scan them easily. Always use PARALLELISM in their wording, capitalization, and typeface. As in OUTLINES, headings have levels: first level, second level, and so on. College essays and research papers rarely call for more than two heading levels. Be consistent in the form you use for each level of heading. For example, if you capitalize or boldface one heading, do the same with other headings at the same level. Here are some common types of headings, with examples.

NOUN PHRASES, FOR A VARIETY OF SUBTOPICS

- Executive Branch of Government
- Legislative Branch of Government
- Judicial Branch of Government

QUESTIONS, FOR EVOKING INTEREST

- When May the President Use Veto Power?
- How Does the Legislative Branch Make Laws?
- How Does the Supreme Court Decide Whether to Consider a Case?

-*ING* PHRASES, FOR EXPLAINING INSTRUCTIONS OR SOLVING PROBLEMS

- Submitting the Congressional Budget
- Updating the Congressional Budget
- Approving the Congressional Budget

IMPERATIVE SENTENCES, FOR ADVICE OR DIRECTIONS

- Identify Problem
- Poll Constituents
- Draft Bill
- Introduce Bill in Legislature

37f When are graphics appropriate in my writing?

Graphics include tables, bar graphs, line graphs, pie charts, timelines, and diagrams that you create or import from the Internet. You can also import photographs, clip art, and drawings. Be sure to check whether you need permission to use imported items—and ask for it according to the instructions on each Web site. Usually, a student who is writing for a college course can use such material for free "one time only." Equally important, be sure to DOCUMENT your source.

Graphics convey information that lends itself to visual presentation. Sometimes, a graphic can condense, compare, and display information more effectively than words can. Most word processing programs offer standard conversion methods to change words into tables. The programs also provide TEMPLATES for some types of graphs and charts. If you have access to a color printer, some of your graphics can look quite dramatic. Never be tempted, however, to present all your information in graphics. Strive instead for a balance between text and graphics; let graphics enhance your writing, not replace it. An excellent site to consult about using graphics is *Online Technical Writing* at <http://www.io.com/~hcexres/tcm1603/acchtml/graphics.html>.

Tables present lists of data or words, as in the MLA-style sample paper (p. 214) and APA-style research papers (p. 263). The table below lists the degree programs offered at the Art Institute of Houston, Texas.

Table 1-1 Degree Programs: The Art Institute of Houston, Texas

Media Arts	Design	Culinary Arts
Web Design & Development	Computer-aided Drafting & Design	Culinary Arts
Multimedia	Interior Design	Restaurant & Catering Management
Video Production	Graphic Design	
	Computer Animation	

Bar graphs compare values, such as the number of different majors at a college, as shown in the graph below.

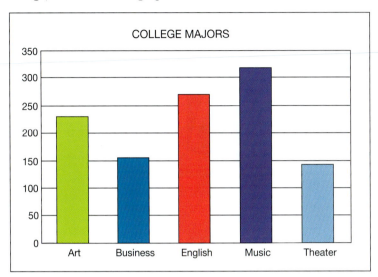

Line graphs indicate changes over time. For example, the graph below shows advertising revenue over an eight-month period.

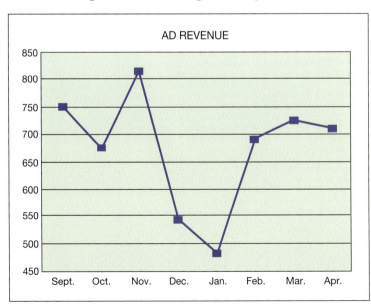

Pie charts show the relationship of each part to a whole, such as a typical budget for a college student, shown in the chart below.

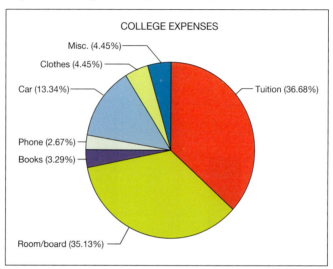

Timelines display events over time, such as the progress of historical events, shown in the chart below.

Diagrams show the parts of a whole, as in this diagram of the human brain, shown in the chart below.

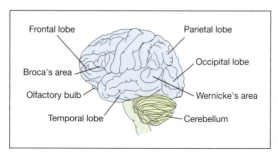

38 WRITING FOR THE WEB

38a What is the Web writing process?

The **Web writing process** is visual as well as verbal. This process has four parts: it starts with writing the content, moves to making decisions about the structure of the content, continues with planning the layout of the material on the computer screen, and ends with checking whether the Web material is usable. Box 45 outlines this process.

BOX 45

⦿ The Web writing process

CONTENT Begin your Web writing project with a content plan that declares your AUDIENCE, your PURPOSE, and the message you want your project to deliver.

STRUCTURE Divide your content into many short computer documents, also called *files*. (Another term for computer documents or files is *writing spaces*, which indicates that the material exists primarily in cyberspace rather than on paper.) Decide on the kind and number of documents you want to include, as well as their level of specialization. Think about the order (called a *path*) in which people will read your documents. Finally, consider linking your documents to supporting sources on the World Wide Web.

LAYOUT Decide how to present the words and graphic elements in each document—the images, backgrounds, and colors—on the computer screen. Think about how to place these elements so that they'll appear to be purposefully arranged.

USABILITY Invite others to try out your Web project by testing all aspects of it. Ask them to make sure that your message suits your audience and purpose; that the structure and layout of your documents support your purpose and reach your audience; that the links you added are appropriate and function well; and that the entire project works effectively as a unit.

The four parts of the Web writing process are interconnected. The decisions you make for one part affect those you make for the other three. The details of your Web writing assignment and the amount of time for its completion influence your decisions for each of the four parts of the Web writing process.

38b How do I plan content for my Web site?

Planning logically

To plan logically, you first need to choose a TOPIC suitable for a Web writing project. You can do this using the strategies suggested in Chapter 5, but with your eye on the unique medium of the Web. The Web differs from other media in distinct ways that affect your writing.

- Web writing calls for smaller sections than print writing.
- Web writing highlights the connections or links between related Web sites.
- Web writing emphasizes visual elements like color and pictures.

Your next step is to plan your writing PURPOSE, choose your AUDIENCE, and analyze your WRITING SITUATION. Ask yourself these questions:

- What is my overall purpose in writing for the Web? Will I aim to create a site that seeks to INFORM, or to PERSUADE, or to combine these purposes?
- What is the size of my Web writing project? Web projects function as collections of computer documents (individual files ending in *htm*, *html*, and the like) linked together and displayed as "pages" on a computer screen. You need to determine the number of documents you want and the amount of content to include in each. Keep in mind that Web readers scan quickly and prefer not to scroll down long sections of information.
- How many links to other **Web sites** should I include? Choose links that directly support your Web project's message by going to an illustration, an explanation, a reference, or other material that can expand your reader's thinking.
- Who will my readers be? Can I assume that they know how to navigate—that is, move—from one document to another? Your Web readers need to be able to move around without getting lost. Many Web writers include a table of contents or a "site map" on the opening document, called the **home page**.

Collaborating effectively

Collaborative writing means sharing and distributing tasks among members of a group. This type of writing is especially suitable for Web writing projects. By working with a team, you can improve each part of your Web writing project, especially at the USABILITY stage in the process. Your Web writing needs to reach and hold the interest of an audience, so the more people who preview your work, the better. Even if you don't complete each part of your Web writing project in collaboration with others, ask one or more of your peers to assess the logic and appeal of your material.

38c How do I create a structure for my Web site?

Web structure is the organization of the content and documents included in a Web project. Often this process begins with the HOME PAGE, which links to all the documents included in the Web project. Many Web writers draw a map of their Web structure so that they can keep track of all their documents and links.

Forming structures and hyperlinks

Just as writers use paragraphing strategies to organize their essays (Ch. 8), you use Web structures to organize your Web writings. When you start writing for the Web, choose only one structure so that your readers are less likely to get lost as they navigate among your documents. Here is a list of the most common structures for Web writing, followed by a figure that illustrates them.

LINEAR STRUCTURE	A series of documents linked in a sequence that establishes expectations of what will come next (number 4 following 3, for example)
OUTLINE STRUCTURE	A series of documents arranged from general to specific or specific to general
CLUSTER STRUCTURE	Groups of documents related to your overall message
MEANDERING STRUCTURE	No apparent structure

To connect your documents into one of these structures, use hyperlinks A **hyperlink** is a direct electronic connection between two documents (*hyper* means "fast" and *link* means "connection"). Combinations of hyperlinks are the glue that holds Web writings together. They also make your Web writings interactive by allowing Web readers to select what they want to see next from among your hyperlink choices.

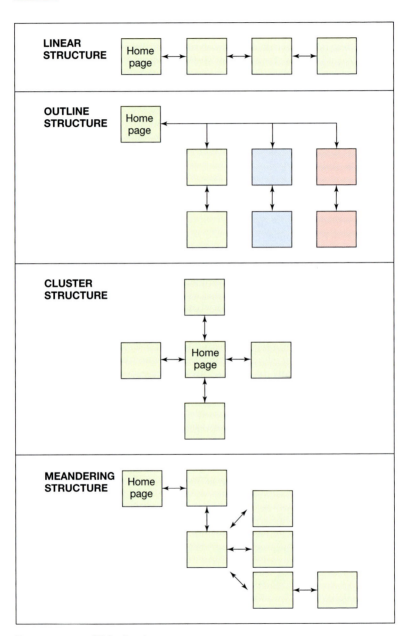

Some common Web structures

At a minimum, each of your Web documents should include two hyperlinks, one of them a **home link** to take people looking at other pages back to where they started—that is, to your home page. With your structure in mind, choose the types of hyperlinks you need to connect your Web documents. The figure below illustrates how hyperlinks work.

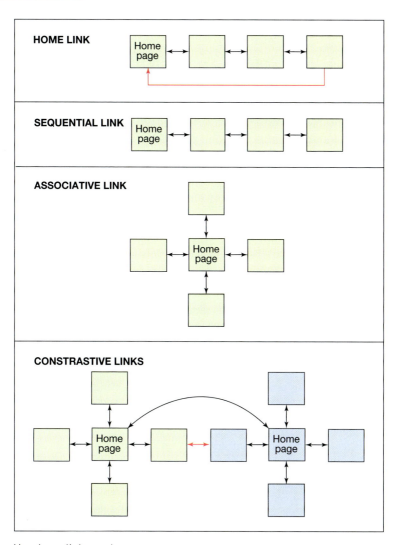

How hyperlinks work

HOME LINK Moves back to the opening document, or home page, on which you might want to include a table of contents and/or a comprehensive list of hyperlinks.

SEQUENTIAL LINK Moves to the next document in an outline or hierarchical progression.

ASSOCIATIVE LINK Moves to a related document with content that supports your Web site's central idea (also called a *related link*).

CONTRASTIVE LINK Moves to a document with content that challenges your Web site's central idea (also called a *refutation link*).

Providing departure and arrival information

Departure and arrival information tells Web readers where they are in your Web project and where they can go next if they follow a hyperlink. This information keeps them from getting lost in your Web project—and helps clarify your message.

- Name your documents to help readers identify their content.

- Start each document in your Web project with a brief heading and perhaps a short description. This gives your readers a rationale for spending time with the document.

- Name your hyperlinks so that people can identify their content, whether they connect to a written document or a graphic.

- Maintain PARALLELISM as you name your documents and hyperlinks so that your Web project conveys a sense of unity and consistency.

38d How do I compose a layout for my Web site?

Web layout is the process of arranging and presenting the elements of your Web project—type styles, headings, lines, colors, graphics, animated images, video, and so on—on the screen. Try to find the right balance among these many elements so that they complement your overall message and communicate it directly. Don't try to pack too much into a single screen or writing space.

Using Web writing software

One early layout decision to make is which kind of software you'll use to compose your documents. Web writing programs such as Netscape Composer, HotMetal Pro, Microsoft FrontPage, and Dreamweaver allow you to construct Web documents in much the same way as you compose word-processed documents—and you don't have to learn HTML code. These programs also allow you to organize and edit your document files, and they even provide ready-made TEMPLATES from which you can select, for a fee, prepared layout choices, including background colors, heading styles, placement or graphic elements, and text styles (font, size, color).

Choosing typefaces

A **typeface**, also called a *font*, is the set of individual letters that make up your Web writings. The typeface you choose greatly affects the appearance of your Web writing. As you lay out your material, consider the size and style of type you want to use.

Selecting the right graphics

Graphics are the visual means of communication that accompany your text. Graphics can increase the effectiveness of your Web writing if you choose them cautiously. To select appropriate graphics, ask yourself these questions.

- What graphics should I include?
- How do I know whether I need permission from its creator to use a graphic on my Web site? Examine the graphic and its surrounding material carefully to see whether a copyright notice announces that permission is required before anyone can use the material. If none is present, you can assume that you can use the graphic. If a notice is present, it usually includes an e-mail address to which you can send a brief note explaining why you want to use the graphic and—most important—whether you intend to make money from your Web project. (Generally, you will be given free permission if you are writing for a class project or another educational purpose, but if you're writing a for-profit Web project, you are expected to pay a fee.)
- How do I DOCUMENT a graphic appropriately to show its source? (For the correct documentation format for your graphic sources, see Ch. 29 for MLA style; Chs. 31 and 32 for APA style.)

Using color

Computer screens can reproduce millions of color combinations. For consistency in appearance, you want to use the same color combinations in all your documents for a particular Web project.

Arranging text and graphics on the screen

Use the following general principles to arrange your text and graphics on the screen.

CONSISTENCY	Keep the overall appearance of your Web documents about the same in terms of typefaces, graphics, and color.
CONTINUITY	Place repeated elements in about the same location in each of your Web documents so that people always know where to find them. These elements include the HOME PAGE link, other HYPERLINKS, your e-mail address, a signature graphic image, and so on.
COHERENCE	Choose words and graphics that go together. For example, if your Web writing project is about outdoor camping, choose graphics that illustrate the activities you describe, such as campfires and canoes.
SIMPLICITY	Keep it simple. Computer screens are small, and most readers move quickly through the Web.

38e How do I make sure my Web writings are usable?

Usability testing helps you measure the success of your Web project according to your audience and purpose. Working collaboratively with your peers and instructor is the best way to test your Web project's effectiveness. Consider the following questions.

• Is my Web project trouble-free? Test to make sure all your HYPERLINKS work and that the documents upload correctly.

• Is my Web project user-friendly? Ask your Web readers to report any sections in which information is difficult to find.

• Does my project's message come through? You need feedback on what your Web readers remember about your message.

• Is everything consistent and correct?

38f How can I publish my Web project?

The final step of your Web project is publishing it on the Internet. This can be a simple or complicated step, depending on the circumstances of your Web assignment. If you wrote your Web project for a class, your instructor may have arranged to provide you with access to the Internet through your college's Web site. If your Web project is unrelated to your class work—for example, if it is a project for a student organization or club—you need to locate a host or purchase space from an Internet service provider.

Grammar Basics

www.prenhall.com/troyka

Grammar Basics

39 PARTS OF SPEECH AND PARTS OF SENTENCES

Parts of Speech

Knowing the parts of speech gives you a basic vocabulary for identifying words and understanding how language works. No part of speech exists in a vacuum. To identify a word's part of speech correctly, you need to see how the word functions in the sentence you are analyzing. Often, the same word functions differently in different sentences.

- We ate **fish.** [*Fish* is a NOUN.* It represents a thing.]

- We **fish** on weekends. [*Fish* is a VERB. It represents an action.]

39a What is a noun?

A **noun** represents a person, place, thing, or idea: *student, college, textbook, education.* Box 46 lists types of nouns.

BOX 46

◎ Types of nouns*

PROPER	names of specific people, places, or things (first letter is always capitalized)	*Garth Brooks, Paris, Buick*
COMMON	general groups, places, people, or things	*singer, city, automobile*
CONCRETE	things experienced through the senses: sight, hearing, taste, smell, and touch	*landscape, pizza, thunder*
ABSTRACT	things not knowable through the senses	*freedom, shyness*
COLLECTIVE	groups	*family, team*
NONCOUNT	"uncountable" things	*beef, dirt*
COUNT	countable items (singular or plural)	*lake (lakes), minute (minutes)*

*Some nouns fit into more than one category. For example, *family* is both a common noun and a collective noun.

* Words printed in small capital letters (such as NOUN) are defined in the Terms Glossary on pages 467–85.

ESL NOTES: (1) Nouns often appear with words that tell how much, how many, whose, which one, and similar information. These words include ARTICLES (*a, an, the*), ADJECTIVES, and other DETERMINERS. (2) Words with these SUFFIXES (word endings) are usually nouns: *-ance, -ence, -ment, -ness,* and *-ty.*

39b What is a pronoun?

A **pronoun** stands for or refers to a NOUN. The word or words a pronoun replaces are called its **antecedents** (42a). Box 47 lists types of pronouns.

- **David** is an accountant. [noun]

- **He** is an accountant. [pronoun]

- The budget committee needs to consult **him.** [The pronoun *him* refers to its antecedent, *David.*]

BOX 47

Types of pronouns

PERSONAL *I, you, they, her, its, ours,* and others	refers to people or things	I saw **her** take a book to **them.**
RELATIVE *who, which, that*	introduces certain NOUN CLAUSES and ADJECTIVE CLAUSES	The book **that** I lost was valuable.
INTERROGATIVE *who, whose, what, which,* and others	introduces a question	**Who** called?
DEMONSTRATIVE *this, these, that, those*	points out the antecedent	Whose books are **these?**
REFLEXIVE; INTENSIVE *myself, themselves,* and other *-self* or *-selves* words	reflects back to the antecedent; intensifies the antecedent	They claim to support **themselves.** I **myself** doubt it.
RECIPROCAL *each other, one another*	refers to individual parts of a plural antecedent	We respect **each other.**
INDEFINITE *all, anyone, each,* and others	refers to nonspecific persons or things	**Everyone** is welcome here.

39c What is a verb?

Main verbs express action, occurrence, or state of being (Ch. 40).

- I **dance.** [action]
- The audience **became** silent. [occurrence]
- Your dancing **was** excellent. [state of being]

👁 **ALERT:** When you are not sure if a word is a verb, try putting it into a different TENSE. If the sentence still makes sense, the word is a verb. (For help with verb tense, see 40e.)

> NO He is a **changed** person. He is a **will change** person. [The sentence does not make sense when the verb *will change* is substituted, so *changed* is not functioning as a verb.]

> YES The store **changed** owners. The store **will change** owners. [Because the sentence still makes sense when the verb *will change* is substituted, *changed* is functioning as a verb.] 👁

39d What is a verbal?

Verbals are verb parts functioning as NOUNS, ADJECTIVES, or ADVERBS. Box 48 on the next page lists types of verbals.

🌐 **ESL NOTES:** The word *to* has several functions. (1) In the following example, *to* is part of the INFINITIVE *to eat*, which MODIFIES the PRONOUN *nothing*. This is one of the few structures in English in which a modifier follows a noun or pronoun.

- He has nothing **to eat.**

(2) In the next example, *to* is part of the MODAL AUXILIARY VERB *have to,* meaning "must" (49b).

- He **has to eat** something.

(3) In this last example, *to* is a preposition that requires a noun, pronoun, or gerund OBJECT—*eating* (48a).

- He is **accustomed to eating** at noon. 🌐

BOX 48

Types of verbals

INFINITIVE *to* + SIMPLE FORM of verb	1. noun: represents an action, state, or condition 2. adjective or adverb: describes or modifies	**To eat** soon is our goal. Still, we have nothing **to eat.**
PAST PARTICIPLE *-ed* form of REGULAR VERB or equivalent in IRREGULAR VERB	adjective: describes or modifies	**Boiled, filtered** water is usually safe to drink.
PRESENT PARTICIPLE *-ing* form of verb	1. adjective: describes or modifies 2. noun:* represents an action, state, or condition	**Running** water may not be safe. **Drinking** contaminated water is dangerous.

*A present participle functioning as a noun is called a **gerund.**

39e What is an adjective?

Adjectives modify—that is, they describe or limit—NOUNS, PRONOUNS, and word groups that function as nouns.

- I saw a **green** and **leafy** tree. [*Green* and *leafy* modify the noun *tree.*]

    Descriptive adjectives, such as *green* and *leafy*, can show levels of intensity: *green, greener, greenest; leafy, more leafy, most leafy* (43e). **Proper adjectives** emerge from PROPER NOUNS: *American, Victorian*. In addition, words with these suffixes (word endings) are usually adjectives: *-ful, -ish, -less,* and *-like*. (For more about suffixes, see 21b.)
    Determiners, sometimes called *limiting adjectives* because they "limit" nouns, reflect the limitations on nouns. Determiners tell whether a noun is general (*a* tree) or specific (**the** *tree*). Determiners also tell which one (***this*** *tree*), how many (***twelve*** *trees*), whose (***our*** *tree*), and similar information. (For more about determiners, see Chs. 43–44.) Box 49 lists types of determiners.

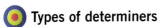

BOX 49

Types of determiners

ARTICLES *a, an, the*	**A** reporter working on **an** assignment is using **the** telephone.
DEMONSTRATIVE *this, these, that, those*	**Those** students rent **that** house.
INDEFINITE *any, each, few, other, some*, and others	**Few** films today have complex plots.
INTERROGATIVE *what, which, whose*	**What** answer did you give?
NUMERICAL *one, first, two, second,* and others	The **fifth** question was tricky.
POSSESSIVE *my, your, their,* and others	**My** dog is older than **your** cat.
RELATIVE *what, which, whose, whatever,* and others	He is the instructor **whose** course I enjoyed.

39f What is an adverb?

An **adverb** modifies—that is, it describes or limits—VERBS, ADJECTIVES, other adverbs, and CLAUSES.

- Chefs plan meals **carefully.** [*Carefully* modifies the verb *plan.*]
- Vegetables provide **very** important vitamins. [*Very* modifies the adjective *important.*]
- Those potato chips are **too** heavily salted. [*Too* modifies the adverb *heavily.*]
- **Fortunately,** people realize that salt can do harm. [*Fortunately* modifies the entire sentence.]

Descriptive adverbs show levels of intensity, usually by adding *more* (or *less*) and *most* (or *least*): *more happily, least clearly*. Many descriptive adverbs are formed by adding *-ly* to adjectives: *sadly, loudly, normally*.

Nevertheless, many adverbs don't end in *-ly: very, always, not, yesterday, well* are a few. Also, some adjectives look like adverbs but are really adjectives: *brotherly, lovely*. (For more about adverbs, see Chapter 43.)

Relative adverbs introduce ADJECTIVE CLAUSES with words such as *where, why,* and *when*.

Conjunctive adverbs modify by creating logical connections in meaning to express relationships as shown in Box 50.

BOX 50

 Conjunctive adverbs and the relationships they express

ADDITION	*also, furthermore, moreover, besides*
CONTRAST	*however, still, nevertheless, conversely, nonetheless, instead, otherwise*
COMPARISON	*similarly, likewise*
RESULT OR SUMMARY	*therefore, thus, consequently, accordingly, hence, then*
TIME	*next, then, meanwhile, finally, subsequently*
EMPHASIS	*indeed, certainly*

39g What is a preposition?

Prepositions include common words such as *in, under, by, after, to, on, over,* and *since*. Prepositions function with other words in PREPOSITIONAL PHRASES. These phrases often express relationships in time or space: *in April, under the orange umbrella*. (For more about prepositions, see Ch. 47.)

- **In** the fall, we will hear a concert **by** our favorite tenor.
- **After** the concert, he will fly **to** Paris.

39h What is a conjunction?

A **conjunction** connects words, PHRASES, or CLAUSES. **Coordinating conjunctions,** which express relationships, join two or more grammatically equivalent structures.

- We hike **and** camp every summer. [*And* joins two words.]
- I love the outdoors, **but** my family does not. [*But* joins two independent clauses.]

━━━━━━━━━━━━━━━━━━━━━━━━━━━━ BOX 51 ━ ▪ ▪

 Coordinating conjunctions and the relationships they express

ADDITION	*and*
CONTRAST	*but, yet*
REASON OR CAUSE	*for*
RESULT OR EFFECT	*so*
CHOICE	*or*
NEGATIVE CHOICE	*nor*

Correlative conjunctions function in pairs to join equivalent grammatical structures. They include *both . . . and, either . . . or, neither . . . nor, not only . . . but (also), whether . . . or,* and *not . . . so much as.*

- **Not only** students **but also** businesspeople should study a second language.

Subordinating conjunctions introduce DEPENDENT CLAUSES. Subordinating conjunctions express relationships that show that dependent clauses are grammatically less important than any independent clause within the same sentence.

- Many people were happy **after** they heard the news.

- **Because** it snowed, the school superintendent canceled all classes.

━━━━━━━━━━━━━━━━━━━━━━━━━━━━ BOX 52 ━ ▪ ▪

 Subordinating conjunctions and the relationships they express

TIME	*after, before, once, since, until, when, whenever, while*
REASON OR CAUSE	*as, because, since*
RESULT OR EFFECT	*in order that, so, so that, that*
CONDITION	*if, even if, provided that, unless*
CONTRAST	*although, even though, though, whereas*
LOCATION	*where, wherever*
CHOICE	*rather than, than, whether*

39i What is an interjection?

An **interjection** is a word or words showing surprise or strong emotion. When it stands alone, punctuate an interjection with an exclamation point: *Hooray!* As part of a sentence, set off an interjection with a comma or commas: *Hooray, you got the promotion.* Use interjections sparingly, if at all, in ACADEMIC WRITING.

Parts of Sentences

When you are aware of the parts of sentences, you have one tool for understanding the art of writing.

39j What are subjects and predicates?

A sentence consists of two basic parts: a subject and a predicate.

A **simple subject** is the word or words that acts, is described, or is acted upon: *The **telephone** rang.* A **complete subject** is the subject and all its MODIFIERS: ***The red telephone** rang.*

The **predicate** contains the VERB: *The telephone **rang**.* The **complete predicate** is the verb and all its modifiers: *The telephone **rang loudly**.*

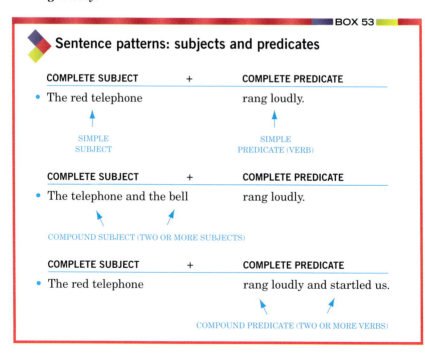

BOX 53

Sentence patterns: subjects and predicates

COMPLETE SUBJECT	+	COMPLETE PREDICATE
• The red telephone		rang loudly.

SIMPLE SUBJECT   SIMPLE PREDICATE (VERB)

COMPLETE SUBJECT	+	COMPLETE PREDICATE
• The telephone and the bell		rang loudly.

COMPOUND SUBJECT (TWO OR MORE SUBJECTS)

COMPLETE SUBJECT	+	COMPLETE PREDICATE
• The red telephone		rang loudly and startled us.

COMPOUND PREDICATE (TWO OR MORE VERBS)

🌐 **ESL NOTE:** Avoid repeating a SUBJECT with a PERSONAL PRONOUN in the same CLAUSE.

> NO **My grandfather he** lived to be eighty-seven.
>
> YES **My grandfather** lived to be eighty-seven. 🌐

39k What are direct and indirect objects?

A **direct object** completes the meaning of VERBS that are TRANSITIVE. To find a direct object, ask *whom?* or *what?* about the verb: *Keisha bought* [what?] ***a sweater.*** To find an **indirect object**, ask *to whom? for whom? to what?* or *for what?* about the verb: *Keisha bought* [for whom?] ***me*** *a sweater.*

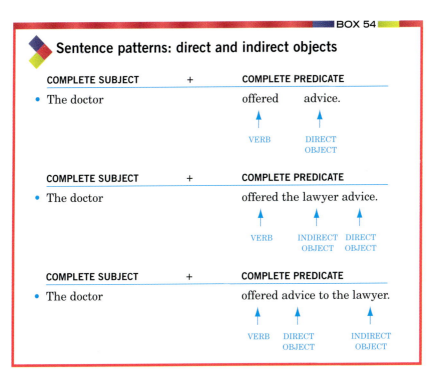

■■■ **BOX 54** ■ ■

◆ Sentence patterns: direct and indirect objects

COMPLETE SUBJECT	+	COMPLETE PREDICATE	
• The doctor		offered	advice.
		↑	↑
		VERB	DIRECT OBJECT

COMPLETE SUBJECT	+	COMPLETE PREDICATE		
• The doctor		offered	the lawyer	advice.
		↑	↑	↑
		VERB	INDIRECT OBJECT	DIRECT OBJECT

COMPLETE SUBJECT	+	COMPLETE PREDICATE		
• The doctor		offered	advice	to the lawyer.
		↑	↑	↑
		VERB	DIRECT OBJECT	INDIRECT OBJECT

🌐 **ESL NOTES:** (1) In sentences with indirect objects that follow the word *to* or *for*, always put the direct object before the indirect object.

> NO Will you please give **to** John this letter?
>
> YES Will you please give this letter **to** John? 🌐

(2) When a PRONOUN works as an indirect object, some verbs that go with the pronoun require *to* or *for* before the pronoun.

> **NO** Please explain **me** the rule. [*Explain* requires *to* before the pronoun *me*, which functions as an indirect object.]

> **YES** Please explain the rule **to me**.

(3) Even if a verb does not require *to* before an indirect object, you may use *to* if you prefer. Make sure, however, that if you do use *to*, you put the direct object before the indirect object.

> **NO** Please give **me** that book. [*Give* does not require *to* before the pronoun *me*, which functions as an indirect object.]

> **YES** Please give that book **to me**.

(4) When both the direct object and the indirect object are pronouns, put the direct object first and use *to* with the indirect object.

> **NO** He gave **me it.** [The indirect object *me* should not go before the direct object *it*.]

> **YES** He gave **it to me.** [The direct object *it* goes first; *to* is used with the indirect object *me*.]⊕

39l What are complements, modifiers, and appositives?

Recognizing complements

A **complement** renames or describes a SUBJECT or an OBJECT. It appears in the PREDICATE of a sentence. A **subject complement** is a NOUN, a PRONOUN, or an ADJECTIVE that follows a LINKING VERB. An **object complement** is a noun or an adjective that follows a DIRECT OBJECT.

Recognizing modifiers

A **modifier** is a word or words that function the same way as an adjective or ADVERB. Modifiers can appear anywhere in a sentence.

- The **large red** telephone rang. [The adjectives *large* and *red* modify the noun *telephone*.]
- The lawyer answered **quickly.** [The adverb *quickly* modifies the verb *answered*.]

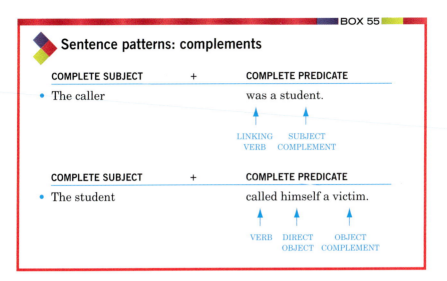

BOX 55

Sentence patterns: complements

COMPLETE SUBJECT + COMPLETE PREDICATE

- The caller was a student.

  LINKING SUBJECT
  VERB COMPLEMENT

COMPLETE SUBJECT + COMPLETE PREDICATE

- The student called himself a victim.

  VERB DIRECT OBJECT
  OBJECT COMPLEMENT

- The person **on the telephone** was **extremely** upset. [The PREPOSITIONAL PHRASE *on the telephone* modifies the noun *person*; also, the adverb *extremely* modifies the adjective *upset*.]

- **Therefore,** the lawyer spoke gently. [The adverb *therefore* modifies the INDEPENDENT CLAUSE *the lawyer spoke gently*.]

- **Because the lawyer's voice was calm,** the caller felt reassured. [*Because the lawyer's voice was calm* is a single ADVERB CLAUSE; it modifies the independent clause *the caller felt reassured*.]

Recognizing appositives

An **appositive** is a word or group of words that renames the noun or pronoun that comes before it.

- The student's **story, a tale of broken promises,** was complicated. [*A tale of broken promises* is an appositive that renames the noun *story*.]

- The lawyer consulted an expert, **her law professor.** [*Her law professor* is an appositive that renames the noun *expert*.]

ALERT: When an appositive is not essential for identifying the noun or pronoun it renames (that is, when an appositive is NONRESTRICTIVE), use a comma or commas to set off the appositive from whatever it renames and from any words following it. (For more about appositives and restriction of clauses, see 50f.)

39m What is a phrase?

A **phrase** is a group of related words that may contain a SUBJECT or a PREDICATE but not both. Never can a phrase stand alone as an independent unit.

A **noun phrase** functions as a NOUN: *The modern population census* started in the seventeenth century.

A **verb phrase** functions as a VERB: The Romans *had been conducting* a census every five years.

A **prepositional phrase,** which starts with a PREPOSITION and contains a noun or PRONOUN, functions as a MODIFIER: *After the collapse of Rome,* censuses were discontinued *until modern times.* (*After the collapse, of Rome,* and *until modern times* are all prepositional phrases.)

An **absolute phrase** is a word group that contains a noun or pronoun and a PARTICIPLE. It modifies the entire sentence: *Censuses being the fashion,* Quebec and Nova Scotia took sixteen counts between 1665 and 1754.

A **verbal phrase** is a word group that contains a VERBAL.

- In 1624, Virginia began **to count** its citizens in a census. [infinitive phrase = direct object]

- **Going from door to door,** census takers interview millions of people. [participial phrase = adjective modifying *census takers*]

- **Amazed by some people's answers,** the census takers always listen carefully. [participial phrase = adjective modifying *census takers*]

The way that a verbal phrase functions tells you the difference between a gerund phrase and a present-tense participial phrase. Although both types of phrases use the *-ing* form, a **gerund phrase** functions only as a noun, while a **present-tense participial phrase** functions only as a modifier.

- **Including each person** in the census was important. [*Including each person* functions as a noun, so it is a gerund phrase.]

- **Including each person in the census,** Abby spent many hours on the crowded city block. [*Including each person* functions as a present-tense participial phrase, so it is an adjective.]

39n What is a clause?

A **clause** is a group of words that contains both a SUBJECT and a PREDICATE. An INDEPENDENT CLAUSE is also known as a *main clause.* A DEPENDENT CLAUSE is also known as a *subordinate clause.*

Recognizing independent clauses

An **independent clause** can stand alone as a sentence as shown in Box 56.

 BOX 56

Sentence patterns: independent clauses

Independent Clause

COMPLETE SUBJECT	+	COMPLETE PREDICATE
• The telephone		rang.

Recognizing dependent clauses

A **dependent clause** contains a subject and a predicate, but it cannot stand alone as a sentence because it contains a SUBORDINATING CONJUNCTION (Box 52). Therefore, you need always to join a dependent clause to an independent clause.

Some dependent clauses start with *subordinating conjunctions.* Such clauses are called **adverb clauses**. They function as ADVERBS, usually answering one of these questions about the independent clause: *How? Why? When? Under what circumstances?*

- **If the bond issue passes,** the city will install sewers. [The adverb clause modifies the verb *install*, explaining under what circumstances.]

- They are drawing up plans **as quickly as they can.** [The adverb clause *as quickly as they can* modifies the verb *are drawing up*, explaining how.]

- The homeowners feel happier **because they know the flooding will soon be better controlled.** [The adverb clause modifies the entire independent clause, explaining why.]

👁 **ALERT:** When an adverb clause comes before its independent clause, the clauses are usually separated by a comma (50b). 👁

Adjective clauses are also dependent clauses and are sometimes called **relative clauses.** These clauses start with RELATIVE PRONOUNS (*who, whom, which, whose,* and *that*) or occasionally with RELATIVE ADVERBS such as *when* or *where.*

- The car **that Jack bought** is practical. [The adjective clause *that Jack bought* describes the noun *car.*]

- The day **when I can buy my own car** is getting closer. [The adjective clause *when I can buy my own car* modifies the noun *day.*]

Noun clauses usually begin with *that, who*, or *which*, but they can also start with *whoever, whichever, when, where, whether, why*, or *how*.

- **Promises** are not always dependable. [noun]
- **What politicians promise** is not always dependable. [noun clause]
- Often, voters do not know **the truth.** [noun]
- Often, voters do not know **that the truth is being manipulated.** [noun clause]

Because noun clauses and adjective clauses start with similar words, they're sometimes confused with each other. A noun clause is a SUBJECT, an OBJECT, or a COMPLEMENT; an adjective clause modifies a subject, object, or complement.

- Politicians understand **whom they must please.** [The noun clause *whom they must please* is an object.]
- Politicians **who make promises** sometimes fail to keep them. [The adjective clause *who makes promises* modifies the noun *politicians*.]

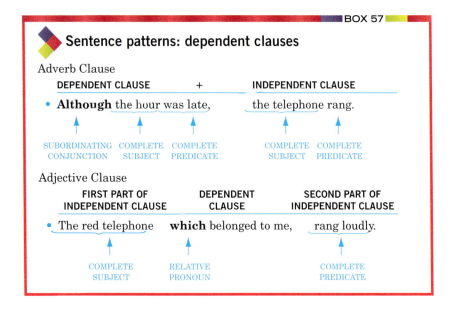

BOX 57

Sentence patterns: dependent clauses

Adverb Clause

DEPENDENT CLAUSE	+	INDEPENDENT CLAUSE

- **Although** the hour was late,   the telephone rang.

SUBORDINATING CONJUNCTION   COMPLETE SUBJECT   COMPLETE PREDICATE   COMPLETE SUBJECT   COMPLETE PREDICATE

Adjective Clause

FIRST PART OF INDEPENDENT CLAUSE	DEPENDENT CLAUSE	SECOND PART OF INDEPENDENT CLAUSE

- The red telephone   **which** belonged to me,   rang loudly.

COMPLETE SUBJECT   RELATIVE PRONOUN   COMPLETE PREDICATE

ALERT: Use a singular verb to agree with a noun clause functioning as a subject: *What most politicians try to do **is** [not are] serve the public. What most politicians need **is** [not are] new careers.*

39o What are sentence types?

A sentence can be simple, compound, complex, or compound-complex.

A **simple sentence** is composed of a single INDEPENDENT CLAUSE with no DEPENDENT CLAUSES.

- Charlie Chaplin was born in London on April 16, 1889.
- As a mime, he was famous for his character the Little Tramp.

A **compound sentence** is composed of two or more independent clauses joined by a comma and COORDINATING CONJUNCTION or a SEMICOLON.

- Chaplin's father died **early, and** his mother spent time in mental hospitals.
- Many people enjoy Chaplin's films; they laugh at his characters.

A **complex sentence** consists of one independent clause along with one or more dependent clauses.

- When Chaplin was performing with a troupe that was touring the United States, he was hired by Mack Sennett, who owned the Keystone Comedies. [This sentence contains a dependent clause starting with *When*, a dependent clause starting with *that*, an independent clause starting with *he*, and a dependent clause starting with *who*.]

A **compound-complex sentence** joins a compound sentence with a complex sentence.

- Once studios could no longer afford him, Chaplin co-founded United Artists, and then he was able to produce and distribute his own films. [This sentence contains a dependent clause starting with *Once*, an independent clause starting with *Chaplin*, and an independent clause starting with *then he was able*.]

40 VERBS

40a How do verbs function?

A **verb** expresses an action (*Many people **overeat***), an occurrence (*Thanksgiving always **falls** on a Thursday*), or a state of being (*Thanksgiving **is** a national holiday*). Verbs also convey other information.

PERSON First person (the speaker: *I* *dance*), second person (the one spoken to: *you* *dance*), or third person (the one spoken about: *the dog* *dances*).

NUMBER Singular (one) or plural (more than one).

TENSE Past (*we* *danced*), present (*we* *dance*), or future (*we* *will dance*); see 40e.

MOOD Moods are indicative (*we dance*), imperative (commands and polite requests: *Dance*), or conditional (speculation, wishes: *if we were dancing* . . .); see 40f.

VOICE Active voice or passive voice; see 40g.

Types of verbs vary as listed in Box 58.

BOX 58

 Types of verbs

MAIN VERB	The word in a PREDICATE that says something about the SUBJECT: *She* ***danced*** for the group.
AUXILIARY VERB	A verb that combines with a main verb to convey information about TENSE, MOOD, or VOICE (40b). The verbs *be, do,* and *have* can be auxiliary verbs or main verbs. The verbs *can, could, may, might, should, would, must,* and others are MODAL AUXILIARY VERBS. They add shades of meaning such as ability or possibility to verbs: *She* ***might dance*** *again*.
LINKING VERB	The verb that links a subject to a **complement,** a word or words that rename or describe the subject: *She* ***was*** *happy dancing. Be* is the most common linking verb; sometimes sense verbs (*smell, taste*) or verbs of perception (*seem, feel*) function as linking verbs. (For a sentence pattern with a linking verb, see Box 55.)
TRANSITIVE VERB	The verb followed by a DIRECT OBJECT that completes the verb's message: *They* **sent** *her a fan letter*. (For sentence patterns with objects, see Box 54.)
INTRANSITIVE VERB	A verb that does not require a direct object: *Yesterday she* ***danced.***

40b What are the forms of main verbs?

- The simple form represents an action, occurrence, or state of being that takes place in the present (*I laugh*) or, with an AUXILIARY VERB, in the future (*I will laugh*).

- The past-tense form represents an action, occurrence, or state completed in the past (*I laughed*). Regular verbs add *-ed* or *-d* to the simple form. Irregular verbs vary as listed in Box 59.

- The past participle form uses the same form as the past tense for regular verbs. Irregular verbs vary (Box 59). To function as a verb, a past participle must combine with one or more auxiliary verbs: *I have laughed*. Used alone, past participles function as ADJECTIVES: *crumbled cookies*.

- The present participle is formed by adding *-ing* to the simple form (*laughing*). To function as a verb, a present participle must combine with one or more auxiliary verbs (*I was laughing*). Used alone, present participles function as NOUNS (*laughing is healthy*) or as adjectives (*my laughing friends*).

- The infinitive uses the simple form, usually but not always following *to* (*I started to laugh*). The infinitive functions as a NOUN or an ADJECTIVE, not as a verb.

Using regular verbs

Most verbs in English are regular. **Regular verbs** form the past tense and past participle by adding *-ed* or *-d* to the simple form: *enter, entered, entered; smile, smiled, smiled*.

👁 **ALERT:** Speakers sometimes skip over or swallow the *-ed* sound in the past tense. If you do not pronounce this sound, you may forget to add it when you write.

- The birthday cake was **supposed** [*not* suppose] to be ready. 👁

Using irregular verbs

More than two hundred English verbs are irregular. You can look in a dictionary for the principal parts of any verb, but memorizing the most common ones, shown in, Box 59 can save you time.

Common irregular verbs

SIMPLE FORM	PAST TENSE	PAST PARTICIPLE
awake	awoke *or* awaked	awaked *or* awoken
be	was, were	been
become	became	become
begin	began	begun
blow	blew	blown
break	broke	broken
bring	brought	brought
build	built	built
buy	bought	bought
catch	caught	caught
choose	chose	chosen
come	came	come
cost	cost	cost
deal	dealt	dealt
dive	dived *or* dove	dived
do	did	done
drink	drank	drunk
drive	drove	driven
eat	ate	eaten
fall	fell	fallen
fight	fought	fought
find	found	found
fly	flew	flown
freeze	froze	frozen
get	got	got *or* gotten
give	gave	given
go	went	gone
grow	grew	grown
have	had	had
hear	heard	heard
hide	hid	hidden
hurt	hurt	hurt

CONTINUED ➝

BOX 59

Common irregular verbs *(continued)*

SIMPLE FORM	PAST TENSE	PAST PARTICIPLE
keep	kept	kept
know	knew	known
lay	laid	laid
lead	led	led
lend	lent	lent
lie	lay	lain
lose	lost	lost
make	made	made
read	read	read
ring	rang	rung
rise	rose	risen
run	ran	run
say	said	said
see	saw	seen
send	sent	sent
shake	shook	shaken
shoot	shot	shot
sing	sang	sung
sink	sank	sunk
sit	sat	sat
sleep	slept	slept
speak	spoke	spoken
stand	stood	stood
steal	stole	stolen
strike	struck	struck
swear	swore	sworn
swim	swam	swum
take	took	taken
teach	taught	taught
throw	threw	thrown
wear	wore	worn
write	wrote	written

Using the -s form of verbs

The -*s* form of a verb functions only in the third-person singular of the present tense. The -*s* ending attaches to the simple form (*laugh, laughs*).

 ALERT: Only the verbs *be* and *have* have irregular forms for third-person singular of the present tense: *is* and *has*. They are the standard third-person singular forms to use in edited American English.

> **NO** Jasper be studying hard because he have to win a scholarship.

> **YES** Jasper **is** studying hard because he **has** to win a scholarship.

40c What are auxiliary verbs?

Auxiliary verbs, also called *helping verbs*, combine with MAIN VERBS to make verb phrases.

AUXILIARY VERB   MAIN VERB

- I **am shopping** for new shoes.
  VERB PHRASE

- Clothing prices **have** [auxiliary verb] **soared** [main verb] recently. [*Have soared* is a verb phrase.]

- Leather shoes **can** [auxiliary verb] **be** [main verb] expensive. [*Can be* is a verb phrase.]

Three frequently used irregular verbs are *be, do*, and *have*. They vary in form more than most other irregular verbs.

FORMS OF *BE*, *DO*, AND *HAVE*

	BE	DO	HAVE
SIMPLE FORM	be	do	have
PAST TENSE	was, were	did	had
PAST PARTICIPLE	been	done	had
-*S* FORM	is	does	has
PRESENT PARTICIPLE	being	doing	having

 ALERTS: (1) For ACADEMIC WRITING, use standard forms of *be*.

- The gym **is** [*not* be] a busy place.

- The gym **is** [*not* be] filling with eager athletes.

(2) If you use an auxiliary verb with a MAIN VERB, the auxiliary verb may change to an *-s* form so that it agrees with a third-PERSON singular subject, but the main verb doesn't change: ***Does*** *the gym* ***close*** [*not* closes] *at midnight?* 👁

The verbs *can, could, may, might, must, shall, should, will, would*, and others are **modal auxiliary verbs.** Modals communicate meanings of ability, permission, obligation, advisability, necessity, or possibility. (For more about modals, see Ch. 49.)

40d Should I use *lie* or *lay?*

Many people confuse the forms of the irregular verbs *lie* and *lay* because the word *lay* is both the PAST-TENSE FORM of *lie* and the SIMPLE FORM of *lay*. Use *lie* ("to recline") and *lay* ("to place something down") with care. *Lie* is intransitive, so a DIRECT OBJECT can never follow it. *Lay* is transitive, so a direct object must follow it.

FORMS OF *LIE* AND *LAY*

	LIE	LAY
SIMPLE FORM	lie	lay
PAST TENSE	lay	laid
PAST PARTICIPLE	lain	laid
***-S* FORM**	lies	lays
PRESENT PARTICIPLE	lying	laying

- The hikers are ~~laying~~ lying down to rest.
- The hikers ~~laid~~ lay down to rest.
- The hikers took off their gear and ~~lay~~ laid it on the rocks.

40e What are verb tenses?

Verb tenses express time. To do this, MAIN VERBS change form and combine with AUXILIARY VERBS. PROGRESSIVE FORMS show ongoing actions or conditions.

SIMPLE TENSES

		PROGRESSIVE FORMS
PRESENT	I talk.	I am talking.
PAST	I talked.	I was talking.
FUTURE	I will talk.	I will be talking

PERFECT TENSES

		PROGRESSIVE FORMS
PRESENT PERFECT	I have talked.	I have been talking.
PAST PERFECT	I had talked.	I had been talking.
FUTURE PERFECT	I will have talked.	I will have been talking.

Using the simple present tense

The simple present tense describes (1) what is happening now, (2) what is true at the moment, (3) what is generally or consistently true, and (4) what event will take place at a fixed time in the future.

- The tourists **are** on vacation. [happening now]
- They **enjoy** the sunshine. [true at the moment]
- Ocean voyages **make** them seasick. [consistently true]
- A cruise **is** an expensive vacation. [generally true]
- Their ship **departs** at midnight. [fixed-time future event]

👁 **ALERT:** Use the present tense to discuss action that takes place in a work of literature.

- In *Romeo and Juliet*, Juliet's father wants Juliet to marry Paris.
- Shakespeare's play depicts the tragedy of ill-fated love. 👁

Using tense sequence accurately

The sequence of verb tenses in your sentence communicates time relationships. Accurate sequence becomes an issue only when your sentence contains both an INDEPENDENT CLAUSE and a DEPENDENT CLAUSE. Box 60 shows how the sequence of verb tenses communicates when something is happening, happened, or will happen.

40f What are indicative, imperative, and subjunctive moods?

The **indicative mood** expresses statements about real things (*The door **opened***) or highly likely ones (*She **seemed** lost*), or questions about fact (***Do** you **need** help?*).

The **imperative mood** expresses commands and direct requests: (*Please **shut** the door. **Watch out!***) When the SUBJECT is omitted in an imperative sentence, assume it to be *you*.

Sequence of tenses with independent and dependent clauses

- If your independent clause contains a simple present-tense verb, then in your dependent-clause verb you can
  - Use the PRESENT TENSE to show same-time action.
  I **avoid** shellfish because I **am** allergic to it.
  - Use the PAST TENSE to show earlier action.
  I **am** sure that I **deposited** the check.
  - Use the PRESENT PERFECT TENSE to show (1) a period of time extending from some point in the past to the present or (2) an indefinite past time.
  They **say** that they **have lived** in Canada since 1979.
  I **believe** that I **have seen** that movie before.
  - Use the FUTURE TENSE for action to come.
  The book **is** open because I **will be reading** it later.
- If your independent clause contains a past-tense verb, then in your dependent-clause verb you can
  - Use the PAST PERFECT TENSE to show earlier action.
  The sprinter **knew** that she **had broken** the record.
  - Use the present tense to state a general truth.
  Christopher Columbus **determined** that the world **is** round.
- If your independent clause contains a present-perfect or a past-perfect-tense verb, then in your dependent-clause verb you can
  - Use the past tense.
  The bread **has become** moldy since I **purchased** it.
  Sugar prices **had** already **declined** when artificial sweeteners first **appeared.**
- If your independent clause contains a future-tense verb, then in your dependent-clause verb you can
  - Use the present tense to show action happening at the same time.
  You **will be** rich if you **win** the prize.
  - Use the past tense to show earlier action.
  You **will** surely **win** the prize if you **remembered** to mail the entry form.

Box 60

Sequence of tenses with independent and dependent clauses (continued)

- Use the present perfect tense to show future action earlier than the action of the independent-clause verb.

  The river **will flood** again next year unless we **have built** a better dam by then.

- If your independent clause contains a future-perfect-tense verb, then in your dependent-clause verb you can

  - Use either the present tense or the present perfect tense.

    Dr. Chang **will have delivered** 5,000 babies by the time she **retires.**

    Dr. Chang **will have delivered** 5,000 babies by the time she **has retired.**

The **subjunctive mood** expresses conditions about wishes, recommendations, demands, indirect requests, and speculations: *If I* **were** *you, I* **would** *ask for directions.*

Using the subjunctive with *if, as if, as though,* and *unless* clauses

Many CLAUSES introduced by *if, as if, as though,* and *unless* require the subjunctive, but some don't. Use the subjunctive only when such clauses describe a speculation or condition contrary to fact.

INDICATIVE **If** she **leaves** late, I will drive her to the party. [fact, not speculation]

SUBJUNCTIVE **If** she **were** [*not* was] **going to leave** late, I would drive her to the party. [speculation]

SUBJUNCTIVE **If** it **were** [*not* was] **raining,** some people would stay home. [condition contrary to fact—it is not raining]

Using the subjunctive in *that* clauses

When *that* clauses express wishes, indirect requests, recommendations, and demands, use the subjunctive.

- I wish **that** this party **were** [*not* was] scheduled for tomorrow. [wish]
- I told the bakery **that** the birthday cake **must be ready** [*not* is needed] at noon. [demand]

40g What is "voice" in verbs?

Voice indicates how the subject relates to the action of the verb. In the **active voice,** the subject performs the action. In the **passive voice,** the subject is acted upon.

> ACTIVE   **Svetlana considers** clams a delicacy. [The subject, *Svetlana,* performs the action: she *considers.*]
>
> PASSIVE   **Clams are considered** a delicacy by Svetlana. [The subject, *clams,* is acted upon—they *are considered*—by Svetlana.]

The active voice—which is usually more direct, concise, and dramatic than the passive voice—emphasizes the doer of an action. The passive voice, however, may be appropriate when who or what did the action is unknown or unimportant.

- The lock **was broken** sometime last night. [The doer of the action is unknown.]
- The formula was discovered years ago. [The doer of the action is unimportant.]

The passive voice is appropriate when an action is more important than who did the action. For example, the person who discovered oxygen is less important information than when it was discovered, because the discovery was a major event in the history of medicine.

ACTIVE VOICE   Joseph Priestley **discovered** oxygen in 1774.

PASSIVE VOICE   Oxygen **was discovered** in 1774 by Joseph Priestley.

Remember not to use the passive voice to make your writing seem "lofty" or to hide who has done an action.

> NO   An experiment **was conducted by me** to demonstrate the existence of carbon. [pointless passive that is trying to sound lofty]
>
> YES   I conducted an experiment to demonstrate the existence of carbon.

41 SUBJECT–VERB AGREEMENT

41a What is subject–verb agreement?

Subject–verb agreement means SUBJECTS and VERBS must match in NUMBER (singular or plural). Singular subjects require singular verbs. Plural subjects require plural verbs. Subjects and verbs must also match in PERSON: *I like you. He likes you.*

Problems can arise with the letter *s* at the end of words. The diagram in Box 61 shows how the *-s* ending works in most cases. The *-s* or *-es* can take only one path at a time, going either to a noun subject (at the top) or to a verb (at the bottom).

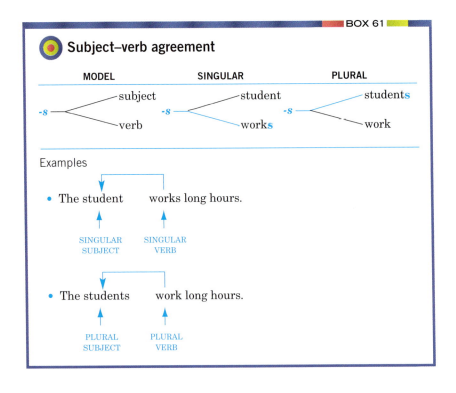

BOX 61

⊙ Subject–verb agreement

MODEL	SINGULAR	PLURAL

-s ⟨ subject / verb

-s ⟨ student / work**s**

-s ⟨ student**s** / work

Examples

• The student → works long hours.

SINGULAR SUBJECT   SINGULAR VERB

• The students → work long hours.

PLURAL SUBJECT   PLURAL VERB

41b Can I ignore words between a subject and its verb?

You can ignore words between a SUBJECT and VERB. Such words do not influence subject–verb agreement.

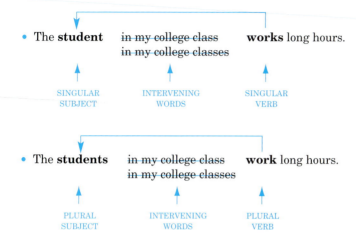

- The **student** ~~in my college class~~ **works** long hours.
  ~~in my college classes~~

  SINGULAR SUBJECT — INTERVENING WORDS — SINGULAR VERB

- The **students** ~~in my college class~~ **work** long hours.
  ~~in my college classes~~

  PLURAL SUBJECT — INTERVENING WORDS — PLURAL VERB

NO The **winners** in the state competition **goes** to the national finals. [*Winners* is the subject, so the verb must agree with it. *In the state competition* is a PREPOSITIONAL PHRASE that comes before the verb, and it does not alter subject–verb agreement.]

YES The **winners** in the state competition **go** to the national finals.

Whenever you need to locate the subject of a sentence, first look over your sentence and eliminate any PHRASES that start with PREPOSITIONS or with the words *including, together with, along with, accompanied by, in addition to,* or *as well as.* What is left in the sentence usually makes the subject stand out more obviously.

NO The **moon,** as well as Venus, **are** visible in the night sky. [*Moon* is the subject, so the verb needs to agree with it. *Are* does not agree with *moon*. The writer forgot to ignore the prepositional phrase *as well as Venus*.]

YES The **moon,** as well as Venus, **is** visible in the night sky.

Using *one of the*

A construction that starts with the words *one of the* takes a singular verb to agree with the word *one*. (This is not true of the construction *one of the . . . who;* see 41g.)

41c How do verbs work when subjects are connected by *and?*

When two or more SUBJECTS are joined by *and,* they become plural as a group. The group requires a plural verb.

- **The student and the instructor work** long hours.

COMPOUND SUBJECT   PLURAL
(USES *AND*)   VERB

Here is another example: ***The Cascade Diner and the Wayside Diner have*** [*not* has] *fried catfish today.*

The only exception occurs when subjects are joined by *and* and the subjects combine to form a single thing or person. In such cases, use a singular verb.

- **Spaghetti and meatballs has** [*not* have] a place on many menus.

Using *each* and *every*

Each and *every* are singular PRONOUNS and require singular verbs. Even when *each* or *every* comes before subjects joined by *and,* use a singular verb.

- **Each** human hand and foot **leaves** a distinctive print. [*Leaves* is a singular verb.]

41d How do verbs work when subjects are connected by *or?*

When SUBJECTS are joined with *or, nor, either . . . or, neither . . . nor,* or *not only . . . but* (*also*) the verb agrees with the subject nearest it. Ignore everything before the final subject.

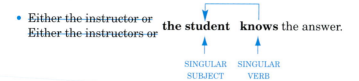

- ~~Either the instructor or~~
  ~~Either the instructors or~~ **the student knows** the answer.

  SINGULAR   SINGULAR
  SUBJECT   VERB

- ~~Either the instructor or~~
  ~~Either the instructors or~~ **the students know** the answer.

  PLURAL   PLURAL
  SUBJECT   VERB

41e How do verbs work with indefinite pronouns?

Indefinite pronouns refer to nonspecific people or things. They are usually singular, so they usually take singular verbs.

INDEFINITE PRONOUNS (MOST COMMONLY USED)

another	each	everything	nothing
anybody	either	neither	somebody
anyone	every	nobody	someone
anything	everyone	no one	something

- Whenever **anyone says** anything, **nothing is** done.
- **Everything** about these roads **is** [*not* are] dangerous.
- **Each** of the roads **has** [*not* have] to be resurfaced.

A few indefinite pronouns—*none, some, more, most, any,* and *all*—can be either singular or plural, depending on the meaning of the sentence.

- **Some** of our streams **are** polluted; **some** pollution **is** reversible, but **all** pollution **is** a threat to the balance of nature. [The first *some* refers to the plural *streams,* so the plural verb *are* agrees with it; the second *some* and *all* refer to the singular word *pollution,* so the singular verbs *is* agree with them.]

41f How do verbs work with *who, which*, and *that?*

When a CLAUSE starts with either *who, which,* or *that,* the verb agrees with the noun or pronoun to which *who, which,* or *that* refers (called its ANTECEDENT).

- The scientist will share the income from her new patent with the graduate students **who work** with her. [*Who* refers to the plural *students*, and *work* is a plural verb.]

- George Jones is the student **who works** in the science lab. [*Who* refers to the singular *student*, and *works* is a singular verb.]

41g How do verbs work with *one of the . . . who?*

In the PHRASES *one of the . . . who,* the verb agrees with what comes before *who*—which is always a plural word. Therefore, the verb is always plural. The same rule applies to the phrase *one of the . . . that* and *one of the . . . which.*

- Tracy is one of the **students who talk** [*not* talks] in class. [*Who* refers to plural *students* and requires the plural verb *talk.*]

However, if the phrase includes the word *only*, as in *the only one of the . . . who,* then the verb has to agree with *only one . . . who*—which is always a singular word. Therefore, the verb is always singular.

- Tracy is **the** only **one** of the students **who talks** [*not* talk] in class. [*Who* refers to the singular *only one* and requires the singular verb *talks.*]

41h How do verbs work in other complicated cases of subject–verb agreement?

Finding the subject in inverted word order

Inverted word order changes the usual order in a sentence: *The mayor walked in* is standard word order. *In walked the mayor* is inverted word order. (Most questions use inverted word order: *Is the mayor here?*) In inverted word order, you want the verb to agree with the SUBJECT that comes after the verb, not before it.

- Across the street **stand** [*not* stands] the protesters. [The subject is *protestors,* and *stand* agrees with it.]

Finding the subject with an expletive construction

Expletive constructions—expressions such as *there is, it is*, and *there were*—put a sentence's verb before the subject. Therefore, you want the SUBJECT to agree with the verb that comes after the subject, not before it.

- There **are** nine **planets** in our solar system. [The verb *are* is plural, so the subject *planets* is also plural.]

Agreeing with the subject, not the subject complement

A SUBJECT COMPLEMENT is a NOUN or ADJECTIVE that follows a LINKING VERB. This means that you want your verb to agree with the subject that comes before it, not after it.

> **NO** The worst **part** of owning a car **are** the bills. [The subject is the singular noun *part,* which requires the singular verb *is. Bills* is a subject complement, so it isn't involved in the subject–verb agreement.]

> **YES** The worst **part** of owning a car **is** the bills. [Now singular *part* agrees with singular *is.*]

> **YES** **Bills are** the worst part of owning a car. [The sentence is rewritten to make the plural noun *bills* the subject so that the plural verb *are* is correct.]

Making verbs agree with collective nouns

A **collective noun** names a group of people or things, such as *family, group, audience, class, number.* When the group acts as one unit, use a singular verb. When the members of the group act individually, use a plural verb.

- The senior *class* **has** [*not* have] 793 people in it. [Here, *class* operates as one unit, so the singular verb *has* agrees with it.]

- The senior *class* **were** [*not* was] **fitted** for their graduation robes today. [Here, *class* means the people in the class acting as individual members within the group, so the plural verb *were fitted* agrees with it.]

Making verbs agree with subjects that specify amounts

Use a singular verb with a subject that specifies an amount of money, time, weight, or distance considered as one unit.

- **Ninety cents is** the current bus fare.

- **Two miles passes** quickly for a serious jogger.

In contrast, when a subject refers to units of measurement, each of which is considered individually rather than as a unit, use a plural verb.

- **Eighteen inches are** marked off on that ruler.

- **Fifty percent** of these peaches **are** rotten.

Making verbs agree with singular subjects in plural form

A singular subject can look like a plural word, but it remains singular. It needs a singular verb, despite its plural appearance. Often, but not always, such words end in *-s* or *-ics*. Some examples are *ethics, economics, mathematics, physics,* and *statistics* when used to refer to a course of study. Other subjects that look like plurals but are really singulars include *news* and *measles.*

- **Statistics is** a requirement for science majors. [Here, *statistics* refers to a course of study, so the singular verb *is* agrees with it.]
- **Statistics show** that a recession is coming. [Here, *statistics* refers to items of data, so the plural verb *show* agrees with it.]

In some cases, the sentence's meaning determines whether a subject ending in *-s* needs a singular or plural verb. For example, *series* and *means* have the same form in singular and plural.

- Six new television **series are** beginning this week. [Here, *six* determines that *television series* is plural, so the plural verb *are* is correct.]
- A **series** of disasters **is** delaying our production. [Here, *series* is a single unit, so the singular verb *is* is correct.]

Using singular verbs with titles, terms, and plural words representing a single unit

The title of a work or a series of words used as a term is a single unit. Therefore, use a singular verb, even when the title or term contains plural words.

- *Cats* **was** [*not* were] a popular musical. [*Cats*, a plural word, acts here as a title; therefore it calls for the singular verb *was*.]
- **"Protective reaction strikes" is** a euphemism for bombing. [*Strikes*, a plural word, acts here as a term; therefore, it calls for the singular verb *is*.]

Used alone, the word *states* is always plural. However, in names such as *the United States* or *Organization of American States,* the word *states* refers to a singular unit, so the names call for singular verbs.

- **The United States has** [*not* have] a large television industry.

42 PRONOUNS: AGREEMENT, REFERENCE, AND CASE

Pronoun–Antecedent Agreement

42a What is pronoun–antecedent agreement?

Pronoun–antecedent agreement means that a PRONOUN must match the grammatical form of the word or words it refers to. That word or words is called the pronoun's **antecedent.** For example, if the antecedent is third-person singular, the pronoun must be third-person singular too.

42b How do pronouns work when *and* connects antecedents?

Two or more antecedents joined by *and* require a plural pronoun, even if each antecedent is itself singular.

- **The United States and Canada** maintain **their** border as the world's longest open frontier.

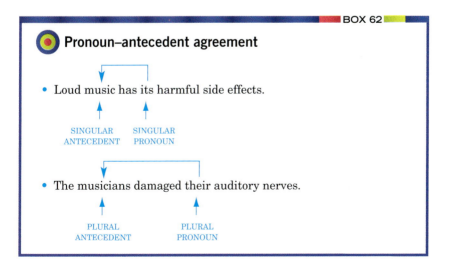

BOX 62

Pronoun–antecedent agreement

- Loud music has its harmful side effects.

  SINGULAR   SINGULAR
  ANTECEDENT PRONOUN

- The musicians damaged their auditory nerves.

  PLURAL   PLURAL
  ANTECEDENT PRONOUN

- **The Cascade Diner and the Wayside Diner** closed for New Year's Eve to give **their** employees the night off.

One exception occurs when *each* or *every* comes before singular nouns joined by *and*. In such cases, a singular pronoun is correct.

- **Every car and truck** that comes through the border station has **its** [*not* their] contents inspected.

Another exception occurs when singular nouns joined by *and* refer to a single person or thing. In such cases, a singular pronoun is correct.

- Our **guide and translator** told us to watch out for traffic as **she** [*not* they] helped us off the tour bus. [The guide is the same person as the translator.]

42c How do pronouns work when *or* connects antecedents?

Some antecedents are joined by the word *or* or *nor*. In addition, CORRELATIVE CONJUNCTIONS such as *either . . . or* and *not only . . . but (also)* can join antecedents. These antecedents can mix masculine and feminine as well as singular and plural. However, for the purposes of agreement, ignore everything before the final antecedent.

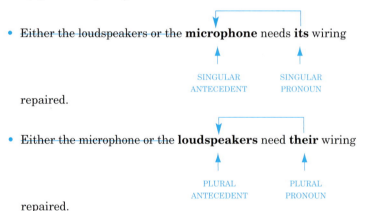

- ~~Either the loudspeakers or the~~ **microphone** needs **its** wiring

  SINGULAR ANTECEDENT   SINGULAR PRONOUN

  repaired.

- ~~Either the microphone or the~~ **loudspeakers** need **their** wiring

  PLURAL ANTECEDENT   PLURAL PRONOUN

  repaired.

42d How do pronouns work when their antecedents are indefinite pronouns?

Indefinite pronouns are pronouns that refer to no particular person, thing, or idea. They carry general meanings, so they take on definite meanings only according to the sentence that they're in.

Indefinite pronouns are usually singular: ***Anyone*** *who knows the answer should raise **his or her** hand*. Some indefinite pronouns can be either singular or plural (*none, some, more, most, any, all*), depending on the meaning of the sentence.

- **None** fear that **they** will fail. [All the people in the group expect to succeed; the plural pronoun *fear* reflects this meaning.]

- **None** fears that **he or she** will fail. [No individual expects to fail; the singular pronoun *he or she* reflects this meaning.]

The indefinite pronouns *each* and *every* are singular, no matter what words follow.

- **Each** of the students handed in ~~their~~ *his or her* final term paper.
- **Every** student in my classes is studying ~~their~~ *his or her* hardest.

Be especially careful about agreement when you use the words *this* (singular) and *these* (plural): ***This*** *kind of hard work has **its** advantages*. ***These*** *kinds of difficult jobs have **their** advantages*.

👁 **ALERT:** The expression *he or she* operates as a single unit and therefore calls for a singular antecedent. 👁

42e How do pronouns work when antecedents are collective nouns?

A COLLECTIVE NOUN names a group of people or things, such as *family, group, audience, class, number*. When the group acts as one unit, use a singular PRONOUN to refer to it. However, when the members of the group act individually, use a plural pronoun to refer to it.

- The **audience** cheered as **it** rose to applaud. [The singular pronoun *it* conveys that the audience is acting as one unit.]
- The **audience** put on **their** coats and walked to the exits. [The plural pronoun *their* conveys that the members of the audience are acting as many individuals.]

Pronoun Reference

If a word or words are replaced by, or stand for, a pronoun, that pronoun must refer precisely to what it replaces or stands for.

42f How can I avoid unclear pronoun reference?

In sentences that contain more than one logical antecedent, meaning can become unclear.

UNCLEAR
PRONOUN
REFERENCE
In 1911, Roald Amundsen reached the South Pole just thirty-five days before Robert F. Scott arrived. **He** [who, Amundsen or Scott?] had told people that he was going to sail north to the Arctic, but then **he** [who, Amundsen or Scott?] turned south for the Antarctic. On the journey back from the South Pole, **he** [who, Amundsen or Scott?] and **his** [whose, Amundsen's or Scott's?] party froze to death just a few miles from safety.

REVISED
In 1911, Roald Amundsen discovered the South Pole just thirty-five days before Robert F. Scott arrived. Amundsen had told people that he was going to sail north to the Arctic, but then he turned south for the Antarctic. On the journey home, Scott and his party froze to death just a few miles from safety.

In addition, when too much material comes between a pronoun and the word or words it refers to, readers can lose track of the meaning.

- Alfred Wegener, a German meteorologist and professor of geophysics at the University of Graz, was the first to suggest that all the continents on earth were originally part of one large land mass. According to his theory, the supercontinent broke up long ago and the fragments drifted apart. Slowly, these fragments formed the pattern of land masses and oceans that we know today. Although they do so slowly over centuries, the land masses are continuing to move. ~~He~~ *Wegener* named this supercontinent Pangaea.

[Although *he* can refer only to *Wegener*, the material about his theory and about land mass patterns takes up three sentences, so using the name *Wegener* again, rather than using *he,* jogs the reader's memory and makes reading easier.]

42g Can I use a pronoun to refer to an adjective?

The rule is that a pronoun can refer to a NOUN or other pronoun. Therefore, because an ADJECTIVE never functions as a noun, a pronoun can't refer to an adjective.

NO   Dan likes to study **geological** formations. **That** is his major. [*Geological* is an adjective, so it is imprecise for the pronoun *That* to refer it.]

YES   Dan likes to study geological formations. **Geology** is his major. [*Geology* is a noun, so the pronoun *That* can refer it.]

42h   How do pronouns work with *it, that, this*, and *which*?

Too often, writers use the words *it, that, this*, and *which* carelessly, so readers have trouble understanding what they refer to.

NO   Comets usually fly by the earth at 100,000 mph, whereas asteroids sometimes collide with the earth. **This** interests scientists. [*This* could refer to the speed of comets, comets flying by the earth, or asteroids colliding with the earth.]

YES   Comets usually fly by the earth at 100,000 mph, whereas asteroids sometimes collide with the earth. **This difference** interests scientists.

In speech, statements sometimes begin with "It said on the news . . ." or "In Washington they say. . . ." Never use these inexact—as well as wordy—expressions in ACADEMIC WRITING.

NO   In California, **they say** that no one feels a minor earthquake.

YES   **Residents of California say** that no one feels a minor earthquake.

42i   When should I use *you* for direct address?

Reserve *you* for **direct address**, writing that addresses the reader directly. *You* is never a suitable substitute with which to refer to people, situations, or occurrences.

NO   Prison uprisings often happen when you allow overcrowding. [The reader, *you*, did not allow the overcrowding.]

YES   Prison uprisings often happen when prisons are overcrowded.

42j When should I use *who, which*, and *that?*

Who refers to people and to animals mentioned by name.

- **Theodore Roosevelt, who** served as the twenty-sixth U.S. president, inspired the creation of the stuffed animal called the teddy bear.

- **Lassie, who** was known for her intelligence and courage, was actually played by a series of male collies.

Which and *that* refer to animals, things, and sometimes anonymous or collective groups of people. Box 63 shows how to choose between *that* and *which*. (For help in using commas with *that* and *which*, see 50f.)

 BOX 63

◉ Choosing between *that* and *which*

- In informal writing, you can use either *that* or *which* in a RESTRICTIVE CLAUSE (a clause that is essential to the sentence's meaning), as long as you do so consistently in each piece of writing. However, in ACADEMIC WRITING, your instructor and peers usually expect you to use *that*.

  The zoos ***that* most delight children** display newborn and baby animals. [The point in this sentence concerns delighting the children. Therefore, the words *most delight children* are essential to the meaning of the sentence.]

- You are required to use *which in* a NONRESTRICTIVE CLAUSE (a clause that isn't essential to the sentence's meaning).

  The zoos, ***which* most delight children,** attract more visitors if they display newborn and baby animals. [The point in this sentence concerns attracting more visitors to the zoos. Therefore, the words *most delight children* are not essential to the meaning of the sentence.]

Pronoun Case

42k What is pronoun case?

Case applies in different ways to PRONOUNS and to NOUNS. For pronouns, case refers to three pronoun forms: **subjective** (pronoun SUBJECTS), **objective** (pronoun OBJECTS), and **possessive** (pronouns that are POSSESSIVE). For nouns, case refers to only one noun form: possessive. (For help in using apostrophes in the possessive case, see Ch. 53.)

42l What are personal pronouns?

Personal pronouns refer to persons or things. Box 64 shows the case forms of personal pronouns (subjective, objective, and possessive) in both the SINGULAR and the PLURAL.

Most questions about pronoun case concern *who/whom* and *whoever/whomever*. For a full discussion, see 42q.

BOX 64

◉ Case forms of personal pronouns

	SUBJECTIVE	OBJECTIVE	POSSESSIVE
SINGULAR	I, you, he, she, it	me, you, him, her, it	mine, yours, his, hers, its
PLURAL	we, you, they	us, you, them	ours, yours, their

42m How can I select the correct case?

Whenever you're unsure whether to use the subjective or the objective case, you can use the "Troyka test." In this three-step test, shown in Box 65, you simply drop some words from your sentence so you can tell which case sounds correct.

BOX 65

◉ Using the "Troyka test"

These examples use pronouns. The test works as well with nouns.

STEP 1 Write the sentence twice, once using the subjective case and once using the objective case. Then cross out enough words to isolate the element you are questioning.

- Janet and me learned about the moon.
- Janet and I learned about the moon.

STEP 2 Omit the crossed-out words and read both sentences aloud to see which one sounds right.

- Me learned about the moon. [No, this doesn't sound right.]
- I learned about the moon. [This sounds right.]

STEP 3 Select the correct version and restore what you crossed out.

- Janet and I learned about the moon.

42n Which case is correct when *and* connects pronouns?

When *and* connects more than one noun and/or pronoun, it forms a compound subject or a compound object. Compounding doesn't affect pronoun case: Use the same case for all pronouns.

COMPOUND PRONOUN SUBJECT **He and I** saw the solar eclipse.

COMPOUND PRONOUN OBJECT That eclipse astonished **him and me.**

Whenever you're unsure of whether to use pronouns in the subjective or objective case, use the Troyka test (Box 65) to get the answer.

- **She and I** [*not* Her and me, She and me, *or* Her and I] learned about the moon.
- The instructor taught **her and me** [*not* she and I, her and I, *or* she and me] about the moon.

ALERT: In PREPOSITIONAL PHRASES, pronouns are always in the objective case.

NO Mrs. Parks gave an assignment to Sam and I. [The prepositional phrase starts with *to*, so the subjective-case *I* is wrong.]

YES Mrs. Parks gave an assignment to **Sam and me.** [The prepositional phrase starts with *to*, so the objective-case *me* is correct.]

Be careful when a pronoun object follows the preposition *between*.

NO Mrs. Parks divided the work between he and I. [The prepositional phrase starts with *between*, so the subjective-case *I* is wrong.]

YES Mrs. Parks divided the work between **him and me.** [The prepositional phrase starts with *between*, so the objective-case *me* is correct.]

42o How can I match case in appositives?

You can match case in APPOSITIVES by putting pronouns and nouns in the same case. Whenever you're unsure of whether to use the subjective or objective case, use the Troyka test (Box 65) to get the answer.

- **We** [*not* us] tennis players practice hard. [Here, the pronoun *we*, which is in the subjective case, comes before the noun *tennis players.*]

- The winners, **she** and **I** [*not* her and me], advanced to the finals. [Here, the pronouns *she and I*, which are in the subjective case, come after the noun *winners.*]

- The coach tells **us** [*not* we] tennis players to practice hard. [Here, the pronoun *us*, which is in the objective case, comes before the noun *tennis players.*]

- The crowd cheered the winners, **her** and **me** [*not* she and I]. [Here, the pronouns *her and me*, which are in the objective case, come after the noun *winners.*]

42p How does the subjective case work after linking verbs?

A pronoun that comes after a LINKING VERB either renames the SUBJECT or shows POSSESSION. In such cases, always use a pronoun in the subjective case.

- The contest winner was **I** [*not* me]. [*I* renames the subject, which is the noun *contest winner,* so the subjective case *I* is correct.]

- The prize was **mine.** [*Mine* shows possession, so the possessive case *mine* is correct.]

42q When should I use *who, whoever, whom,* and *whomever?*

The pronouns *who* and *whoever* are in the SUBJECTIVE CASE. The pronouns *whom* and *whomever* are in the OBJECTIVE CASE.

Informal spoken English tends to blur distinctions between *who* and *whom,* so with these words some people can't rely entirely on what "sounds right." Whenever you're unsure of whether to use the subjective case *who* and *whoever,* or the objective case *whom* or *whomever,* use a variation of the Troyka test (Box 65). For *who* and *whoever,* substitute *he, she,* or *they.* For *whom* and *whomever,* substitute *him, her,* or *them.* Doing so, you get the following results:

- Volunteers enrolled **whoever/whomever** was eligible to vote.

- Volunteers enrolled **he/him.** [By temporarily substituting the subjective case *he* and the objective case *him* for *whoever/whomever,* you see that *him* is correct. Therefore, the objective case *whomever* is correct.]

Sometimes you will need to add a word to make the test work. In this example, you add the word *if*.

- I wondered **who/whom** would vote for her.
- I wondered **if he/him** would vote for her. [The subjective-case *who* is correct because the sentence works when you substitute *if **he*** for *who/whom*. In contrast, the objective-case *whom* is wrong because the sentence doesn't work when you substitute *if **him*** for *who/whom*.]

At other times you will need to invert the word order to make the test work.

- Babies **who/whom** mothers cuddle grow faster and are happier.
- Mothers cuddle **they/them.** [By inverting the word order of the phrase *whom mothers cuddle* (*mothers cuddle whom*) and substituting *they/them* for *who/whom,* you can see that *them* is correct. Therefore, the objective-case *whom* is correct.]

When *who* or *whom* comes at the beginning or end of a question, use *who* if the question is about the subject and *whom* if the question is about the object. To determine which case to use, recast the question into a statement, substituting *he* or *him* (or *she* or *her*).

- **Who** watched the Space Shuttle liftoff? [*He* (*not* Him) *watched the Space Shuttle liftoff* uses the subjective case, so *Who* is correct.]
- Ted admires **whom?** [*Ted admires him* (*not* he) uses the objective case, so *whom* is correct.]
- **Whom** does Ted admire? [*Ted admires him* (*not* he) uses the objective case, so *whom* is correct.]
- To **whom** does Ted speak about becoming an astronaut? [*Ted speaks to them* (*not* they) uses the objective case, so *whom* is correct.]

42r What case should I use after *than* and *as?*

When a pronoun follows *than* or *as,* choose the pronoun case according to the meaning you want to convey. The following two sentences convey very different messages simply because of the use of *me* or *I* after *than.*

SENTENCE 1 My sister loved that dog more than me.

SENTENCE 2 My sister loved that dog more than I.

Sentence 1 means "My sister loved that dog more than she loved me" because the pronoun *me* is in the objective case. Sentence 2 means "My sister loved that dog more than I loved it" because the pronoun *I* is in the subjective case.

To make sure that your sentences using *than* or *as* deliver the message you intend, mentally fill in the implied words.

42s What case should I use with infinitives and -*ing* words?

When you use INFINITIVES, make sure that your pronouns are in the objective case. This rule holds whether the pronoun is the SUBJECT or the OBJECT of the infinitive.

- Our tennis coach expects **me *to serve.*** [*Me* is the subject of the infinitive *to serve.*]
- Our tennis coach expects him ***to beat* me.** [*Me* is the object of the infinitive *to beat.*]

With -*ing* words, the POSSESSIVE CASE can change a sentence's meaning entirely. For example, the following two sentences convey very different messages simply because of the change in case of the noun *man.* The same distinction applies to both NOUNS and pronouns.

SENTENCE 1   The detective noticed the **man** staggering. [objective case]

SENTENCE 2   The detective noticed the **man's** staggering. [possessive case]

Sentence 1 means that the detective noticed the *man.* In contrast, sentence 2 means that the detective noticed the *staggering.* The same differences exist for the following two sentences, which use pronouns.

SENTENCE 3   The detective noticed **him** staggering. [objective case]

SENTENCE 4   The detective noticed **his** staggering. [possessive case]

42t What case should I use for -*self* pronouns?

Pronouns that end in -*self* (singular) or -*selves* (plural) usually refer back to the subject of the sentence. They have a limited number of case forms.

FIRST PERSON	*myself; ourselves*
SECOND PERSON	*yourself; yourselves*
THIRD PERSON	*himself, herself, itself; themselves*

-Self pronouns are called **reflexive pronouns** when they are the object of a verb or preposition, or when they otherwise complete the meaning of a verb.

- She freed **herself** from a difficult situation.
- They allowed **themselves** another break from work.
- He is not **himself** today.
- Their new business can't possibly pay for **itself.**

Never use a reflexive pronoun in place of a subject or an object.

> **NO** The detective and **myself** had a long talk. He wanted my partner and **myself** to help him. [The reflexive pronoun *myself* cannot serve as a subject or an object; it can only reflect back on a subject or object.]

> **YES** The detective and **I** had a long talk. He wanted my partner and **me** to help him.

-Self pronouns are called **intensive pronouns** when they provide emphasis by intensifying the meaning of a nearby word: *The detective felt that his **career itself** was at risk.*

43 ADJECTIVES AND ADVERBS

43a What are the differences between adjectives and adverbs?

Both **adjectives** and **adverbs** are MODIFIERS. Modifiers describe other words. The key to distinguishing between adjectives and adverbs is understanding that they modify very different parts of speech.

WHAT ADJECTIVES MODIFY

NOUNS The *busy* **lawyer** rested.

PRONOUNS **She** felt *tired.*

WHAT ADVERBS MODIFY

VERBS The lawyer **spoke** *quickly.*

ADVERBS The lawyer spoke *very* **quickly.**

ADJECTIVES   The lawyer was *extremely* busy.

INDEPENDENT CLAUSES   *Undoubtedly*, **the lawyer needed a rest.**

Many adverbs end in *-ly* (*run **swiftly***), but some do not (*run **often***). Also, some adjectives end in *-ly* (***friendly dog***). Therefore, never depend on an *-ly* ending to identify a word as an adverb.

43b When should I use adverbs—not adjectives— as modifiers?

NO   The candidate made promises careless. [The adjective, *careless,* cannot modify a verb, *made.*]

YES   The candidate made promises **carelessly.** [The adverb, *carelessly*, is correctly modifying the verb, *made.*]

NO   The candidate felt unusual energetic today. [The adjective, *unusual,* cannot modify another adjective, *energetic.*]

YES   The candidate felt **unusually** energetic today. [The adverb, *unusually,* is correctly modifying the verb, *made.*]

43c What is wrong with double negatives?

A **double negative** is nonstandard form. In standard English, use only one negative (for example, *no, not, never, none, nothing*, or *hardly*) in a sentence.

NO   The union members did **not** have **no** money in the reserve fund. [Two negatives, *not* and *no,* are in the same sentence.]

YES   The union members did **not** have **any** money in the reserve fund. [Only one negative, *not,* is in this sentence.]

YES   The union members had **no** money in the reserve fund. [Only one negative, *no,* is in this sentence.]

43d Do adjectives or adverbs come after linking verbs?

LINKING VERBS use adjectives as COMPLEMENTS. In contrast, ACTION VERBS use adverbs.

- Anne **looks happy.** [Here, *looks* functions as a linking verb, so the adjective *happy* is correct.]

- Anne **looks happily** at the sunset. [Here, *looks* functions as an action verb, so the adverb *happily* is correct.]

Using *bad* and *badly*

Never substitute *bad* (an adjective) for *badly* (an adverb). These words are often misused with linking verbs such as *feel, grow, smell, sound,* and *taste.*

> **NO** The student felt badly. [Here, *felt* functions as a linking verb, so the adverb *badly* is wrong.]

> **YES** The student felt **bad.** [Here, *felt* functions as a linking verb, so the adjective *bad* is correct.]

Using *good* and *well*

Good is always an adjective. *Well* is an adjective only when it is referring to health; otherwise, *well* is an adverb.

- You look **well.** [This means "You look to be in fine health." *Well* functions as an adjective.]

- You write **well.** [This means "You write skillfully." *Well* functions as an adverb.]

43e What are correct comparative and superlative forms?

When comparisons use adjectives and adverbs, the forms of the adjectives and adverbs are either regular or irregular.

Regular forms of adjectives and adverbs

Regular adjectives and adverbs show comparisons in two ways. First, they add either an *-er* ending or the word *more* or *less* (**comparative**). Second, they add either an *-est* ending or the word *most* or *least* (**superlative**).

POSITIVE [1]	COMPARATIVE [2]	SUPERLATIVE [3+]
green	greener	greenest
happy	happier	happiest
selfish	less selfish	least selfish
beautiful	more beautiful	most beautiful

[1]   That tree is **green.**

[2]   That tree is **greener** than this tree.

[3+]   That tree is the **greenest** tree on the block.

The number of syllables in the adjective or adverb usually determines whether you choose -er or more. Similarly, the number of syllables determines whether you choose -est or most.

- Add -er and -est to one-syllable adjectives and adverbs: *large, larger, largest* (adjective); *far, farther, farthest* (adverb).
- Use *more* and *most* for two-or-more syllable adverbs. For example, for the adverb *easily*, use *more easily* and *most easily*.
- Use either the -er or -est ending or *more* and *most* for two-syllable adjectives. The only way to know which forms are correct is to check the dictionary. The forms vary greatly.
- Add *more* and *most* to adjectives and adverbs of more than two syllables: *more protective* [not "protectiver"] and *most protective* [not "protectivest"].

◉ **ALERT:** Never use *more* or *most* together with the -er or -est ending. For example, *more louder* and *most happiest* are incorrect forms. ◉

Irregular forms of adjectives and adverbs

A few adjectives and adverbs have irregular forms in the comparative and superlative.

POSITIVE [1]	COMPARATIVE [2]	SUPERLATIVE [3+]
good [adjective]	better	best
well [adverb]	better	best
well [adjective]		
bad [adjective]	worse	worst
badly [adverb]	worse	worst
many	more	most
much	more	most
some	more	most
little	less	least

[1] The Millers had **little** trouble finding jobs.

[2] The Millers had **less** trouble finding jobs than the Smiths did.

[3+] The Millers had the **least** trouble finding jobs of everyone.

◉ **ALERT:** Never use *less* and *fewer* interchangeably. Use *less* with UNCOUNTABLE ITEMS and *fewer* with numbers or other COUNTABLE ITEMS: *They consumed **fewer calories**. The sugar substitute had **less aftertaste**.* ◉

43f Why should I avoid using too many nouns as modifiers?

Sometimes NOUNS function as MODIFIERS of other nouns.

- *truck* [modifier as well as noun] *driver* [noun]
- *train* [modifier as well as noun] *track* [noun]
- *security* [modifier as well as noun] *system* [noun]

The problem arises when modifying nouns pile up. This makes it difficult for your reader to tell which nouns are being modified and which nouns are doing the modifying. You can use several strategies to revise a long string of nouns.

SENTENCE REWRITTEN

> **NO** I asked my adviser to write **two college recommendation** letters for me.

> **YES** I asked my adviser to write **letters of recommendation** to **two colleges** for me.

ONE NOUN REVISED TO POSSESSIVE CASE AND ANOTHER TO ADJECTIVE FORM

> **NO** Some students might take the **U.S. Navy examination** for **navy engineering training.**

> **YES** Some students might take the **U.S. Navy's** examination for **naval** engineer training.

NOUN REVISED TO PREPOSITIONAL PHRASE

> **NO** Our student adviser training program has won awards for excellence.

> **YES** Our training program **for student advisers** has won awards for excellence. [Notice here that this revision also requires the plural *advisers.*]

Tips for Multilingual Writers

www.prenhall.com/troyka

Tips for Multilingual Writers

Tips for Multilingual Writers 359–379

Message from Lynn Troyka to Multilingual Writers

If you ever worry about your English writing, you have much in common with me and with many U.S. college students. Still, I recognize that because you are a multilingual writer, you face special challenges. In becoming a skilled writer in English, you need to consider almost every word, phrase, sentence, and paragraph in ways native speakers of English do not.

The good news is that errors you make demonstrate the reliable truth that you are moving normally through the unavoidable, necessary stages of second-language development. Unfortunately, there are no shortcuts. As with your progress in speaking, listening, and reading in a new language, development of writing skills takes time. The process is like learning to play a musical instrument. Few people learn to play fluently without making many errors.

What can you do to progress as quickly as possible from one writing stage to another? I recommend that you start by bringing to mind what school writing is like in your first language. Specifically, recall how ideas are presented in your written native language, especially when information is explained or a topic requires a logical argument.

Most college writing in the United States is very direct in tone and straightforward in structure. In a typical essay or research paper, the reader expects to find a THESIS STATEMENT* that clearly states the central message of the entire piece of writing. Usually, the thesis statement falls in the first paragraph, or in a longer piece, perhaps in the second paragraph. Then, each paragraph that follows relates in content directly to the essay's thesis statement. In addition, each paragraph begins with a TOPIC SENTENCE that contains the main point of the paragraph, and the rest of the paragraph supports the point made in the topic sentence. This support consists of RENNS (8d) that provide specific details. The final paragraph brings the piece of writing to a logical conclusion that grows out of the rest of the essay.

Writing structures typical of your native language most likely differ from those in the United States. Always honor your culture's writing traditions and structures, for they reflect the richness of your heritage. At the same time, try to adapt to and practice the academic writing style characteristic of the United States. Later, some college instructors might encourage you to practice other, more subtle English writing styles that allow greater liberty in organization and expression.

Distinctive variations in school writing styles among people of different cultures and language groups have interested researchers for the past twenty years. Such research is ongoing, so scholars hesitate to generalize. Even so, interesting differences have been observed. Many

---

* You can find the definition of a word printed in small capital letters (such as THESIS STATEMENT) in the Terms Glossary on pages 467–85.

Spanish-speaking students feel that U.S. school writing lacks grace because writers do not include any wide-ranging background material: in fact, U.S. writing teachers usually say such broad introductory material is wordy or not really relevant to the central message. Japanese school writing customarily begins with references to nature. In some African nations, a ceremonial, formal opening is expected to start school writing as an expression of respect for the reader. As a person, I greatly enjoy discovering the rich variations in the writing traditions of the many cultures of the world. As a U.S. college teacher, however, my responsibility is to explain the expectations in the United States.

If you were in my class, I would say "Welcome!" and then ask you to teach me about writing in your native language. Using that knowledge, I would respectfully teach you the U.S. approach to writing so that I could do my best to help you succeed in a U.S. college.

L.Q.T.

44 SINGULARS AND PLURALS

44a What are count and noncount nouns?

Count nouns represent items that can be counted: *radio, fingernail, street, idea.* **Noncount nouns** represent things that cannot be counted: *knowledge, rain, traffic.*

Count nouns can be SINGULAR (*radio, street*) or PLURAL (*radios, streets*), so they may use singular or plural VERBS. Noncount nouns (Box 66) are used in singular form only, so they use only singular verbs.

👁 **ALERT:** If you are not sure whether a noun is count or noncount, look it up in a learner's dictionary such as the *Longman Dictionary of American English.* 👁

Some nouns can be countable or uncountable depending on their meaning in a sentence. Most of these nouns represent things that can be meant either individually or as "wholes" made up of individual parts. See Box 66.

COUNT   Two hairs were on his collar. [individual, countable hairs]

NONCOUNT   His hair was cut very short. [all the hairs on his head considered together]

When you are EDITING your writing, be sure you have not added a plural *s* to any noncount nouns, which are always singular in form.

 BOX 66

Uncountable items

- Groups of similar items making up "wholes": *clothing, equipment, furniture, luggage, mail, money.*
- Abstractions: *equality, fun, health, ignorance, knowledge, peace, respect.*
- Liquids: *blood, coffee, gasoline, water.*
- Gases: *air, helium, oxygen, smog, smoke, steam.*
- Materials: *aluminum, cloth, cotton, ice, wood.*
- Food: *beef, bread, butter, macaroni, meat, cheese.*
- Collections of particles or grains: *dirt, dust, hair, rice, salt, wheat.*
- Languages: *Arabic, Chinese, Japanese, Spanish.*
- Fields of study: *biology, computer science, history, physics, literature, math.*
- Natural phenomena: *electricity, heat, moonlight, sunshine, thunder.*

ALERT: Be sure to use a singular verb with any noncount noun that functions as a SUBJECT in a CLAUSE.

44b Which determiners should I use with singular and plural nouns?

Determiners, including expressions of quantity, are used to tell *which, how much,* or *how many* about NOUNS. Choosing the right determiner to use with a noun can depend on whether the noun is NONCOUNT or COUNT. For count nouns, you must also decide whether the noun is SINGULAR or PLURAL. See Box 67.

 BOX 67

Using determiners with count and noncount nouns

GROUP 1: DETERMINERS FOR SINGULAR COUNT NOUNS

With singular count nouns, use one of these determiners.

- *an, the*
  - **a** house, **an** egg; **the** egg, **the** house
- *one, any, some, every, each, either, neither, another, the other*
  - **any** book, **each** person, **another** year

CONTINUED →

BOX 67

 Using determiners with count and noncount nouns *(continued)*

- *my, our, your, his, her, its, their, nouns with 's or s'*
  - **your** father, **its** cover, **Connie's** car
- *this, that*
  - **this** week, **that** desk
- *one, no, the first, the second, etc.*
  - **one** example, **no** reason, **the fifth** chair

GROUP 2: DETERMINERS FOR PLURAL COUNT NOUNS

All the determiners listed in Group 2 can be used with plural count nouns. Plural count nouns can also be used without determiners (45b).

- *the*
  - **the** bicycles, **the** rooms, **the** ideas
- *some, any, both, many, more, most, few, fewer, the fewest, a number of, other, several, all, all the, a lot of*
  - **some** people, **many** jobs, **all** managers
- *my, our, your, his, her, its, their, nouns with 's or s'*
  - **our** coats, **her** books, **students'** grades
- *these, those*
  - **these** days, **those** computers
- *no, two, three, four, etc.; the first, the second, the third, etc.*
  - **no** exceptions, **four** students, **the first** month

GROUP 3: DETERMINERS FOR NONCOUNT NOUNS

All determiners in Group 3 can be used with noncount nouns (always singular). Noncount nouns can also be used without determiners (45b).

- *the*
  - **the** rice
- *some, any, much, more, most, other, the other, little, less, the least, enough, all, all the, a lot of*
  - **enough** snow, **a lot of** equipment, **more** food
- *my, our, your, his, her, its, their, nouns with 's or s'*
  - **their** training, **India's** heat, **your** leadership
- *this, that*
  - **this** staff, **that** expertise
- *no, the first, the second, the best, etc.*
  - **no** smoking, **the first** rainfall, **the best** vocabulary

👁 **ALERTS:** (1) *Many, most,* and *some* require *of the* for a noun that is specific, but not for a noun that is a generalization.

- Most supervisors are well qualified. [general]
- Most **of the** supervisors **here** are well qualified. [specific]

(2) The phrases *a few* and *a little* convey the meaning "some": *I have **a few** rare books* means "I have some rare books." *They are worth **a little** money* means "They are worth some money." Without the word *a,* the meaning of *few* and *little* is "almost none": *I have **few** [or *very few*] books* means "I have almost no books." *They are worth (**very**) **little** money* means "They are worth almost no money." (3) A phrase with *one of the* always has a plural noun as the OBJECT of the PREPOSITION *of*. The verb agrees with *one,* not with the plural noun, so it is always singular: *One of the most important inventions of the twentieth century is* [*not* *are*] *television* (see 41g). 👁

44c What forms are correct for nouns used as adjectives?

Some words that function as NOUNS can also function as ADJECTIVES. In English, adjectives do not have plural forms. If you use a noun as an adjective, do not add *s/es* to the adjective, even when the noun or PRONOUN it modifies is PLURAL.

- Many Americans students are basketball fans.
- My nephew likes to look at pictures books.

EXCEPTION   a sports car

45 ARTICLES

The words *a, an,* and *the* are **articles.** Articles are one type of DETERMINER. They signal that a NOUN will follow and that any MODIFIERS between the article and the noun refer to that noun. See Box 68.

- **a** chair, **the** computer
- **a** cold metal chair, **the** lightning-fast computer

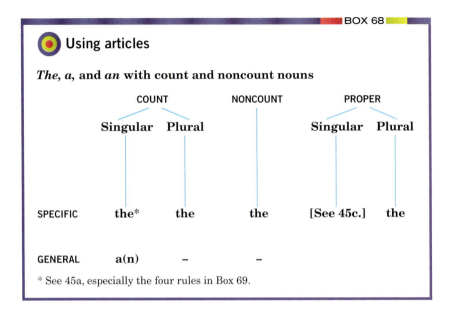

BOX 68

Using articles

***The*, *a*, and *an* with count and noncount nouns**

	COUNT		NONCOUNT	PROPER	
	Singular	**Plural**		**Singular**	**Plural**
SPECIFIC	**the***	**the**	**the**	[See 45c.]	**the**
GENERAL	**a(n)**	–	–		

* See 45a, especially the four rules in Box 69.

45a How should I use articles with singular count nouns?

When you use a singular COUNT NOUN (Box 69), it requires a DETERMINER; see Group 1 in Box 67. If you have to choose between *a/an* and *the,* decide whether the noun is specific or nonspecific. A noun is considered specific when a reader can understand from the context exactly and specifically what the noun is referring to.

For nonspecific singular count nouns, use *a/an.* When the singular noun is specific, use *the* or some other determiner. Box 69 can help you decide when a singular count noun is specific and therefore requires *the.*

ALERT: *An* is used before words that begin with a vowel sound; *a* is used before words that begin with a consonant sound. Sound, not spelling, is the key. Words that begin with *h* or *u* can have either a vowel or a consonant sound; check your dictionary. Choose *a/an* based on the sound of the first word after the article, even if that word is not the noun.

- **an** idea, **a** good idea
- **an** umbrella, **a** useless umbrella
- **an** honor, **a** history book

BOX 69

 ## Using *the* with singular count nouns

RULE 1

A noun is specific and requires *the* when it names something either unique or commonly known.

- **The** sun has risen above **the** horizon. [Because only one *sun* and one *horizon* exist, they are specific nouns.]

RULE 2

A noun is specific and requires *the* when it names something used in a representative or abstract sense.

- Benjamin Franklin favored **the** turkey as **the** national bird of the United States. [Because *turkey* and *national bird* are representative references rather than references to a particular turkey or bird, they are specific nouns in this context.]

RULE 3

A noun is specific and requires *the* when it names something that is defined elsewhere in the same sentence or in an earlier sentence.

- **The** ship *Savannah* was the first steam vessel to cross **the** Atlantic Ocean. [*The Savannah* names a specific ship, and *the Atlantic Ocean* identifies one of the world's oceans.]

- **The** carpet in my bedroom is new. [*In my bedroom* defines exactly which carpet is meant, so *carpet* is a specific noun in this context.]

- I have a computer and a fax machine in my office. **The** computer is often broken. [*Computer* is introduced in the first sentence, so it uses *a*. *Computer* has been made specific by the first sentence, so the second sentence uses *the* to refer back to the same noun.]

RULE 4

A noun is specific and requires *the* when it represents something that can be inferred from the context.

- I need an expert to fix **the** problem. [If you read this sentence after the example about a computer in Rule 3, above, you understand that *problem* refers to the broken computer, *problem* is specific in this context. Here the word *the* is similar to the word *this*.]

👁 **ALERT:** One common exception affects Rule 3 in Box 69. A noun may still require *a/an* after the first use if one or more descriptive adjectives come between the article and the noun: *I bought a sweater today. It was a* [*not* the] ***red** sweater.* 👁

45b How should I use articles with count and noncount nouns?

Like singular count nouns, PLURAL COUNT NOUNS and NONCOUNT NOUNS that are *specific* usually use *the* according to the rules in Box 69. When a noun has a *general* meaning, it usually does not use *the*.

Using articles with plural count nouns

• Geraldo planted tulips and roses this year. **The** tulips will bloom in April.

The plural count noun *tulips* is used in a general sense in the first sentence, without *the*. Because the first sentence identifies *tulips,* the second sentence refers to them specifically as ***the** tulips*. This example is related to Rule 3 in Box 69.

Using articles with noncount nouns

• Kalinda served rice and chicken to us. She flavored **the** rice with curry.

Rice is a noncount noun. By the second sentence, *rice* has become specific, so *the* is used. This example is related to Rule 3 in Box 69.

Generalizing with plural and noncount nouns

Omit *the* in generalizations using plural or noncount nouns.

• ~~The~~ tulips are the flowers that grow from ~~the~~ bulbs.

Compare this sentence to a generalization with a singular count noun.

• **A** tulip is **a** flower that grows from **a** bulb.

45c How should I use *the* with proper nouns?

Proper nouns represent specific people, places, or things. Most proper nouns do not require ARTICLES: *We visited Lake Mead* [*not* **the** Lake Mead] *with Asha and Larry.* However, certain types of proper nouns do require *the*.

- Nouns with the pattern *the . . . of . . . the United States of America, the president of Mexico* [*not* **the** Mexico].
- Plural proper nouns: *the Johnsons, the Chicago Bulls, the United Arab Emirates.*
- Collective proper nouns (nouns that name a group): *the Society of Friends, the AFL-CIO.*
- Some, but not all, geographical features: *the Amazon, the Gobi Desert, the Indian Ocean.*

46 WORD ORDER

46a What are standard and inverted word orders?

Standard word order is the most common pattern for DECLARATIVE SENTENCES in English. The SUBJECT comes before the VERB: *That book* [subject] *was* [verb] *heavy.*

Inverted word order, with a verb coming before the subject, is common for direct questions in English: *Was* [verb] *that book* [subject] *heavy? Were* [verb] *you* [subject] *close to it when it fell?*

A common way to form questions with MAIN VERBS other than *be* is to use inverted order with a form of the verb *do* as an AUXILIARY VERB before the subject and the SIMPLE FORM of the main verb after the subject: ***Do you want*** *me to put the book away?* ***Do you have*** *my pencil?*

Use *do* with inverted order when a question begins with a question-forming word such as *what, why, when, where,* or *how:* ***Where does*** *the* ***book*** *belong?*

When a question has more than one auxiliary verb, put the subject after the first auxiliary verb: ***Would you*** *have replaced the book?*

ALERT: Do not use inverted word order with indirect questions: *She asked where I saw the book* [*not* She asked where did I see the book].

Verb–subject word order is also required by certain ADVERBS at the beginning of a sentence.

- Only once **did she** ask my advice.
- Never **have I** seen such a mess!

Verb–subject word order rules also apply to emphatic exclamations: ***Was*** *that* ***book*** *heavy!* ***Did she*** *enjoy that book!* (For advice about using word order to create emphasis in declarative sentences, see 46c.)

BOX 70

Word order for adjectives

1 Determiner, if any: *a, an, the, my, your, Jan's, these,* etc.

2 Expressions of order, including ordinal numbers, if any: *first, second, next, last, final,* etc.

3 Expressions of quantity, including cardinal numbers, if any: *one, two, few, each, every, some,* etc.

4 Adjectives of judgment or opinion, if any: *smart, happy, interesting, sad, boring,* etc.

5 Adjectives of size and/or shape, if any: *big, small, short, round, rectangular,* etc.

6 Adjectives of age and/or condition, if any: *new, young, broken, dirty, shiny,* etc.

7 Adjectives of color, if any: *red, green, beige, turquoise,* etc.

8 Adjectives that can also be used as nouns, if any: *French, metal, Protestant, cotton,* etc.

9 The noun.

1	2	3	4	5	6	7	8	9
A		few		tiny		red		ants
The	last	six					Thai	drums
My			fine		old		oak	table

46b Where should I place adjectives?

In English, an ADJECTIVE ordinarily comes directly before the NOUN it modifies. Box 70 shows the most common order for positioning several adjectives that modify the same noun.

46c Where should I place adverbs?

Adverbs and adverbial PHRASES modify VERBS, ADJECTIVES, other adverbs, or whole sentences. They can go in three different places in a CLAUSE: first, middle, or last. ("Middle" usually means just after the auxiliary verb, if any.) See Box 71.

ALERT: If a sentence begins with a negative adverb of frequency (*never, rarely, only once, seldom,* etc.), the subject–verb word order must be inverted (41h). This creates emphasis.

• **Never** has Nick been bitten by a dog.

BOX 71

Types and positions of adverbs

- Adverbs of manner describe how something is done and usually go in middle or last position.
  - Nick **carefully** groomed the dog. Nick groomed the dog **carefully.**
- Adverbs of time describe when an event occurs or how long it lasts and usually go in first or last position.
  - **First**, he shampooed the dog. He shampooed the dog **first.**
- Adverbs of place describe where an event takes place and usually go after the object.
  - He lifted the dog **into** the tub.
- Adverbs of frequency describe how often an event takes place and go in the middle position to modify a verb, or in the first position to modify an entire sentence.
  - Nick has **never** been bitten by a dog.
  - **Occasionally,** he is scratched while shampooing a cat.
- Adverbs of degree or emphasis indicate *how much* or *to what extent* about other modifiers, and come directly before the word they modify. They include *only*, which is easy to misposition (14a).
  - Nick is **rather** quiet around animals.
- Sentence adverbs modify an entire sentence. They include transitional words and expressions, as well as *maybe, probably, possibly, fortunately, incredibly,* and others, and they go in the first position.
  - **Incredibly,** he once had to groom a squirrel.

47 PREPOSITIONS

Prepositions, along with their OBJECTS, form prepositional PHRASES, which often describe relationships in time or space. Prepositions, when combined with certain verbs, sometimes have idiomatic meanings in American English. A dictionary such as the *Longman Dictionary of Contemporary English* or the *Oxford Advanced Learner's Dictionary* can be especially helpful when you need to find the correct preposition for these idiomatic uses.

47a How should I use *in*, *at*, and *on* to show time and place?

TIME

- *in* a year or a month (*during* is also correct but less common): *in 1999*, *in May*

- *in* a period of time: *in a few months* (*seconds, days, years*)

- *in* a period of a day: *in the morning* (*afternoon, evening*), *in the daytime* (*morning, evening*) but *at night*

EXCEPTIONS

- *on* a specific day: *on Friday*, *on my birthday*, *on May 12*

- *at* a specific time or period: *at noon*, *at 2:00*, *at dawn*, *at nightfall*, *at takeoff* (the time a plane leaves), *at breakfast* (the time a specific meal takes place)

PLACE

- *in* a location surrounded by something else: *in the province of Alberta*, *in Utah*, *in downtown Bombay*, *in the kitchen*, *in my apartment*, *in the bathtub*

- *at* a specific location: *at your house*, *at the bank*, *at the corner of Third Avenue and Main Street*, *at 376 Oak Street*, *at home*

- *on* a street: *on Oak Street*, *on Third Avenue*, *on the road*

47b How should I use prepositions in phrasal verbs?

Phrasal verbs are verbs that combine with PREPOSITIONS to deliver their meaning. The meaning of many phrasal verbs is idiomatic, not literal; *pick on,* for example, means "annoy" or "tease" rather than anything associated with either *pick* or *on*. Also, many phrasal verbs are informal and more appropriate for conversation than for academic writing. For a research paper, for example, *propose* or *suggest* would usually be better choices than *come up with.*

In some phrasal verbs, the verb and the preposition should not be separated by other words: *Look at the moon* [not *Look the moon at*]. In other phrasal verbs, called *separable phrasal verbs,* words can separate the verb and the preposition without interfering with meaning: *I threw my homework away* [or *I threw away my homework*]. When a separable phrasal verb has a PRONOUN OBJECT, that object should be positioned between the verb and the preposition: *I threw it away* [not *I threw away it*]. Object PHRASES or CLAUSES with more than four or five words should usually be positioned after the preposition: *I* ***threw away*** *the homework that was assigned last week.*

Here is a list of some common phrasal verbs. The ones that cannot be separated are marked with an asterisk (*).

SELECTED PHRASAL VERBS

ask out	find out	look into*
break down	get along with*	look out for*
bring about	get back	look over
call back	get off*	make up
call off	go over*	run across*
call up	hand in	speak to*
drop off	keep up with*	speak with*
figure out	leave out	throw away
fill out	look after*	throw out
fill up	look around*	turn down

47c How should I use prepositions with passive verbs?

PASSIVE verbs usually follow the pattern *be* + PAST PARTICIPLE + *by: The child* ***was frightened by*** *a snake.* However, many passive verbs require other prepositions instead of *by: The child is frightened* ***of*** *all snakes.* Here is a list of some of these passive verbs with their prepositions. Look in a dictionary for others. (See 48a on using GERUNDS after some of these expressions.)

SELECTED PASSIVE VERBS + PREPOSITIONS

be accustomed to	be interested in
be acquainted with	be known for
be composed of	be located in
be concerned/worried about	be made of (*or* from)
be disappointed with (*or* in someone)	be married to
be discriminated against	be pleased/satisfied with
be divorced from	be prepared for
be excited about	be tired of (*or* from)
be finished/done with	

47d How should I use prepositions in expressions?

In many common expressions, different PREPOSITIONS convey great differences in meaning. For example, check a dictionary to see that four prepositions can be used with the VERB *agree* to create different meanings: *agree to, agree about, agree on,* and *agree with.*

Many ADJECTIVES also require certain prepositions: *afraid of, familiar with, famous for, friendly toward* (or *with*), *guilty of, patient with, proud of.*

You can find entire books filled with English expressions containing prepositions, and comprehensive dictionaries often give meanings for verb–preposition combinations as part of the entry for the verb.

48 GERUNDS AND INFINITIVES

GERUNDS and INFINITIVES are types of verbals. **Verbals** are VERB forms that function as NOUNS or MODIFIERS. Like all nouns, gerunds and infinitives can be DIRECT OBJECTS. Some verbs call for gerund objects to follow them; other verbs must be followed by infinitive objects. Still other verbs can be followed by either gerund or infinitive objects. A few verbs change meaning depending on whether a gerund object or an infinitive object is used.

48a What verbs use a gerund, not an infinitive, object?

Certain VERBS cannot be followed by INFINITIVES as DIRECT OBJECTS; they require GERUNDS: *Yuri considered **calling** [not to call] the mayor.*

VERBS THAT USE GERUND OBJECTS

acknowledge	complain about	detest
admit	consider	discuss
advise	consist of	dislike
anticipate	contemplate	dream about
appreciate	defer from	enjoy
avoid	delay	escape
cannot help	deny	evade

favor	mention	recommend
finish	mind	resent
give up	object to	resist
have trouble	postpone	risk
imagine	practice	suggest
include	put off	talk about
insist on	quit	tolerate
keep (on)	recall	understand

Using a gerund after *go*

Although *go* is usually followed by an infinitive object (*We can **go to see** [not go to seeing] a movie*), *go* is followed by a gerund in such phrases as *go swimming, go fishing, go shopping,* and *go driving: I will **go swimming** [not go to swim] tomorrow.*

Using gerunds after *be* + complement + preposition

A COMPLEMENT often follows a form of *be.* Some complements require certain prepositions (47c).

SELECTED *BE* + COMPLEMENT + PREPOSITION EXPRESSIONS

be (get) accustomed to	be interested in
be angry about	be prepared for
be bored with	be responsible for
be capable of	be tired of (*or* from)
be committed to	be (get) used to
be concerned about	be worried about
be excited about	

- We are excited about **voting** [*not* to vote] in the election.
- They were interested in **hearing** [*not* to hear] the candidates' debate.

 ALERT: Always use a gerund, not an infinitive, as the object of a preposition. Be especially careful when the word *to* is functioning as a preposition in a phrasal verb (47b): *We are committed to **saving** the elephants* [*not* committed to save].

48b What verbs use an infinitive, not a gerund, object?

Certain VERBS cannot be followed by GERUNDS as DIRECT OBJECTS; they use INFINITIVES: *Three people decided to question [not decided questioning] the speaker.*

VERBS THAT USE INFINITIVE OBJECTS

afford	demand	plan
agree	deserve	prepare
aim	expect	pretend
appear	fail	promise
arrange	give permission	refuse
ask	hesitate	seem
attempt	hope	struggle
be able (unable)	intend	tend
be left	know how	threaten
beg	learn	try
care (not care)	like	volunteer
claim	manage	wait
consent	mean	want
decide	offer	would like
decline		

Using infinitives after *be* + some complements

- We are eager **to go** [*not* going] to the mountains.
- I am ready **to sleep** [*not* sleeping] in a tent.

Using unmarked infinitive objects

An **unmarked infinitive** uses a verb's SIMPLE FORM, but not the word *to*. Some common verbs that are followed by unmarked infinitive objects are *feel, have, hear, let, listen to, look at, make* (meaning "compel"), *notice, see,* and *watch.*

- Please **let** me **take** [*not* to take] you to lunch.[*Take* is an unmarked infinitive used after *let.*]
- I want **to take** you to lunch. [*To take* is a marked infinitive used after *want.*]

The verb *help* can be followed by either a marked or an unmarked infinitive: *Help me put* [or *Help me to put*] *these groceries away*.

👁 **ALERT:** Be careful about parallel structure when you use two or more verbals as objects after one verb. Put the verbals into the same form.

- We went sailing and to scuba ~~dive.~~ *diving.*

- We heard the wind blow and the waves ~~crashing.~~ *crash.*

But if you are using verbal objects in a COMPOUND PREDICATE, be sure to use the kind of verbal that each verb requires.

- We enjoyed scuba diving but do not want ~~sailing~~ *to* sail again.

  [*Enjoyed* requires a gerund object and *want* requires an infinitive object.] 👁

48c How does meaning change if an infinitive object or a gerund follows *stop, remember,* or *forget?*

Followed by a GERUND, *stop* means "finish, quit": *We stopped eating* means "We finished our meal." Followed by an INFINITIVE, *stop* means "stop or interrupt one activity to begin another": *We stopped to eat* means "We stopped doing something [such as driving or painting the house] to eat."

Followed by a gerund, *remember* means "recall a memory": *I remember talking to you last night*. Followed by an infinitive, *remember* means "not to forget to do something": *I must remember to talk with Isa*.

Followed by a gerund, *forget* means "to do something and not recall it": *I forget having put my keys in the refrigerator*. Followed by an infinitive, *forget* means "to not do something": *If you forget to put a stamp on that letter, it will be returned*.

48d Do sense verbs change meaning with a gerund or an infinitive object?

Sense VERBS such as *see, notice, hear, observe, watch, feel, listen to*, and *look at* usually do not change meaning whether a GERUND or an INFINITIVE is used as an OBJECT. *I saw the water rising* and *I saw the water rise* (unmarked infinitive—see 48b) both deliver the same message.

48e How should I choose between *-ing* and *-ed* forms of adjectives?

Deciding whether to use the *-ing* form (PRESENT PARTICIPLE) or the *-ed* form (PAST PARTICIPLE of a REGULAR VERB) as an ADJECTIVE in a specific sentence can be difficult. For example, *I am amused* and *I am amusing* are both correct in English, but their meanings are very different.

- **I am amused** by something. [I experience amusement.]
- **I am amusing** to other people. [I cause the amusement of other people.]

To make the right choice, decide whether the modified NOUN or PRONOUN is causing or experiencing what the participle describes.

Use a present participle (*-ing*) to modify a noun or pronoun that is the agent or the cause of the action. This meaning is ACTIVE.

- Mica explained your interesting plan. [The noun *plan* caused interest, so *interesting* is correct.]
- I find your plan exciting. [The noun *plan* causes excitement, so *exciting* is correct.]

Use a past participle (*-ed* in regular verbs) to modify a noun or pronoun that experiences or receives whatever the modifier describes. This meaning is PASSIVE.

- An interested committee wants to hear your plan. [The noun *committee* experiences interest, so *interested* is correct.]
- Excited by your plan, I called a board meeting. [The noun *I* experiences excitement, so *excited* is correct.]

Here is a list of some frequently used participles that require your close attention when you use them as adjectives. To choose the right form, decide whether the noun or pronoun *experiences* or *causes* what the participle describes.

amused, amusing	frightened, frightening
annoyed, annoying	insulted, insulting
appalled, appalling	offended, offending
bored, boring	overwhelmed, overwhelming
confused, confusing	pleased, pleasing
depressed, depressing	reassured, reassuring
disgusted, disgusting	satisfied, satisfying
fascinated, fascinating	shocked, shocking

49 MODAL AUXILIARY VERBS

Modal auxiliary verbs include *can, could, may, might, should, had better, must, will, would*, and others. Like the auxiliary verbs *be, do,* and *have*, modal auxiliary verbs help main verbs convey more information. Modal auxiliary verbs convey meaning about ability, necessity, advice, possibility, and other conditions.

49a How do modal auxiliary verbs differ from *be, do,* and *have?*

Modal auxiliary verbs are always followed by the SIMPLE FORM of a main verb: *I might go tomorrow.*

One-word modal auxiliary verbs usually do not have an *-s* ending in third-person singular: *She* **could** *go with me, you* **could** *go with me,* and *they* **could** *go with me.* Exceptions include modals such as *have to* and *need to*, which make the third-person singular changes that *have* and *need* ordinarily do (for example, *I* **have** *to stay, she* **has** *to stay; you* **need** *to smile, he* **needs** *to smile*).

👁 **ALERT:** *Ought to* does not add *-s* in third-PERSON singular. *Be* (*supposed*) *to* makes all the usual changes to *be*. 👁

49b Which modal auxiliary verbs express ability, necessity, advisability, or probability?

Expressing ability

Can means "ability in the present." *Could* sometimes means "ability in the past." These words deliver the meaning of "able to."

- You **can work** late tonight.
- I **could play** the piano when I was younger.

Could often expresses some condition that must be fulfilled.

- If you **could** come early, then we can start on time.
- I **could** have gone to bed at 10:00 if I had finished my homework.

Adding *not* between a MODAL AUXILIARY VERB and the MAIN VERB makes the sentence negative: *I could* **not** *work late last night.*

👁 **ALERT:** Negative forms of modal auxiliary verbs are often turned into contractions: *can't, couldn't, won't, wouldn't,* and so on. Because contractions can be considered informal usage, you will never be wrong to avoid them in academic writing. 👁

Expressing necessity

Must, have to, and *need to* express a requirement to do something. *Must* implies future action. *Have to* and *need to* are used in all verb tenses.

- You **must leave** before midnight. She **has to leave** when I leave. We **needed to be** with you last night. You **will need to be** here before dark.

👁 **ALERT:** *Must* has no past tense form when it expresses necessity. Use *had to.* 👁

Expressing advice or the notion of a good idea

Should and *ought to* mean that doing the action of the main verb in the present or future is a good idea. The PAST TENSE forms are *should have* and *ought to have;* they are followed by the PAST PARTICIPLE.

- You **should call** your sister tonight. I **ought to have** gone to the dentist last week.

The modal *had better* expresses the meaning of good advice or warning or threat.

- You **had better see** a doctor before your cough gets worse.

Expressing probability

May, might, could, and *must* usually express probability, possibility, or likelihood.

- We **might** see a tiger in the zoo. We **could** go this afternoon.

The past-tense forms for *may, might, could,* and *must* add *have* and the main verb's past participle to the modals.

- I'm hungry; I **must have neglected** to eat breakfast.

49c Which modal auxiliary verbs express preference, plan, or past habit?

Expressing preferences

Would rather (present tense) and *would rather have* (past tense) express a preference. In the past tense, the modal is also followed by a past participle.

- We **would rather see** a comedy than a mystery. We **would rather have seen** a movie last night.

Expressing a plan or obligation

A form of *be* followed by *supposed to* and the SIMPLE FORM of a MAIN VERB, in both present and past tense, delivers a meaning of something planned or an obligation.

- I **was supposed to meet** them at the bus stop.

  The word *supposed* may be omitted with no change in meaning.

- I **was to meet** them at the bus stop.

Expressing past habit

Used to and *would* mean that something happened repeatedly in a time that has passed.

- I **used to hate** getting a flu shot. I **would dread** the injection for weeks beforehand.

⊚ **ALERT:** Both *used to* and *would* can be used for repeated actions in the past, but *would* cannot be used for a situation that lasted for a period of time in the past.

- I ~~would~~ used to live in Arizona.⊚

Punctuation

and Mechanics

Punctuation
and Mechanics

www.prenhall.com/troyka

Punctuation and Mechanics

50 COMMAS

The comma separates sentence parts for greater clarity. You can avoid most comma errors with these two bits of advice. (1) While you're writing or reading what you've written, don't insert a comma whenever you pause to think or take a breath before moving on. (2) If you are unsure about a comma, insert it and circle the spot. Later, when you're editing, look in this book for the rule you need to check.

50a When do I use commas?

For quick answers to most comma questions, see Box 72. If you want more information about a rule, go to the section of this chapter shown in parentheses.

50b How do I use a comma to set off introductory words?

When a DEPENDENT CLAUSE,* PHRASE, expression, or word comes before an INDEPENDENT CLAUSE, place a comma after the introductory material.

- **When the topic is dieting,** many people say sugar craving is their worst problem. [introductory DEPENDENT CLAUSE (in bold) followed by a comma]

- **Between 1544 and 1689,** sugar refineries appeared in London and New York. [introductory PREPOSITIONAL PHRASE (in bold) followed by a comma]

- **Beginning in infancy,** we develop lifelong tastes for sweet and salty foods. [introductory PARTICIPIAL PHRASE (in bold) followed by a comma]

- **Sweets being a temptation for many adults,** parents need to know that most commercial baby foods contain sugar. [introductory ABSOLUTE PHRASE (in bold) followed by a comma]

- **For example,** fructose comes from fruit, but it is still sugar. [introductory TRANSITIONAL EXPRESSION (in bold) followed by a comma]

- **Nevertheless,** many people think fructose is not harmful. [introductory CONJUNCTIVE ADVERB (in bold) followed by a comma]

---

*Words printed in small capital letters (such as DEPENDENT CLAUSE) are defined in the Terms Glossary on pages 467–85.

BOX 72

 ## When to use commas

COMMAS AFTER INTRODUCTORY ELEMENTS (50b)

- **Although most postcards cost only a dime,** one recently sold for thousands of dollars. [clause]
- **On postcard racks,** several designs are usually available. [phrase]
- **For example,** animals are timeless favorites for postcards. [transitional expression]
- **However,** most postcards show local landmarks. [word]

COMMAS WITH COORDINATING CONJUNCTIONS LINKING INDEPENDENT CLAUSES (50c)

- Postcards are ideal for brief greetings, **and** they are sometimes miniature works of art.

COMMAS WITH ITEMS IN SERIES (50d)

- **Places, paintings, and people** appear on postcards. [The word *and* comes between the last two items.]
- **Place, painting, people, animals** occupy dozens of postcard display racks. [The word *and* is not used between the last two items.]

COMMAS WITH COORDINATE ADJECTIVES (50e)

- Some postcards feature **appealing, dramatic** scenes.

NO COMMAS WITH CUMULATIVE ADJECTIVES (50e)

- Other postcards feature **famous historical** scenes.

COMMAS WITH NONRESTRICTIVE ELEMENTS (50f)

- **Four years after the first postcard appeared,** the U.S. government began to issue prestamped postcards. [Nonrestrictive element (in bold) introduces independent clause.]
- The Golden Age of postcards, **which lasted from about 1900 to 1929,** yielded many especially valuable cards. [Nonrestrictive element (in bold) interrupts independent clause.]
- Collectors attend postcard shows, **which are similar to baseball-card shows.** [Nonrestrictive element (in bold) ends independent clause.]

CONTINUED →

BOX 72

 When to use commas *(continued)*

NO COMMAS WITH RESTRICTIVE ELEMENTS (50f)

- Collectors **who attend these shows** may specialize in a particular kind of postcard. [Restrictive clause (in bold)]

COMMAS WITH QUOTED WORDS (50g)

- One collector told me, **"Attending a show is like digging for buried treasure."** [Quoted words (in bold) at end of sentence]
- **"I always expect to find a priceless postcard,"** he said. [Quoted words (in bold) at start of sentence]
- **"Everyone there,"** he joked, **"believes a million-dollar card is hidden in the next stack."** [Quoted words (in bold) are interrupted mid-sentence.]

50c How do I use a comma before a coordinating conjunction?

When you link INDEPENDENT CLAUSES, place a comma before a COORDINATING CONJUNCTION (*and, but, for, or, nor, yet, so*).

- The sky turned black, **and** the wind blew fiercely. [A comma and *and* link two independent clauses.]
- The sky began to brighten, **but** the wind continued blowing strongly. [A comma and *but* link two independent clauses.]

In one particular situation, you need to use a SEMICOLON instead of a comma and coordinating conjunction to link independent clauses. When commas are already part of one or both independent clauses, the semicolon clearly shows exactly where the link between independent clauses occurs.

- With temperatures below freezing, the snow did not melt; **and** people wondered, gazing at the white landscape, when they would see grass again. [Each of the two independent clauses contains one or more commas. Therefore, a semicolon with *and* does the linking of the independent clauses.]

ALERTS: (1) Never put a comma *after* a coordinating conjunction that joins independent clauses.

NO A house is renovated in two weeks **but,** an apartment takes a week.

YES A house is renovated in two weeks**, but** an apartment takes a week.

(2) Never use a comma when a coordinating conjunction links only two words, PHRASES, or DEPENDENT CLAUSES.

NO Habitat for Humanity depends on volunteer **labor, and donations** for its construction projects. [Only two words are linked by *and*, so the comma is incorrect.]

YES Habitat for Humanity depends on volunteer **labor and donations** for its construction projects.

(3) Never use a comma between independent clauses unless you also use a coordinating conjunction. (If you make this error, you create a COMMA SPLICE).

NO Five inches of snow fell in two **hours, driving** was hazardous.

YES Five inches of snow fell in two **hours, and driving** was hazardous.

50d How do I use commas with a series?

A **series,** which always calls for commas, consists of three or more elements with the same grammatical form. The elements in a series can be words, PHRASES, or CLAUSES.

WORDS The earliest clothing fabrics were made from natural fibers such as **cotton, silk, linen,** and **wool.**

PHRASES Fabrics today are made **from natural fibers, from synthetic fibers,** and **from natural and synthetic fiber blends.**

CLAUSES **Natural fibers are durable as well as absorbent, synthetic fibers resist wrinkling as well as fading,** and **blends of the two fibers offer the advantages of both.**

Although some professional writers omit the comma before a final CO-ORDINATING CONJUNCTION in a series, most instructors prefer that you use that comma. The comma helps readers understand the sentence.

NO Ivan wears only **natural fibers, nylon** and **thinsulate.**
[This sentence says that Ivan wears clothes made only from natural fibers, specifically nylon and thinsulate. In this sentence, *nylon and thinsulate* function as an APPOSITIVE.]

YES Ivan wears only **natural fibers, nylon,** and **thinsulate.**
[Ivan wears clothes made from three types of fabric: natural fibers, nylon, and thinsulate.]

Items in a series often appear as numbered or lettered lists within a sentence. In such cases, use commas to separate three or more items.

- Three synthetic fibers predominate in clothing manufacture: **(1) rayon, (2) polyester,** and **(3) acrylic.**

When, however, some or all of the items in a series already contain commas (or other punctuation), or when the items are long and complex, use semicolons instead of commas to separate the items. (This also holds for the rule explained in 50c.)

👁 **ALERTS:** (1) Never use a comma before the first item or after the last item in a series, unless another rule makes it necessary.

NO We decorated with**, red, white,** and **blue** ribbons for the Fourth of July.

NO We decorated with **red, white,** and **blue,** ribbons for the Fourth of July.

YES We decorated with **red, white,** and **blue** ribbons for the Fourth of July.

(2) Never use a comma when only two items are linked by a COORDINATING CONJUNCTION.

NO Everyone enjoyed the **parade,** and **the concert.**

YES Everyone enjoyed the **parade** and **the concert.** 👁

50e When do I use a comma between adjectives?

The question of whether to use a comma between ADJECTIVES comes up when the adjectives are coordinate. **Coordinate adjectives** are two or more adjectives that carry equal weight in modifying a NOUN. Equality is the key point. Use a comma between coordinating adjectives (that is, adjectives that have equal weight) unless a COORDINATING CONJUNCTION (such as *and* or *but*) already links them.

BOX 73

 ## Test for coordinate and cumulative adjectives

- Can the order of the adjectives be changed without changing the meaning or creating nonsense? If the answer is yes, the adjectives are coordinate and need commas.
  - The **restless, large, noisy** crowd wanted the concert to start. [The order of adjectives can be changed (*noisy, restless,* and *large*) and the sentence still makes sense, so these are coordinate adjectives that need commas.]
  - The concert featured **several familiar backup** singers. [*Several familiar backup* cannot be changed to *backup familiar several* and make sense, so these are cumulative adjectives that do not need commas.]
- Can *and* be inserted between the adjectives without changing the meaning or creating nonsense? If the answer is yes, the adjectives are coordinate and need commas.
  - The **large and noisy and restless** crowd wanted the concert to start. [Inserting *and* does not change the meaning of the sentence. Therefore, the adjectives are coordinate. Drop the *and*'s and insert commas.]
  - The concert featured **several and familiar and backup** singers. [Inserting *and* creates nonsense. Therefore, the adjectives are cumulative. Drop both the *and*'s and do not use commas.]

In contrast, never use a comma between **cumulative adjectives,** which do not carry equal weight in modifying a noun. The role of cumulative adjectives is to build up—that is, accumulate—meaning as they move toward the noun.

To determine whether adjectives are carrying equal weight in a sentence, use the test in Box 73.

50f How do commas work with nonrestrictive and restrictive elements?

A **nonrestrictive element** (also called a *nonessential element*) adds information to a sentence without changing the general meaning of the basic sentence. Nonrestrictive elements can be clauses, phrases, or appositives. Always use commas to set off nonrestrictive elements.

In contrast, a **restrictive element** (also called an *essential element*) limits and creates the specific meaning of the basic sentence.

Like nonrestrictive elements, restrictive elements can be clauses, phrases, or appositives. Never use commas to set off restrictive elements, because they provide essential information.

Punctuating nonrestrictive and restrictive clauses

Set off nonrestrictive ADJECTIVE CLAUSES with commas. Most adjective clauses begin with *who, which*, or *that*. Never put commas around restrictive clauses.

NONRESTRICTIVE CLAUSE
Farming**, which is our major source of food production,** is relentlessly affected by the weather. [Here, the focus is on the fact that farming is relentlessly affected by the weather. Therefore, *which is our major source of food production* is not essential information, so the clause is nonrestrictive and needs commas.]

RESTRICTIVE CLAUSE
Much food **that consumers buy canned or frozen** is processed. [Here, the focus is on *food that consumers buy canned or frozen*. Therefore, *that consumers buy canned or frozen* is essential information, so the clause is restrictive and does not need commas.]

Punctuating nonrestrictive and restrictive phrases

Set off nonrestrictive phrases with commas. Never put commas around restrictive phrases.

NONRESTRICTIVE PHRASE
Farmers**, trying to enhance crop growth,** use pesticides and fertilizers. [Here, the focus is on the fact that farmers use pesticides and fertilizers. Therefore, *trying to enhance crop growth* is not essential information, so the clause is nonrestrictive and needs commas.]

RESTRICTIVE PHRASE
Farmers **trying to enhance crop growth** use pesticides and fertilizers. [Here, the lack of commas indicates that the meaning of *farmers* depends on *trying to enhance crop growth* for its complete meaning. Therefore the phrase *trying to enhance crop growth* is restrictive and does not need commas.]

Punctuating nonrestrictive and restrictive appositives

An **appositive** renames the noun preceding it. Most appositives are nonrestrictive. Occasionally, depending on their context, appositives are restrictive. Set off nonrestrictive appositives, but not restrictive appositives, with commas.

NONRESTRICTIVE APPOSITIVE	Agricultural scientists**, a new breed of farmer,** control the farming environment. [Here, the focus is on the fact that agricultural scientists control the farming environment. Therefore, the appositive *a new breed of farmer* is not essential information, so the appositive is nonrestrictive and needs commas.]
RESTRICTIVE APPOSITIVE	The agricultural scientist **Wendy Singh** has helped develop a crop rotation system. [Here, the lack of commas indicates that *The agricultural scientist* depends on the name *Wendy Singh* for its complete meaning. Therefore, the appositive is restrictive and does not need commas.]

50g How do I use commas with quoted words?

Use a comma to set off quoted words from explanations anywhere in the same sentence.

- The poet William Blake wrote**,** "Love seeketh not itself to please." [The explanatory words *The poet William Blake wrote* come before the quoted words.]

- "I love you**,**" Mary told John**,** "but I cannot marry you." [The explanatory words *Mary told John* interrupt the quoted words.]

- "My love is a fever**,**" declared William Shakespeare. [The explanatory words *declared William Shakespeare* come after the quoted words.]

However, when you use *that* before or after a quotation, never use a comma before or after *that*. This rule holds whether you write a DIRECT QUOTATION or an INDIRECT QUOTATION.

NO	Mary claims**,** that "our passion is strong, but we have nothing else in common." [A comma never comes before *that*.]
NO	Mary claims that**,** "our passion is strong, but we have nothing else in common." [A comma never comes after *that*.]
YES	Mary claims that "our passion is strong, but we have nothing else in common."

50h What other word groups do I set off with commas?

Additional word groups that call for a comma to set them off from the rest of a sentence include TRANSITIONAL EXPRESSIONS, CONJUNCTIVE ADVERBS, asides, contrasts, words addressed directly to a reader or listener, and tag questions. The following examples show where in the sentence these word groups may fall. Contrasts act like an appositive and always fall right after the word they contrast with.

TRANSITIONAL EXPRESSIONS

- **For example,** California is a major food producer.
- California, **for example,** is a major food producer.
- California is a major food producer, **for example.**

CONJUNCTIVE ADVERBS

- **However,** the Midwest section of the United States is the world's breadbasket.
- The Midwest section of the United States, **however,** is the world's breadbasket.
- The Midwest section of the United States is the world's breadbasket, **however.**

ASIDES

- Most large growers, **I imagine,** hope to export food.
- Most large growers hope to export food, **I imagine.**

CONTRASTS

- Food, **not technology,** tops the list of U.S. exports.

WORDS ADDRESSED DIRECTLY TO READER

- **All you computer majors,** perhaps the future lies in soybeans rather than software.
- Perhaps the future, **all you computer majors,** lies in soybeans rather than software.
- Perhaps the future lies in soybeans rather than software, **all you computer majors.**

TAG QUESTIONS (CAN INTERRUPT OR END A SENTENCE)

- You know, **don't you,** what tag questions are?
- You know what tag questions are, **don't you?**

50i How do I use commas in dates, names, addresses, letter format, and numbers?

Punctuating dates

Use a comma between the day and the month. In addition, use a comma between a day of the week and the month.

- July 20, 1969
- Sunday, July 20, 1969

When you use month-day-year order for dates, use a comma after the day and the year.

- Everyone watched television on July 20, 1969, to see Neil Armstrong walk on the moon.

When you use day-month-year order for dates, never use commas.

- Everyone watched television on 20 July 1969 to see Neil Armstrong walk on the moon.

Never use a comma between only a month and year, only a month and day, or only a season and year.

- The major news story in July 1969 was the moon landing; news coverage was especially heavy on July 21. Many older people will always remember summer 1969.

Punctuating names, places, and addresses

When an abbreviated title (*Jr., M.D., Ph.D.*) comes after a name, use a comma between the name and the title (60b). When a sentence continues after a name and title, also use a comma after the title.

- Rosa Gonzales, M.D., was the principal witness for the defense.

Use a comma between the last and first names in an inverted name (last name first).

- Troyka, David

Use a comma between a city and state. When a sentence continues after a city and state, also use a comma after the state.

- Philadelphia, Pennsylvania, is home to the Liberty Bell.

When a sentence includes a complete address, use a comma to separate all the items in the address except the zip code (60d). The zip code follows the state after a space and no comma.

- I wrote to Mr. U Lern, 10-01 Rule Road, Classgate, NJ 07632 for the instruction manual.

Punctuating letter openings and closings

Use a comma after the opening of an informal letter. Use a COLON after the opening of a formal letter.

- Dear Betty,   - Dear Ms. Renshaw:

After the closing of a formal or informal letter, use a comma.

- Sincerely yours,
- Love,

Punctuating numbers

Counting from the right, not the left side, of a number, put a comma after every three digits in numbers longer than four digits.

- 150,567,066
- 72,867

In four-digit numbers, a comma is optional for money, distance, amounts, and most other measurements. Be consistent in each piece of writing.

- $1776
- 1776 miles
- 1776 potatoes

- $1,776
- 1,776 miles
- 1,776 potatoes

Use a comma to separate related measurements written in words.

- five feet, four inches

Use a comma to separate the act and scene numbers in plays. In addition, use a comma to separate a page reference in any SOURCE from a line reference.

- act ii, scene iv [or act 2, scene 4]
- page 120, line 6

50j How can a comma prevent a misreading?

Use a comma to clarify the meaning of a sentence, even if no other rule calls for one.

NO   Those who can practice many hours a day.

YES   Those who can, practice many hours a day.

NO   George dressed, and performed for a sellout crowd.

YES   George dressed and performed for a sellout crowd.

50k When are commas wrong?

In explaining comma rules in this chapter so far, I've covered the errors associated with those rules. The list below summarizes what I've already discussed; see the sections in parentheses for a full explanation.

COMMA ERRORS ALREADY COVERED IN THIS CHAPTER

- Commas with introductory words, phrases, clauses (50b)
- Commas with coordinating conjunction to link independent clauses (50c)
- Commas with items in a series (50d)
- Commas with coordinate adjectives (50e)
- Commas with nonrestrictive elements (50f)
- Commas with quoted words (50g)
- Commas with other material—transitional expressions, conjunctive adverbs, asides, contrasts, directly addressed words, and tag questions (50h)
- Commas in dates, names, places, addresses, letters, and numbers (50i)
- Commas to prevent misreading (50j)

THE OVERRIDING RULE FOR USING COMMAS

If advice in this handbook against using a comma clashes with a rule that requires a comma, *use the comma*.

- Kitty Hawk**,** North Carolina**,** attracts thousands of tourists each year. [Although the comma after *North Carolina* could be wrong because it separates the subject and verb, the comma here is correct because it is required to set off a city–state combination from the rest of the sentence.]

ADDITIONAL TYPES OF COMMA ERRORS

Comma errors can occur in ten additional ways.

1. Never put a comma in a number in an address or in a page reference.

   - 11263 Dean Drive
   - see page 1338

2. Never put a comma in years that are expressed in four figures. If the year is expressed in five or more figures, use a comma.

   - 1995, 1998, 2002
   - 25,000 B.C.E.

3. Never put a comma after *such as*.

   NO The Wright brothers were fascinated by other vehicles, **such as,** bicycles and gliders.

YES The Wright brothers were fascinated by other vehicles, **such as** bicycles and gliders.

4. Never put a comma before *than* in a comparison.

   NO The 1903 airplane sustained its flight **longer, than** any other engine-powered aircraft had.

   YES The 1903 airplane sustained its flight **longer than** any other engine-powered aircraft had.

5. Never put a comma before an opening parenthesis. When a comma is required, put it *after* the closing parenthesis.

   NO Because aviation enthralls many of **us, (especially children)** a popular spot to visit is Kitty Hawk's flight museum.

   YES Because aviation enthralls many of **us (especially children),** a popular spot to visit is Kitty Hawk's flight museum.

6. Never put a comma after a PREPOSITION.

   NO People expected more damage **from,** the high winds.

   YES People expected more damage **from the** high winds.

7. Never put a comma after a SUBORDINATING CONJUNCTION.

   NO **Although,** winds exceeded fifty miles an hour, little damage occurred.

   YES **Although** winds exceeded fifty miles an hour, little damage occurred.

8. Never put a comma between a SUBJECT and its VERB.

   NO **Orville and Wilber Wright, made** their first successful airplane flights in 1903.

   YES **Orville and Wilber Wright made** their first successful airplane flights in 1903.

9. Never put a comma between a verb and its OBJECT.

   NO These inventors enthusiastically **tackled, the problems** of powered flight.

   YES These inventors enthusiastically **tackled the problems** of powered flight.

10. Never put a comma between a verb and its COMPLEMENT.

> **NO** Flying has **become, an important industry** and a popular hobby.

> **YES** Flying has **become an important industry** and a popular hobby.

51 SEMICOLONS

Use a semicolon in only two situations. (1) A semicolon can replace a period between two sentences when they're closely related in meaning. (2) Use a semicolon to replace a comma when you use a COORDINATING CONJUNCTION to link INDEPENDENT CLAUSES that already contain commas.

51a When can I use a semicolon instead of a period between independent clauses?

You can choose whether to use a semicolon to replace a period, but do so only between two independent clauses that relate closely in meaning.

- The desert known as Death Valley became a U.S. National Park in 1994; it used to be a National Monument.

 ALERT: Never use a semicolon between a DEPENDENT CLAUSE and an independent clause.

> **NO** Although Death Valley is a desert; its mountain peaks are covered with snow.

> **YES** Although Death Valley is a desert, its mountain peaks are covered with snow.

You can also choose to use a semicolon to replace a period between closely related sentences when the second sentence starts with a CONJUNCTIVE ADVERB or a TRANSITIONAL EXPRESSION.

CONJUNCTIVE ADVERB
- Death Valley gets little rain each year; **nevertheless,** in the spring its mountains have spectacular wildflower displays.

TRANSITIONAL EXPRESSION
- Many plant roots in Death Valley burrow dozens of feet below the surface; **in contrast,** some Death Valley plant roots run only slightly below the surface.

51b When do I need to use a semicolon to replace a comma?

A semicolon replaces a comma when you use a COORDINATING CONJUNC-TION to link INDEPENDENT CLAUSES that already contain commas.

- Because Death Valley is the hottest place in North America, some people think that no animals live there**; but** visitors, especially, are amazed to see many tiny and a few larger animals emerge at night, when the temperatures drop, to find food.

In addition, when individual items in a series (50d) contain commas, use a semicolon instead of a comma to separate the items. By doing so, you help your reader to understand your meaning.

- The animals in Death Valley include **spiders,** such as black widows and tarantulas**; snakes,** such as coral snakes and sidewinders**;** and **small mammals,** such as kangaroo rats, which can convert seeds into water; and trade rats, which nest around cactus.

ALERT: Never use a semicolon to introduce a list of items. Use a COLON instead (52a).

NO Many animals live in Death Valley**;** spiders, snakes, and small mammals.

YES Many animals live in Death Valley**:** spiders, snakes, and small mammals.

52 COLONS

52a How do I use a colon with a list, an appositive, or a quotation?

When you introduce a list, an appositive, or a quotation with an INDEPENDENT CLAUSE use a colon. This rule applies when the words *the following* and *as follows* end an independent clause. In contrast, when the words you use to introduce a list, an appositive, or a quotation form an incomplete sentence, never use a colon. This rule applies after the words *such as, like,* and *including*—never use a colon.

LISTED ITEMS

- The students demanded the following: an expanded menu in the cafeteria, improved janitorial services, and more up-to-date textbooks.

APPOSITIVE

- Museums in New York and Florida own the best known works from Louis Tiffany's studio: those wonderful stained-glass windows. [*Stained-glass windows* is an appositive that renames *best known works*.]

QUOTATION

- The little boy in *E.T.* did say something neat: "How do you explain school to a higher intelligence?"

  —George F. Will, "Well, I Don't Love You, E.T."

👁 **ALERT:** If an incomplete sentence introduces a direct quotation, use a comma, not a colon (50g). 👁

52b When can I use a colon between sentences?

When a sentence serves as an introduction to a second sentence, you can choose to use a colon between the two sentences.

- We will never forget the first time we made dinner at home together: He got food poisoning and was too sick to work for four days.

👁 **ALERTS:** (1) Never use a colon when a DIRECT OBJECT consists of a series or list of items.

> NO We bought: eggs, milk, cheese, and bread.
>
> YES We bought eggs, milk, cheese, and bread.

(2) Never separate a DEPENDENT CLAUSE from an INDEPENDENT CLAUSE with a colon. Use a comma instead.

> NO After the drought ended: water restrictions were lifted.
>
> YES After the drought ended, water restrictions were lifted.

(3) You can choose whether to capitalize the first word of an independent clause following a colon. Be consistent in each piece of writing. 👁

52c What conventional formats call for colons?

BETWEEN TITLE AND SUBTITLE

- *Literature: An Introduction to Critical Reading*

BETWEEN HOURS AND MINUTES AND MINUTES AND SECONDS

- The runner passed the halfway point at 1:23:02.

BETWEEN NUMBERS IN RATIOS

- a proportion of 7:1
- a 3:5 ratio

AFTER WORDS IN MEMO HEADINGS

- To: Dean Kristen Joy
- From: Professor Daniel Black
- Re: Student work-study program

AFTER FORMAL LETTER OPENINGS

- Dear Ms. Carter:

BETWEEN BIBLE CHAPTERS AND VERSES

- Psalm 23:1–3

⊙ **ALERT:** In MLA STYLE, a period takes the place of the colon: *Psalm 23.1.* ⊙

53 APOSTROPHES

53a How do I use an apostrophe to show that a noun is possessive?

The **possessive case** communicates ownership (*the writer's pen*) or other relationships (*the writer's parent*). In general, to indicate possession in NOUNS, you can choose to use *-'s* (*the instructor's comments*, which calls for an apostrophe; or a PHRASE beginning with *of* (*a comment of the instructor*), which doesn't call for an apostrophe. Here are some applications of this general rule.

1. Add *-'s* to nouns not ending in *-s*.
   - She felt a **parent's** joy. [*Parent* is a singular noun not ending in *-s*.]
   - They care about their **children's** education. [*Children* is a plural noun not ending in *-s*.]

2. Add *-'s* to singular nouns ending in *-s*.
   - The **business's** system for handling complaints is inefficient. [*The business* is a singular noun.]
   - Lee **Jones's** car insurance is expensive. [*Lee Jones* is one person—a singular noun.]

3. Add only an apostrophe to plural nouns ending in *-s*.
   - The **boys'** eyewitness statements helped solve the crime. [*Boys* is a plural noun, so only an apostrophe comes after the *s*.]
   - Three **months'** maternity leave is in the **workers'** contract. [*Months* and *workers* are plural nouns, so only an apostrophe comes after them.]

4. Add *-'s* to the last word in compound words and phrases.
   - His **mother-in-law's** company makes scuba gear. [The *-'s* comes at the end of the compound noun *mother-in-law*.]

5. Add *-'s* to each noun in individual possession.
   - **Avery's and Jimmy's** houses are next to each other. [Avery and Jimmy each own a house; they do not own the houses jointly.]

6. Add *-'s* to only the last noun in joint or group possession.
   - **Lindsey and Ryan's** house has a screened porch. [Lindsey and Ryan jointly own one house together, so the *-'s* follows only the final name.]

ALERTS: (1) Never use an apostrophe at the end of a nonpossessive noun ending in *-s*.

> **NO**   A medical **crisis'** often involves a heart attack. [*Crisis* is a singular noun that ends in *s*, but the sentence expresses no possession.]

> **YES**   A medical **crisis** often involves a heart attack.

(2) Never use an apostrophe with a nonpossessive plural noun.

> **NO**   **Team's** of doctors are researching the effects of cholesterol. [*Teams* is a plural noun that ends in *s*, but the sentence expresses no possession.]

> **YES**   **Teams** of doctors are researching the effects of cholesterol.

53b How do I use an apostrophe to show that an indefinite pronoun is possessive?

INDEFINITE PRONOUNS refer to general or nonspecific persons or things: *someone, somebody, anyone, anything, no one, else.* (For a complete list of types of pronouns, see Box 47, on p. 312.) To indicate possession in an indefinite pronoun, follow it with *-'s.*

- I need **someone's** help in studying for the test.
- Are **anyone else's** notes more complete than mine are? [When one indefinite pronoun follows another (*anyone else*), the second one takes the possessive *-'s.*]

53c Do I ever use an apostrophe with *hers, his, its, ours, yours,* and *theirs?*

Never use an apostrophe with **possessive pronouns:** *hers, his, its, ours, yours,* and *theirs.* As possessive pronouns, they already carry possessive meaning.

> **NO** Because cholesterol has been widely publicized, **it's** role in heart disease is well known.

> **YES** Because cholesterol has been widely publicized, **its** role in heart disease is well known.

👁 **ALERT:** Never confuse *its,* the possessive pronoun, with the contraction *it's,* which stands for *it is.* A similar confusion arises between *you're* and *your, who's* and *whose,* and *they're* and *their.* 👁

53d Do I ever add an apostrophe to a verb that ends in *-s?*

Never add an apostrophe to a VERB that ends in *-s.*

> **NO** Cholesterol **play's** a key role in longevity.

> **YES** Cholesterol **plays** a key role in longevity.

53e How do I use apostrophes in contractions?

In **contractions,** an apostrophe indicates that one or more letters have been omitted from a word or a term: *can't, don't, I'm, isn't, it's, let's, they're, wasn't, weren't, we've, who's, won't,* and *you're.*

- **It's** [*not* its] still snowing.

Many college instructors and other readers think that common contractions aren't appropriate in ACADEMIC WRITING. Indeed, the fifth edition of the *MLA Handbook* says they are "rarely acceptable in research papers" (61). However, the *MLA Handbook* does permit contractions such as *the nineties* and *the 1990s,* meaning the decade 1990–1999 (neither calls for an apostrophe); and *the '90s,* another shortened form for the decade 1990–1999 (this form calls for an apostrophe at the start, to take the place of *19*).

53f Do I use an apostrophe with letters, numerals, symbols, and terms?

Use an apostrophe before the *-s* to form the plurals of letters, numbers written as figures, symbols, and words used as terms.

LETTERS	Printing *w*'s is hard for some first graders.
NUMBERS IN FIGURES	The address includes six *2*'s.
SYMBOLS	A line of *&*'s onscreen may mean the keyboard is jammed.
WORDS USED AS TERMS	All the *for*'s were misspelled *four*.

● **ALERT:** When you use letters as letters or words as words, you can choose to underline them, put them in italics, or enclose them in quotation marks (54e). Whatever you choose, be consistent in each piece of writing. ●

54 QUOTATION MARKS

54a How do I use quotation marks with short direct quotations?

Direct quotations are exact words of prose or poetry copied from a SOURCE, either print or electronic. In MLA STYLE, a **short quotation** of prose runs four or fewer lines in your handwriting or on your word processor. In APA STYLE, a short quotation contains no more than forty words of prose or three lines of poetry. Whenever you write a short quotation, enclose it in quotation marks and allow it to run in with the rest of your sentence.

👁 **ALERT:** At the end of a short quotation, place the page number or the author's name and the page number (if you don't mention the author's name in the sentence that leads into the quotation) in parentheses. Put the period that ends the sentence *after the parentheses*, not before them. 👁

A LONG QUOTATION needs to be *set off* or *displayed* as a whole block of words (54b).

Using double quotation marks (" ")

Use double quotation marks to enclose a SHORT QUOTATION.

- Edward T. Hall explains the practicality of close conversational distances: **"If you are interested in something, your pupils dilate: if I say something you don't like, they tend to contract"** (47). Some cultures prefer arm's length for all but the most intimate conversations.

- As W. H. Auden wittily defined personal space, **"Some thirty inches from my nose / The frontier of my person goes"** (539).

Using single quotation marks (' ')

The only time you can use single quotation marks in short quotations is to replace any double quotation marks that appear in the original source.

ORIGINAL SOURCE

- He has also said that he does not wish to be the arbiter for what is or is not an **"official"** intelligence.

  —Thomas Hoerr, "The Naturalistic Intelligence," n.p.

EXAMPLE FROM A RESEARCH PAPER

- As Thomas Hoerr reports, Gardner "does not wish to be the arbiter for what is or is not an **'official'** intelligence."

👁 **ALERT:** (1) When you quote short passages of poetry, use a slash with a space on either side of it to signal where one line ends and the next line starts in the original. (2) Capitalize and punctuate quotations of poetry exactly as in the original, even if they do not follow the rules in this book. 👁

54b How do I use quotation marks with long direct quotations?

In MLA STYLE, a **long quotation** of prose runs five or more lines. In APA STYLE, a long quotation contains more than forty words of prose or more than three lines of poetry. A long quotation needs to start on a new line and should be indented, or *displayed* as a whole block of words, one inch from the left margin (MLA style) or half an inch from the left margin (APA style).

Never use quotation marks to enclose indented blocks of prose or poetry. The block indentation signals that the material is a quotation. Of course, if within a long quotation, some words in the original are in quotation marks, use them exactly as in the original. In the example below, the words *wrist distance* are in double quotation marks in the original source, so they are in double quotation marks in the long quotation as well.

- As Desmond Morris explains, personal space varies among cultures:

    When you are talking to someone in the street or in any open space, reach out with your arm and see where the nearest point on his body comes. If you hail from western Europe, you will find that he is at roughly fingertip distance from you. In other words, as you reach out, your fingertips will just about make contact with his shoulder. If you come from eastern Europe you will find you are standing at "wrist distance." If you come from the Mediterranean region you will find that you are much closer to your companion. (23)

👁 **ALERT:** At the end of a long quotation, place the page number or the author's name and the page number (if you don't mention the author's name in the sentence that leads into the quotation) in parentheses. Put the period that ends the sentence *before the parentheses*, not after them. 👁

54c How do I use quotation marks to indicate spoken words?

Spoken words are called **direct discourse.** When you quote direct discourse or you want to write dialogue, use quotation marks to enclose the speaker's words. Start a new paragraph—that is, indent the first line—each time the speaker changes.

- "I don't know how you can see to drive," she said. "Maybe you should put on your glasses."

"Putting on my glasses would help you to see?"
"Not me; you," Macon said. "You're focused on the windshield
instead of the road."

—Ann Tyler, *The Accidental Tourist*

If the same speaker's words continue for more than one paragraph, use
quotation marks at the start of each paragraph. However, do not use a
quotation mark at the end of a paragraph until you come to the final
paragraph.

👁 **ALERT:** Never enclose INDIRECT DISCOURSE (54f) in quotation marks.

- The mayor said that he was tired. [This indirect discourse needs no
  quotation marks. As a direct quotation, this sentence would read *The mayor
  said, "I am tired."*]👁

54d How do I use quotation marks with titles?

Use quotation marks around the titles of short published works: poems,
short stories, essays, articles from periodicals, pamphlets, brochures,
song titles, and individual episodes of a television or radio series. In
contrast, use italics (or underlining) for longer works. Box 79 (p. 423)
shows when to use quotation marks, italics or underlining, or neither.

54e How do I use quotation marks to indicate terms, translations, and irony?

You can choose to use either quotation marks or italics (or underlining)
to indicate words that are technical terms; words that are used as terms;
words in another language; translated words; and words that are meant
ironically. Whichever you choose, be consistent in each piece of writing.

TECHNICAL   "Plagiarism"—the unacknowledged use of another
TERM   person's words or ideas—is a serious offense. Plagiarism
    by students can result in expulsion. [Once the term has
    been introduced, it needs no further quotation marks.]

WORD USED   Many people confuse "affect" and "effect."
AS A TERM

TRANSLATED   My grandfather usually ended arguments with an old say-
WORDS   ing: *De gustibus non disputandum est* ("there is no argu-
    ing about tastes"). [If you italicize or underline the words
    being translated and enclose the translation in quotation marks,
    your reader's job is easier.]

IRONIC WORD   The proposed "reform" is actually a tax increase.

54f When are quotation marks wrong?

Never use quotation marks around CLICHÉS, SLANG, or other language that is inappropriate in ACADEMIC WRITING. Instead, revise by replacing it with specific, appropriate, fresh wording.

> **NO** They "eat like birds" in public and "stuff their faces" in private.

> **YES** They nibble in public and gorge themselves in private.

Never enclose a word in quotation marks merely to call attention to it.

> **NO** Remember, the "customer" matters to your business.

> **YES** Remember, the customer matters to your business.

Never enclose INDIRECT DISCOURSE in quotation marks.

> **NO** The College Code of Conduct points out that "plagiarism can result in expulsion." [The original words are "Grounds for expulsion include plagiarism." Here, the quotation is indirect, so quotation marks are wrong.]

> **YES** The College Code of Conduct points out that plagiarism can result in expulsion.

Never use quotation marks around the title of your own paper, whether you place it at the top of the page or on a title page or mention it in the body of your paper. One exception exists: If the title of your paper includes another title, use quotation marks (or italics or underlining, if the title is of a short work) around the other title only (Box 79, p. 424).

> **NO** "The Elderly in Nursing Homes: A Case Study"

> **YES** The Elderly in Nursing Homes: A Case Study

> **NO** Character Development in Shirley Jackson's The Lottery

> **YES** Character Development in Shirley Jackson's "The Lottery"

54g How do I use quotation marks with other punctuation?

1. Put commas and periods *inside* closing quotation marks.

- Having enjoyed F. Scott Fitzgerald's **"The Freshest Boy,"** we were eager to read his longer works.
- Edward T. Hall coined the word **"proxemics."**

2. Put colons and semicolons *outside* closing quotation marks.

   - We try to discover **"how close is too close":** We do not want to invade others' personal space.
   - Esther DiMarzio claims that the current job market **"offers opportunities that never existed before";** others disagree.

3. Put question marks, exclamation points, and dashes inside or outside closing quotation marks, depending on their function. If a question mark, exclamation point, or dash punctuates the words enclosed in quotation marks, put that punctuation *inside* the closing quotation mark.

   - "Did I Hear You Call My Name**?"** was the winning song.
   - They shouted, "We won the lottery**!"**

   If a question mark, exclamation point, or dash punctuates words *not* enclosed in quotation marks, put that punctuation *outside* the closing quotation mark.

   - Have you read Nikki Giovanni's poem "Knoxville, Tennessee**"?**
   - Edward T. Hall's coined word "proxemics"**—**a term based on proximity—can now be found in the dictionary.

55 PERIODS, QUESTION MARKS, AND EXCLAMATION POINTS

55a When should I use a period?

A period is correct after a statement, a mild command, or an **indirect question,** which reports a question that someone asks. An indirect question never calls for quotation marks. (For help in punctuating direct questions, see 54a. For help with periods in abbreviations, see Ch. 60.)

STATEMENT Mountain climbers enjoy the outdoors**.**

MILD COMMAND Pack warm clothes for the climb**.**

INDIRECT QUESTION I asked whether they wanted to climb Mt. Everest**.**

55b When should I use a question mark?

A question mark is correct after a direct question, a directly quoted question, a series of questions, or a polite request. A **direct question**, which asks a question outright, and a **directly quoted question** call for quotation marks and end with a question mark *outside* the quotation marks. (For help in punctuating an indirect question, see 55a.) Questions in a series can be either complete or incomplete sentences. For either type, use a question mark after each.

👁 **ALERT:** When questions in a series are incomplete sentences, you can choose whether to capitalize the first letter of each. Whatever your choice, be consistent in each piece of writing. 👁

DIRECT QUESTION	Have you ever wanted to climb Mt. Everest**?**
DIRECTLY QUOTED QUESTION	I asked, "Do you want to climb Mt. Everest**?"**
SERIES OF QUESTIONS WITH CAPITALS	The mountain climbers debated what to do: Turn back**? M**ove on**? R**est**?**
SERIES OF QUESTIONS WITH LOWERCASE	The mountain climbers debated what to do: turn back**? m**ove on**? r**est**?**

To end a **polite request,** you can choose between a question mark and a period.

- Would you please send me the report**?** [This version emphasizes the politeness more than the request.]
- Would you please send the report**.** [This version emphasizes the request.]

To communicate IRONY or sarcasm, depend on words, not a question mark in parentheses, to communicate your message.

NO Having altitude sickness is a pleasant **(?)** experience.

YES Having altitude sickness is as pleasant as having a terrible case of the flu.

55c When should I use an exclamation point?

An exclamation point is correct after a strong command (*Look out!*), an emphatic declaration (*Those cars are going to crash!*), or an **interjection,** a word that conveys surprise or other emotion (*Oh! You're afraid of heights.*). Avoid using exclamation points in your

ACADEMIC WRITING. Reserve them for dialogue. Otherwise, use words that have enough impact to communicate a strong message.

> **NO** Each day in Nepal, we tried to see Mt. Everest. Each day we failed**!** The summit remained shrouded**!** Clouds defeated us**!**

> **YES** Each day in Nepal, we tried to see Mt. Everest. Each day we failed**.** The summit remained shrouded**.** Clouds defeated us**!**

To communicate amazement or sarcasm, depend on words, not an exclamation point in parentheses, to communicate your message.

> **NO** At 29,035 feet **(!)**, Mt. Everest is the world's highest mountain.

> **YES** At a staggering 29,035 feet, Mt. Everest is the world's highest mountain.

56 OTHER PUNCTUATION MARKS

56a When should I use a dash?

Dashes let you interrupt a sentence's structure to add information. They can also insert a little suspense, if the meaning calls for it. Use dashes sparingly so that you don't dilute their effect by overexposure.

COMPUTER TIP: You create a dash on a computer by typing two hyphens with no space before, between, or after them. In some word processing software, the two hyphens automatically turn into one unbroken line to form a dash, but only when you type a word after the hyphens and hit the space bar on your keyboard.

You can use a dash to add information such as examples, definitions, APPOSITIVES, contrasts, and asides. Sometimes parentheses (56b) serve the same purposes, but while dashes tend to emphasize material, parentheses tend to speak in quieter voice.

- Two of the strongest animals in the jungle are vegetarians—the elephant and the gorilla. [examples]

  —Dick Gregory, *The Shadow That Scares Me*

- Although the emphasis at the school was mainly language—speaking, reading, writing—the lessons always began with an exercise in politeness. [definition]
—Elizabeth Wong, *Fifth Chinese Daughter*

- The care-takers—the helpers, nurturers, teachers, mothers—are still systematically devalued. [appositive]
—Ellen Goodman, "Just Woman's Work"

- Tampering with time brought most of the house tumbling down, and it was this that made Einstein's work so important—and controversial. [contrast]
—Banesh Hoffman, "My Friend, Albert Einstein"

- I live on an income well below the poverty line—although it does not seem like poverty when the redbud and dogwood are in bloom together—and when I travel I have to be careful about expenses. [aside]
—Sue Hubbell, *Beekeeper*

👁 **ALERTS:** (1) If the words within a pair of dashes are a complete sentence and call for a question mark or an exclamation point, place such punctuation *before* the second dash: *A first love—do you remember?—stays in the memory forever.* (2) Never use commas, semicolons, or periods next to dashes. Revise your writing to avoid these types of double punctuation. 👁

56b When should I use parentheses?

Like dashes (56a), **parentheses** let you interrupt a sentence's structure to add information. Parentheses tend to de-emphasize whatever they enclose; dashes tend to call attention to whatever they set off.

Using parentheses to add information

Parentheses can enclose the same kind of material that dashes can, such as explanations, definitions, examples, contrasts, and asides.

- In division (also known as partition), a subject commonly thought of as a single unit is reduced to its separate parts. [definition]
—David Skwire, *Writing with a Thesis*

- Though other cities (Dresden, for instance) had been utterly destroyed in World War II, never before had a single weapon been responsible for such destruction. [example]
—Lawrence Behrens and Leonard J. Rosen,
Writing and Reading Across the Curriculum

- The sheer decibel level of the noise around us is not enough to make us cranky, irritable, or aggressive. (It can, however, affect our mental and physical health, which is another matter.) [aside]
  —Carol Tavris, *Anger: The Misunderstood Emotion*

Using parentheses to enclose numbers or letters

Conventional uses for parentheses include enclosing numbers or letters of listed items: *The topics to be discussed are (1) membership, (2) fundraising, (3) networking, and (4) special events.* Another conventional use occurs in business writing when parentheses sometimes enclose a number written as a figure immediately after its spelled-out version: *The order of fifteen (15) cartons was shipped yesterday.*

Using parentheses with other punctuation

Never put a comma *before* an opening parenthesis, even if what precedes the parenthetical material requires a comma. Always put the comma *after* the closing parenthesis.

> **NO** Although different from the first film we watched**, (***The Wizard of Oz***)** *Gone with the Wind* is also worth studying.

> **YES** Although different from the first film we watched **(***The Wizard of Oz***),** *Gone with the Wind* is also worth studying.

If a sentence in parentheses stands on its own, rather than within another sentence, place whatever ending punctuation is called for *before* the closing parentheses.

If a complete sentence in parentheses falls within another sentence, never use a period to signal the end of the parenthetical sentence. In addition, never start such a sentence in parentheses with a capital letter—unless the first word is a PROPER NOUN. In contrast, if the complete sentence within parentheses calls for a question mark or an exclamation point, use it.

> **NO** Searching for his car keys **(H**e had left them in the kitchen**.)** wasted an hour.

> **YES** Searching for his car keys **(h**e had left them in the kitchen**)** wasted an hour.

> **YES** Searching for his car keys **(w**hy can't he learn to put them in the same place all the time**?)** wasted an hour.

> **YES** Searching for his car keys wasted an hour**. (H**e had left them in the kitchen**.)**

56c When should I use brackets?

Brackets enclose one or more words that a writer inserts into SHORT QUOTATIONS or LONG QUOTATIONS. As a writer, you would use brackets

- to fit the wording of the quotation into the structure of your own sentence;

- to enclose explanatory words within quoted material in order to help your reader understand the quotation.

ORIGINAL SOURCE

- For a variety of reasons, the system attempts to maintain stability and resist temporal change.
  > —Peter Bonner, "Travel Rhythms," *Sky Magazine*, p. 72

SOURCE IN A QUOTATION

- In "Travel Rhythms," Bonner explains that **"maintain[ing]** stability and **resist[ing]** temporal change" are natural goals for human beings. [Brackets are used to fit the quotation's wording into the rest of sentence structure.]

SOURCE IN A QUOTATION

- Bonner pointed out that a "system **[undergoing large and sudden time shifts]** attempts to maintain stability and resist temporal change" (72). [Brackets are used for explanatory words added by the writer, not the original author, Bonner.]

👁 **ALERT:** You can use the bracketed term [sic] when you've found an error in something you are quoting—perhaps a wrong date or an error of fact. Because no one can change the wording in the original source, adding [sic] says to a reader, "It is this way in the original." In MLA STYLE, use regular (roman) type, not italics or underlining, for the term. When this term falls within a sentence, use brackets around it; use parentheses when the term falls at the end of a sentence, and place puctuation after them. In APA STYLE, underline or italicize the term sic, but never use brackets. 👁

56d When should I use ellipses?

An **ellipsis** is a set of three spaced periods. The most important function of an ellipsis is to indicate that in copying a quotation into your writing, you've omitted some of the words in the original source. This rule applies only when the omission is a word or a short phrase from the original source—in such cases, simply use quotation marks.

👁 **ALERTS:** (1) Never put a space before the first period or after the last period in an ellipsis. (2) Place any punctuation from the original source *after* the ellipsis. 👁

Using ellipses in prose quotations

MLA STYLE distinguishes between (1) an ellipsis that signals your personal omissions *from* the quoted material and (2) an ellipsis that appears in the original source. For your own omissions, use three spaced periods . . . to create an ellipsis. **The sixth edition of the *MLA Handbook for Writer's of Research Papers* no longer requires the use of brackets surrounding an ellipsis.** If an ellipsis appears in the original source, include it. Never split an ellipsis between the end of a line and the beginning of the next.

ORIGINAL SOURCE

> For over a century, twins have been used to study how genes make people what they are. Because they share precisely the same genes but live in different surroundings under different influences, identical twins reared apart are helping science sort out which qualities of body and mind are shaped by our genes and which by upbringing. Researchers needn't worry about running out of subjects: according to the Twins Foundation, there are approximately 4.5 million twin individuals in the United States alone, and about 70,000 more are born each year.
>
> —Sharon Begley, "Twins," p. 84

MLA STYLE

- According to Begley, "identical twins reared apart are helping science sort out which qualities of body and mind are shaped by our genes and which by upbringing" (84). [Ellipsis unnecessary; quotation is worked into a sentence.]

- Begley says, "Because they share precisely the same genes ... , identical twins reared apart are helping science sort out which qualities of body and mind are shaped by our genes and which by upbringing" (84). [Ellipsis shows that the writer has omitted words from the quoted sentence or a longer passage.]

- Begley says, "Because they share precisely the same genes but live in different surroundings under different influences, identical twins reared apart are helping science ..." (84). [Ellipsis shows that the writer has omitted words from the quoted sentence or a longer passage.]

- Begley says, "For over a century, twins have been used to study how genes make people what they are. ... Researchers needn't worry about running out of subjects" (84). [Even if one or more entire sentences are omitted, use an ellipsis.]

APA STYLE

APA STYLE calls for three spaced periods without brackets.

1. Use an ellipsis to signal your personal omissions from the middle of a sentence of quoted material.

2. Never use an ellipsis to signal your omission from the start or end of a sentence, unless you need to call attention to the fact that the quoted words come from the middle of a sentence.

3. Add a fourth period to the ellipsis in two cases: (a) to stand for sentence-ending punctuation or (b) to indicate the omission of one or more sentences from the quotation.

- Begley says, "Because they share precisely the same genes **. . .** , identical twins reared apart are helping science sort out which qualities of body and mind are shaped by our genes and which by upbringing" (p. 84). [Ellipsis shows that the writer has omitted words from the middle of the quoted sentence in APA style.]

- Begley says, "Identical twins reared apart are helping science sort out which qualities of body and mind are shaped by our genes and which by upbringing" (p. 84). [Here, the writer omits words from the beginning of the quoted sentence but does not use an ellipsis to indicate the omission. APA style permits a writer to change the lowercase letter that starts the quotation to a capital letter.]

- Begley says, "Because they share precisely the same genes but live in different surroundings under different influences, identical twins reared apart are helping science." (p. 84). [Here, the writer omits words from the end of the quoted sentence but does not need to use an ellipsis to indicate the omission in APA style.]

- Begley says, "For over a century, twins have been used to study how genes make people what they are**. . . .** Researchers needn't worry about running out of subjects" (84). [Here, the writer uses an additional period to indicate the omission of one or more sentences from the quoted material in APA style.]

Using ellipses in quotations from poetry

In MLA style, show omissions from SHORT QUOTATIONS of poetry—that is, quotations of three lines or less—with an ellipsis. In LONG QUOTATIONS of poetry, show an omission of a few words with an ellipsis, and show an omission of a full line or more with an entire line of spaced periods. In APA style, follow the same rules.

ORIGINAL SOURCE

Fear no more the heat o' the sun
Nor the furious winter's rages;
Though thy worldly task has done,
Home art gone, and ta'en thy wages;
Golden lads and girls all must,
As chimney-sweepers, come to dust.

—William Shakespeare, from *Cymbeline*

MLA STYLE

- Ultimately, however, as Shakespeare reminds us, "Golden lads and girls all must, . . . come to dust." [short poetry quotation with a few words omitted]

- Fear no more the heat o' the sun
  Nor the furious winter's rages;
  . . . .
  Golden lads and girls all must,
  . . . come to dust.
  [long poetry quotation with lines and words omitted]

APA STYLE

- Ultimately, however, as Shakespeare reminds us, "Golden lads and girls all must, . . . come to dust." [short poetry quotation with a few words omitted]

- Fear no more the heat o' the sun
  Nor the furious winter's rages;
  . . . .
  Golden lads and girls all must,
  . . . come to dust.
  [long poetry quotation with lines and words omitted]

56e When should I use a slash?

When quoting three or fewer lines of poetry, use a slash to divide one line from the next. Leave a space on each side of the slash.

- Consider the beginning of Anne Sexton's poem "Words": "Be careful of words, / even the miraculous ones."

To type numerical fractions that don't appear on your keyboard, use the slash to separate the numerator and denominator, leaving no space before or after the slash.

- 1/16
- 1 2/3

Avoid word combinations like *and/or* when writing in the humanities. Revise your sentence to avoid such a combination. In academic disciplines in which the use of word combinations is acceptable, separate the two words with a slash, leaving no space before or after it.

57 HYPHENS

57a When should I hyphenate at the end of a line?

When you use a word processing program, set the default to allow no hyphenation. If you write by hand, follow the rules in Box 74.

BOX 74

Hyphenating at the end of a line

- Never divide very short words, one-syllable words, or words pronounced as one syllable.

  we-alth ~~we-alth~~ *(wealth)*   en-vy ~~en-vy~~ *(envy)*   scream-ed ~~scream-ed~~ *(screamed)*

- Never leave or carry over only one or two letters.

  a-live ~~a-live~~ *(alive)*   o-pen ~~o-pen~~ *(open)*   cover-ed ~~cover-ed~~ *(covered)*

- Divide words only between syllables. (If you're unsure about a word's syllables, look it up in a dictionary.)

  proc-ess ~~proc-ess~~ *(pro-cess)*

- Divide between consonants, keeping pronunciation in mind.

  ful-lness ~~ful-lness~~ *(full-ness)*   omitt-ing ~~omitt-ing~~ *(omit-ting)*   asp-halt ~~asp-halt~~ *(as-phalt)*

- Divide a hyphenated word only at the hyphen, and divide a closed compound word only between complete words.

  self-con-scious ~~self-con-scious~~ *(self-conscious)*   mas-terpiece ~~mas-terpiece~~ *(master-piece)*

  sis-ter-in-law ~~sis-ter-in-law~~ *(sister-in-law)*   stom-achache ~~stom-achache~~ *(stomach-ache)*

BOX 75

🎯 Hyphenating prefixes and suffixes

- Use hyphens after the prefixes *all-, ex-,* and *self-*
  - all-inclusive, self-reliant
- Never use a hyphen when *self* is a root word onto which a prefix is attached.
  - selfishness, selfless, selfhood
- Use a hyphen to avoid a distracting string of repeated letters.
  - anti-intellectual, bell-like
- Use a hyphen between a prefix and the first word of a compound word.
  - anti-gun control
- Use a hyphen to prevent confusion in meaning or pronunciation.
  - re-dress ("dress again"), un-ionize ("remove the ions")
  - redress ("set right"), unionize ("form a union")
- Use a hyphen when two or more prefixes apply to one root word.
  - two-, three-, or four-year program
  - pre- and postwar eras
- Use a hyphen before the suffix *-elect.*
  - president-elect
- Use a hyphen when a prefix comes before a number or before a word that starts with a capital letter.
  - post-1950, pro-American

57b When should I hyphenate prefixes and suffixes?

Prefixes and **suffixes** are syllables attached to words—prefixes at the beginning and suffixes at the end. Some prefixes and suffixes call for hyphens, but others don't (Box 75).

57c When should I hyphenate compound words?

A **compound word**—two or more words combined to express one concept—can be written in one of three ways: as separate words (*night shift*), as hyphenated words (*tractor-trailer*), or as one word (*handbook*). Follow the rules in Box 76 on the next page.

BOX 76

Hyphenating compound words

- Use a hyphen for most compound modifiers that precede the noun. Never use a hyphen for compound modifiers *after* the noun.
  - well-researched report; two-inch clearance [before the noun]
  - report is well researched; clearance of two inches [after the noun]
- Use a hyphen between compound nouns joining two units within a measure.
  - light-year, kilowatt-hour, foot-pound
- Never use a hyphen when a compound modifier starts with an *-ly* adverb.
  - happily married couple
- Never use a hyphen when a compound modifier is in the comparative (*-er, more, less*) or superlative (*-est, most, least*) form.
  - better fitting shoe, least welcome guest
  - most significant factor
- Never use a hyphen when a compound modifier is a foreign phrase.
  - post hoc fallacies
- Never use a hyphen with a possessive compound modifier.
  - a full week's work, eight hours' pay

57d When should I hyphenate spelled-out numbers?

For help in deciding when to use numerals and when to spell out numbers, see Chapter 61. Box 77 shows how to hyphenate spelled-out numbers.

👁 **ALERTS:** Use figures for any fraction that requires more than two words in its spelled-out form. If you cannot avoid spelling out a fraction in three or more words, follow these rules. (1) Use a hyphen between all words in the numerator. (2) Use a hyphen between all words in the denominator. (3) Use a space (no hyphen!) to separate the numerator from the denominator.

- 2/100 *or* two one-hundredths
- 33/10,000 *or* thirty-three ten-thousandths 👁

Hyphenating spelled-out numbers

- Use a hyphen between two-word numbers from twenty-one through ninety-nine.
  - thirty-five, two hundred thirty-five
- Use a hyphen in a compound modifier formed from a number and a word.
  - fifty-minute class [*also* 50-minute class]
  - three-to-one odds [*also* 3-to-1 odds]
- Use a hyphen between the numerator and the denominator of a two-word fraction.
  - one-half, two-fifths, seven-tenths

58 CAPITALS

See 58a–58c for when to use capital versus lowercase letters. For more examples, see Box 78 at the end of this chapter.

58a When should I capitalize a "first" word?

1. Capitalize the first word in a sentence.
   - **F**our inches of snow fell last winter.

2. If you wish, capitalize the first word of a complete sentence after a colon. When a complete sentence follows a colon, you can begin the first word with either a capital or a lowercase letter, but be consistent in each piece of writing. When the words after a colon are not a complete sentence, never capitalize.
   - Only one solution occurred to her: **S**he picked up the ice cream and pushed it back into the cone. [The capital letter is acceptable after the colon because a full sentence comes after it.]
   - Only one solution occurred to her: **s**he picked up the ice cream and pushed it back into the cone. [A lowercase letter is acceptable after the colon.]
   - She bought four pints of ice cream: **v**anilla, chocolate, strawberry, and butterscotch swirl. [A lowercase letter is required because the words following the colon are not a full sentence.]

3. Capitalize the first word in a series of complete questions. When questions in a series are *not* complete sentences, you can begin the first word of each question with either a capital or a lowercase letter. Be consistent within each piece of writing.

- What facial feature would most people like to change? **E**yes? **E**ars? **N**ose?

- What facial feature would most people like to change? **e**yes? **e**ars? **n**ose?

ALERT: The rule for capitalizing a series of incomplete *questions* is different (55b).

4. Capitalize the first word in a list of items that are complete sentences.

- Three problems caused the shortage: (1) **B**ad weather delayed delivery. (2) **P**oor scheduling created slowdowns. (3) **I**nadequate maintenance caused equipment breakdowns.

Never capitalize listed items that are *not* complete sentences.

- The delays resulted from (1) **b**ad weather, (2) **p**oor scheduling, and (3) **e**quipment breakdowns.

5. Capitalize the first word of a complete sentence that stands alone inside parentheses. A complete sentence enclosed in parentheses may stand alone or fall within another sentence. A complete sentence that stands alone within parentheses starts with a capital letter and ends with a period, a question mark, or an exclamation point. A complete sentence that falls *within* another sentence does *not* start with a capital letter or end with a period. However, if the sentence is a question, it ends with a question mark; if it is an exclamation, it ends with an exclamation point.

- I didn't know till years later that they called it the Cuban Missile Crisis. But I remember Castro. (**W**e called him Castor Oil and were awed by his beard—beards were rare in those days**.**) We might not have worried so much (**w**hat would the Communists want with our small New Hampshire town**?**) except that we lived 10 miles from an air base.

  —Joyce Maynard, *An 18-Year-Old Looks Back on Life*

58b How should I capitalize quotations?

Capitalize the first word in a prose quotation.

- Encouraging students to study in other countries, Mrs. Velez says, "**Y**ou will absorb a good accent with the food."

When you interrupt quoted words, never capitalize the continued part of the quoted words.

- "You will absorb a good accent," says Mrs. Velez, "**w**ith the food."

If the quoted words are part of your own sentence, never capitalize the first quoted word unless it is a PROPER NOUN. Phrases such as *writes that,* *thinks that,* and *says that* usually signal this kind of quotation.

- Mrs. Velez believes that "**y**ou will absorb a good accent with the food" if you study in another country.

When you quote poetry in your writing, use (or don't use) capitals exactly as they appear in the original source.

If you need help using quotation marks, see Chapter 54.

58c When should I capitalize nouns and adjectives?

Capitalize PROPER NOUNS (*Mexico, Arthur*) and PROPER ADJECTIVES (*a Mexican diplomat, the Arthurian legend*). Capitalize certain COMMON NOUNS when you add specific names or titles to them: *We visit a lake every summer. This summer we went to Lake Ontario.* See Box 78.

ALERTS: (1) Never capitalize DETERMINERS and other words just because they accompany proper nouns or proper adjectives: *Here is a Canadian penny* [not *A Canadian penny*]. (2) Be aware that some proper nouns and proper adjectives become so common that they lose their capital letters: *french fries, italics, pasteurized.*

BOX 78

Capitalization guide

	CAPITALS	LOWERCASE LETTERS
NAMES	Mother Teresa [*also* used as names: Mother, Dad, Mom, Pa, etc.]	my mother [relationship]
	Doc Holliday	the doctor [role]
TITLES	President Truman	the president
	Democrat [party member]	democrat [believer in democracy]
	Representative Harold Ford	the congressional representative
	Senator Edward M. Kennedy	the senator
	Queen Elizabeth II	the queen

CONTINUED ⟶

■ BOX 78 ■ ■

 Capitalization guide *(continued)*

	CAPITALS	LOWERCASE LETTERS
GROUPS OF PEOPLE	Caucasian [race]	white, black [*also* White, Black]
	African American, Hispanic [ethnic group]	
	Irish, Korean, Canadian [nationality]	
	Jew, Catholic, Protestant, Buddhist [religious affiliation]	
ORGANIZATIONS	Congress	legislative branch of the U.S. government
	the Ohio State Supreme Court	the state supreme court
	the Republican Party	the party
	National Gypsum Company	the company
	Chicago Cubs	baseball team
	American Medical Association	professional group
	Sigma Chi	fraternity
	Alcoholics Anonymous	self-help group
PLACES	Los Angeles	the city
	the South [region]	turn south [direction]
	the West Coast	the U. S. states along the western seaboard
	Main Street	the street
	Atlantic Ocean	the ocean
	the Black Hills	the hills
BUILDINGS	the Capitol [in Washington, DC]	the state capitol
	Ace High School	a high school
	China West Café	a restaurant
	Highland Hospital	a hospital

CONTINUED →

BOX 78

Capitalization guide *(continued)*

	CAPITALS	LOWERCASE LETTERS
SCIENTIFIC TERMS	Earth [as a planet]	the earth beneath our feet
	the Milky Way	the galaxy, the moon, the sun
	Streptococcus aureus	a streptococcal infection
	Gresham's law	the theory of relativity
LANGUAGES SCHOOL COURSES	Spanish, French, Chinese	
	Chemistry 342	a chemistry course
	English 111	my English class
	Introduction to Photography	a photography class
NAMES OF SPECIFIC THINGS	the *Boston Globe*	the newspaper
	Time	the magazine
	Purdue University	the university
	Heinz ketchup	ketchup
	a Dodge Cobra	a car
TIMES, SEASONS, HOLIDAYS	Friday	spring, summer, fall, autumn, winter
	August	
	Passover, New Year's Day, Ramadan, Kwanza	
HISTORICAL EVENTS AND DOCUMENTS	World War II	a war
	the Roaring Twenties	a decade
	the Great Depression [of the 1930s]	a depression
	the Paleozoic, the Reformation	an era, an age, the eighteenth century
	the Bill of Rights	fifth-century manuscripts
RELIGIOUS TERMS	God	a god, a goddess
	Buddhism	a religion
	the Torah, the Koran, the Bible	
LETTER PARTS	Dear Ms. Kupperman:	
	Sincerely,	
	Yours truly,	

CONTINUED →

BOX 78

⦿ Capitalization guide *(continued)*

	CAPITALS	LOWERCASE LETTERS
TITLES OF PUBLISHED AND RELEASED WORKS	"The Lottery" *A History of the United States to 1877* *Jazz on Ice*	[Capitalize the first letter of the first word and all other words except ARTICLES, short PREPOSITIONS, and short CONJUNCTIONS.]
ACRONYMS AND INITIALISMS	NATO, FBI, AFL-CIO, UCLA, DNA, CD	
COMPUTER TERMS	Gateway, Dell	a computer company
	Microsoft Word, WordPerfect	computer software
	Netscape Navigator	a browser
	World Wide Web, the Web	
	Web site, Web page	a home page, a link
	the Internet	a computer network
PROPER ADJECTIVES	Victorian	biblical
	Midwestern	transatlantic
	Indo-European	alpine

59 ITALICS (UNDERLINING)

Most printed material is set in roman type. Type that slants to the right is called italic type. If your word processing program does not have italic type, use the underline function. Italics and underlining mean the same thing.

HANDWRITTEN AND UNDERLINED

Great Expectations

TYPED AND UNDERLINED

Great Expectations

ITALIC TYPE

Great Expectations

How do I choose between italics and quotation marks?

Generally, use italics for titles of long works or works that contain subsections. Use quotation marks for titles of shorter works or titles of subsections within a larger work. Consult Box 79 for specifics.

BOX 79

⊙ Italics, quotation marks, or nothing

	ITALICIZE	**NEVER ITALICIZE**
TITLES AND NAMES	*The Bell Jar* [a novel]	
	Death of a Salesman [a play]	
	Collected Works of O. Henry [a book]	"The Last Leaf" [a story in the book]
	Simon & Schuster Handbook for Writers [a book]	"Agreement" [a chapter in the book]
	The Prose Reader [a collection of essays]	"Putting in a Good Word for Guilt" [one essay]
	The Iliad [a book-length poem]	"Nothing Gold Can Stay" [a short poem]
	Almost Famous [a film]	
	the *Los Angeles Times**** [a newspaper]	
	Scientific American [a magazine]	"The Molecules of Life" [an article in a magazine]
	Aida [an opera]	
	Symphonie Fantastique [a long musical work]	Concerto in B-flat Minor [a musical work identified by form, number, and key—neither quotation marks nor underlining]

**Even if *The* is part of the title printed on a newspaper, don't capitalize it and don't underline it in the body of your paper. In MLA-style documentation, omit the word *The*.

CONTINUED ⟶

BOX 79

 Italics, quotation marks, or nothing *(continued)*

ITALICIZE	NEVER ITALICIZE
Twilight Zone [a television series]	"Terror at 30,000 Feet" [an episode of a television series]
The Best of Bob Dylan [an album]	"Mr. Tambourine Man" [one recording]
the U.S.S. *Intrepid* [a ship; U.S.S. is not italic]	aircraft carrier [a class of ship]
Voyager 2 [specific aircraft, spacecraft, satellites]	Boeing 787 [names shared by classes of aircraft, spacecraft, or satellites]

OTHER WORDS		
semper fidelis [words in a language other than English]	burrito, chutzpah [widely understood non-English words]
What does *our* imply? [a word referred to as such]	
the *abc*'s; confusing *3*'s and *8*'s [letters and numerals referred to as such]	

59b When should I use italics for emphasis?

Use italics or underlining sparingly for emphasis. Your choice of words and sentence structure normally conveys the emphasis you want to give.

- The pain from my injury was <u>severe</u>.
- The pain from my injury was so severe that I could not breathe. [more effective description]

---

60 ABBREVIATIONS

The guidelines in this chapter apply to general writing and writing in the humanities. Guidelines in other disciplines vary. If you're in doubt about a particular abbreviation, check your college dictionary for correct capitalization, spacing, and use of periods.

👁 **ALERTS:** (1) When the period of an abbreviation falls at the end of a sentence, it serves also as a sentence-ending period. (2) When a question mark or exclamation point ends a sentence, place it after the abbreviation's period. 👁

60a What abbreviations can I use with times and amounts?

Use the abbreviations *a.m.* (or *A.M.*) and *p.m.* (or *P.M.*) with exact times. You can use capital or lowercase letters for *a.m.* and *p.m.* as long as you are consistent in each piece of writing.

- 7:15 a.m.
- 7:15 A.M.
- 3:47 p.m.
- 3:47 P.M.

Use *A.D.* (or *C.E.* for "common era") before the year and *B.C.* (or *B.C.E.* for "before the common era") following the year.

- A.D. 934
- C.E. 934
- 1200 B.C.
- 1200 B.C.E.

As a rule, avoid symbols in the body of your writing for classes in the humanities. Still, let common sense and a concern for clarity guide you. If you mention temperatures once or twice in a paper, spell them out: *ninety degrees, minus twenty-six degrees*. However, if you mention temperatures throughout your work, use numbers and symbols: *90°, −26°*.

In tables, you can abbreviate amounts and measurements when they're used with exact numbers (such as *in., mi., cm., km., gal., ml., lb., kg.*) as well as days and months (such as *Mon., Jan., Aug.*).

Use *$* with exact dollar-and-cent amounts expressed in numerals or numerals and words.

- $4.95
- $34 million

60b How should I use abbreviations with people's names?

Use the abbreviations *Mr., Mrs., Ms.*, and *Dr.* with either full names or last names only.

- Dr. Anna Freud
- Dr. Freud
- Mr. Daljit Singh
- Mr. Singh

Use most other abbreviated titles only with a full name.

FULL NAME	LAST NAME ONLY
Col. [Col. Lee Potts]	Colonel [Colonel Potts]
Gen.	General
Gov.	Governor
Rep.	Representative
Rev.	Reverend
Sen.	Senator

Abbreviations of professional and academic degrees follow the person's name.

- Betty Sun, M.D.
- Bruce Freund, D.D.S.
- Georgia Newman, Ph.D

ALERT: Never use both a title of address before a name and an abbreviated degree after a name.

   NO **Dr.** Jill Sih, **M.D.**

   YES Jill Sih, **M.D.**

   YES **Dr.** Jill Sih

Abbreviations indicating family generations—such as *Jr., Sr.,* and *III*—are part of the names themselves. Do not use a comma between the name and the generational abbreviation. Use a comma before other abbreviations.

- **Mr.** Kenneth Huizinga **Jr.**
- Roy J. Modugno **Sr., D.D.S.**

ALERTS: (1) Use a comma between a name and most abbreviations following it (50i). Some people omit the comma for the generation designations *II* and *III* (*Fred D. Fumia II*), but you need to use a comma for *Jr.* and *Sr.* (*Andrew Watson, Jr.*). (2) Separate abbreviations following a name with a comma: *Fred D. Fumia II, M.D.*

60c When can I abbreviate names of countries, organizations, and government agencies?

In general, do not abbreviate the names of countries. The abbreviation *U.S.* (or *US*) can be used as an ADJECTIVE form for *United States* (*the U.S. ski team*) but not as a NOUN: *The United States* [not *The U.S.*] *plays a major role in today's global economy.*

When you refer to an organization throughout your document and want to use its abbreviation, spell out the full name the first time you use it and then, immediately afterward, put the abbreviation in parentheses. Thereafter, you can use the abbreviation alone.

- Spain voted to continue as a member of the **North Atlantic Treaty Organization (NATO)**, to the surprise of other **NATO** members.

60d What abbreviations can I use in addresses?

You can use abbreviations such as *St.* for *Street* and *Blvd.* for *Boulevard* for addresses. You can also use abbreviations for *North* (*N.*); *South* (*S.*); *East* (*E.*); and *West* (*W.*). In the United States, use the two-letter postal abbreviations for state names in addresses.

If you include a full address—(street, city, state, zip code)—in one of your sentences, spell out all words except the two-letter postal abbreviation. If you are referring to a city and state or a state alone, spell out the city and the state.

- I wrote to Mr. U. Lern, 10-01 Rule Road, **Classgate, NJ** 07632 for the instruction manual. He had moved to **Falstaff, Arizona,** before my letter arrived.

ALERT: When you use a city–state combination within a sentence, use a comma between the city and state names and after the state name.

- My sister in **Norcross, Georgia,** studied in China.

60e When can I use *etc.* and other Latin abbreviations?

The abbreviation *etc.* comes from the Latin word *et cetera,* which means "and the rest." When you're writing for classes in the humanities, never use this abbreviation. Acceptable substitutes are *and the like, and so on*, and *and so forth.*

61 NUMBERS

61a When should I spell out numbers in words?

When a number can be expressed in one or two words, use words. If, however, numbers occur frequently in your paper, spell out *one* through *nine* and use numerals for all others.

- Between them, the two families own 126 sheep and 493 chickens.

👁 **ALERT:** With two-word numbers from *twenty-one* through *ninety-nine*, use a hyphen between the words. 👁

If a sentence starts with a number, spell it out rather than using a numeral. Better still, revise the sentence so that the number doesn't come first.

ACCEPTABLE **Three hundred seventy-five dollars** per credit is the tuition rate for nonresidents.

BETTER The tuition rate for nonresidents is **$375** per credit.

Never mix spelled-out numbers and figures when they refer to the same thing. In the following example, all numbers referring to volunteers need to be figures; *four* needs to be spelled out because it refers to days, not volunteers.

- In the past 4 days, our volunteers increased from ~~five~~ to ~~eight~~ to ~~seventeen~~ to 233. On Saturday, ~~thirty-seven~~ people who usually volunteer on weekdays joined the regular Saturday staff of ~~forty-one~~ volunteers.

61b How should I write dates, addresses, times, and other numbers?

Box 80 shows how to write numbers in some common forms.

BOX 80

● Using numbers

DATES	August 6, 1941
	1732–1845
	34 B.C.E. to A.D. 230
ADDRESSES	237 North 8th Street
	Export Falls, MN 92025
TIMES	8:09 a.m., 4:00 p.m. [*but* four o'clock, *not* 4 o'clock; 4 p.m. *or* four in the afternoon, *not* four p.m. *or* 4 in the afternoon]
CHAPTERS AND PAGES	Chapter 27, page 245
ACT, SCENE, AND LINE NUMBERS	act II, scene ii, lines 75–79 [*or* act 2, scene 2]
SCORES AND STATISTICS	a 6–0 score
	a 5 to 3 ratio [*or* a 5:3 ratio]
	29 percent
IDENTIFICATION NUMBERS	93.9 on the FM dial
	call 1-212-555-3930
MEASUREMENTS	2 feet
	67.8 miles per hour
	1.5 gallons, 3 liters
	8 1/2″ × 11″ paper [*or* 8 1/2 × 11 inch]
TEMPERATURES	43°, 4° Celsius
MONEY	$1.2 billion
	$3.41
	25 cents [*or* 25¢ *but not* twenty-five ¢]
DECIMALS AND FRACTIONS	5.55
	98.6
	3.1416
	7/8
	12 1/4
	3/4 [*or* three-fourths *or* three-quarters, *but not* 3-quarters]

Special Kinds of Writing

www.prenhall.com/troyka

Special Kinds of Writing

62 WRITING ABOUT LITERATURE

62a What is literature?

Literary works include **fiction** (novels and stories), **drama** (plays, scripts, and some films) and **poetry** (poems and lyrics), as well as non-fiction with artistic qualities (certain memoirs, personal essays, and so on). Since ancient times, literature has been important for the ways it represents human experience. Literature is designed to entertain and often to disrupt—and it always enlarges your perspective.

62b Why write about literature?

Writing about literature leads you to shape your reading experiences and insights. It helps you understand other people, ideas, times, and places. It shows you how authors use language to stir the imaginations, emotions, and intellects of their readers. Finally, writing is a way to share your own reading experiences and insights with other readers.

62c What general strategies can help me write about literature?

When you write about literature, you want to read the work closely as well as actively (2c). Of course, you may initially read a literary work for sheer enjoyment. During further readings, however, you want to pay careful attention to various aspects of the text. Readers are sometimes surprised to find that close, active reading actually enhances their enjoyment. Such reading includes asking what the work means, why the author made a particular choice, and why readers react to the work as they do. Box 81 (p. 433) lists several questions that encourage active reading. Boxes 82 and 83 (pp. 434 and 435) suggest other elements to think about as you read.

Sometimes instructors ask students to answer questions that deal with material on a literal level: to say what is on the page. If a question asks what happens in the plot or what a passage means, you need to write a SUMMARY* or PARAPHRASE of part of the work. If a question asks for the historical context of a work or background information about the author, you will need to do some research and report what you find.

*Words printed in small capital letters (such as SUMMARY or PARAPHRASE) are defined in the Terms Glossary on pages 467–85.

As often, assignments might call for you to make INFERENCES (2b). Making inferences means reading between the lines to figure out what is implied but not stated—an essential activity when you read literature, which tends to show rather than tell. Literature depicts events, conversations, settings, and so on, but the author doesn't come out directly and say exactly what the work means. To figure out the meaning, you need to read closely and actively. Inferential thinking is necessary when your instructor asks you to discuss why a character does something for which the author provides no explicit reason. Alternatively, your instructor might ask you to explain the effect of images in a poem, to discuss how a work implies the author's stance on a social issue, or to analyze how the author depicts the role of women. Your instructor may ask you to describe your personal reaction to reading a literary work. In such papers you analyze not only the literary text but also your own experiences and beliefs (62d).

Writing effective papers about literature involves more than summarizing the plot. It involves CRITICAL THINKING and SYNTHESIS. In such papers, you state a CLAIM (an observation or a position about the work of literature) and convince your readers that the thesis is reasonable. To be effective, you want your papers to be thorough and well supported. For support, you make direct references to the work, by writing summaries, paraphrases, and quotations of specific passages and by explaining precisely *why* and *how* the selected passages support your interpretation. What specifically do your readers need to understand about the passages?

62d How do I write different types of papers about literature?

When you read a literary work closely, look for details or passages that relate to your claim or thesis. Mark up the text as you read by selectively underlining passages or by writing notes, comments, or questions in the margin. Alternatively, take notes separately, on paper or on a computer.

Writing a personal response

A **personal response paper** is an essay in which you explain your reaction to a literary work or some aspect of it. You might write about why you did or did not enjoy reading it. You might discuss whether situations in the work are similar to your personal experiences. You might explain whether you agree or disagree with the author's point of view— and *why*. You might answer a question or explore a problem that the work raised for you. For example, how do you react if a likable character breaks the law? Similarly, how do you respond to racial, gender, or class prejudice? As with all effective papers about literature, you need to explain your response through discussions of specific passages or elements from the text.

Writing an interpretation

An interpretation explains what you think the work means—that is, the message or viewpoint that you think it conveys. Most works of literature are open to more than one interpretation. Your task, then, is not to discover the single right answer. Instead, your task is to determine a possible interpretation and provide an argument that supports it. The questions in Box 81 can help you write an effective interpretation paper.

BOX 81

 ### Questions for an interpretation paper

1. What is the central theme of the work?
2. How do particular parts of the work relate to the theme?
3. What meaning does the author create through the elements listed in Box 82?
4. Why does the work end as it does?

Writing a formal analysis

A formal analysis explains how elements of a literary work function to create meaning or effect. Your instructor may ask you to concentrate on one of these elements (for example, "How does the point of view in the story affect its meaning?") or to discuss how a writer develops a theme through several elements (for example, "How do setting, imagery, and symbolism reveal the author's viewpoint?").

To prepare to write your formal analysis, read the work thoroughly, looking for patterns and repetitions. Take notes as you go along, because the act of writing helps you form insights about the patterns and repetitions you discover. For example, to analyze a character, you want to pay attention to everything that character says or does, everything other characters say about him or her, and any descriptions of the character.

BOX 82

Major elements to analyze in literary works

PLOT	Events and their sequence
THEME	Central idea or message
STRUCTURE	Organization and relationship of parts to each other and to the whole
CHARACTERIZATION	Traits, thoughts, and actions of the people in the work
SETTING	Time and place of the action
POINT OF VIEW	Perspective or position from which a narrator or a main character presents the material
STYLE	How words and sentence structure present the material
IMAGERY	Mental pictures created by the work (19e)
TONE	Author's attitude toward the subject of the work—and sometimes toward the reader—as expressed through choice of words, imagery, and point of view
FIGURES OF SPEECH	Unusual use or combination of words, such as a METAPHOR or SIMILE, for enhanced vividness or effect
SYMBOLISM	Meaning beneath the surface of the words or images
RHYTHM	Beat, meter
RHYME	Repetition of similar sounds for their auditory effect

Box 82 describes some of the major literary elements that you might expect to use in formal analyses.

Writing a cultural analysis

A **cultural analysis** relates a literary work to broader historical, social, cultural, or political situations. Instructors might ask you to explain how events or prevailing attitudes influenced the writing of a work or the way readers understand it. For example, they might ask, "How did Maxine Hong Kingston's experience as a Chinese American affect the way she tells her story in *The Woman Warrior?*" or "How do differences between the institution of marriage in the early nineteenth century and today affect readers' interpretations of *Pride and Prejudice?*" Box 83 lists some common topics appropriate for a cultural analysis.

BOX 83

Major topics for cultural analyses

GENDER	How does a work portray women or men—and define, or challenge, their roles in society?
CLASS	How does a work portray relationships among the upper, middle, and lower classes? How do characters' actions or perspectives result from their wealth and power—or from their poverty and powerlessness?
RACE AND ETHNICITY	How does a work portray the influences of race and ethnicity on the characters' actions, status, and values?
HISTORY	How does a work reflect—or challenge—past events and values in a society?
AUTOBIOGRAPHY	How did the writer's life experiences influence his or her work?
GENRE	How is the work similar to or different from other works of its type (for example, plays, sonnets, mysteries, comic novels, memoirs, and so on)?

62e What special rules apply to writing about literature?

Using correct verb tenses

Always use the PRESENT TENSE when you describe or discuss a literary work or any of its elements.

- Walter [a character] **makes** a difficult decision when he **turns down** Linder's offer to buy the house.

In addition, always use the present tense for discussing what an author has done in a specific work.

- Lorraine Hansberry, author of *A Raisin in the Sun,* **explores** not only powerful racial issues but also common family dynamics.

Always use a PAST-TENSE VERB to discuss historical events or biographical information.

- *A Raisin in the Sun* **was** the first play by an African-American woman produced on Broadway.

Using your own ideas and using secondary sources

Some assignments call only for your own ideas about the literary work. Other assignments call for you to use SECONDARY SOURCES. Secondary sources include books and articles in which experts discuss some aspect of the literary text or other material related to your topic. You might use secondary sources to support your own ideas, perhaps by citing a literary scholar who agrees with you. Alternatively, when you have a new or different interpretation, you might summarize, analyze, or critique what others have written in order to provide a framework for your own analysis. No matter what your assignment, never PLAGIARIZE (62f) by pretending that the ideas of others are your own. Always DOCUMENT your secondary sources. In addition, use appropriate verbs effectively so that your writing smoothly integrates your QUOTATIONS, PARAPHRASES, and SUMMARIES into your paper. (For a list of useful verbs, see Box 38.)

You can locate secondary sources by using the research process explained in Chapter 22. A particularly important resource for writing about literature is the *MLA International Bibliography,* which many researchers consider the most comprehensive index to literary scholarship. It is available in nearly every college library, both in print and online through the library's computer system or Web site. (Because the online version is too expensive for individuals to purchase, libraries pay for it and provide it free to people who want to use it.)

62f How do I avoid plagiarism in writing about literature?

To avoid **plagiarism,** always DOCUMENT your sources, whether PRIMARY or SECONDARY. By documenting, you reveal to your readers exactly where to find the specific passages in the literary work from which you are quoting. Readers often want to read the source material directly, to confirm that what you have written correctly reflects the original meaning of the material. Perhaps more important, by documenting your sources, you're behaving as a person who never intentionally or unintentionally steals from others.

The DOCUMENTATION STYLE of the Modern Language Association (MLA) (Chs. 28–29) is the standard reference that most instructors require students to use for writing about literature. Some instructors, however, prefer a different documentation style (see Chs. 31–36), so always ask which to use.

Identify passages from short poems by line numbers (for example, "Theme for English B," lines 4–5). Refer to passages from plays by act and scene (for example, *Othello* 3.4). For other types of literature, use page numbers.

62g The final draft of student's essay about literature

Working on the assignment

Michael Choi, a student in first-year English, fulfilled an assignment to write an interpretation of the images and metaphors in Yusef Komunyakaa's poem "Blackberries." When Michael first read "Blackberries," several of the images puzzled him. He wondered how they connect to an apparently simple scene of a boy picking, eating, and selling blackberries. In the process of writing his essay, Michael came to understand how those previously puzzling images and metaphors help to shape the poem's deeper meaning. His final draft is reproduced here.

Learning about the poet, Yusef Komunyakaa

Yusef Komunyakaa is an African-American poet who was born in 1947 and raised in Louisiana. His father was a carpenter. Komunyakaa was educated at the University of Colorado, at Colorado State University, and at the University of California–Irvine. He served a tour of duty in Vietnam and was awarded the Bronze Star. In 1994, he won the Pulitzer Prize for poetry—one of the most prestigious honors a poet can receive in the United States—for his book *Neon Vernacular*. Komunyakaa currently teaches at Princeton University. Here is his poem "Blackberries."

BLACKBERRIES
Yusef Komunyakaa

They left my hands like a printer's
Or thief's before a police blotter
& pulled me into early morning's
Terrestrial sweetness, so thick
The damp ground was consecrated   5
Where they fell among a garland of thorns.

Although I could smell old lime-covered
History, at ten I'd still hold out my hands
& berries fell into them. Eating from one
& filling a half gallon with the other,   10
I ate the mythology & dreamt
Of pies & cobbler, almost

Needful as forgiveness. My bird dog Spot
Eyed blue jays & thrashers. The mud frogs
In rich blackness, hid from daylight.   15
An hour later, beside City Limits Road
I balanced a gleaming can in each hand,
Limboed between worlds, repeating *one dollar.*

The big blue car made me sweat.
Wintertime crawled out of the windows.   20
When I leaned closer I saw the boy
& girl my age, in the wide back seat
Smirking, & it was then I remembered my fingers
Burning with thorns among berries too ripe to touch.

Student's essay about literature

Michael Choi

Professor May

English 100

8 November 2003

Images, Metaphors, and Meaning in "Blackberries"

In Yusef Komunyakaa's poem "Blackberries," the poet
describes himself as "limboed between worlds" (line 18). At
that moment, he is a boy standing beside City Limits Road—a
symbolic line between the city and the country—selling berries
that he has just picked. Yet, the boy is also caught between his
familiar natural world and a world of wealth and privilege.
One of the poem's key issues is whether the boy is responsible
for his situation. Komunyakaa uses a rich set of images and
metaphors to suggest the boy's complicated position.

Some plain and direct images connect the boy to the
world of nature. As he picks blackberries, the poet describes

continued ⟶

(Proportions shown in this paper are adjusted to fit space limitations of this book.
Follow actual dimensions shown in this book and your instructor's directions)

the "bird dog Spot" watching blue jays and thrashers (lines 13-14), and he mentions "mud frogs" hiding in the dark (lines 14-15). Readers form an impression of a rustic boy trying to earn some money from a countryside that is familiar and comfortable to him. He eats as he fills "gleaming" half-gallon cans (line 17) and dreams of "pies & cobbler" (line 12). The day is "thick" with "terrestrial sweetness," (line 4) and the atmosphere is peaceful, almost sleepy.

When the boy moves beyond the country to the City Limits Road to sell his harvest, however, his pleasant morning is shattered. After a customer drives up, the boy says, "The big blue car made me sweat" (line 19). Partly, he sweats because the car's air-conditioning makes him aware of heat that had not bothered him until that very moment. Komunyakaa uses the strong image that "Wintertime crawled out of the windows" to heighten the contrast between the artificial environment of the car and the natural environment of the boy (line 20). More importantly, the boy sweats because he is suddenly self-conscious. He feels uncomfortable at the gap between himself and "the boy / & girl my age, in the wide back seat" (lines 21-22). The emphasis on the air-conditioning and the width of the seat make clear that these children come not only from the city but also from wealthier circumstances. When they smirk at him, he remembers his berry-stained fingers. Those stained hands are a metaphor for how different he is from the children in the car, both socially and economically. He feels ashamed.

Yet, should he feel this way? Several complicated images and metaphors in the poem make this question difficult

continued ⟶

to answer. For example, at the beginning, the poet says that the berries "left my hands like a printer's" (line 1). This image not only calls attention to the inky stains on his hands but also likens berry picking to printing. Both are forms of honest manual labor. Furthermore, picking ripe berries is similar to the messy job of shedding ink-saturated type from a printing press—the typesetting method used before computers. This printing metaphor suggests a subtle connection between the boy's work and the poet's. Komunyakaa immediately complicates the first image with a second that compares the boy's hands to a "thief's before a police blotter" (line 2). The common element between the two metaphors is the ink, which in the second is used for fingerprinting.

Note that the person whose fingerprints are being taken by the police is not simply a 'suspect' but rather a thief (line 2). The person is already guilty of a crime. Has the boy been stealing berries that do not belong to him, and does he feel guilty when he is caught? This possible interpretation does not completely fit the encounter with the big blue car. The "smirking" response of the children in the car seems snobbish (line 23). Rather than accusing him of being a thief, the children make fun of his getting dirty while picking berries, which they can buy in cool comfort. For his efforts, which even involved his "fingers / Burning with thorns" (lines 23-24), the boy receives ridicule. The reader's sympathies lie with the boy selling the berries. Even if he did steal the berries, his crime does not seem that great.

Another set of metaphors, more mythic in nature, suggests an answer to the question of whether the boy should

continued ⟶

feel guilty. The boy reports that he "could smell old lime-covered / History" as he picks and eats (lines 7-8). While lime could refer simply to a bright shade of green or, more strangely, to the citrus fruit, another meaning seems to apply here. The chemical substance lime has two uses. Farmers use it to reduce acidity in soil, where it serves as a kind of fertilizer. Alternatively, quicklime spread over the bodies of dead animals speeds their decomposing. To cover history in lime, therefore, means either to cultivate it or to bury it. Later, the boy states that he "ate the mythology & dreamt / of pies & cobbler" (lines 11-12). Obviously, no one can literally eat mythology. This metaphor suggests that the boy is consuming the berries with little thought of any deeper significance his actions might have. There is a mythic dimension to picking blackberries, but the boy focuses on pleasant physical sensations and, eventually, the chance to make some money. Similarly, history is something to consume or ignore. If the boy is a criminal at all, maybe he is unaware that he is doing anything wrong. Furthermore, perhaps no one owns the berries and he is merely "stealing" from nature.

  The poem's most profound images and metaphors have religious overtones. The poet describes the ground beneath the berry bushes as "consecrated" (line 5). This powerful word choice characterizes the ground as somehow holy. The berries do not fall simply among thorns but among "a garland of thorns" (line 6). The image of a garland suggests the crown of thorns placed upon the head of Jesus after his trial, and these images draw out the deepest meaning of the poet's being "limboed between worlds" (line 18). In some religious traditions, limbo is a place where souls temporarily go before entering

continued ⟶

heaven or where innocent but unbaptized babies permanently dwell. In addition to standing between the world of wealth and status that is represented by the car and the simpler world of bird dogs and mud frogs, the boy stands outside paradise. He has left and knows that he cannot go back.

Although mythic and religious elements are present in "Blackberries," Komunyakaa's poem ultimately supports interpretations on several levels. The poet uses religious images to give depth to the boy's situation. When the boy picks the berries, he is in a peaceful, natural environment that is almost sacred, even if he does not realize it. When he sells the berries, he encounters a foreign world of wealth and privilege. Because of his background, he cannot easily join that world. Yet, he cannot easily go back to his familiar ways because he now sees his actions differently. He perceives there may be something wrong with picking blackberries. Whether or not he <u>should</u> feel guilty, he <u>does</u> feel guilty. The poet is truly limboed between worlds.

Work Cited

Komunyakaa, Yusef. "Blackberries." <u>Pleasure Dome: New and Collected Poems</u>. Middletown: Wesleyan UP, 2001. 280-81.

63 BUSINESS WRITING

Format and content are important in all forms of business writing. Today, **e-mail** is the most common form of business communication.

63a How do I format and write business e-mail?

The physical format of e-mail, which resembles some memo formats, varies slightly depending on the program you use. Whenever you start a new job, take time to learn the company's e-mail system, including special features such as address books and electronic "filing cabinets."

Formatting business e-mail

Single-space the text of your e-mail; double-space between paragraphs and before your complimentary closing. Always fill in the exact topic of your message on the "Subject" or "Re" line of the e-mail form. Because the subject line tells your recipients and you how to sort, file, and prioritize e-mails, being specific about your topic shows that you're a professional who respects the importance of time management. In fact, if you need to write to the same person about more than one topic at the same time, send a separate e-mail on each topic so that the subject line for each one can be specific.

Use the "Cc" or "Copies" space for the e-mail addresses of recipients who need to see the message, even if you don't expect them to respond. Send copies only to those who really need the information. If you overload people with e-mails they don't need to see, you'll waste their time. Soon people will stop paying attention to all your e-mails, no matter what the topic.

Use the "Bcc" space sparingly to send a copy to someone else without your recipient knowing it (for example, you might need to send your manager a blind copy of your message to a customer). Remember that the "Bcc" feature can reflect negatively on the sender if it's used for the sake of gossip, personal opinion, put-downs, jokes, or chain letters. If you overuse this feature, people might begin to distrust the way you are handling your e-mails to them. Never forget that recipients of a blind copy can easily forward it to others, publicly revealing what you have written. And even if a recipient deletes blind copies you send, technical experts can retrieve them years later.

Spaces for To, Copies, and Subject

Click to send

Mail-handling choices

Format choices

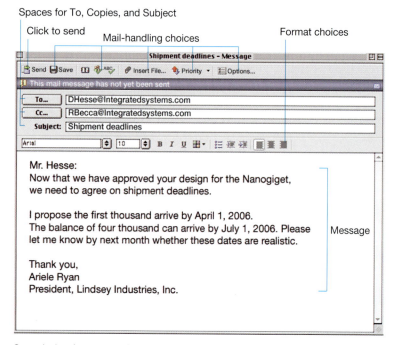

Sample business e-mail

Source: Microsoft® Internet Explorer reprinted by permission from Microsoft® Corporation.

Writing business e-mail

Business e-mail has PURPOSES and AUDIENCES quite different from those of the informal e-mail messages you exchange with friends and family. The purpose of business e-mail is to communicate about planning, procedures, processes, purchases, and other issues that pertain to a company's business. The audience for business e-mail is other business-people who require information, want to exchange and discuss ideas, or need to take or request action. Because businesspeople are busy people, your writing needs to be brief, well organized, and to the point. Box 84 suggests some guidelines for writing business e-mail.

Because any e-mail you write as a business employee represents your company and yourself, you want to appear professional, focused, and well informed. Remember, too, that when a business matter takes on legal importance, even your most casually written messages can become official evidence in a court case. Choose your words carefully.

Netiquette, a word coined from *etiquette,* demands that you address business recipients by their full names, including any title such as *Ms., Mr.,* or *Dr.* Give the same information about yourself in the closing of

BOX 84

⊙ Guidelines for writing business e-mail

- Start your e-mail with a sentence that tells what your memo is about.
- If you want your recipients to take action as a result of your e-mail, alert them in your opening paragraph—though you can save the specific action(s) for the end of your message.
- Put the essence of your message in the second paragraph. Supply background information only if your recipients aren't already aware of it or might have forgotten it.
- Conclude your e-mail in the third paragraph, by asking for a specific action if one is needed or by restating your reason for writing (for example, keeping someone apprised of a situation or reporting on a meeting).
- If your e-mail runs longer than three to four paragraphs, add topic headings to help your readers speed through the material.

your e-mail. Especially when you start communicating with business-people you've never met or corresponded with before, use titles and last names. After you get to know your co-workers and customers well, you might decide to loosen your LEVEL OF FORMALITY. A good time to do so is after those you are writing to begin to end their messages with their first names. Wait for a few exchanges before using the first name of someone with a position considerably above yours, however.

A medium to formal level of word choice is best for your business e-mail. This level of formality calls for no slang, abbreviations, or informal words or expressions. Use standard grammar, spelling, and punctuation. Never write in all-capital letters, which are difficult to read and are considered the equivalent of shouting, or in all-lowercase letters, which suggest laziness and show a lack of respect for your recipient. At the end of your message, before your full name and position, use a commonly accepted complimentary closing, such as *Sincerely* or *Cordially*.

Business e-mail travels quickly, so writers usually expect a reply within one or two days. When you can't respond quickly, always acknowledge that you've received a message. Say when you'll reply, and don't forget to follow up. Unless an e-mail explicitly grants permission to forward it, never do so without first getting the writer's approval.

Finally, know your company's **e-mail policy** covering issues such as use of business e-mail accounts for personal purposes, the length and tone of most e-mail, whether for internal or external use; your legal responsibilities concerning your e-mail; and restrictions on visiting Web sites unrelated to work. Increasingly, businesses monitor their employees' e-mail. Never forget that your superiors—or perhaps an entity called the Office of Technology and Compliance—might be reading all the e-mail you send and receive at work.

63b How do I format and write business letters?

Use the following guidelines for the format and content of your business letters.

- **Paper:** Use $8\frac{1}{2} \times 11$ inch paper for business writing. (Business correspondence from outside the United States may have different page measurements.) The most suitable colors for letters are white, slightly off-white, and light beige. Fold your business letters horizontally into thirds to fit into a standard business envelope. Never fold a page in half and then into thirds.

- **Letterhead:** Use the official letterhead stationery (name, address, and logo, if any) of the business where you are employed. If no letterhead exists, create your own. To do this, center your full name, address, and phone number at the top of the page; use a larger font than for the content of your letter. Avoid fancy, loud fonts.

- **Format:** Use single spacing within paragraphs and double spacing between paragraphs. The two most frequently used formats for business writing are block style and modified block style. **Block style** has single-spaced paragraphs with a double space between paragraphs and no indentations (see the letter on p. 447). **Modified block style** is the same as block style except that the first line of each paragraph is indented, the letterhead sits at the left margin rather than in the middle, and the complimentary closing and signature begin halfway across the page (see the letter on p. 453).

- **Recipient's name:** Use the full name of your recipient whenever possible. If you can't locate a name, either through a phone call to a central switchboard or on the Internet, use a specific category— for example, "Dear Billing Department"—and place the key word first ("Billing Department," not "Department of Billing"). The old-fashioned "To Whom It May Concern" rarely reaches the right person in an organization.

- **Content:** Write CONCISELY, clearly, and to the point; never repeat yourself. Announce the purpose of your letter in the opening. Make sure your information is accurate and complete and that your letter includes all relevant facts and dates.

Jan Dubitz
742 Lincoln Hall Northeast College
2038 Washington Blvd.
Chicago, IL 60132
(210)555-3723

September 14, 2003

▲
4 spaces
▼

Ms. Yolanda Harper
Abco Rental Company
1249 Logan Rd.
Chicago, IL 60312

Dear Ms. Harper:

SALUTATION: Use an appropriate title (Mr., Ms., Dr., Professor) and the person's name. If you do not know the name, use a title (Dean of Students, Personnel Director). Add a colon at the end of the salutation.

▲
2 spaces
▼

I rented a refrigerator from your company on August 27. After only two weeks, the freezer compartment no longer keeps food frozen. Per the rental agreement, this is my written request for a replacement refrigerator. The agreement states that you will replace the refrigerator within five business days from the receipt of my letter.

I will call you next week to arrange the exchange. Thank you for your prompt attention.

Sincerely,

CLOSING: Capitalize only the first word (Yours truly, Sincerely yours) and follow with a comma.

4 spaces *Jan Dubitz*

Jan Dubitz

SIGNATURE: If you have a title, type it underneath your name. Sign letter in space above your name.

Enc: Copy of rental agreement

OTHER: Use *Enc:* or *Enclosure:* if you include material *with* your letter. Use *cc:* to indicate that you have sent any courtesy copies.

Sample business letter in block style

- **Tone:** Remember that your writing reflects on your company and you. Choose words that achieve a medium to formal LEVEL OF FORMALITY. Try to take an evenhanded approach: Express disappointment or make a complaint without resorting to BIASED LANGUAGE. A reasonable, mature tone gets better results than an angry accusation.

- **Envelope:** Use the official envelope of the company where you work. If none exists or if you write business correspondence on your own behalf, use the standard number 10 envelope ($9\frac{1}{2} \times 4$ inches), which fits a properly folded business letter

```
Jan Dubitz                    ENVELOPE: Fold letter in thirds horizontally
742 Lincoln Hall              and insert in an appropriate-size envelope.
Northeast College             Place your return address in the upper left
2038 Washington Blvd.         corner and the mailing address in the middle
Chicago, IL 60132             of the envelope.



              Ms. Yolanda Harper
              Abco Rental Company
              1249 Logan Rd.
              Chicago, IL   60312
```

Sample envelope when no letterhead exists

63c How do I format and write memos?

Memos are communications that are usually exchanged within an organization or business. For communications with people outside your company, a business letter (63b) is more appropriate. In the past, businesspeople wrote their memos on paper so that they would have a "paper trail." Today, however, e-mail is taking the place of memos. The guidelines for writing e-mail (63a) also pertain to memos, which share the same PURPOSES and AUDIENCES and require the same conciseness and care in word choice. The form of communication you choose—paper memos or e-mail—depends on your assessment of the situation in which you are writing.

Most word processing software provides **templates,** or preprogrammed formats, for memos. The standard format of a memo includes two major parts: the headings and the content (see the sample memo below). The headings should appear as follows:

To: [Name your audience—a specific person or group.]

From: [Give your name and your title, if any.]

Date: [Give the date on which you write the memo.]

Re: [State your subject.]

Your recipient(s) need to determine the importance of your memo quickly by scanning these headings, so be as specific as possible in the "Subject" or "Re" line. The content can run for as many paragraphs as you need, as along as you don't ramble. However, if you write more than three or four paragraphs, add headings that name your subtopics.

TO: English Teaching Assistants

FROM: Professor Thomas Nevers, Director,
           First-Year Composition

DATE: December 1, 2003

SUBJECT: New Computer Programs

Several new writing programs will be installed in the English computer labs. Training sessions are scheduled during the week before classes begin next semester.

    Tuesday, January 6   9:00–11:00 a.m.

    Wednesday, January 7   1:00–3:00 p.m.

    Thursday, January 8   8:30–10:30 a.m.

    Friday, January 9   1:30–3:30 p.m.

Please stop by my office by December 12 to sign up for one of the two-hour workshops.

Sample memo

If you need more than one or two pages, change your format to that of a brief report rather than a memo. A report consists of the same content, but it always includes headings for major sections (introduction, central topic, conclusion) as well as for subtopics within sections. Follow these guidelines.

- **Introduction:** State your purpose for writing and explain why your memo is worth your readers' attention. In addition, mention whether the recipient needs to take action because of your memo. You can save the specifics of the action until the conclusion of your memo, if you wish.

- **Central topic:** Write the essential information on your topic, including facts the recipient needs to know and a deadline for any action that is required. If you write more than three or four paragraphs, use headings to break down the information into subtopics.

- **Conclusion:** End with a one- to two-sentence summary or a specific recommendation. If your memo is short, end with instructions or a "thank you" line.

63d How do I format and write a resume?

A **resume** details your accomplishments and employment history. The AUDIENCE for your resume is a potential employer. Most employers scan the resumes of several applicants at a time to compare their qualifications. The impression your resume makes on your audience determines whether you are seriously considered for employment.

To make a favorable impression, you want your resume to be easy to read. Label its sections clearly, and target it to the position you want. Don't forget to proofread carefully; even one spelling error can eliminate you from consideration. A helpful Web site for writing resumes is <http://www.umn.edu/ohr/ecep/resume/>. Here are some additional guidelines for writing a resume.

- Include all appropriate information.
- Put your most recent job and/or degree first.
- Adjust the emphasis of your resume to fit your PURPOSE. For example, if you are applying for a job as a computer programmer, you want to emphasize different facts than you would if you were applying for a retail sales job.
- Try to fit all the information on one page. If you need a second page, make sure the most important information is on the first page.
- Use headings to separate blocks of information (see the sample resume on p. 451). Include the following, as appropriate: name,

Margaret Lorentino
1338 Sunflower Lane
Rochelle, IL 61068
(815) 555-3756

OBJECTIVE: Seeking a full/part-time position as a medical transcriptionist to utilize my medical, computer, and office skills

EDUCATION: Certificate of Completion, Medical Transcription
Kishwaukee College, Malta, IL, December 2000
Bachelor of Science, Marketing
Northern Illinois University, DeKalb, IL, May 2000
Associate in Arts; Studied Nursing and Business
Harper Junior College, Palatine, IL, December 1987

EMPLOYMENT: Kishwaukee College, Malta, IL, January 2000—Present
Lab Assistant and Computer Skills Teacher
RTD Real Estate, Muncie, IN, August 1994—August 1995
Receptionist, Accounting Assistant
Northwestern Mutual Life, Schaumburg, IL,
May 1991—July 1992, Sales Assistant
Reliable Personnel, Park Ridge, IL, May 1990—May 1991
Temporary Employment Manager

SKILLS: Computer
• Experienced with Microsoft Office 2000 and WordPerfect
• Type 60 wpm
• Have experience with Lotus, Excel, and Access
• Teach WordPerfect and basic computer skills in first-year college English classes

Organizational
• Girl Scout leader, soccer coach, Sunday school teacher
• Trained employees in data entry and accounting principles
• Managed a temporary work force of 20-30 employees

REFERENCES: Available on request

Sample resume

address, e-mail address, and telephone number; position desired or career objective; education; experience; licenses and certifications; other experience that might relate to the job you're applying for; honors or awards; publications or presentations; activities and interests; special abilities, skills, and knowledge; and references.

- Write telegraphically. Start with verb phrases, not with the word *I,* and omit *a, an,* and *the.* For example, write "Created new computer program to organize company's spreadsheets" instead of "*I* created *a* new computer program to organize *the* company's spreadsheets."
- Never pad your resume with irrelevant information.
- Never lie on your resume. Even if you get the job, when the lies catch up with you, you'll likely be fired.
- Include references, or state that you can provide them on request (be sure to have them at hand so you can respond speedily to such a request).
- Use high-quality paper that is white, off-white, or light beige.

ALERT: Note to multilingual writers: In applying for a job in the United States, never include personal information, even if employers in your home country might expect it. For example, never give your age, marital status, religion, or political party.

63e How do I format and write a job application letter?

A job application letter needs to accompany your resume. Avoid simply repeating what is already on the resume. Instead, make a connection between the company's expectations and your experience by emphasizing how your background has prepared you for the position. Your job application letter, more than your resume, reflects your personality. See the sample letter on page 453 by Margaret Lorentino. Here are some guidelines for writing a job application letter.

- Use one page only.
- Think of your letter as a polite sales pitch. Don't be shy, but don't exaggerate what you can do for the company if you get the job.
- Use the same name, content, and format guidelines as for a business letter (63b).
- Address the letter to a specific person. If you can't discover a name, use a title such as *Personnel Director.*
- Open your letter by identifying the position you are applying for.

(*continued on p. 454*)

1338 Sunflower Lane
Rochelle, IL 61068
December 1, 2003

Ms. Arlene Chang
Employment Coordinator
Rockford Medical Center
820 N. Main St.
Rockford, IL 61103

Dear Ms. Chang:

   I had a chance to talk with you last spring about your company at the Kishwaukee College Job Fair. I am very interested in the medical transcription position that I noticed in the Rockford Register Star on November 29.

   I will be completing my Medical Transcription Certificate at the end of December. I have taken courses in medical transcription, medical office procedures, keyboarding, as well as numerous computer courses. I have a bachelor's degree in marketing from Northern Illinois University and also studied nursing for almost a year at Harper Junior College. I believe that this background would help me in this position.

   The enclosed resume will give you the details of my experience and qualifications. I think that my experience and education make a great combination for this position. I am available for an interview at your convenience. My home phone number is (815) 555-3756.

                                        Sincerely yours,

                                        Margaret Lorentino

                                        Margaret Lorentino

Sample job application letter in modified block style

- Mention your qualifications for the position, and explain how your background will meet the requirements for the job.
- Let the reader know that you are familiar with the company or organization.
- End by being specific about what you can do for the company. If the job would be your first, give your key attributes—but make sure they are relevant and true. For instance, you might state that you are punctual, self-disciplined, a team player, and eager to learn and work hard for the company.
- State when you are available for an interview and how the potential employer can reach you.
- Edit and proofread the letter carefully.

64 ORAL PRESENTATIONS

Preparing an **oral presentation** and writing an essay involve many of the same processes. In each, you determine your PURPOSE, analyze your AUDIENCE, and work to develop a well-supported THESIS STATEMENT. Chapters 5–10 discuss the writing process in general. This chapter explains the special demands of adapting the writing process to developing and delivering an oral presentation.

These are the overriding principles in an oral presentation: (1) Keep the volume of your voice high without shouting; (2) Never rush as you speak; (3) Speak slowly enough that your listeners have an extra second or two to absorb each point (listening takes more time than reading); and (4) Pronounce all your words fully and clearly so that your delivery enhances your message.

Preparing an Oral Presentation

64a How do I determine my purpose and topic?

Once your instructor assigns a TOPIC or you have chosen one (Ch. 5), you need to decide whether your purpose is INFORMATIVE or PERSUASIVE. To help you focus your speech, type or write in large letters a statement of your chosen purpose. (If you want, tack the statement over your desk to help you remember your purpose while you work.) Always use one of these two lead-ins, making sure that it contains an INFINITIVE PHRASE.

- I am going **to inform** my audience that. . . .
- I am going **to persuade** my audience that. . . .

Other informative infinitives include *to explain why, to clarify, to show how, to report, to define, to describe,* and *to classify.* Other persuasive infinitives include *to convince, to argue, to agree with, to disagree with, to win over,* and *to influence.* You might need to revise or add words to write a logical sentence using these alternatives.

64b How do I adapt my message to my audience?

Adapting your presentation to your audience doesn't mean that you need to say only what your listeners might want to hear. Rather, you need to grab and hold their interest. Consider your listeners' prior knowledge of your topic, their desire to learn more, and whether or not they agree with your point of view. You'll find that your audience falls into one of three categories: *uninformed, informed,* or *mixed.* Box 85 suggests how to adapt your message to each type of audience.

BOX 85

Adapting an oral presentation to your audience

UNINFORMED AUDIENCE — Start with the basics, and then move to a few new ideas. Define new terms and concepts, and avoid unnecessary technical terms. Use visual aids and give examples. Repeat key ideas—but not too often.

INFORMED AUDIENCE — Never give more than a quick overview of the basics. Devote most of your time to new ideas and concepts.

MIXED AUDIENCE — In your introduction, acknowledge the more informed audience members who are present. Explain that you're going to review the basic concepts briefly so that everyone can build from the same knowledge base. Move as soon as possible toward more complex concepts.

64c How do I organize my presentation?

An oral presentation has three parts: INTRODUCTION, BODY, and CONCLUSION. Within the body you present your major points, with two to three supports for each point. You can use the RENNS formula (8d) to help you think of specific supporting details. As you outline and then expand on

BOX 86

⦿ Organizational outline for an oral presentation

Title: _____

Topic: _____

Specific purpose: _____

Thesis statement: _____

_____

   I. Introduction (followed by a clear transition to point 1 in the body)
  II. Body
     A. Major point and specific supporting examples (followed by a clear transition from point 1 to point 2, perhaps with a brief reference to the introduction*)
     B. Major point and specific supporting examples (followed by a clear transition from point 2 to point 3, perhaps with a brief reference to point 1 and the introduction)
     C. Major point and specific supporting examples (followed by a clear transition from point 2 to point 3, perhaps with a brief reference to points 1 and 2 and the introduction)
 III. Conclusion

* Refer back to your introduction sparingly or your audience will lose interest.

what you plan to say, use complete sentences rather than phrases. Doing so gets you closer to your final form, and just as important, forces you to sharpen your thinking.

Box 86 presents a typical organizational outline for a speech, including points where you might need a clear transition. Use only a few of these suggestions for transitions—not all of them—or your speech will become repetitive.

Introducing yourself and your topic

All audience members want to know three things about a speaker: Who are you? What are you going to talk about? Why should I listen? To respond effectively to these unasked questions, try these suggestions.

- Grab your audience's attention with an interesting question, quotation, or statistic; an anecdote; a compliment; or a bit of background information. Even if someone has introduced you, briefly—and always humbly—mention your qualifications as a speaker about your topic.

- Give your audience a road map of your talk: Tell where you're starting, where you're going, and how you intend to get there. Your listeners need to know you won't waste their time. (As you revise your drafts, make sure that you deliver what you have promised.)

Following your road map

Listening to a speech is very different from reading an essay. Audiences for oral presentations generally need special help from the speaker in staying on track and following the speaker's line of reasoning. Here are some strategies to keep your listeners' minds from wandering and to make sure they understand where you—and they—are going.

- Signal clearly where you are on your road map by using words such as *first, second,* and *third.* Show that you're discussing CAUSE AND EFFECT by using words such as *subsequently, therefore,* and *furthermore.* Signal that you're telling a story or explaining a process by using a locator word such as *before, then,* or *next.*

- Define unfamiliar terms and concepts, and follow up with strong examples, so that your audience can understand the new ideas you present.

- Comment on your own material. Tell the audience what you consider significant, memorable, or especially relevant, and why. Do so sparingly; if you overuse this strategy, you'll lose credibility and people will stop listening.

- Provide occasional summaries at a point of transition. Recap what you've covered and say how it relates to what's coming next.

Wrapping up your presentation

You don't need to bring every point you've made to a neat closure in your conclusion. Still, you need to demonstrate that you haven't let key points simply float away. Try these suggestions.

- Never let your voice volume fall or your clarity of pronunciation falter because the end is in sight.

- Signal the end with verbal cues ("In conclusion," "Finally") and body language (facial expressions, gestures). Use these cues only when you are truly at the end of your speech.

- Restate your main message; do not introduce new ideas at the last minute.

- Make a dramatic, decisive statement; cite a memorable quotation; or issue a challenge.

64d What language and tone are appropriate for oral presentations?

An oral presentation calls for the same awareness of your language as your writing does. Review especially Chapters 18–20. For help with TONE, see 5d. Here are some tips on using language in oral presentations.

- Recognize the power of words. For example, read this statement by Winston Churchill, made after World War II: "Never in the field of human conflict was so much owed by so many to so few." Now try substituting the word *history* for "the field of human conflict." Note that while the single word *history* is more direct, using it destroys the powerful impact of the original words.
- Do not alienate your audience; avoid words, phrases, or examples that could offend your listeners or people connected with them.
- Use GENDER-NEUTRAL LANGUAGE; avoid sexist pronouns and nouns and other inappropriate words and expressions (20b).
- Use the ACTIVE VOICE (40g) to help listeners to grasp your point. Consider which of these two sentences is easier to follow:
  - Gun control is an issue that must be considered by all citizens. [passive]
  - All citizens must consider the issue of gun control. [active]
- Present yourself with dignity, not only in your choice of words but also in your body language, tone of voice, and dress.

Delivering an Oral Presentation

64e How do I choose a presentation style?

Presentation style is the way you deliver your speech. You may memorize it, read it, map it, or speak without notes. As a student, you want to avoid the last style until you have considerable experience giving speeches.

Memorizing your speech

Memorized speeches often sound unnatural. Unless you've mastered memorized material well enough to recite it in a relaxed way, choose another presentation style. After all, no safety net exists if you forget a word or sentence. Fortunately, instructors rarely require you to memorize long speeches.

Reading your speech

Reading a speech aloud often bores your audience. Burying your nose in sheets of paper creates an uncomfortable barrier between you and your audience, and most listeners lose interest. In addition, you may appear unfamiliar with your topic, unprepared, or insincere.

If you have no choice but to read your speech, avoid speaking in a monotone voice. Without variations in voice tone, few people can manage to listen to a speech for long. In addition, try these tips.

- Memorize your words as much as possible so that you can make frequent eye contact with your audience.
- Instead of holding the sheets of paper, place them on a podium—or even on an inverted wastepaper basket on top of a table, if no podium is available.
- Keep your hands out of your pockets. Use them to gesture instead.
- Turn your body—not just your head—to look at all members of your audience.

Mapping your speech

After you've written out your speech—or thought through every word of it—outline it. On a single page or on numbered index cards, write the key words of each part of your speech. Use one color of ink for each major point and a different color for examples and illustrations. Use a highlighter for material that you want to emphasize. Practice your presentation repeatedly so that you're thoroughly familiar with the major points and examples each key word signals you to recall. Box 87 contains additional suggestions for preparing your note cards. Always in-

---

BOX 87

 Preparing oral presentation aids

- Type your material in a large font for easier reading.
- Highlight the most important point(s) you want to make.
- Use only one side of a page or card to avoid confusion.
- Number your pages or cards in large type in case you drop them.
- Clearly separate—with different ink colors or colored index cards—your introduction, body, and conclusion.
- Mark cues for pauses, use of visuals, or emphasis.

clude information on your sources so that you can briefly mention them (and offer to give more details after your speech).

Speaking without notes

When you speak without notes, you need not only to master your content but to pace yourself. Unless you are highly experienced, you will tend to ramble, stray off the topic, or lose track of time when speaking without notes. No audience respects such a speaker.

64f How do I vary my voice and use nonverbal communication?

Your voice is the focus of any oral presentation. If you're unsure of your volume in a particular setting, speak briefly and then ask your listeners whether they can hear you. When you use a microphone, speak into it without raising your voice. If the sound system "screeches" with feedback, stay away from speaker units set up on the stage or around the room.

Speak naturally but clearly. Articulate your words, and speak slowly and deliberately—but not so slowly that your words have no rhythm or pace. Vary your tone of voice for emphasis and clarity. Pause every now and then to let your points sink in.

Eye contact is your most important nonverbal tool; it communicates confidence and shows respect for your listeners. Smile or nod at your audience and make eye contact with them as you begin. To do this smoothly, you need to memorize your first few sentences.

Your body language can either add to or detract from your message. If you use a podium, stand squarely behind it before you begin speaking. Use appropriate facial expressions to mirror the emotions in your message. Gestures, if not overdone, contribute to your message by adding emphasis; they are best when they appear to be natural rather than forced or timed. When gestures aren't needed, rest your hands on the podium—don't scratch your head, dust your clothing, or fidget. You may step slightly forward or backward from a microphone to indicate transitions in your message, but never sway from side to side.

64g How do I incorporate visual aids into my presentation?

Good visual aids make a speaker's ideas clear and understandable, but they cannot take the place of a well-prepared and rehearsed speech. Never show a visual of the points you're going to make and then read them aloud—unless you can use *PowerPoint* animation to reveal each point separately as it comes up—or you'll lose your audience's attention. Rather, save time by reinforcing your major points with illustrations or concrete images.

Well-prepared, well-delivered visuals add to your credibility and maintain an audience's attention. Number your visuals so that you don't have to shuffle them by hand or "find" them on a projector. Arrive early to double-check the equipment. For many types of visual aids, you need to dim the lights, but don't turn them off completely or you won't be able to see your notes and your audience won't be able to take notes. To avoid PLAGIARISM, always include the DOCUMENTATION for information drawn from other sources.

There are various types of visual aids you can prepare. Don't combine different types or your audience will sense that your material is too scattered for you to deliver a cohesive speech.

- **Slides of photographs, scientific material, etc.** Make sure that your slides are in the proper order and correctly placed in the projector. Turn off the projector or cover its lens when you don't need to show a slide. Keep the screen in one position—that is, don't raise and lower it during your presentation.

- **Overhead transparencies.** These are handy for when you want to write on the visual—for example, to illustrate a revision or emphasize a point. If you can draw quickly and well, you can sketch on a blank transparency as your audience watches.

- **PowerPoint.** This Microsoft product allows you to prepare slides on a computer and project them for your audience. Not every classroom is equipped to handle a computerized slide system, however, so find out what technology is available. You may need to bring your own laptop or submit a CD of your slides to a network administrator. If your classroom can't support PowerPoint, don't despair. Though the technology is impressive, other visual aids can work just as well. Finally, use PowerPoint only as an enhancement. Your information—spoken with clarity and authority—is the main attraction.

- **Poster.** Large posters can dramatize a point. Keep them covered until you're ready for them or they'll lose their impact.

- **Dry-erase boards.** Because dry-erase colors are visually appealing, these boards are often preferable to chalkboards. Use them sparingly to emphasize an occasional technical word or to do a rough sketch when illustrating a process.

- **Handouts.** You can use handouts with other visuals. Audiences often appreciate being able to take away something tangible. Handouts are indispensable if you're conducting an interactive workshop and need your audience to participate in writing. Opinions vary about when to distribute them—in a packet before your speech, one by one as you need them, or at the end of your presentation. If you hand them out in advance, people will read through them all as you speak. If you hand them out one by one, you need to ask for help so that you can maintain your audience's attention. Handing them out at the end works best when you want your listeners to have a record of your illustrations and other materials.

Visuals enhance a speech, but you should be able to give your presentation without them if the need arises. Bringing backup material can help you in a pinch. You might, for example, put key illustrations on transparencies in addition to a PowerPoint file. If something does go wrong during your presentation, relax; it happens to everyone! Take a deep breath, apologize to the audience if necessary, and keep going. Here are some tips for using visuals.

- Make visuals large enough for the entire audience to see.
- Use simple layouts or drawings—nothing cluttered or overly complicated.
- Proofread your written visuals carefully.
- Use no more than one or two visuals for each major point in the body of your speech.
- Practice with the visuals you plan to use; never let the mechanics of using visuals distract you from your audience or your speech.
- During your presentation, maintain eye contact with your audience; don't turn away to read or look at your visual.

64h What can I do to practice for my presentation?

Good delivery requires practice. Plan at least four complete runthroughs of your presentation, using visuals if you have them. Time yourself and cut or expand material accordingly. Practice in front of a mirror or a friend. If possible, videotape yourself. As you watch yourself, notice your gestures. Do you look natural? Do you make nervous movements that you are not aware of as you speak?

If you suffer from stage fright—as almost everyone does—remember that the more prepared and rehearsed you are, the less frightened you will be. Your aim is to communicate, not to perform. If you worry that your audience will see that you're nervous, Box 88 suggests ways to overcome physical signs of anxiety. The truth is that once you're under way, the momentum of your presentation will carry you onto another plane and you'll forget to be nervous. Try it.

■■■■ BOX 88 ■■■

 Overcoming anxiety during an oral presentation

- **Pounding heart.** Don't worry: No one else can hear it!
- **Trembling hands.** Rest them on the podium. If there is no podium, put your hands behind your back or hold your outline or notes until the shaking stops. It always does once you're under way.
- **Shaky knees.** Stand behind the desk or podium. If there is no desk, step forward to emphasize a point. Walking slowly from one place to another can also help you get rid of nervous energy.
- **Dry throat and mouth.** Place water at the podium. Never hesitate to take an occasional sip, especially at a transition point.
- **Quavering voice.** Speaking louder can help until this problem disappears on its own, which it always does. The sooner you ignore the quaver, the faster it will stop.
- **Flushed face.** Although you might feel as if you're burning up, audiences don't notice. The heat always fades as you continue speaking.

65 WRITING UNDER PRESSURE

All writers, student and professional, sometimes find themselves under pressure to get words down on paper without losing organization, focus on a central message, and control of their WORD CHOICE and GRAMMAR. This happens to journalists, for example, when they need to write a news story in a hurry to meet a deadline. It happens in the business world when a manager wants a report from a team member before the end of the day. And it happens to students when instructors require them to write an essay exam during class. Although many students resent the pressure of writing an essay exam under strict time limits, doing so is practical preparation for the real world.

65a What strategies can I use to write essay exams?

Writing essay exams is like writing other essays, but with firm limitations on the time available. Therefore, you need to go through all the steps in the WRITING PROCESS, but at a highly stepped-up speed. Here are some time-tested strategies that students use to write essay exams under pressure.

STRATEGIES FOR WRITING ESSAY EXAMS

- **Breathe.** Never begin writing immediately. Instead, take a deep breath and let it out slowly. Research shows that deliberate deep breathing is an effective way to relax and focus your thoughts.

- **Read.** Read the test from beginning to end without skimming, so that you understand the questions completely. If you have a choice among topics, and equal credit is given to each, select those topics you know the most about.

- **Plan your time.** If the instructor indicates what percentage of your grade each question will affect, allot your time to your greatest advantage. Jot down the total time available and divide it up to match the steps in the writing process; allot most of the time to drafting. Always allow time to reread and fix your material after you have finished. Some—but definitely not all—instructors make allowances for the time limit and are less strict than usual about grammar, spelling, and other mechanical details.

- **Underline cue words.** These words tell you what you must do in your essay. Look for words such as *analyze, classify,* and *criticize.* An essay question might read like this:
  - **Analyze** Socrates' discussion of "good life" and "good death." [Separate the concepts of "good life" and "good death" into parts and discuss each part.]
  - **Classify** the different stages of the digestive system in action. [Arrange the parts of the digestive system in groups based on their functions.]
  - **Criticize** the architectural function of the modern football stadium. [Give your opinion of the modern football stadium's architectural function.]

  Box 89 lists some common cue words with their meanings.

- **Circle key content words.** Look for the keywords or major terms in a statement or question. An essay question might ask:
  - Compare and contrast a **book** with its **movie version.** [The key content words are *book* and *movie version.*]
  - Justify the existence of **labor unions** in the **U.S. economy.** [The key content words are *labor unions* and *U.S. economy.*]
  - Prove that **smoking** is a major **cause of lung cancer.** [The key content words are *smoking* and *cause of lung cancer.*]

- As you begin writing, take a few minutes to jot down major ideas, the support you'll give for each one, and the order you think best for presenting the ideas.

Some common cue words

CUE WORD	MEANING
ANALYZE	Separate into parts and discuss each.
CLASSIFY	Arrange in groups based on shared characteristics or functions.
CRITICIZE	Give your opinion and explain why you approve or disapprove of something.
COMPARE	Show similarities and differences.
DEFINE	Tell what something is to differentiate it from similar things.
DISCUSS	Consider in an organized way the various issues or elements involved.
EXPLAIN	Make clear a complex thing or process that needs to be illuminated or interpreted.
INTERPRET	Explain the meaning of something.
REVIEW	Evaluate or summarize critically.
SUMMARIZE	Lay out the major points of something.
SUPPORT	Argue in favor of something.

- Dive into the actual writing and allow your notes to carry you along. Never get distracted from your time plan. If your instructor allows students to leave the room before class time is over, never assume that they know more than you do. Even if no one but you remains in the room, keep working. The best writers use every second available to write and polish. (Trust me, I've been in that spot often and have never regretted working right up to the time limit.)

TERMS GLOSSARY

This glossary defines important terms used in your *Quick Access Reference for Writers*. Terms printed throughout the book in SMALL CAPITAL LETTERS are defined here. Many of these glossary entries include parenthetical references to the handbook section(s) where the specific term is most fully discussed.

absolute phrase   A phrase containing a subject and a participle that modifies an entire sentence: *The semester* [subject] *being* [present participle of *be*] *over the campus looks deserted.* (39m)

abstract noun   A noun that names things not knowable through the five senses: *idea, respect.* (39a)

academic writing   Writing people do for college and scholarship. (5b)

action verb   A verb that describes an action or occurrence done by or to the subject. (15e)

active voice   An attribute of verbs showing that the action or condition expressed in the verb is done by the subject; in contrast with the *passive voice,* which conveys that the action or condition of the verb is done *to* the subject. (40g)

adjective   A word that describes or limits (modifies) a noun, a pronoun, or a word group functioning as a noun: *silly, three.* (39e, Ch. 43, 46b)

adjective clause   A dependent clause also known as a *relative clause.* An adjective clause modifies a preceding noun or pronoun and begins with a relative word (such as *who, which, that,* or *where*) that relates the clause to the noun or pronoun it modifies. Also see *clause.* (39n)

adverb   A word that describes or limits (modifies) verbs, adjectives, other adverbs, phrases, or clauses: *loudly, very, nevertheless, there.* (39f, Ch. 43, 46c)

adverb clause   A dependent clause beginning with a subordinating conjunction that establishes the relationship in meaning between the adverb clause and its independent clause. An adverb clause modifies the independent clause's verb or the entire independent clause. Also see *clause, conjunction.* (Box 22, Ch. 43)

agreement   The required match of number and person between a subject and verb (Ch. 41) or between a pronoun and antecedent (Ch. 42). A pronoun that expresses gender must match its antecedent in gender also.

analogy   An explanation of the unfamiliar in terms of the familiar. Like a simile, an analogy compares things not normally associated with each other; but unlike a simile, an analogy does not use *like* or *as* in making the comparison (19e). Analogy is also a rhetorical strategy for developing paragraphs (8f).

analysis   A process of critical thinking that divides a whole into its component parts in order to understand how the parts interrelate (Ch. 1, 26e). Sometimes called *division,* analysis is also a rhetorical strategy for developing paragraphs (8f).

antecedent   The noun or pronoun to which a pronoun refers. (Ch. 42)

antonym   A word opposite in meaning to another word.

APA style   Guidelines developed by the American Psychological Association (APA) for preparing and documenting papers. (Chs. 31–33)

appositive   A word or group of words that renames a preceding noun or noun phrase: *my favorite month,* **October**. (39l, 50f)

argument   A rhetorical attempt to convince others to agree with a position about a topic open to debate. (Ch. 10)

articles   Also called *determiners* or *noun markers,* articles are the words *a, an,* and *the. A* and *an* are indefinite articles; *the* is a definite article. Also see *determiner.* (39e, Ch. 45, Box 68)

assertion   A statement. In the process of developing a thesis statement, an assertion is a sentence that makes a statement and expresses a point of view about a topic (5h)

audience   The readers to whom a piece of writing is directed. (5c)

auxiliary verb   Also known as a *helping verb,* an auxiliary verb is a form of *be, do, have, can, may, will,* and others, that combines with a main verb to help it express tense, mood, and voice. Also see *modal auxiliary verb.* (40c)

balanced sentences   Sentences consisting of two short independent clauses that serve to compare or contrast. (17d)

base form   See *simple form.*

bias   Writer slants the material towards beliefs or attitudes and away from the facts or evidence. (2b)

bibliography   A list of information about sources. (23f, Chs. 29, 32, 34–36)

brainstorming   Listing all ideas that come to mind on a topic, and then grouping the ideas by patterns that emerge. (5g)

case   The form of a noun or pronoun in a specific context that shows whether it is functioning as a subject, an object, or a possessive. In modern English, nouns change form in the possessive case only (*city* is the form for subjective and objective cases; *city's* is the possessive-case form). Also see *pronoun case.* (42k–42t)

cause and effect   The relationship between outcomes (effects) and the reasons for them (causes). Cause-and-effect analysis is a rhetorical strategy for developing paragraphs. (8f)

chronological order   Also called *time order;* an arrangement of information according to time sequence; an organizing strategy for sentences, paragraphs, and longer pieces of writing. (8f)

citation   Information to identify a source referred to in a piece of writing. Also see *documentation.* (Chs. 26, 28, 31, 34a, 35a, 36a)

claim   States an issue and then takes a position on a debatable topic related to the issue. A claim is supported with evidence and reasons, moving from broad reasons to specific data and details. (10a)

clause   A group of words containing a subject and a predicate. A clause that delivers full meaning is called an *independent* (or *main) clause.* A clause that lacks full meaning by itself is called a *dependent* (or *subordinate) clause.* Also see *adjective clause, adverb clause, nonrestrictive element, noun clause, restrictive element.* (39n)

cliché   An overused, worn-out phrase that has lost its capacity to communicate effectively: *flat as Kansas, ripe old age.* (19f)

climactic order   Sometimes called *emphatic order,* climactic order is an arrangement of ideas or information from least important to most important. (8f)

clustering   An invention technique based on thinking about a topic and its increasingly specific subdivisions; also known as *mapping* and *webbing.* (5g)

coherence   The clear progression from one idea to another using transitional expressions, pronouns, selective repetition, and/or parallelism to make connections between ideas. (8e)

collaborative writing   Sharing and distributing writing tasks among members of a group. (38b)

collective noun   A noun that names a group of people or things: *family, committee.* (Box 46, 41h, 42e)

comma fault   See *comma splice.*

comma splice   The error that occurs when only a comma connects two independent clauses. (Ch. 12)

common noun   A noun that names a general group, place, person, or thing: *dog, house.* (Box 46)

comparative   The form of a descriptive adjective or adverb that expresses a different degree of intensity between two: *bluer, less blue; more easily, less easily.* Also see *positive, superlative.* (43e)

comparison and contrast   A rhetorical strategy for organizing and developing paragraphs by discussing a subject's similarities (comparison) and differences (contrast). (8f)

complement   An element after a verb that completes the predicate, such as a direct object after an action verb or a noun or adjective after a linking verb. Also see *object complement, subject complement, predicate adjective, predicate nominative.* (39l, Box 55)

complete predicate   See *predicate.*

complete subject   See *subject.*

complex sentence   See *sentence types.*

compound-complex sentence   See *sentence types.*

compound predicate   See *predicate.*

compound sentence   See *sentence types.*

compound subject   See *subject.*

concrete noun   A noun naming things that can be seen, touched, heard, smelled, or tasted: *smoke, sidewalk.* (Box 46)

conjunction   A word that connects or otherwise establishes a relationship between two or more words, phrases, or clauses. Also see *coordinating conjunction, correlative conjunction,* and *subordinating conjunction.* (39h)

conjunctive adverb   An adverb that creates a relationship, such as of addition, contrast, comparison, result, time, or emphasis, between words. (Box 50)

connotation   Ideas implied by a word; connotations convey associations such as emotional overtones beyond a word's direct, explicit definition. (19b)

contraction   A word in which an apostrophe takes the place of one or more omitted letters: *can't, don't I'm, isn't, it's, let's, they're, wasn't, weren't, we've, who's, won't* and *you're.* (53e)

coordinate adjectives   Two or more adjectives that equally modify a noun (***big, friendly*** *dog*). The order of coordinate adjectives can be changed without destroying meaning. Also see *cumulative adjectives.* (Box 73, 50e)

coordinating conjunction   A conjunction that joins two or more grammatically equivalent structures: *and, or, for, nor, but, so, yet.* (Box 51)

coordination The use of grammatically equivalent forms to show a balance or sequence of ideas. (Box 51, 16a–16b)

correlative conjunction A pair of words that joins equivalent grammatical structures, including *both . . . and, either . . . or, neither . . . nor, not only . . . but also.* (39h)

count noun A noun that names items that can be counted: *radio, street, idea, fingernail.* (Box 46, 44a, 45b)

critical response Formally, an essay summarizing a source's central point or main idea and then presenting the writer's synthesized reactions in response. (4b)

cumulative adjectives Adjectives that build up meaning from word to word as they get closer to the noun (***familiar rock** tunes*). The order of cumulative adjectives cannot be changed without destroying meaning. Also see *coordinate adjectives.* (50e)

dangling modifier A modifier that attaches its meaning illogically, either because it is closer to another noun or pronoun than to its true subject or because its true subject is not expressed in the sentence. (14e)

declarative sentence A sentence that makes a statement: *Sky diving is exciting.* Also see *exclamatory sentence, imperative sentence, interrogative sentence.*

definite article See *article.*

denotation The dictionary definition of a word. (19b)

dependent clause A clause that cannot stand alone as an independent grammatical unit; also called *subordinate clause.* Also see *adjective clause, adverb clause, noun clause.* (39n)

descriptive adjective An adjective that describes the condition or properties of the noun it modifies and (except for a very few, such as *dead* and *unique*) has comparative and superlative forms: *flat, flatter, flattest.*

descriptive adverb An adverb that describes the condition or properties of whatever it modifies and that has comparative and superlative forms: *happily, more happily, most happily.*

determiner A word or word group, traditionally identified as an *adjective,* that limits a noun by telling "how much" or "how many" about it. Also called *expressions of quantity, limiting adjectives,* or *noun markers.* (Box 49, Box 67, 39e, 44b, Ch. 45)

diction Word choice. (19b)

direct discourse In writing, words that repeat speech or conversation exactly and so are enclosed in quotation marks. Also see *indirect discourse.* (13d)

direct object   A noun or pronoun or group of words functioning as a noun that receives the action (completes the meaning) of a transitive verb. (39k, 40d)

direct question   A sentence that asks a question and ends with a question mark: *Are you going?*

direct quotation   See *quotation.*

discovery draft   See *drafting.*

documentation   The acknowledgment of someone else's words and ideas used in any piece of writing by giving full and accurate information about the person whose words were used and about where those words were found; for example, for a print source, documentation usually includes author name(s), title, place and date of publication, and related information. (Chs. 23–26, 28, 31, 32, 34–36)

documentation style   Any of various systems for providing information about the source of words, information, and ideas quoted, paraphrased, or summarized from some source other than the writer. Documentation styles discussed in this handbook are MLA, APA, CM, CSE, and COS (23e, Chs. 28, 29, 31, 32, 34–36)

double negative   A nonstandard negation using two negative modifiers rather than one. (42c)

draft   See *drafting.*

drafting   A part of the writing process in which writers compose ideas in sentences and paragraphs; the documents produced by drafting are often called *drafts.* A *discovery draft* is an early, rough draft. (6a)

edited American English   English language use that conforms to established rules of grammar, sentence structure, punctuation, and spelling; also called *standard English.* (19d)

editing   A part of the writing process in which writers check a document for the technical correctness of its grammar, spelling, punctuation, and mechanics. (7d–7e, Box 11)

elliptical construction   A sentence structure that deliberately omits words that are expressed elsewhere or words that can be inferred from the context. (13f)

essential element   See *restrictive element.*

euphemism   Language that attempts to blunt certain realities by speaking of them in "nice" or "tactful" words. (19g)

evidence   Facts, data, examples, and opinions of others used to support assertions and conclusions. (8f, 27b)

exclamation   A word or words expressing strong feeling and ending in an exclamation point.

exclamatory sentence   A sentence beginning with *What* or *How* that expresses strong feeling: *What a ridiculous statement!*

expletive   The phrase *there is (are), there was (were), it is,* or *it was* at the beginning of a clause, changing structure and postponing the subject: *It is Mars that we hope to reach* (compare *We hope to reach Mars*). (15c, 41h)

faulty predication   A grammatically illogical combination of subject and predicate. (13e)

first person   See *person.*

freewriting   Writing nonstop for a period of time to generate ideas by free association of thoughts. *Focused freewriting* may start with a set topic or may build on one sentence taken from earlier freewriting. (5g)

fused sentence   The error of running independent clauses together without the required punctuation that marks them as complete units. (Ch. 12)

future perfect progressive tense   The form of the future perfect tense that describes an action or condition ongoing until some specific future time: *I will have been talking.*

future perfect tense   The tense indicating that an action will have been completed or a condition will have ended by a specified point in the future: *I will have talked.*

future progressive tense   The form of the future tense showing that a future action will continue for some time: *I will be talking.*

future tense   The form of a verb, made with the simple form and either *shall* or *will,* expressing an action yet to be taken or a condition not yet experienced: *I will talk.*

gender   Concerning languages, the classification of words as masculine, feminine, or neuter. In English, a few pronouns show changes in gender in third-person singular: *he, him, his; she, her, hers; it, its, its.* A few nouns naming roles change form to show gender difference: *prince, princess,* for example. (20a)

gender-neutral language   See *sexist language.*

gerund   A present participle functioning as a noun: *Walking is good exercise.* Also see *verbal.* (Ch. 48)

gerund phrase   A gerund, along with its modifiers, and/or object(s), which functions as a subject or an object. (39m)

helping verb   See *auxiliary verb.*

homonyms   Words spelled differently that sound alike: *to, too, two*. (21d, Box 24)

idiom   A word, phrase, or other construction that has a different meaning from its usual or literal meaning: *He lost his head. She hit the ceiling.*

illogical predication   See *faulty predication.*

imperative mood   The mood that expresses commands and direct requests, using the simple form of the verb and often implying but not expressing the subject, *you: Go.* (40f)

imperative sentence   A sentence that gives a command: *Go to the corner and buy me a newspaper.*

indefinite article   See *article, determiner.*

indefinite pronoun   A pronoun, such as *all, anyone, each,* and others, that refers to a nonspecific person or thing. (39b, 41e, 42d)

independent clause   A clause that can stand alone as an independent grammatical unit. (39n)

indicative mood   The mood of verbs used for statements about real things or highly likely ones: *I think Grace is arriving today.* (40f)

indirect discourse   Reported speech or conversation that does not use the exact structure of the original and so is not enclosed in quotation marks. (13d)

indirect object   A noun or pronoun or group of words functioning as a noun that tells to whom or for whom the action expressed by a transitive verb was done. (39k)

indirect question   A sentence that reports a question and ends with a period: *I asked if you are going.*

indirect quotation   See *quotation.*

infinitive   A verbal made of the simple form of a verb and usually, but not always, *to,* which functions as a noun, adjective, or adverb.

infinitive phrase   An infinitive, its modifiers, and/or object, which functions as a noun, adjective, or adverb.

informal language   Word choice that creates a tone appropriate for casual writing or speaking. (19d)

informative writing   Writing that gives information and, when necessary, explains it; also known as *expository writing.*

intensive pronoun   A pronoun that ends in *-self* and that intensifies its antecedent: *Vida **himself** argued against it.* Also see *reflexive pronoun.* (Box 47)

interjection An emotion-conveying word that is treated as a sentence, starting with a capital letter and ending with an exclamation point or a period: *Oh! Ouch!* (39i, 55c)

interrogative pronoun A pronoun, such as *whose* or *what,* that implies a question: *Who called?* (Box 47)

interrogative sentence A sentence that asks a direct question: *Did you see that?*

intransitive verb A verb that does not take a direct object. (39k, 40d)

invention techniques Ways of gathering ideas for writing. (5g)

inverted word order In contrast to standard order, the main verb or an auxiliary verb comes before the subject in inverted word order. Most questions and some exclamations use inverted word order. (17h, 46a)

irony Using words to imply the opposite of their usual meaning. (19e)

irregular verb A verb that forms the past tense and past participle in some way other than by adding *-ed* or *-d.* (40b, Box 59)

jargon Specialized vocabulary of a particular field or group that a general reader is unlikely to understand. (19g)

keywords Main words in a source's title, or that the author or editor has identified as central to that source. Sometimes keywords are called *descriptors* or *identifiers.* (24d)

levels of formality The degree of formality of language, reflected by word choice and sentence structure. A highly formal level is used for ceremonial and other occasions when stylistic flourishes are appropriate. A medium level, which is neither too formal nor too casual, is acceptable for most academic writing. (19d)

limiting adjective See *determiner.*

linking verb A main verb that links a subject with a subject complement that renames or describes the subject. Linking verbs convey a state of being, relate to the senses, or indicate a condition. (Box 55, Box 58)

literal meaning What is stated by words. (2b)

logical fallacies Flaws in reasoning that lead to illogical statements. (10f)

main clause See *independent clause.*

main verb A verb that expresses action, occurrence, or state of being and that shows mood, tense, voice, number, and person. (39c)

mapping See *clustering.*

mechanics Conventions governing matters such as the use of capital letters, italics, abbreviations, and numbers. (Chs. 58–61)

metaphor   A comparison implying similarity between two things; a metaphor does not use words such as *like* or *as,* which are used in a simile and which make a comparison explicit: *a mop of hair* (compare the simile *hair like a mop*). (19e)

misplaced modifier   Describing or limiting words that are wrongly positioned in a sentence so that their message either is illogical or relates to the wrong word(s). (14a)

mixed construction   A sentence that unintentionally changes from one grammatical structure to another, incompatible one, thus garbling meaning. (13e)

mixed metaphors   Incongruously combined images. (19e)

MLA style   Guidelines developed by the Modern Language Association (MLA) for preparing and documenting papers. (Chs. 28–30)

modal auxiliary verb   A group of auxiliary verbs that add information such as a sense of needing, wanting, or having to do something or a sense of possibility, likelihood, obligation, permission, or ability. (Ch. 49)

modifier, modify   A word or group of words functioning as an adjective or adverb to describe or limit (modify) another word or word group. (Chs. 14, 43)

mood   The attribute of verbs showing a speaker's or writer's attitude toward the action by the way verbs are used. English has three moods: imperative, indicative, and subjunctive. Also see *imperative mood, indicative mood, subjunctive mood.* (40f)

Netiquette   Good manners when using e-mail, the Internet, and on-line sites such as bulletin boards, chatrooms, etc. Netiquette is coined from the word *etiquette.* (63a)

noncount noun   A noun that names "uncountable" things: *water, time.* (Box 46, 44a, 45a–45b)

nonessential element   See *nonrestrictive element.*

nonrestrictive element   A descriptive word, phrase, or dependent clause that provides information not essential to understanding the basic message of the element it modifies; it is therefore set off by commas. Also see *restrictive element.* (50f)

nonsexist language   See *sexist language.*

nonstandard   Language usage other than edited American English. Also see *edited American English.* (19d)

noun   A word that names a person, place, thing, or idea. Nouns function as subjects, objects, or complements. (39a, 39k, 39l)

noun clause   A dependent clause that functions as a subject, object, or complement. (39n)

noun complement See *complement.*

noun determiner See *determiner.*

noun phrase A noun along with its modifiers functioning as a subject, object, or complement. (39m)

number The attribute of some words indicating whether they refer to one (singular) or more than one (plural). (44a)

object A noun, pronoun, or group of words functioning as a noun or pronoun that receives the action of a verb (direct object); tells to whom or for whom something is done (indirect object); or completes the meaning of a preposition (object of a preposition). (39k)

object complement A noun or adjective renaming or describing a direct object after certain verbs, including *call, consider, name, elect,* and *think: I call **joggers** [object] **fanatics** [object complement].*

objective case The case of a noun or pronoun functioning as a direct or indirect object or as an object of a preposition or of a verbal. A few pronouns change form to show case (*him, her, whom*). Also see *case.* (42k–42t)

oral presentation A speech or other spoken presentation in front of an audience. (Ch. 64)

paragraph A group of sentences that work together to develop a unit of thought. (8a)

paragraph development Using specific, concrete details (RENNS) to support a generalization in a paragraph; rhetorical strategies for arranging and organizing paragraphs. (8d, 8f)

parallelism The use of equivalent grammatical forms or matching sentence structures to express equivalent ideas. (8e)

paraphrase A restatement of someone else's ideas in language and sentence structure different from that of the original. (4a, 26g)

parenthetical documentation See *parenthetical reference.*

parenthetical reference Information enclosed in parentheses following quoted, paraphrased, or summarized material from another source to alert readers to the use of the material from that source. Parenthetical references and a list of bibliographic information about each source used in a paper document the writer's use of sources. (Chs. 28–30 [MLA], Chs. 31–33 [APA])

participial phrase A phrase that contains a present participle or a past participle and any modifiers and that functions as an adjective. Also see *verbal.*

participle A verb form. See *past participle, present participle.*

passive construction See *passive voice.*

passive voice   The form of a verb in which the subject is acted upon; if the subject is mentioned in the sentence, it usually appears as the object of the preposition *by: I was frightened by the thunder* (compare the active-voice version *The thunder frightened me*). The passive voice emphasizes the action, in contrast to the active voice, which emphasizes the doer of the action. (40g)

past participle   The third principal part of a verb, formed in regular verbs by adding *-d,* or *-ed* to the simple form, as with the past tense. In irregular verbs, it often differs from the simple form and the past tense: *break, broke, broken.* (40b, Box 59)

past perfect progressive tense   The past-perfect-tense form that describes an ongoing condition in the past that has been ended by something stated in the sentence: *(Before the curtains caught fire,) I had been talking.*

past perfect tense   The tense that describes a condition or action that started in the past, continued for a while, and then ended in the past: *I had talked.*

past progressive tense   The past-tense form that shows the continuing nature of a past action: *I was talking.*

past-tense form   The second principal part of a verb, in regular verbs formed by adding *-d* or *-ed* to the simple form. In irregular verbs, the past tense may change in several ways from the simple form. (40b)

perfect tenses   The three tenses—the present perfect (*I have talked*), the past perfect (*I had talked*), and the future perfect (*I will have talked*)—that help to show complex time relationships between two clauses. (40e)

person   The attribute of nouns and pronouns showing who or what acts or experiences an action. *First person* is the one speaking (*I, we*); *second person* is the one being spoken to (*you, you*); and third person is the person or thing spoken about (*he, she, it; they*). All nouns are third person.

personal pronoun   A pronoun that refers to people or things: *I, you, them, it.*

persuasive writing   Writing that seeks to convince the reader about a matter of opinion. (Ch. 10)

phrasal verb   A verb that combines with one or more prepositions to deliver its meaning: *ask out, look into.* (47b)

phrase   A group of related words that does not contain a subject and predicate and thus cannot stand alone as an independent grammatical unit. A phrase can function as a noun, a verb, or a modifier. (39m)

plagiarism A writer's presenting another person's words or ideas without giving credit to that person. Documentation systems allow writers to give proper credit to sources in ways recognized by scholarly communities. Plagiarism is a serious offense, a form of intellectual dishonesty that can lead to course failure or expulsion. (26a–26c)

planning An early part of the writing process in which writers gather ideas. When combined with shaping, planning is sometimes called *prewriting*. (5a)

plural See *number*.

positive The form of an adjective or adverb when no comparison is being expressed: *blue, easily*. Also see *comparative, superlative*. (43e)

possessive case The case of a noun or pronoun that shows ownership or possession. Also see *case*. (53a–53c)

predicate The part of a sentence that contains the verb and tells what the subject is doing or experiencing or what is being done to the subject. A *simple predicate* contains only the main verb and any auxiliary verb(s). A *complete predicate* contains the verb, its modifiers, objects, and other related words. A *compound predicate* contains two or more verbs and their objects and modifiers, if any. (39j)

predicate adjective An adjective used as a subject complement: *That tree is **leafy***.

predicate nominative A noun or pronoun used as a subject complement: *That tree is a **maple***.

prefix Letters added at the beginning of a root word to create a new word.

preposition A word that conveys a relationship, often of space or time, between the noun or pronoun following it and other words in the sentence. The noun or pronoun following a preposition is called its *object*. (39k, Ch. 47, 48a–48b)

prepositional phrase A group of words beginning with a preposition and including a noun, which is called the object.

present participle A verb's *-ing* form. Used with auxiliary verbs, present participles function as main verbs (40a). Used without auxiliary verbs, present participles function as nouns or adjectives (39d).

present perfect progressive tense The present-perfect-tense form that describes something ongoing in the past that is likely to continue into the future: *I have been talking*. (40b)

present perfect tense The tense indicating that an action or its effects, begun or perhaps completed in the past, continue into the present: *I had talked*. (40b)

present progressive tense   The present-tense form of the verb that indicates something taking place at the time it is written or spoken about: *I am talking*. (40b)

present tense   The tense that describes what is happening, what is true at the moment, and what is consistently true. It uses the simple form (*I talk*) and the *-s* form in the third-person singular (*he, she, it talks*). (40b)

presentation style   The way a person delivers an oral presentation. (64e)

prewriting   A term for all activities in the writing process before drafting. (51a)

primary sources   "Firsthand" work: write-ups of experiments and observations by the researchers who conducted them; taped accounts, interviews, and newspaper accounts by direct observers; autobiographies, diaries, and journals; expressive works (poems, plays, fiction, essays); also known as *primary evidence*. Also see *secondary sources*. (23d, Chs. 24–25)

principle parts   Verb forms. (40b)

progressive forms   Verb forms made, in all tenses, with the present participle and forms of the verb *be* as an auxiliary. Progressive forms show that an action, occurrence, or state of being is ongoing. (40e)

pronoun   A word that takes the place of a noun and functions in the same ways that nouns do. Types of pronouns are demonstrative, indefinite, intensive, interrogative, personal, reciprocal, reflexive, and relative. The word (or words) a pronoun replaces is called its antecedent. (39b, Ch. 42)

pronoun–antecedent agreement   The match required between a pronoun and its antecedent in number and person, and for personal pronouns, in gender as well. (42a–42e)

pronoun case   The way a pronoun changes form to reflect its use as the agent of action (subjective case), the thing being acted upon (objective case), or the thing showing ownership (possessive case). (42k–42t)

pronoun reference   The relationship between a pronoun and its antecedent. (42f–42j)

proofreading   Reading a final draft to find and correct any spelling or mechanics mistakes, typing errors, or handwriting illegibility; the final step of the writing process. (7f)

proper adjective   An adjective formed from a proper noun: *Victorian, American.*

proper noun   A noun that names specific people, places, or things; it is always capitalized: *Rob Reiner, Buick.*

purpose   The goal or aim of a piece of writing: to express oneself, to provide information, to persuade, or to create a literary work. (2b)

quotation   Repeating or reporting another person's words. *Direct quotation* repeats another's words exactly and encloses them in quotation marks. *Indirect quotation* reports another's words without quotation marks except around any words repeated exactly from the source. Both direct and indirect quotation require documentation of the source to avoid plagiarism. Also see *indirect discourse*. (Ch. 26, 54a–54c)

reciprocal pronoun   The pronouns *each other* and *one another,* referring to individual parts of a plural antecedent: *We respect **each other**.*

References   In many documentation styles, including APA, the title of a list of sources cited in a research paper or other written work. (Chs. 32, 35)

reflexive pronoun   A pronoun that ends in *-self* and that reflects back to its antecedent: *They claim to support **themselves.***

regular verb   A verb that forms its past tense and past participle by adding *-ed* or *-d* to the simple form. Most English verbs are regular. (40b)

relative adverb   An adverb that introduces an adjective clause: *The lot **where I usually park my car** was full.* (39f)

relative clause   See *adjective clause.*

relative pronoun   A pronoun, such as *who, which, that, who whom, whoever,* and a few others, that introduces an adjective clause or sometimes a noun clause. (Box 47)

restrictive clause   A dependent clause that gives information necessary to distinguish whatever it modifies from others in the same category. In contrast to a nonrestrictive clause, a restrictive clause is not set off with commas. (39n, 50f)

restrictive element   A word, phrase, or dependent clause that provides information essential to the understanding of the element it modifies. In contrast to a nonrestrictive element, a restrictive element is not set off with commas. Also see *nonrestrictive element.* (50f)

revising, revision   A part of the writing process in which writers evaluate their rough drafts and, on the basis of their assessments, rewrite by adding, cutting, replacing, moving, and often totally recasting material. (7a–7c, Box 10)

rhetoric   The area of discourse that focuses on arrangement of ideas and choice of words as a reflection of the writer's purpose and sense of audience.

rhetorical strategies   In writing, various techniques for presenting ideas to deliver a writer's intended message with clarity and impact.

Reflecting typical patterns of human thought, rhetorical strategies include arrangements such as chronological and climactic order; stylistic techniques such as parallelism and planned repetition; and patterns for organizing and developing writing such as description and definition. (Ch. 8)

run-on (run-together) sentence See *fused sentence.*

second person See *person.*

secondary source A source that reports, analyzes, discusses, reviews, or otherwise deals with the work of someone else, as opposed to a primary source, which is someone's original work or firsthand report. A reliable secondary source should be the work of a person with appropriate credentials, should appear in a respected publication or other medium, should be current, and should be well reasoned. (23b, Chs. 24–25)

sentence See *sentence types.*

sentence fragment A portion of a sentence that is punctuated as though it were a complete sentence. (Ch. 12)

sentence types A grammatical classification of sentences by the kinds of clauses they contain. A *simple sentence* consists of one independent clause. A *complex sentence* contains one independent clause and one or more dependent clauses. A *compound-complex sentence* contains at least two independent clauses and one or more dependent clauses. A *compound sentence* contains two or more independent clauses joined by a coordinating conjunction. Sentences are also classified by their grammatical function; see *declarative sentence, exclamatory sentence, imperative sentence,* and *interrogative sentence.* (39o)

sexist language Language that unfairly or unnecessarily assigns roles or characteristics to people on the basis of gender. Language that avoids gender stereotyping is called *gender-neutral* or *nonsexist language.* (20b)

shift An unnecessary change in person, number, voice, tense, or other grammatical framework that makes a sentence unclear. (Ch. 13)

simile A comparison, using *like* or *as,* of otherwise dissimilar things. (19e)

simple form The form of the verb that shows action, occurrence, or state of being taking place in the present. It is used in the singular for first and second person and in the plural for first, second, and third person. It is also the first principal part of a verb. The simple form is also known as the *dictionary form* or *base form.* (40b)

simple predicate See *predicate.*

simple sentence See *sentence types.*

simple subject   See *subject.*

simple tenses   The present, past, and future tenses, which divide time into present, past, and future. (40e)

singular   See *number.*

slang   Coined words and new meanings for existing words, which quickly pass in and out of use; inappropriate for most academic writing. (19d)

source   A book, article, document, other work, or person providing information.

split infinitive   One or more words coming between the two words of an infinitive. (14c)

standard English   See *edited American English.*

standard word order   The most common order for words in English sentences: The subject comes before the predicate. (17h, 46a)

subject   The word or group of words in a sentence that acts, is acted upon, or is described by the verb. A *simple subject* includes only the noun or pronoun. A *complete subject* includes the noun or pronoun and all its modifiers. A *compound subject* includes two or more nouns or pronouns and their modifiers. (39j)

subject complement   A noun or adjective that follows a linking verb, renaming or describing the subject of the sentence; also called a *predicate nominative.* (39l, 41h)

subjective case   The case of the noun or pronoun functioning as subject. Also see *case.*

subject–verb agreement   The required match between a subject and verb in expressing number and person. (Ch. 41)

subjunctive mood   The verb mood that expresses wishes, recommendations, indirect requests, speculations, and conditional statements: *I wish you were here.* (40f)

subordinate clause   See *dependent clause.*

subordinating conjunction   A conjunction that introduces an adverbial clause and expresses a relationship between the idea in it and the idea in the independent clause. (16c, Box 52)

subordination   The use of grammatical structures to reflect the relative importance of ideas. A sentence with logically subordinated information expresses the most important information in the independent clause and less important information in dependent clauses or phrases. (16c–16d)

suffix   An ending added to a basic (root) word to change function or meaning.

summary An extraction of the main message or central point of a passage or other discourse; a critical thinking activity preceding synthesis. (4a, 26h)

superlative The form of an adjective or adverb that expresses comparison among three or more things: *bluest, least blue, most easily, least easily.* (43e)

synonym A word that is close in meaning to another word. (19a)

synthesis A component of critical thinking in which material that has been summarized, analyzed, and interpreted is connected to what is already known (one's prior knowledge). (4b, 26e)

tag question An inverted verb-pronoun combination, added to the end of a sentence and creating a question, that "asks" the audience to agree with the assertion in the first part of the sentence: *You know what a tag question is,* ***don't you?*** A tag question is set off from the rest of the sentence with a comma. (50h)

tag sentence See *tag question.*

template A preprogrammed format in word processing software. (37d)

tense The time at which the action of the verb occurs: in the present, the past, or the future. (40e)

tense sequence In sentences that have more than one clause, the accurate matching of verbs to reflect logical time relationships. (40e, Box 60)

thesis statement A statement of an essay's central theme that makes clear the main idea, the writer's purpose, the focus of the topic, and perhaps the organizational pattern. (5h, 7b)

third person See *person.*

tone The writer's attitude toward his or her material and reader, especially as reflected by word choice. (19g)

topic The subject of discourse.

topic sentence The sentence that expresses the main idea of a paragraph. (8c)

transition The connection of one idea to another in discourse. Useful strategies for creating transitions include transitional expressions, parallelism, and planned repetition of key words and phrases. (8e)

transitional expressions Words and phrases that signal connections among ideas and create coherence. (8e, Box 14)

transitive verb A verb that must be followed by a direct object. (39k, 40d)

unity The clear and logical relationship between the main idea of a paragraph and the evidence supporting the main idea. (Ch. 8)

unmarked infinitive   A base verb functioning as an infinitive without the word *to* in front of it.

usage   A customary way of using language. (Ch. 18, Usage Glossary)

valid   A term applied to a deductive argument when the conclusion follows logically from the statements that create the terms of the argument. Validity describes the structure of an argument, not its truth. (10f)

verb   A class of words that show action or occurrence or that describe a state of being. Verbs change form to show time (tense), attitude (mood), and role of the subject (voice). Verbs occur in the predicate of a clause and can be in verb phrases, which may consist of a main verb, any auxiliary verbs, and any modifiers. Verbs can be described as transitive or intransitive, depending on whether they take a direct object. (39c, Ch. 40)

verb phrase   A main verb, along with any auxiliary verb(s) and any modifiers.

verbal   A verb part functioning as a noun, adjective, or adverb. Verbals include infinitives, present participles (functioning as adjectives), gerunds (present participles functioning as nouns), and past participles. (39d)

verbal phrase   A group of words that contains a verbal (an infinitive, participle, or gerund) and its modifiers. (39m)

voice   An attribute of verbs showing whether the subject acts (active voice) or is acted upon (passive voice). (40g)

warrants   The writer's underlying assumptions, which are often implied rather than stated. Warrants may also need support (also called *backing*). (10d)

Works Cited   In MLA documentation style, the title of a list of all sources cited in a research paper or other written work. (Ch. 29)

writing process   Stages of writing in which a writer gathers and shapes ideas, organizes material, expresses those ideas in a rough draft, evaluates the draft and revises it, edits the writing for technical errors, and proofreads it for typographical accuracy and legibility. The stages often overlap. (Chs. 5–9)

INDEX

QUICK ACCESS BOXES

CONTINUED ⟶

CONTINUED ⟶

Where can I find what I need to know about . . . ?